SLOUCHING TOWARDS SIRTE

Maximilian C. Forte

SLOUCHING TOWARDS SIRTE

NATO's War on Libya and Africa

Baraka
Books
Montreal

Library and Archives Canada Cataloguing in Publication

Forte, Maximilian C., 1967-

Slouching towards Sirte: NATO's war on Libya and Africa /Maximilian Forte.

Includes bibliographical references and index. ISBN 978-1-926824-52-9

1. Libya–History–Civil War, 2011-. 2. Libya–History–Civil War, 2011- –Causes. 3. North Atlantic Treaty Organization–Libya. 4. North Atlantic Treaty Organization–Africa. 5. Imperialism. I. Title.

DT236.F67 2012   961.204'2   C2012-906868-3

@ 2012 by Baraka Books

Cover photo: European Pressphoto Agency
Cover by Folio infographie
Book design by Folio infographie

ISBN 978-1-926824-52-9 (paper)
ISBN 978-1-926824-74-1 (ePub)
ISBN 978-1-926824-75-8 (PDF)

Legal Deposit, 4th quarter, 2012

Bibliothèque et Archives nationales du Québec
Library and Archives Canada

Published by Baraka Books of Montreal.
6977, rue Lacroix
Montréal, Québec H4E 2V4
Telephone: 514 808-8504
info@barakabooks.com
www.barakabooks.com

Printed and bound in Quebec

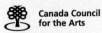

Baraka Books acknowledges the generous support of its publishing program from the Société de développement des entreprises culturelles du Québec (SODEC) and the Canada Council for the Arts.

Trade Distribution & Returns
Canada
LitDistCo
1-800-591-6250
ordering@litdistco.ca

United States
Independent Publishers Group
1-800-888-4741
orders@ipgbook.com

Contents

Preface

Why did NATO intervene militarily in Libya? When did the intervention really begin, and what forms did it take? Was NATO's military campaign really about saving lives, as the key political leaders of NATO member states claimed? Or was this just another war over oil? What have been the consequences of foreign intervention? What do we learn about our governments, our media, and our ideologies, particularly as represented in Western humanitarianism? These are the primary questions addressed in this book, which began as a research and writing project from the start of the first street protests in Libya in February until the aftermath of the first national elections in July 2012.

My argument, which focuses on foreign intervention, is that NATO's campaign represents the continued militarization of Western and especially U.S. foreign policy and the rise of the new "military humanism." NATO's war in Libya was advertised as a humanitarian intervention—bombing in the name of "saving lives." Attempts at diplomacy were stifled. Peace talks were undermined and rendered impossible. Libya was barred from representing itself at the UN, where shadowy NGOs and "human rights" groups held full sway in propagating exaggerations, outright falsehoods, and racial fear mongering that served to sanction atrocities and ethnic cleansing in the name of democracy. Nothing could impede a rush to war that was far speedier than George W. Bush's invasion of Iraq. A consistent refusal to examine contexts, causes, and the dire consequences of intervention speaks to the proliferation of myths that were used to justify and explain the war, heralded as a success at NATO headquarters, and proclaimed as a "high watermark" by proponents of the interventionist doctrine known as the "Responsibility to Protect."

This book takes us through the documentary history of events, processes and decisions that led up to NATO's war, the conduct of the war, and its immediate consequences. It shows us that Western relations with a "rehabilitated" Libya after 2003 were at best shaky, mired in distrust, and exhibited a U.S. preference for regime change. Yet the foreign powers' preferred alternative, the National Transitional Council, had more legitimacy in Europe and North America than in Libya, a fact that opened the door to new and ongoing violence in that country. NATO's war was not about human rights, despite official propaganda. Moreover, neither "saving lives," nor the alleged nature of the "human rights record" of the "Gaddafi regime" could ever justify what NATO wrought. Many more lives have been lost, and continue to be lost, than if there had been no foreign intervention at all. NATO not only failed to respect the UN mandate to protect civilians, it threatened many more, and entirely neglected civilian lives at risk. NATO claimed to have saved Benghazi from a massacre, and yet Sirte was devastated with the aid of NATO bombing. If this war was not about human rights, it was also not exclusively about oil, though oil remains a factor of critical importance.

NATO's war should instead be seen as part of a larger process of militarizing U.S. relations with Africa, where the Pentagon's AFRICOM seeks to counter Pan-Africanist initiatives such as those spearheaded by the late Muammar Gaddafi. In a broader scope, it is part of an ongoing contest between U.S. power (in decline) against the interests of China, Russia, and other ascendant regional hegemons, to secure access to both material and political resources in an effort to stall the impending demise of the U.S. while making the world safe for transnational capital. Finally, the intervention was an attempt to control the direction of uprisings in a region of critical geopolitical and economic significance to the U.S. and Europe. Libya, once prosperous, independent and defiant, is now faced with ruin, dependency and prolonged civil strife, precisely at a time of extreme political and economic volatility and uncertainty in the world system. This is the kind of Libya that has finally met with Western approval.

In writing this book, my aim was to survey, synthesize, and interpret a substantial amount of the documentation produced by the key actors in the intervention, as produced especially by diplomats, military and political leaders, human rights activists, journalists, and others. Given that NATO's military operations were primarily aerial ones—ordered and planned from a distance—the book does not cover key local actors "on the ground," with ethnographic detail about their personal biographies and description of everyday life in Libya. Instead the focus is on the ideological smokescreen that was raised across the world of international and especially Western public opinion, judged in light of what has been revealed by first-hand accounts of the war in Libya and its aftermath.

The perspective of "being there" that that this book embodies might come as a surprise to some Western readers. But all of us have always "been there" if we understand the central unit of analysis—the "there" in question—as one composed of our militaries, our ideologies, our fantasies of control, our preferred self-image, and our political contests. To these, we are all first hand witnesses and participants. No amount of field research in Libya will ever, in and of itself, help to explain and understand the motor forces and psychological operations of militarism and inter-ventionism, and the cover of humanitarianism that stem from our societies and from our economic drives. This book intends to sketch out that context, while providing a critique of the political culture of late imperialist societies in the West, the kind of morality that is being refashioned for mass consumption, and the vision of humanity that is embedded within NATO and U.S. foreign policy narratives and their calls for public outrage.

The sources relied upon are varied, consisting primarily of published documents, press releases, private and independent intelligence analyses, and reports from journalists and members of human rights groups that spent time in Libya during the war and after. As always, extreme care and source criticism are essential.

Among key sources are the U.S. Embassy cables published by WikiLeaks. These cables were primarily written by diplomats attached to the U.S. Department of State, and therefore cannot represent other, unknown reports produced by military and intelligence agencies that would have actually been involved in drafting plans for the overthrow of Gaddafi. In addition, we do not have all of the cables that were written for the time period covered—I examined the 598 cables originating in the U.S. Embassy in Tripoli alone, plus more than 600 others from other U.S. Embassies on the African continent and in the Caribbean, none of which is dated after 2010. The cables were written by Americans, for American purposes, informed by American prejudices, and using a limited range of contacts within Libyan society. For these and other reasons, it would be unwise to takes these cables as representing "the truth" of Libya. Where they are useful is as a window onto issues of interest to the U.S. and insight into its network of contacts in Libya.

NATO documents are even more limited, especially when in the form of the daily press releases about "Operation Unified Protector." These tend to be mere lists of numbers of sorties flown and targets struck, which ask the public to take them at face value when in many cases they mask strikes on civilian targets and against particular individuals, such as Muammar Gaddafi.

Reports by human rights organizations also merit source criticism. The leading ones supported foreign intervention, and until the very late stages of the war they persistently magnified their criticism of "Gaddafi forces" while somewhat minimizing any direct criticism of insurgent actions and downplaying criticisms of NATO operations even more. Only after the end of NATO operations did they begin to criticize and condemn the human rights abuses of the new regime more firmly, while making a rather half-hearted effort to document civilian deaths caused by NATO bombings.

Other government documents of value were those produced in reports by members of the U.S. Congress, by the Congressional Research Service, the White House Office of the Press Secretary, the Department of Defense press services, AFRICOM's Public Affairs unit, and others. Most of the statements, interviews, and documents emanating from these sources are designed as officially sanctioned state propaganda, and must be read in that light, and in dialogue with actual events as they unfolded. Sometimes, of course, they can be extremely telling of actual interests and motivations, as well as useful presentations of the prejudices that guide U.S. policies.

Journalistic accounts can be useful if double-edged: useful when multiple reporters in a given location corroborate each other and show some independence by departing from NATO's preferred narrative. This happened on occasion. Yet they are misleading when the reports are filed from a distance, relying excessively on one side of the conflict for "information," or forming a chorus that simply reproduces official NATO statements without question and without fact-checking. In other cases, journalists' editorial narratives produced important insights into the interventionist mindset and the extent to which culturally instituted forms of demonizing Gaddafi have become entrenched, having accumulated over nearly four decades of mass socialization from the media replaying the vitriol of political leaders in the West, often without question. It is also important to be aware of the fact that some media organizations barely hid the foreign policy agendas that they served, most notably Al Jazeera, which relayed National Transitional Council propaganda without question, just as its paymaster, the Emir of Qatar, had also deployed jets and troops in the fight against Libya, but also CNN, with its narrative on Libya almost exactly matching that of the U.S. State Department, if not exceeding it in its interventionist zeal and breathless demonization of Gaddafi.

On the other hand, the first-hand reports of some of the foreign supporters of the Libyan government sometimes proved to be problematic for simply repeating the claims of government spokespersons without first scrutinizing the evidence for their claims—for example, that the opposition in Misrata had been totally vanquished by the government on the very eve of the collapse of Tripoli. Yet they too furnished vital documentary evidence of mass destruction and civilian casualties caused by NATO bombings that few in the mass media ever showed; their critical commentaries usually brought into bold relief the contradictions, myths, and underlying intent of NATO actions and public narratives. Whenever possible, I have also relied on reports from Libyan state television and from high officials in the former Libyan government, first to avoid reliance on what others claimed they said, and second to provide some balance to the dominance of Western officialdom in the mainstream media.

The reports of private intelligence firms, such as STRATFOR, were sometimes useful as they were often written for paid subscribers in the media, diplomatic corps, and military and intelligence circles, and were produced by individuals who in many cases had military and intelligence backgrounds. Finally, previously published works on Libyan history published before the NATO intervention were particularly valuable in providing an historical mooring that better contextualized what some might mistakenly see as merely a single "event" in 2011, that event being the war.

Acknowledgments

First and foremost, I must thank Robin Philpot, the senior editor behind Baraka Books, for inviting me to produce this manuscript, for his advice, questions, and encouragement from start to finish, and for his extraordinary patience. It is a very rare experience for me to have developed such a warm and productive collaboration with a publisher, and to benefit from the insights of one with the experience, learning, and critical investigative mindset of Robin Philpot. This has been, by very far, the happiest relationship I have yet had with a publisher. I would also like to particularly thank Josée Lalancette for her wonderful work on the layout and design of the book. I wish to also thank Mahdi Darius Nazemroaya for his many reports from Libya, and for his generosity in allowing free reproduction of his photos for this book. Especially important was the groundbreaking research and correspondence from the French independent documentary filmmaker, Julien Teil, whose work helped to complement much of my own, and to fill in important gaps. Several Libyan correspondents also provided input, advice, and in some cases severe criticism—I of course take responsibility for anything they would perceive as lingering shortcomings in my work. I am also thankful to Oxford Research International and the Institute of Human Sciences at the University of Oxford for sharing the detailed data from their first national survey of Libya. I am particularly thankful to WikiLeaks for its publication of unedited U.S. Embassy cables which helped to dispel many false interpretations, while acknowledging the significant risks to which WikiLeaks was exposed. Finally, I wish to particularly thank my wife, Allison, who shouldered far more daily work than she should have just to allow me more time and peace of mind to write this book, and who especially helped me by allowing me to engage in interminable conversations with her about the war in Libya.

Abbreviations

ADA	Libyan Foundation for African Development Aid
AFRICOM	U.S. Africa Command
AI	Amnesty International
AOPIG	African Oil Policy Initiative Group
AQIM	Al Qaeda in the Maghreb
AU	African Union
BISC	Sahel-Saharan Bank for Investment and Commerce
CDA	Chargé d'Affaires
CEN-SAD	Community of Sahel-Saharan States
CIA	U.S Central Intelligence Agency
ECOWAS	Economic Community of West African States
EU	European Union
Eximbank	U.S. Export-Import Bank
FATL	Forum for African Traditional Leaders
GDF	Gaddafi Development Foundation
GMR	Great Man-made River Project
HRW	Human Rights Watch
ICC	International Criminal Court
ICRC	International Committee for the Red Cross
LAICO	Libyan Arab African Investment Company
LAFICO	Libyan Arab Foreign Investment Company
LAP	Libyan African Investment Portfolio
LIA	Libyan Investment Authority
LIFG	Libyan Islamic Fighting Group
NATO	North Atlantic Treaty Organization
NDI	National Democratic Institute (U.S.)
NGO	Non-governmental Organization
NTC	National Transitional Council (also Interim Transnational National Council, also Transitional National Council)
OAU	Organization of African Unity
OPIC	U.S. Overseas Private Investment Corporation
POTUS	President of the United States
SADC	Southern African Development Community
TSCTP	Trans-Sahara Counter-Terrorism Partnership
UNECA	United Nations Economic Commission for Africa
UNGA	United Nations General Assembly
UNHRC	United Nations Human Rights Council
UNSC	United Nations Security Council
UNSCR	United Nations Security Council Resolution
USAID	U.S. Agency for International Development
USEAA	U.S. Embassy, Addis Ababa, Ethiopia
USEM	U.S. Embassy, Monrovia, Liberia
USET	U.S. Embassy, Tripoli, Libya
USSR	Union of Soviet Socialist Republics
WICS	World Islamic Call Society

Liberal Imperialism and the New Scramble for Africa

"There is a growing belief, not least within the ranks of latter-day new Labour missionaries, that appears to favour the reconquest of Africa. No one really suggests how this would come about, nor is there a 'plan' available for discussion. Yet the implicit suggestion of recent reporting from Sierra Leone, Zimbabwe and Nigeria, sometimes echoed in London, is that imperial intervention might indeed be welcomed by peoples threatened with mayhem, anarchy and civil war. In the process, several decades of revisionist imperial history and leftist criticism of 'neocolonialism' have been easily ignored or forgotten, and external interference is once again being made respectable." (Gott, 2001/1/15)

A single "plan" as such there may not be, even if the commentary on British interventions by Richard Gott above already flagged some of the key elements of the new imperial mission in Africa. These are military interventions in the name of humanitarian protection, the restoration of order to nations inevitably seen as helpless and in need of external assistance, and the reformulation of dominant ideologies. Yet that is still just part of an explanation, for it retains the suggestion that intervention may occur simply and only because "we" believe that our actions are conducted in order to benefit "them." Gott is right to pinpoint the ideological sources of the new imperialism. In the war against Libya some of the most prominent anti-war criticisms did not come from "liberals" or vaguely self-nominated "leftists," but rather from avowed "conservatives" and those in the Realist school of U.S. foreign policy: Ron Paul (2011/8/29), Patrick Buchanan (2011/3/8), George Will (2011/3/8), and Leslie Gelb (2011/3/8) among others. Few recognized that liberal imperialism was the driving force in new American conquests even under putative conservatives such as George W. Bush, and thus many did not recognize "neoconservativism" whose ideological principles and goals are that of a "new" liberal imperialism: direct intervention, regime-change, nation-building, counterinsurgency, pacification, aid, development. The hard-line conservatives in the U.S. instead proclaim that America is a republic, and not an empire. Others clearly disagree. The result is the creation of a renewed hierarchy that not accidentally mirrors old ethnocentric theories of "cultural evolution" from the nineteenth century and some of the racial typologies of the time: the West, white, developed, and superior has the right to intervene in Africa, and Africa has the "right" to be intervened in, and should be barred from even intervening in its own affairs. We are not dealing with coincidences and accidents, not at this level of expenditure and obsessive strategizing: the U.S. military's new Africa Command (AFRICOM), the African Growth and Opportunities Act (AGOA), the work of the USAID, and the International Criminal Court (ICC) with its nearly exclusive focus on Africa—none of these things are "accidents."

"What Africa really needs," Gott continued, highlighting conclusions of published works on Africa funded by George Soros and the U.S. Institute for Peace, "is the advice of a new generation of foreign missionaries, imbued with the new, secular religion of good governance and human rights." As Gott also rightly spotlights:

> "Other contemporary witnesses, the innumerable representatives of the non-governmental and humanitarian organisations that clog the airwaves and pollute the outside world's coverage of African affairs with their endless one-sided accounts of tragedy and disaster, echo the same message. With the reporting and analysis of today's Africa in the hands of such people, it is not surprising that public opinion is often confused and disarmed when governments embark on neocolonial interventions. The new missionaries are much like the old ones, an advance guard preparing the way for military and economic conquest." (Gott, 2001/1/15)

It also helps when, within "public opinion," the anxious motivators, the militarized altruists, and the imperial humanists are working as amplifiers and repeaters of interventionist doctrine, seeking to rally public support for the causes of the U.S. State Department. Sometimes, they even provide the appropriate emotional cues hoping to spread outrage: "my hand is trembling as I write this," or "no time to play with my five-year old daughter, she can't understand why, and I dare not tell her of these horrors" (conveyed by the endless supply of Internet videos posted by unidentified "activists"). One scathing and very memorable British op-ed characterized this element of public opinion as consisting of "iPad imperialists":

> "From the comfort of his Home Counties home, possibly to the sound of birds tweeting on the windowsill, the liberal interventionist will write furious, spittle-stained articles about the need to invade faraway countries in order to topple their dictators. As casually and thoughtlessly as the rest of us write shopping lists, he will pen a 10-point plan for the bombing of Yugoslavia or Afghanistan or Iraq and not give a second thought to the potentially disastrous consequences. Now, having learned nothing from the horrors that they cheer-led like excitable teenage girls over the past 15 years, these bohemian bombers, these latte-sipping lieutenants, these iPad imperialists are back. This time they're demanding the invasion of Libya." (O'Neill, 2011/2/25)

Rather than stopping and taking comfort from mocking caricatures, this book takes the tenets and claims of the assemblage of "humanitarian" arguments for military intervention in Libya seriously. But taking them seriously does not mean the same thing as taking them at face value, or being unduly deferential. Instead, if we take them on their very own terms the arguments for "humanitarian" intervention and "protection" soon fall apart in the face of actual evidence from practice. The real challenge is not to get the humanitarian interventionists to stake a position, but rather to get them to maintain that position when events and processes go exactly counter to all of their stated ideals, when "saving lives" soon becomes overwhelmed by the deliberate destruction of lives, and when "protection" becomes a mere fig-leaf for regime change. It is not enough to dismiss them after showing and recognizng the nullification of dogma by practice. We still need to see why such arguments were deployed to begin with and what purposes they serve, and in turn, what purposes we are called upon to serve when orchestrators of mass opinion pointedly ask us, "how can we stand idly by?"

That question has always perplexed me. We can stand idly because we have been well trained to do so, just like the majority of U.S. and British citizens stood idly by as their troops wrought destruction, death and pain on Iraq. Citizens of NATO states whose troops went to Afghanistan did the same, as was the case in our countless other ongoing covert wars and employment of proxy torture states. We even stand idly by as protesters in our own societies get beaten, arrested, or worse, for daring to exercise their supposed rights to assembly without first submitting notice and asking the authorities for permission, sometimes well in advance—indeed, the protest-ers are inevitably excoriated by mass mediated opinion. So what is so special about Libya that we could not continue to stand idly by? Had all of us developed a strong, intimate affection for these people? What did we know about these protesting Libyans that we could so readily commit ourselves to some undefined cause that mouthed suspiciously predictable buzzwords of democracy and freedom but only when spoken in some grand hall in a European capital, under the glare of camera lights? On what basis would we always be willing to credit these "rebels" with noble intentions and always give them the benefit of the doubt, while launching flaming invective at those defending the existing social order? And how could we engage with such intense evangelical sternness that we could permit ourselves to denounce and condemn those among us who would hold back and ques-tion the campaign to demolish another state? Perhaps some of us saw how we could benefit from being on "the right side of history," which was code for being pro-military intervention by *our side*. Suddenly, we could feel very comfortable about being on the same team with the CIA, the Pentagon, and a battery of so-called "neocon" commentators who all supported the war; we would all be on "the winning team," Team West.

This book is thus largely about our intervention, and about making ourselves accountable for it. It is true that some Libyans, often expatriates, complained loudly and severely against "anti-imperialists" and "Gaddafi apologists." However, since they invited Western intervention, appealed to us to spend money on bombs, missiles, jets and ships to change their history for them, then whether they like it or not they invited *all* of us into their conflict and the least they could have done was to courteously desist from demanding silence of those whose support they requested. This too offered an important lesson: neocolonialism is not just about Western agency, but also of local collaborators and upholders of Western power. Anti-imperialism, most clearly and persistently articulated by some African and Latin American leaders during the war against Libya, was therefore never just a confrontation with Western opponents alone.

Among the ranks of those who remain critical of U.S. adventures are those who would entirely dismiss as nonsensical propaganda all U.S. government talk of supporting democracy, freedom, and human rights abroad (often for excellent reasons). Nonetheless, it is still necessary to take these claims ser-iously by understanding what they are *meant to mean* in actual practice.

"Democracy," defined by way of comparison to the U.S. political sys-tem, can represent a significant strategic gain of importance for the U.S.

A society unprotected by a hard shell of state-organized resistance is one that can be more easily penetrated when it has multiple parties in competition, subject to external lobbying, influence, and financing. The U.S. has thus worked covertly in manipulating electoral outcomes to its advantage even in supposed ally states such as Italy and the Philippines, on numerous occasions, while able to cover its tracks with a gloss of legitimacy. Currently, one of the favourite vehicles for the U.S. to pursue its interests are local NGOs. They are funded and aided in other ways by U.S.-government funded bodies, such as the National Endowment for Democracy, or NGOs affiliated with either of the two dominant political parties in the U.S., such as the National Democratic Institute, or the International Republican Institute, or trade union bodies such as the AFL-CIO. Thus far the U.S. has been very successful in convincing many that they should confuse a method with a process, namely that they should equate multi-party elections with democracy. In practical and strategic terms, "democracy" means access, and in Libya as the U.S. Embassy cables published by WikiLeaks have shown, U.S. officials routinely complained of the frustrations, setbacks, unpredictability, and unreliability of access to local authorities and competing local interests.

As with "democracy," the idea of "freedom" also means a great deal in the pursuit of U.S. interests, but what can it mean when the U.S. has over many decades intervened directly or indirectly to install or support repressive regimes around the globe? Freedom, when one examines the corrollaries outlined by U.S. officials, especially in the speeches of presidents, State Department officials, or in legislation passed by Congress, usually involves free enterprise, free markets, free trade, and a general withdrawal of the state from a given economy. Freedom also means the relatively unrestrained ability of wealthy private interests to operate and act to maximize their gains, such as by launching or acquiring media companies in order to better influence public opinion in their favour, and to advance the culture of international consumption. Freedom can additionally mean the unfettered action of those who wish to mobilize to make their society more and more like a replica of American, i.e. "developed" society. Freedom can mean that foreign investors are free to strike deals with local agents and collaborators, without having to answer too much to state authorities.

In U.S. strategic thinking, "human rights" performs similar functions to the above. This is especially the case as the concept focuses on the rights of the individual, further reduced by U.S. political action in international and other fora to mean essentially individual civil liberties, not social and economic rights, and even less so the rights of collectivities. It is strategically valuable then to multiply the access points for U.S. influence, to act while appearing to be legitimate, to open economies to U.S. corporate control and foster greater consumerism, and to create networks that can unsettle a society should its leadership pursue greater independence or outright defiance. In other words, ideological and symbolic strategies matter even if they often appear to be tissue-thin.

It cannot be denied that the key motor force of historical change in Libya would be symbolized by the air-dropped bomb. Interestingly, 2011 was the 100th anniversary of aerial bombardment. It began in 1911 with Italy bombing Libya, and in 2011 Italy was bombing Libya again, this time as part of NATO, and with the pleas and thanks of Benghazi "revolutionaries." Some may wish to argue the point of agency, of who won the "war against Gaddafi," but the argument is without merit. The central protagonist in the story of the war became NATO, led by the U.S., with aerial bombardment and special forces on the ground. Whatever happened in Libya, happened because of this presence, and it cannot be erased from any credible analysis. Mustafa Abdul Jalil, formerly the Libyan justice minister, who then defected immediately to lead the rebel National Transitional Council (NTC), candidly admitted to the press: "We asked for a no-fly zone to be imposed from day one" (AFP, 2011/3/13). This was not the only such indication of where the rebels were placing the power to chart their course, as evidenced by numerous appeals and early frustration when there was even a hint that their calls might not get the intended response. Either way a relationship of dependency was articulated and made clear to anyone closely watching the Libyan crisis unfold. The following statements illustrate this dependency.

"'The international community has failed us,' Mr. [Ahmed] Omar [a rebel commander] said by phone." (Koring, 2011/3/16)

"'People are fed up. They are waiting impatiently for an international move,' said Saadoun al-Misrati, a rebel spokesman in the city of Misrata, the last rebel-held city in western Libya, which came under heavy shelling Wednesday. 'What Gadhafi is doing, he is exploiting delays by the international community. People are very angry that no action is being taken against Gadhafi's weaponry'." (Michael, 2011/3/16)

"Gheriani, the rebel spokesman, said by telephone from Benghazi that the opposition was hoping for a positive U.N. Security Council vote." (Lucas, 2011/3/17)

"'We think that in the coming hours we will see real genocide in Ajdabiya,' he said. 'The international community has to act within the next 10 hours'— Dabbashi said Gadhafi's forces would unleash 'ethnic cleansing' on villages in the mountain region of the western part of the country. 'I think something will be in the resolution to allow air strikes'." (Charbonneau, 2011/3/16)

"'The world is sleeping,' he [a rebel fighter interviewed by AP] said. 'They (the West) drunk of Gadhafi's oil and now they won't stand against him. They didn't give us a no-fly zone'." (Lucas & Hadid, 2011/3/15)

"'We feel so, so, isolated here. We are pleading with the international community to help us in this very difficult time'." (AP, 2011/3/15)

"Libya's revolutionary leadership is pressing western powers to assassinate Muammar Gaddafi and launch military strikes against his forces to protect rebel-held cities from the threat of bloody assault. Mustafa Gheriani, spokesman for the revolutionary national council in its stronghold of Benghazi, said the appeal was to be made by a delegation meeting the French president, Nicolas Sarkozy, and the US secretary of state, Hillary Clinton, in Paris on Monday, as G8 foreign ministers gathered there to consider whether to back French and British calls for a no-fly zone over Libya…. 'We are telling the west we want a no-fly zone, we want tactical strikes against those tanks and rockets that are being used against us and we want a strike against Gaddafi's compound,' said Gheriani. 'This is the message from our delegation in Europe.'….'The west is missing the point. The revolution was started because people were feeling despair from poverty, from oppression. Their last hope was freedom. If the west takes too long—where people say it's too little, too late—then people become a target for extremists who say the west doesn't care about them. Most people in this country are moderates and extremists have not been able to penetrate them. But if they get to the point of disillusionment with the west there will be no going back'." (McGreal, 2011/3/14)

"The founding statement of the ITNC (later changing its name to NTC) said: 'Finally, even though the balance of power is uneven between the defenceless protestors and the tyrant regime's mercenaries and private battalions, we will relay on the will of our people for a free and dignified existence. Furthermore, we request from the international community to fulfill its obligations to protect the Libyan people from any further genocide and crimes against humanity without any direct military intervention on Libyan soil'." (Boyle, 2011/3/13)

"'This was a rare decision of the Arab League,' rebel spokesman Abdul Basit al-Muzayrik told Al-Jazeera. 'We call on the international community to quickly make a firm decision against these crimes'." (CBC, 2011/3/13)

"'Where is the West? How are they helping? What are they doing,' shouted one fighter." (AJE, 2011/3/12)

"'People are losing faith in the international community,' said Essam Gheriani, a spokesman for the rebel movement in Libya.... 'They are not pleased with all the procrastination,' Gheriani said. 'What are they waiting for?'.... 'The United States has a lot it can do to support the Libyans,' Ali said. 'I wonder why they are taking it slow?'" (Michaels, 2011/3/12)

U.S. Senator John Kerry also wrote an influential op-ed, urging immediate, high-speed intervention, which would of course limit the time for debate, for formulating and answering questions, and for stronger Congressional criticism to emerge. Repairing damage to the image of the U.S. as a result of Iraq and Afghanistan, clearly weighed on Kerry's mind: "The US and the world community should also make clear—as we did in Bosnia and Kosovo—that we are taking a united stand against a thug who is killing Muslims" (Kerry, 2011/3/14). In virtually erecting himself to the position of "protector of Muslims," Kerry eerily echoed another leader who took on the name, "Protector of Islam": Benito Mussolini, waving a gold sword as he entered Tripoli on horseback on March 20, 1937.

Not to "appear to be seen" (as Washington strategists like to say) to be leading the crusade against Libya, the U.S. attempted various poorly executed magic tricks in public. The desire was to be seen as "leading from behind" (which is still leading), or having followed others into war. First the stated desire was to have the African Union and the Arab League call for a no-fly zone and a UN resolution calling for intervention in Libya. The AU resisted. The Arab League, with only half of its members present, and two of those abstaining, voted for foreign intervention. It then seemed that the AU's consent and approval was no longer important. While the U.S. led the war campaign with the majority of bombs, missiles, drones, jets and ships, it still had to masquerade as something else: hence Obama proudly, perhaps carelessly, revealed that even French jets were sometimes flown by U.S. pilots. Leading from behind NATO is also a peculiar notion, as the U.S. is NATO's own commanding power: the U.S. ran the show that ran the show.

The political leaders of NATO states at the forefront of the war against Libya also seemed to have some recurring difficulty in trying a duplicitous rhetorical balancing act, arguing that they really were not determining what Libya's internal affairs should be, but that they would and should.

Thus UK Prime Minister David Cameron in his opening speech at the "London Conference on Libya" on March 29, 2011 stated:

> "Today is about a new beginning for Libya—a future in which the people of Libya can determine their own destiny, free from violence and oppression. But the Libyan people cannot reach that future on their own....we must help the Libyan people plan for their future after the conflict is over....A new beginning for Libya is within their grasp....and we will help them seize it." (Cameron, 2011/3/29)

UK Foreign Secretary William Hague fared no better, seemingly unable to make one plea of innocence without immediately contradicting it. He stated, "We agreed that it is not for any of the participants here today to choose the government of Libya: only the Libyan people can do that." But then he said, "Participants agreed that Qadhafi and his regime have completely lost legitimacy and will be held accountable for their actions." Then Hague reaffirmed that, "the Libyan people must be free to determine their own future," and then he reversed himself saying, "participants recognised the need for all Libyans..." etcetera (Hague, 2011/3/29). Which participants agreed to that? Not even the NTC was invited to the event. Indeed, the "participants" referred to in the speeches above, besides representatives of multilateral institutions such as the UN, NATO and EU, and one priest, were: Albania, Belgium, Bulgaria, Canada, Croatia, the Czech Republic, Denmark, Estonia, France, Germany, Greece, Hungary, Iceland, Italy, Iraq, Jordan, Kuwait, Latvia, Lebanon, Lithuania, Luxembourg, Malta, Morocco, Netherlands, Norway, Poland, Portugal, Qatar, Romania, Slovakia, Slovenia, Spain, Sweden, Tunisia, Turkey, UAE, and the U.S. One has difficulty imagining how Estonia thought that it too should have a say in Libya's future, but at least its presence helped to complete the portrait of imperial whiteness we see in Figure I.1.

The U.S. stood to gain in many ways from intervening in Libya. Having such a diverse range made the intervention much more attractive to those who had to first conceive it and weigh its possible results, and then commit when a "window of opportunity" presented itself in the form of street protests that sought to emulate those of Egypt, Tunisia and elsewhere. Among the gains were: 1) increased access for U.S. corporations to massive Libyan expenditures on infrastructure development (and now reconstruction), from which U.S. corporations had frequently been locked out when Gaddafi was in power; 2) warding off any increased acquisition of Libyan oil contracts by Chinese and Russian firms; 3) ensuring that a friendly regime was

FIGURE I.1. Group photograph of the participants in the London Conference on Libya, March 29, 2011. (Source: UK Foreign and Commonwealth Office, in the public domain.)

in place that was not influenced by ideas of "resource nationalism;" 4) increasing the presence of AFRICOM in African affairs, in an attempt to substitute for the African Union and to entirely displace the Libyan-led Community of Sahel-Saharan States (CEN-SAD); 5) expanding the U.S. hold on key geostrategic locations and resources; 6) promoting U.S. claims to be serious about freedom, democracy, and human rights, and of being on the side of the people of Africa, as a benign benefactor; 7) politically stabilizing the North African region in a way that locked out opponents of the U.S.; and, 8) drafting other nations to undertake the work of defending and advancing U.S. political and economic interests, under the guise of humanitarianism and protecting civilians.

This book does not readily subscribe to a number of arguments commonly made in either the mainstream or independent electronic media. One is usually summed up colloquially as, "Gaddafi was in bed with the West" since at least 2003 when sanctions were lifted and the U.S. and Libya appeared to pursue a mutual strategy of reconciliation and normalization. That reveals a superficial understanding of the actual content of their relations, which remained tense, on the brink of breaking on numerous occasions, and fraught with mutual suspicion. Ample evidence exists of course to show increased cooperation, exchange, and even the appearance of friendship between Gaddafi and certain Western leaders, as well as his heightened desire to be admitted into the mainstream of Western capitalism. Few (if any) commentators seem prepared to consider that it was this very "friendliness" that made Gaddafi more of a liability to those states that had previously attacked and isolated Libya, previously plotted his overthrow, supported previous uprisings, and continued to be a home to several opposition groups. Gaddafi became more of a liability because Western powers had now allowed a historical enemy to buy his way into the circuits of influence. Now he appeared to be using the momentary peace to pursue new goals that were ultimately far more threatening than any supply of weapons to the IRA had been, and those goals involved a central Libyan leadership role in an integrated Africa. In addition, no sanctions, new wealth, and influential friends in the West, along with promised reforms, threatened to extend the life of the Libyan Jamahiriya under Gaddafi. Otherwise, as revealed in the diplomatic cables, the Libyan government was constantly seeking assurances from the U.S. that it would not be undermined or attacked, seeking a defensive pact, and worrying that it had given up too much (support for armed groups, and advanced weapons programs of a chemical and nuclear nature), for too little in return. Indeed, the Libyan experience will, and arguably already has been, a piercingly loud wakeup call to those states considering "coming in from the cold" by engaging in compromise and surrendering the weapons programs that appear now, more than ever, to be their best bet against U.S. aggression.

Another prominent and entrenched viewpoint holds that in any analysis of what happened in Libya, attention must be devoted to the Gaddafi government's "human rights record" (usually framed in terms that exclude social and economic rights that are also recognized as human rights in the U.N. Charter). In other words, that we must reinforce the portrait of Gaddafi as a "brutal dictator," as if this somehow explains either the rebellion or justifies the need for foreign military intervention. I will therefore state boldly and directly that Gaddafi's so-called human rights record is almost completely irrelevant. That is except insofar as it featured in roughly hewn, everyday propaganda that served to demonize him and to reduce the discussion of Libya down to one man, while deflecting attention away from the human rights records of the accusers, or the atrocities of the insurgents whose abuses have now amply rivalled all of those of which Gaddafi had ever been accused. Attacking one man is an approach that makes for good caricatures and graffiti, and for awful analysis, and so such viewpoints will not be dignified in this book. At least on paper, regime change is still illegal under international law—it does not become more permissible depending on what we may think is the nature of a regime.

It is also not the case that the rebellion happened either because of high unemployment or anger with dictatorial rule. That is a very poor theory of political revolt and has little currency among serious scholars of politics, probably because nowhere has it been proven to be valid. Nor is it tenable that the best way to understand the rebellion is by isolating Libyan affairs, actors, social relations and political processes from the wider world that impinged upon and shaped them. For example, the sanctions imposed on Libya, the inevitably diminished consumption of foreign goods, and the diminished ability to hire foreign services, clearly had an impact on the Libyan leadership's ability to respond to heightened demands and expectations for an "improved" lifestyle. But by no measure were Libyans living in poverty—indeed, one of the crying complaints phoned in to CNN during one of the nights of the protests, purportedly from someone in Libya, lamented that daily life consisted only of eating, sleeping and working. The lifting of sanctions only exacerbated these tensions: suddenly Libya was awash in many billions of dollars, and while hundreds of new infrastructure projects were undertaken, with tens of thousands of new homes being built, the issue of how the money would be spent was hotly debated and caused dissatisfaction. The Libyan leadership was very aware of that discontent, as the cables published by WikiLeaks repeatedly show. The idea that Gaddafi would steer some of that newly acquired wealth toward Africa and to pursuing ambitious plans for accelerated African integration, irked many Libyans. The discontent with the leadership's Pan-African realignment was thus ever present well before 2011, and it converged with U.S. interests in also seeking unrivalled dominance in shaping African initiatives.

Sirte is the starting point of this book, for in many ways the story of Sirte—and not Benghazi—is central to understanding the war against Libya and Africa. From even before Gaddafi was born in Sirte, to when he came to power, and through the war in 2011 and the bombing campaign that ended in Sirte with Gaddafi's horrific murder and the near total devastation of the city, Sirte is what offers the central reference point for understanding what happened. Place of birth, final resting place, Sirte was also envisioned as a possible new capital for a United States of Africa. That dream has been abruptly and brutally terminated, with the determined persecution of African migrants in Libya, extending to black Libyans, and the new regime promising to close the door on Africa. In some ways, however, some in Africa have decided to slam the door back in Libya's face: witness the deliberate refusal of Algeria, Mauritania, and Niger to comply with demands from the new regime in Libya to hand over government officials and Gaddafi family members who fled to their countries. The loop locking Libya out of Africa is thus pulled tighter. In Libya, what was much romanticized in the media and by activists as the "Arab Spring," was wedded to xenophobia, racism, and a Eurocentric alliance of NATO states. The two chapters on Sirte, offering painful detail on the destruction of the city, also trace the historical role of Sirte in the development of the Libyan Jamahiriya, and its site as one of confrontation with imperialism, from bombings that occurred when Ronald Reagan was president, to attempted assassinations of Gaddafi that occurred with covert support from British intelligence. Sirte in post-sanctions Libya also offers key insights on the nature of Libyan relations with the West, and U.S. anxiety about its own inability to steer developments exactly as it wished. The chapters on Sirte also put to a severe test the claims that NATO's intervention was humanitarian and intended to protect civilians, while also showing the nature of the insurgency and its conceptions of what human rights practice meant.

As described and analyzed throughout, the U.S. had many more pressing and pertinent reasons to pursue regime change in Libya than that of supposedly saving lives. This is not to say that boasting of its success in saving Benghazi could not help satisfy some of its larger aims, while also enabling local forces on the ground to do some of the dirty work of the war. "Protecting civilians" in and of itself—as a stated goal—could, if unchallenged, help to enhance U.S. credibility and legitimacy in international arenas, while also creating the basis for forging alliances with local proxies, and open the door to regime change. Regime change in turn, while not an end in itself, would help to open the door to achieving some larger U.S. goals on the African continent: disrupting an emerging pattern of independence and network of collaboration that would facilitate increased African self-reliance, at odds with the geostrategic and political economic ambitions of the U.S. The creation of AFRICOM directly followed suit from U.S. policy makers and strategists identifying Africa as a key source of oil and minerals. Libya, along with China, was named as one of the adversaries of U.S. interests in Africa. As Sirte symbolizes a resurgent Pan-Africanism in the making, so the termination of NATO's military operations in that city and the insurgents' devastation of it and the overthrow of Gaddafi would spell the unmaking of the Pan-Africanist project, as some might have hoped.

Following two chapters showing how Sirte was a stage for many of the currents and developments leading up to and following from the U.S.-led NATO intervention, two chapters focus on Pan-Africanism and AFRICOM. In as much detail as possible we learn of the strong bonds formed between Gaddafi and key African leaders; the development of Gaddafi's Pan-Africanist thinking; the resurgence of Kwame Nkrumah's ideals for African integration; and the extensive nature of Libyan aid and investment throughout Africa. The second chapter on Africa deals with AFRICOM and Libyan defiance, followed by a detailed presentation of the argument that war against the Libyan Jamahiriya was a fundamentally racist one.

Chapter 5 provides a wider discussion of humanitarian intervention and the protection of civilians, as well as claims that Benghazi was saved, and that "genocide" was prevented. The popular myths that worked to legitimate military intervention are critically examined and put to the test in light of available evidence. The role of the UN and human rights NGOs in ensuring that only one story of events in Libya could be told in international fora is also examined. That story was the one told by the opposition. We look at how Libya was repeatedly prevented from speaking for itself at the UN, and also at the revolving door between some NGOs and the U.S. State Department. The chapter then asks the reader to consider what were the alternatives to foreign intervention.

The concluding chapter ends with an extension of one of the key themes in this book, namely that the war against Libya was also a war against Africa. This is best illustrated by the critical perspectives on regime change in Libya as voiced by prominent African leaders. In addition, we look at the impact of the war on leadership within the African Union itself, which has had an unsettling effect to say the least. We end by considering how the war in Libya has destabilized the immediate region, and how this too represents further opportunity for U.S. intervention, and a thus continued need on our part for vigilance and skepticism in the face of the heady claims of our own inherent goodness which can only find its highest expression in the form of aerial bombardment.

CHAPTER ONE

Sirte: Keystone of Independence

"I welcome you in the city of Sirte," Colonel Muammar Gaddafi told those gathered for the Fifth Ordinary Summit of the African Union in 2005. He told his guests that Sirte is the place "which the Libyans call the frontline city because it confronted the colonial onslaughts and resisted several colonial campaigns aimed at the heart of Africa since the Roman, Byzantine, Turkish and Italian colonial eras, alongside other incursions by the Vandals who were seeking to penetrate deep into the African continent." Gaddafi then instructed the audience: "Sirte was always the first line of defence against those campaigns" (Gaddafi, 2005, p. 31).

FIGURE 1.1 Muammar Gaddafi, President of the Libyan Arab Jamahiriya, speaking at the opening of the Fifth Summit of the African Union in Sirte, Libya, on July 4, 2005. (Source: courtesy of the United Nations, photograph by Evan Schneider.)

Welcome to Sirte Today

"It used to be a beautiful city, one of the most beautiful in Libya," said Zarouk Abdullah, 42, a university professor, standing outside his badly damaged family home: "Today it looks like (postwar) Leningrad, Gaza or Beirut" (AP, 2011/10/28). "It looks today like Ypres in 1915, or Grozny in

1995 after the Russian Army had finished with it," a journalist with *The Independent* reported with similar comparisons (Randall, 2011/10/23).

Other visitors, writing for *The Sunday Telegraph*, wrote much the same: "The shattered remains of housing blocks and the wreckage…are more reminiscent of the grimmest scenes from Grozny, towards the end of Russia's bloody Chechen war, than of anything seen in Libya so far" (Farmer & Sherlock, 2011/10/15). Sirte was found "almost without an intact building," with "nearly every house…pulverized by a rocket or mortar, burned out or riddled with bullets"—"the infrastructure of a city upon which the Libyan leader lavished many millions has simply ceased to exist" (Randall, 2011/10/23). Sirte has been "reduced to rubble, a ghost town filled with the stench of death and where bodies litter the streets" (Bastian, 2011/10/23). "So far, we visited 7,000 houses and 6,000 are damaged," said Ahmed Qurbaj who was charged with assessing the scale of destruction in this city (Gumuchian, 2012/2/29). "Much of the Mediterranean city of palm tree-lined boulevards has been destroyed. Whole neighborhoods are uninhabitable" (AP, 2011/10/28). "The air rankles with the smell of rotting bodies" (Bastian, 2011/10/23). "There's no electricity or water. Debris-filled streets are flooded from broken pipes" (AP, 2011/10/28). Well before the assault on Sirte ended, the BBC's Wyre Davies reported: "the city is more badly damaged than any other Libyan city affected by the 'war'—flattened in places."[1] "Utterly ravaged" is what *The Telegraph*'s Ben Farmer (2011/10/22) said when he saw Sirte, "a skeleton of a city—a place without food, water or light; a city without citizens. Its streets were turned into rivers by burst pipes, as fighters battled through waist-high swathes of mud brown water, street by bloody street." Another journalist made the following report from the scene of the devastation that our victors morbidly hailed as "liberation."

> "Gaddafi's home town appeared Saturday to have been largely destroyed, with most of its population fled and holes the size of manhole covers blown in apartment buildings and the ousted leader's showcase convention center. A drive through some of Sirte's 'liberated' neighborhoods revealed the pounding the city has taken. In one area, block after block of small mustard-yellow apartments were peppered with small-arms fire. Artillery fire had blasted holes in the walls, and front doors were ripped off their hinges. The burned-out carcasses of a truck and car littered one empty street. Gabriele Rossi, the

---

1. Reporting live via Twitter: < http://twitter.com/#!/WyreDavies/status/1269366277 32955136>

emergency coordinator in Sirte for the aid group Doctors Without Borders, said the city appeared to have sustained some of the greatest damage of the war. 'The part we have seen is almost completely destroyed,' he said." (Sheridan, 2011/10/15)

"What happened in our town is a disaster," one girl in Sirte told the BBC, "they attacked us in our houses and looted them, they destroyed everything" (Head, 2012/2/9).

Sirte suffered a catastrophe according to these and many more eyewitness descriptions of endless rows of buildings on fire, corpses of the executed lying on hospital lawns, mass graves, homes looted and burned by insurgents, apartment blocks flattened by NATO bombs. This is what "protecting civilians" actually looks like, and it looks like crimes against humanity. Far from the romantic image of all of Libya having risen up against "the evil tyrant," this was one side of Libya destroying the other with the aid (to say the least) of foreign forces. "Sirte is over. There is nothing left for me here," said Ahmad Ali as he drove away from the city (Bastian, 2011/10/23).

Sirte, once promoted by Colonel Muammar Gaddafi as a possible capital of a future United States of Africa, and one of the strongests bases of support for the revolution he led, was found to be in near total ruin by visiting journalists who came after the end of the bombing campaign by members of the North Atlantic Treaty Organization (NATO).

"Four months after Libya's leader met his end in his hometown Sirte, the fishing village he turned into a model city lies in ruins....In a city that once served as a showcase to foreign dignitaries, nearly every building bears the scars of war.... In the once favoured seafront neighbourhood known as District Two, scene of some of the heaviest fighting and where Gaddafi is believed to have hidden in his last days, some houses have entire walls missing. Windows are shattered or blown off, fallen balcony railings hang to one side. Street lampposts are riddled with bullet holes." (Gumuchian, 2012/2/29)

Testifying to the indiscriminate nature of the assault on residential areas, aimed at overthrowing the government, a BBC reporter said "it is hard to find a building undamaged by bullets or shells," adding, "occasionally you see grotesquely twisted concrete structures, barely recognisable now, that were blown apart by NATO bombs" (Head, 2012/2/9). Sometimes "indiscriminate" can suggest accidental, merely a result of poor targeting, careless but unintentional. Yet the same BBC reporter tells us: "I have met many people in Misrata who believe Sirte should be wiped off the map" (Head, 2012/2/9). This would suggest that at least some of the attackers forming part of militias from Misrata, were driven to pursue total war against the population. Another report indicated that this is how the residents of Sirte perceived the NATO-supported assault on their city: "Residents now believe the Misrata fighters intentionally destroyed Sirte, beyond the collateral damage of fighting" (AP, 2011/10/28). At an earlier stage in the rebels' drive to take over Libya, as they unsuccessfully tried to take Ajdabiya from government supporters in March 2011, one of the rebels told *The Telegraph* that NATO should bomb the town even if it meant civilian casualties, that entirely razing the town was the best way to "free" the country: "Even if they blow up Ajdabiya we don't care" (Crilly, 2011/3/21).

That such desires, which the Western media would have otherwise labeled "genocidal" if expressed by Gaddafi or his supporters, received so little notice and even less comment from the Western humanitarians who were anxious to intervene to "save lives" in Libya, is a testament to the manufacture of a moral dualism that could justify as much atrocity as it claimed to abhor. In this scheme, the rebels could only be divine, and their victims could only be sacrificed; hence the vast destruction of Sirte which occurred with the commanding support of our Western intervention. In Sirte, we did far worse than "standing idly by" (the favourite phrase used by "humanitarian interventionists" when imploring action): we actively participated in the slaughter, and without a hint of remorse. The United Nations Security Council passed no resolutions to initiate action to stop the rebels. There were no calls from "the international community" to protect the people of Sirte from slaughter. Those who militated for action to uphold the new norm called the "Responsibility to Protect" (R2P) were mostly able to avert their eyes. Few were willing to admit that force was not being used to enforce a doctrine, but rather that the doctrine served as a legitimizing pretext for force. The entire NATO campaign, culminating and coming to a stop in Sirte, was instead roundly hailed as a "success story," even a "model," not just by the Secretary-General of NATO, but by most NATO leaders, by leading R2P advocates, and by the Secretary-General of the United Nations (UN). Weaponizing morality as an instrument of warfare is not new, but it deserves a prominent place in any account of the ideological structures of what some call "the new imperialism" and how it plastered Libya with bombs.

An account of our intervention in Libya must, as a central feature, contextualize it properly by bringing a symbolically central case such as Sirte's back into history. Otherwise, we are left with simplistic formulas, of the kind proferred by the talk-show punditry, which are as lacking in analytical depth as they are deficient of credibility: that this war was about "human rights," that Gaddafi was a "brutal dictator," that we needed to "protect civilians" or that "the world" looked to "us" to "do something." The nature of the "Gaddafi regime" neither explains nor justifies Western intervention: "This is not about who Gaddafi is. It's about who we are and how our good name is hijacked by leaders who order violence without any restraint" (Collins, 2011).

The story of Sirte is important because of the symbolic and strategic centrality of this location, which does not mean that what happened there happened nowhere else in Libya. However, almost all commentators agree that what Sirte suffered was the worst. Sirte is symbolic of the ends of this war: it rests at the intersection between being the place of birth of Gaddafi and the place of his torture and execution; born to loving parents in the region adjoining Sirte, it was in this city that Gaddafi was killed at the hands of a hate-filled mob; the city that shone under Gaddafi, was reduced to rubble by NATO bombardments and by the blanketing firepower by rebels; a city developed by the revolution Gaddafi led and then looted by fighters who proclaimed a new revolution. He was a target of regime change, with an end brought about by NATO bombing his convoy as he tried to escape, struck by NATO on the pretext that even his fleeing convoy could "threaten civilians." In broader terms, Sirte was the proposed capital for a new, united Africa, to which the doors have been closed by a combination of racism, xenophobia, a rival Arabism, and an alliance with North American and European powers. And Sirte was the city that could be destroyed because for some reason we were told that the more important imperative was to "save Benghazi." Believing that some lives are better and more important than others logically takes us out of the realm of "universal human rights" and moves us into the arena of conquest and domination.

From a Tent outside Sirte: Defining a New Libya

"His [Gaddafi's] birthplace was the low tent of his father, a semi-nomad, pitched somewhere south of Sirte in the open desert that formed the family's traditional range-lands. The Sirtica, although administratively part of Tripolitania in the west and part of Cyrenaica in the east, has always been an extended frontier district, a historically ungovernable no man's land between the main centres of population round Tripoli, Benghazi and the southern oases. In being born there, [Muammar Gaddafi] acquired the politically

invaluable credential of being neither a true Tripolitanian, nor a Cyrenaican,
nor even a Fezzanese, but a *bedu* of the open desert that is common to all
Libya, and from which many Libyans like to think they themselves once
came." (Wright, 1981, p. 124)

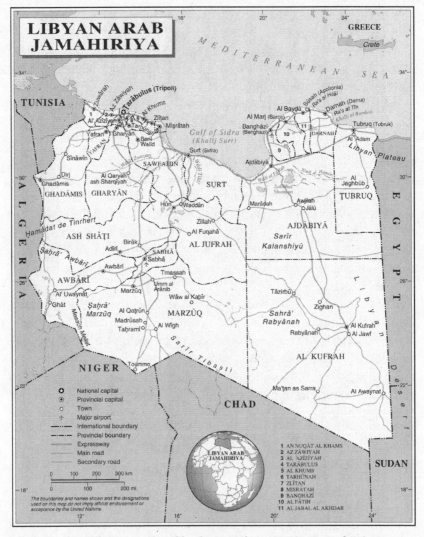

FIGURE 1.2 Map of Libya produced by the United Nations Cartographic Section.
Sirte (Surt) is almost in the centre of the coast, and the Fezzan region lies to its
south. (Source: UN via WikiMedia Commons)

"How can a soldier remain passive and salute a king who has filled the coun-try with foreign forces? How can you accept being stopped on the street by an American? That happened to me personally. When I wanted to enter Wheelus base, I was turned away....When I told them of my position as an officer in the Libyan army, I was told, 'true, but you will not enter!' I replied, 'it is Libyan territory.' Response, 'it is futile to argue, you will not enter, per-iod!'." (Gaddafi quoted in Vandewalle, 1998, p. 61)

Muammar Gaddafi was born in Sirte circa 1942, to a poor family. His relatives fought for many years against Italian colonial rule, just as mem-bers of his tribe, the Gaddadfa, had fought against the Turkish occupation (Simons, 1996). Gaddafi's family was Bedouin, a people who were "par-ticularly known for their ferocity in defending their freedom;" indeed, even Gaddafi's father served time in prison for his resistance against the Italians (Sullivan, 1999, p. 22). Though not a central plank in the Italian domination of Libya, Sirte itself was a destination of the only Italian air service in Africa, run by SANA (Burchall, 1933, p. 69).

After the defeat of the Italians in the Second World War, another col-onial power, this time Britain, sought to lay claim over Sirte. The British aimed to include the region encompassing Sirte, under a trusteeship estab-lished by the UN (Strausz-Hupé & Possony, 1950, p. 306). Thus the UN too, from the time before Libya even gained formal political independ-ence, had already inserted itself as a central actor in managing and defin-ing Libya. On November 21, 1949, the UN decided that Libya should become independent by January 1, 1952, and the transfer of power to King Idris I was overseen by a Dutch UN Commissioner, Adriaan Pelt. The fol-lowing year, King Idris held Libya's first elections, and when opposition parties contested the results, all political parties and programs were sup-pressed (Lea, 2001, p. 252). In July 1953, Libya signed a 20-year treaty with Great Britain granting permission for it to maintain military bases in Libya in return for a nominal sum to aid development (Lea, 2001, p. 252). Libya agreed to a similar pact with the U.S. in September 1954, which saw the establishment of U.S. air bases in Libya in return for $40 million U.S. over 20 years (Lea, 2001, p. 252). For Gaddafi and his fellow officers who led the overthrow of King Idris, the monarch had sold out Libya to for-eign, imperial powers.

"My parents are still living in a tent near Sirte," Gaddafi said years after overthrowing the King in a bloodless revolt in 1969 (Anderson, 1983, p. 139; see also McDermott, 1973, p. 400, and Anderson, 1982, p. 519). "We are not rich people," Gaddafi said about his fellow officers and himself,

FIGURE 1.3 King Idris I of Libya shaking hands with U.S. Vice-President Richard Nixon in March of 1957. (Source: Mohamed Yousef el-Magariaf via WikiMedia Commons)

"the parents of the majority of us are living in huts" (Anderson, 1983, p. 139). Indeed, according to his own mother, Gaddafi told his parents that they would continue living in their tent until every Libyan had been allotted proper housing (BBC, 1976).

At the age of ten, and at great sacrifice to his family, Gaddafi was sent to a Quranic school in Sirte (Anderson, 1983, p. 139), where his schoolmates "looked down on him as a poor desert *bedu*; at night he slept in the mosque and at holidays he trudged back to the family encampment" (Wright, 1981, p. 124). Simons similarly related that Gaddafi, "as a rural Bedouin," was "viewed by his classmates as something of a country bumpkin" (1996, p. 170).

This grounding, in the desert tent, in the Quranic school, later in his training at the British Royal Military Academy in Sandhurst, Surrey, and then in the struggle against broad global forces such as Western imperialism, is a critical part of understanding both Sirte and its son, Gaddafi.

FIGURE 1.4 Colonel Muammar Gaddafi, in his tent in the desert outside Sirte, speaking in an interview with the BBC in 1976.

FIGURE 1.5 Muammar Gaddafi's famous tent, in the Bab-al-Aziziya complex in Tripoli. (Source: Ricardo Stuckert, Agência Brasil, Creative Commons)

Sirte, like many other formerly colonized places, was an area that may have seemed utterly peripheral, but which instead spanned forces of world-historic importance. The elusive dream, then and especially now, is that which lies in between these forces: the idea of a nation, united and self-reliant. Beyond the Bedouin Fezzan, we are suddenly shifted to colonial rule, Islam, oil, Pan-Arabism and then Pan-Africanism—what seems mirage-like is, however, the idea of a "Libya." While Gaddafi was a dedicated nationalist, his own vision of the nation constantly shifted boundaries, moving beyond Libya to include, at different times, Syria, Egypt, Tunisia, Morocco, and so on. Born of a people who were pastoral nomads, dwellers of the open desert (always retained as a motif by Gaddafi, who greeted visitors in his tent, see Figure 1.5), it is perhaps not surprising that Gaddafi's horizons were always open and shifting. This sense of ceaseless movement, indicative of Libya as a whole, was perhaps best summed up by Anderson (1982, pp. 533-534).

"Libyans often remark on the vertigo with which their recent history has left them. From Ottoman province to Italian colony, from the devastation of a colonial war to the destruction of World War II, from abject poverty to splendid riches, from conservative monarchy to radical revolution, the Libyans have had barely a decade of peace, stability and continuity in the last 80 years. Many educated Libyans acknowledge that this had confused their sense of what their country should be, has undermined efforts at calculation and investment for the future, and has created a cynicism and alienation well beyond what is already typical of the Third World."

Until Gaddafi came to power, Sirte itself and the broader Fezzan region to the south were largely neglected (Anderson, 1983, p. 139). It was Cyrenaica, dominated by Benghazi, which the deposed King Idris favoured. Some have gone as far as arguing that "the 1969 revolution was, in essence, the overthrow of the traditional Cyrenaican tribal dominance over the country, on which the Libyan monarchy was based because of its origins in the Sanusi [Senussi] order which, in turn, controlled these tribes" (Joffé, 2009, p. 939). As Gaddafi's own tribe, the Gaddadfa, is based in Sirte, his opponents in Benghazi inevitably treated his efforts to redress this historic imbalance as favouritism, as practicing divide and rule, but of course they never mentioned their own privileged treatment under King Idris. The other options—to do nothing about Sirte's neglect or to pretend that both Sirte and Benghazi were equal—would have still proven unsatisfactory. As some observers have noted, Gaddafi abhorred regionalism and was dedicated to nationalism and unity, and he spoke with "an Arabic accent typical of the frontier between the major regions" (Anderson, 1983, p. 139; 1982, p. 519). Others have reported that members of the Gaddadfa tribe, and tribes linked to it (the Maghraha and Warfalla), "penetrated deep into the administration and the security services, as well as the army command, originally the preserve of Libya's Berber minority" (Joffé, 2009, p. 939). Moreover, it is not settled among researchers the extent to which Gaddafi could be understood as a nationalist, even if not a tribalist: "As he frequently declared, the Libyan revolution was based on an international ideology, not on a national movement" (Anderson, 1982, p. 525).

Regardless of his orientations, whether tribal, national, or internationalist, Gaddafi's background as a "bumpkin" from Sirte has consistently been held against him by opponents in other regions of Libya. In a cable from the U.S. Embassy in Tripoli, John T. Godfrey, the Chargé d'Affaires (CDA), wrote that "average Libyans" tend to "view the al-Qadhafi family as unsophisticated upstarts from a historically inconsequential part of the country (Sirte) who routinely embarrass Libya" (USET, 2008/7/22). (While the U.S. Chargé d'Affaires generalizes across all "average Libyans," a broad category with which he would have had little personal familiarity, the comment may likely be representative of the feelings of the kinds of regime opponents and dissastified members of the elite that the U.S. Embassy regularly consulted.)

Where there were tensions between regionalism and nationalism, between tribal affiliation and national unity, there were tensions in the social policies of the Al-Fateh Revolution. Having been raised in poverty, and then faced with increased oil wealth, both Gaddafi and members of his generation were ambivalent about material wealth and what it could acquire. The same ambivalence was shown toward Western technology, both admiration and fear. Gaddafi was also aware that Libyans, "toiled very little to earn the 9,000-dollar annual per capita income they enjoyed in the early 1980s, and this awareness translated into a domestic policy which oscillated between wasteful spending and artificial austerity and arbitrary traditionalism" (Anderson, 1982, p. 519). The primary economic stratum which continued to support Gaddafi throughout his rule "was comprised of those who had owned little or nothing before 1975" (Anderson, 1982, p. 522).

Travelling to Sirte in 1999, Milton Viorst, a veteran Middle East correspondent and author, described the kind of development that Sirte finally enjoyed:

> "Our next stopover was Sirte, chosen by Qaddafi as Libya's new capital. Money was clearly pouring in. Some state offices had already relocated to temporary quarters in the city, and handsome housing was going up. A huge, modern government complex, the work of Italian builders, was nearly completed and is to house the General People's Congress and most ministries. Qaddafi, who talks of bringing government closer to the people, dislikes Tripoli for its vestiges of Italian colonialism and chose Sirte for its centrality. Most important, Sirte is also Qaddafi's home turf. He was born south of the city in 1942, in the desert where his father, a Bedouin tribesman, herded sheep and goats. Libyans say the desert surrounding Sirte remains in Qaddafi's blood." (Viorst, 1999, p. 64)

Sirte: An African Dream Turned into a Nightmare

While observing the destruction of Sirte throughout the course of NATO's intervention, and particularly in the period from late August to late October 2011, or when visiting the aftermath of the catastrophic shattering of this small city (varyingly described as containing between 70,000 and 150,000 inhabitants), journalists repeatedly noted just how far from grace Sirte had been taken down. While many of their comments repeated the "favouritism" theme, they collectively paint a picture of the centrality that Sirte had acquired since 1969, of both its strategic and symbolic value, both locally and more internationally. That the slaughter in Sirte should have barely raised an eyebrow among the kinds of Western audiences and opinion leaders who just a few months before clamoured for "humanitarian intervention," is thus all the more striking.

First, media reports frequently noted the newly acquired administrative position of Sirte, stressing that whereas it had once been a "sleepy" fishing village, it had become the de facto capital of Libya (Bastian, 2011/10/23).[2] *The Christian Science Monitor* (2011) spoke of the decentralization of Libya's administration, with the result being a large move of government offices to Sirte. A BBC reporter wrote of "the imposing ministries and conference centres" and the "outsized ministry buildings and other prestige Gaddafi projects," that in the reporter's opinion were "disproportionate to a population of around 70,000" (Head, 2012/2/9). (One might think they were disproportionate, until one visits other capitals in small cities, such as Ottawa and Canberra.) A reporter for the Associated Press commented about how Gaddafi had turned Sirte into "a second capital," and that he spent unspecified millions "to build conference halls and hotels to use it as a venue for Arab and African summit meetings." As if to indicate its proper, natural state, the reporter states that Sirte had been "a sleepy town... traditionally a trading and agricultural community," but had now been "filled out by large numbers of government employees" and that it "comes alive only when Gadhafi hosts summit meetings in its luxurious convention center" (Hendawi, 2011/3/28). Saying that it had instead been a fishing village, but nonetheless still "sleepy," a writer for *The Washington Post* wrote that Sirte had been "favored with some of the country's finest buildings and public services" (Sheridan, 2011/10/15).

On the one hand, by making Sirte appear to be little more than an undeserving pet project of Gaddafi's, such reports tended to reaffirm the invidious complaints of inhabitants of Benghazi whose position pre-1969 had been central, and privileged, and whose narrative about Gaddafi ruled virtually without challenge in the Western media. On the other hand, these reports also accentuated just how far the city had been severely degraded. Perhaps some in Libya will now feel content that matters have been "equalized."

Second, numerous media reports spoke of how much the residents had benefited from the years that Gaddafi was in power. This is closely related

---

2. Indeed, one account, based on the words of an unnamed European diplomat in Tripoli, was that when Gaddafi chose to relocate many government offices from Tripoli to Sirte, numerous high-ranking officials balked: "One morning, the prime minister drove to his office in Tripoli, only to find it a pile of rubble." Frustrated by the refusal, Gaddafi apparently ordered direct action and had the office bulldozed (Timmerman, 2004, p. 21).

to the first point above, underscoring Sirte as a new centre of administration, except that the spotlight was now on residential improvements and popular support for Gaddafi. "But the money Col. Gaddafi lavished on Sirte is also evident," a BBC reporter remarked, noting the "neat, whitewashed housing estates, the grand avenues and parks" (Head, 2012/2/9). For *The Christian Science Monitor* (2011), Gaddafi had "showered the city with development projects and wealth since becoming Libya's leader," which was an apparent explanation for why the "residents of Sirte are fiercely loyal" to Gaddafi. Given how well aligned Western media reports were with the dominant narratives of the opposition National Transitional Council (NTC), the following statement from a Reuters reporter is the sort of comment that seemed to "naturally" fit in with the rest above: "Fighters for the National Transitional Council say they believe some residents of the city, which Gaddafi transformed from a remote fishing village into a modern city, still support him and a few may have taken up arms to defend him" (Dziadosz, 2011/9/22). In almost identical terms, *The Washington Post* wrote: "Under Gaddafi, Sirte grew from a sleepy fishing village to a city of 100,000....Many residents were staunch supporters of the former Libyan leader" (Sheridan, 2011/10/15). Again, these reports can have different effects. On the one hand, they can serve to cast Sirte's residents as deserving targets of aggression, by casting them as pampered supporters of the man vilified as being on the wrong side of history. On the other hand, the reports undermine the simplistic assertions that Gaddafi had no popular support whatsoever, and that the only way he could maintain himself in power for so many months of sustained NATO bombing was that he had hired foreign (African) mercenaries.

But they also introduced yet another element that few at the high levels of the UN, NATO, or human rights NGOs, barely noted or remarked upon: that many of those fighting the opposition militias were, like the militias, largely composed of armed civilians. This not only introduces the "civil war" dimension that the NTC actively repudiated (because then the war would appear to be Libyans versus Libyans, and not Libyans versus Gaddafi, as they preferred to promote their campaign), but this also jeopardized the "humanitarian protection" motive. If the UN and NATO could work to protect armed civilians supposedly represented by the NTC, then why not the armed civilians of Sirte, who were literally fighting for their lives? This ought to have been a clear signal that NATO acted to effect regime change, as a participant on one side of a civil war. Nonetheless, UN Secretary-General Ban Ki-Moon would confidently assert that NATO had acted fully within the UN mandate established in UN Security Council Resolution 1973.

Third, writing of Sirte as another sort of de facto capital, this time for a united Africa, was another consistent feature of reports. Sirte was the staging ground for numerous international events of considerable significance, to Libya, its African partners, and world powers for that matter, as we shall see below. Many reports mentioned the Ouagadougou Conference Centre, "a showpiece venue in Sirte where Gaddafi hosted the launch of the African Union," which was besieged and then largely destroyed by "NTC forces" (Sky News, 2011; see also Sheridan, 2011/10/15); "a luxurious conference centre where only last year [2010] he [Gaddafi] hosted an Arab summit.... All that now is devastated" (Bastian, 2011/10/23). "The showpiece of Gaddafi's future continental capital," today the Ouagadougou Conference Centre, "resembles an architectural model that has been stamped on and then burned" (Randall, 2011/10/23). This was to be the centerpiece city of a United States of Africa as envisioned by Gaddafi (Kaijun & Xiaolong, 2011/10/26); a "shimmering, futuristic capital of a United Africa" (Randall, 2011/10/23); "envisaged by Colonel Muammar Gaddafi as a model of what a modern African city should be: a brilliant panoply of university and hospitals, with a glittering seafront and a marble-lined conference centre to host leaders from around the world" (Farmer & Sherlock, 2011/10/15).

Sirte, the New Pan-Africanism, and U.S. Scrutiny

In order to critically examine the practice of militarized humanitarianism and more importantly to contextualize and historicize NATO's war, it is necessary to clear the brush of accumulated assumptions and instantaneous opinions that would reduce the war either to a mere response to a "human rights crisis" or a single-minded grab for oil, or that access to oil is a sufficient explanation by itself. Nor is it my position that regime change was an end in itself, a kind of anti-Gaddafi reflex that produced actions motivated by some visceral, personal revulsion among world leaders.

Instead, a key argument and analytical point is that the purpose of NATO's *rehearsed* military expedition[3] was to disrupt an emerging pat-

---

3. For more on this, see Chossudovsky (2011) on "Operation Southern Mistral" against the fictitiously labelled dictatorship of Southland—and see the website for

tern of independence and a new network of collaboration that could facilitate increased African self-reliance, which was at odds with the geostrategic and political economic ambitions of extra-continental powers, namely the U.S. As Sirte symbolizes a resurgent Pan-Africanism in the making, so the termination of NATO's military operations there and the insurgents' unmaking of Gaddafi's plans bring to a bloody end any immediate prospects for greater African independence through the more ambitious forms of integration championed by Gaddafi. In this vein, it is interesting to note what was brief, passing news: a month before Gaddafi was murdered, the EU decided not to unfreeze the assets of the Libyan African Investment Portfolio, among others, but did release funds used for "resuming Libyan production and sale of hydrocarbons" (O'Connor, 2011/9/26). Put simply, investment funds benefiting Libya's African partners were blocked, but the production of oil and natural gas for European consumption was enabled.

Sirte served as a centrally important site in the new Pan-Africanism that was sweeping the continent, and for which Gaddafi, in the eyes of his African colleagues themselves, arose as a leading visionary. On September 9, 1999, the Fourth Extraordinary Session of the Assembly of Heads of State and Government took place in Sirte—and produced what is now known as "the Sirte Declaration." At that session, following a Libyan initiative, it was decided to establish the African Union (AU), thus replacing its predecessor, the Organization of African Unity (OAU) (AU, 1999; Nowak, 2003). Regarding Gaddafi's leadership, Article 7 of the Sirte Declaration stated:

> "In our deliberations, we have been inspired by the important proposals submitted by Colonel Muammar Ghaddafi, Leader of the Great Al Fatah Libyan Revolution and particularly, by his vision for a strong and united Africa, capable of meeting global challenges and shouldering its responsibility to harness the human and natural resources of the continent in order to improve the living conditions of its peoples." (AU, 1999)

Permanently commemorating the Sirte Declaration, Afriqiyah Airways, owned by the Libyan state and founded in April of 2001, featured "9.9.99" as the logo that appeared on the tails of all its aircraft (also noted in USET, 2009/3/23). Slowly, the Pan-African orientation was becoming part of the

---

the joint French-British exercise, Southern Mistral 2011, of the Air Defence and Operations Command at http://www.southern-mistral.cdaoa.fr/GB/index.php?option=com_content&view=article&id=57&Itemid=127.

official state identity of Libya, as it displayed itself to the wider world. As
the old website of the airline explained:

> "The African Union contract, a vital part of the self-awareness of modern
> Africa, was completed on 09.09.'99 in Sirte/Libya. As this historical date is a
> milestone in the recent African history Afriqiyah Airways has chosen 9.9.99
> for the company logo, which shall address to all African nationals. This shall
> create a common feeling of confidence and self-esteem for our African guests."
> (Air Afriqiyah, 2009)

Inside the aircraft, seats were upholstered in green, the colour of the
Libyan Arab Jamahiriya flag, a colour most associated with Gaddafi and
his political philosophy. Following Gaddafi's overthrow, the new regime
grounded the fleet, prohibiting it from flying to European Union nations,
and apparently not for safety reasons (Marghani, 2012/4/6). The airline
website continues, several months after, to be "down for maintenance."

FIGURE 1.6 Afriqiyah Airways, with the 9.9.99 logo on both the tail and engines.
(Source: Konstantin von Wedelstaedt via WikiMedia Commons)

In March 2001, at the OAU's Fifth Extraordinary Summit, again in
Sirte, the Constitutive Act establishing the African Union was tabled and
it was fully ratified by April 26 (Lea, 2001, p. 268). The meeting also called
for the immediate lifting of sanctions imposed on Libya for the Lockerbie
affair (the downing of Pan Am 103 in December 1988), a point pressed by
former South African President Nelson Mandela also in attendance. In a
welcome address to the summit, Gaddafi described the event as coming
at the end of a long process of struggles for decolonization, stretching back

a century. Gaddafi told those gathered that the proclamation of the African Union in Sirte was, "the crowning of a thirst for freedom and a unity dream which successive generations of Africans have all upheld" (PANA, 2001/3/1). This was a promising and exciting new phase of African integration efforts. If carried through, they could have achieved far greater independence, self-reliance, and improved lives for Africans than anything offered by foreign banks, mining companies, or a U.S. military keen on showing its "humanitarian" side by engaging in token acts of charity staged for photo opportunities.

As we will see from the U.S. Embassy-Tripoli cables published by WikiLeaks, the U.S. maintained a close watch on all of the summits that took place in Sirte. Apart from cables dealing with oil, investment opportunities, and Gaddafi's political opponents, these are some of the lengthiest cables in the published set of 598 emanating from that embassy alone. They can also be among some of the ostensibly pettiest in tone. U.S. officials were apparently reluctant to concede that a non-Western other could master the civilized arts of diplomacy—as if Gaddafi, an old hand at international manoeuvring, were instead stuck in some irredeemable stage of infancy. U.S. embassy officials frequently detailed "conference atmospherics": how successful Gaddafi had been in organizing conference logistics and how "last minute" some of the preparations were. They seem hopeful to paint a poor picture, judging Gaddafi as if he aspired to be a wedding planner. Yet the superficial frivolity hides deeper meanings. The cables paint an even poorer picture of U.S. interpretations and intentions, namely that there had been no "reconciliation" with Gaddafi, that he was still viewed with hostility (seemingly more so since Barack Obama became the U.S. President), and that there was considerable envy for Gaddafi's African prominence. Now that Sirte has effectively been destroyed, U.S. embassy officials at least will no longer need to trouble themselves with reports on African Union "conference atmospherics."

To offer some preliminary examples of the observations made above, numerous cables on Sirte's role as a front stage for the new African Union focused on Gaddafi's rise to continental prominence, with a special focus on 2009. In 2009, several cables mentioned how propitious that particular year was for Gaddafi. One of the cables marked "secret" stated:

"Qadhafi's increased international profile as AU Chair coincides with the 40th anniversary of the Fatah Revolution (September 1) and the tenth anniversary of the Sirte Declaration that created the AU (September 9). Libya's current roles on the UNSC and as UNGA President add to the importance of this year for Qadhafi. Libyan officials will be looking toward Qadhafi's appearance at UNGA as the capstone of an extraordinary year." (USET, 2009/7/21; see also: USET, 2009/1/21; 2009/2/11; 2009/5/18; 2009/7/15)

Another "secret" cable also wisely noted that Gaddafi "seeks symbolic gains as much as he does substantive ones, and 2009 is full of symbolic milestones."

"In September, he will celebrate both 40 years as Libya's leader and 10 years since the Sirte Proclamation—a foundational document of the African Union signed in al-Qadhafi's hometown. His February election to the African Union chairmanship provides al-Qadhafi with a high-profile platform from which he can trumpet his vision of Africa and rail against Western interference on the continent and serves as confirmation of his regional importance. In March, Libya presided over the Security Council and al-Qadhafi expects to send his top Africa diplomat [Ali Treiki] to preside over the 64th session of the UN General Assembly in the fall. Al-Qadhafi has played host to Tony Blair, Vladimir Putin, Nicolas Sarkozy, and Juan Carlos of Spain." (USET, 2009/4/17)

Writing about Gaddafi's ascension to the chairmanship of the AU in 2009, on the tenth anniversary of the Sirte Declaration, a U.S. cable was only barely able to contain its underlying disdain. Speaking of how "the King of Kings" entered "the scene," the cable cast the event as "an attempt to frame him as the popular choice of ordinary Africans," and with obvious worry added that Gaddafi's "flashy entrance to the AU Summit with a retinue of tribal kings shortly before his election as the AU chairman on February 2 did little to dispel the perception that he sees the AU as a bully pulpit" (USET, 2009/2/11). Revisiting the September 9, 1999, Sirte Declaration, the U.S. Embassy remarked that the formation of the AU "was seen by the regime as the foundation of a new and larger sphere of influence that could eventually lead to al-Qadhafi's leadership of a unified African continent" (USET, 2009/2/11). This remained a central focus of concern in the U.S. Embassy cables that questioned the prospects for success, yet with clear apprehension about possible successes for Libya. The cable noted that there has been "a domestic propaganda campaign designed to represent Libya as an African state," and referred to "billboards and larger-than-life murals [that] depict al-Qadhafi emerging, Messiah-like, from a glowing green Libya into an embracing African continent." It did not spare the detail about Gaddafi's "personal designers (he employs two full-time)," who, "have incorporated the continent's shape into all types of clothing (favorites include a large green Africa-shaped brooch on a white double-breasted blazer, a pseudo-camouflaged tunic comprised of Africa-shaped patterns and a jersey emblazoned with pictures of prominent African leaders like Kwame Nkrumah)" (USET, 2009/2/11).

Symbolism matters, not just to anthropologists, but apparently it also matters in understanding imperialist ideology, the texts produced under that ideology, and the wide-range of methods chosen to pursue aims therein. Symbolism may well be one of the few neglected areas of theories of imperialism. However, one must also remember that the U.S. Embassy cables are written by diplomats, who themselves are merely one ever-diminishing part of the U.S. apparatus, and not by military strategists, intelligence officers, or Obama's economic advisers. As such, U.S. Embassy officials tended to also see Gaddafi's chairmanship of the AU in symbolic terms: "chairmanship of the AU will be a significant symbolic victory for al-Qadhafi, who sees himself as the father of both the AU and an eventual united African government" (USET, 2009/1/29).

Despite all of Gaddafi's apparent international achievements, the U.S. Embassy cables held out a meeting between Gaddafi and Obama as a special achievement that Gaddafi was to be denied (see Figure 1.8), which also points to the low-intensity hostility that the U.S. maintained against his government. As one cable noted, "any potential interaction with POTUS

FIGURE 1.7 Muammar Gaddafi makes his first speech as Chairperson of the African Union in Addis Ababa, Ethiopia, during the 12th African Union Summit on February 2, 2009. (Source: U.S. Navy photo by Mass Communication Specialist 2nd Class Jesse B. Awalt via WikiMedia Commons)

[president of the United States] will have long-lasting implications for our bilateral relationship" (USET, 2009/7/21). Another cable boldly stated that "the 'Holy Grail' for al-Qadhafi, a meeting with the U.S. President, has eluded him thus far," explaining that, "the bottom line for the Qadhafi clan is respect which they believe comes from high-level interaction and formal agreements" (USET, 2009/4/17). The respect earned from symbolic gains could in the officials' view: a) help Gaddafi show the Libyan public that the country was acquiring greater international respect and winning powerful new friends, thus assuring them of a more prosperous future; and/or b) bolster one or the other of Gaddafi's competing sons, as one secured an international agreement, that proved that he was more competent in laying the groundwork for the future of the nation , than another son. These cables suggest a "soft power" play on symbols, respect, status, and influence, and that the U.S., even during times of superficial amicability with Libya, never ceased to grind away at the Libyan government.

FIGURE 1.8 Muammar Gaddafi in a fleeting moment manages to obtain a handshake from Barack Obama, on July 9, 2009, at the G8 meeting in L'Aquila, Italy. (Source: courtesy of the United Nations, photograph by Mark Garten.)

A photograph of a "meeting" can be ambiguous at best, and Figure 1.8 deserves further elaboration. Apart from this passing encounter, Obama consistently refused all Libyan invitations for any meeting between himself and Gaddafi. Cables from the U.S. Embassy in Tripoli tell of multiple Libyan requests for a formal meeting with Obama at the G8 summit, none of which met with favour. Libyan officials, up to Gaddafi, were keen on such a meeting as a sign of positive intent on the part of the U.S. to develop an amicable bilateral relationship. Note the direction in which the delegates are moving and Obama's awkward posture: Gaddafi apparently called out to Obama from behind, insisting on even the briefest greeting. That Gaddafi had to go as far as he did, in calling Obama back for this handshake, says more than the picture can convey by itself (see USET, 2009/2/18, 2009/5/3, 2009/5/26). We should also note, as will be discussed in chapter 4, that this apparent coldness followed the visit to Washington in April, 2009 by Libyan National Security Adviser Muatassim Gaddafi. At that visit he rejected U.S. plans for supplanting or appropriating regional counter-terrorism and peacekeeping efforts, with the apparent intent of diminishing the African Union and installing the U.S. Africa Command as the real power broker (USET, 2009/4/17).

However, if one goes just a little further back, to February 2009, it was Muatassim Gaddafi who, in his first meeting with U.S. Ambassador Gene Cretz,[4] made it clear to Cretz that the Libyan government "hoped President Obama would be able to meet the Leader [Muammar Gaddafi] during the July G8 session in Sardinia [*sic*]. For Libya, such a meeting would be *a critical signal that a page had truly been turned in the relationship*. It would also be an important gesture in light of Muammar al-Qadhafi's recent election as Chairman of the African Union. The Ambassador undertook to convey the request to Washington" (USET, 2009/2/18, emphasis added). Cretz again told Foreign Minister Musa Kusa that he would convey the request to Washington (USET, 2009/5/3). Clearly, these multiple requests were declined. This too is an interesting point for another reason: in several televised election debates during Obama's 2007-2008 run for the White House, Obama-the-candidate promised and insisted repeatedly that he

---

4. Gene F. Cretz had a long career in states whose regimes the U.S. would overthrow, or seek to overthrow, that is when not serving in Israel. Cretz served as a Peace Corps Volunteer in Kabul, Afghanistan from 1975-1977. From 1986-88, Cretz was a political officer in Damascus, Syria. Cretz served in Tel Aviv (1991-1994) where he was responsible for the Arab affairs portfolio, including the Gaza Strip. In 2001 he was transferred to Cairo, Egypt where he served as Minister-Counselor for Economic and Political Affairs. He returned to Damascus, Syria in August 2003 as Deputy Chief of Mission and subsequently served as Chargé d'Affaires of the Embassy until January 2004. Most recently he has been the Deputy Chief of Mission in Tel Aviv from August 2004 until August 2007. From his biography posted by the U.S. Embassy in Tripoli, Libya, at: <http://web.archive.org/web/20110716093827/ http://libya.usembassy.gov/principal.html>.

would talk with the U.S.' presumed greatest adversaries. The G8 meeting in L'Aquila came a mere six months into Obama's term in office, and there Obama would not even meet with the leader of a nation which George W. Bush himself had admitted into the sphere of U.S. diplomatic and trade relations. Clearly, a major shift in stated U.S. policy had occurred under Obama, an administration more severe towards Libya than Bush's, with little awareness by the U.S. public and with all of the "strategic ambiguity" that Obama swore he would eliminate.[5]

In other cables on Gaddafi's manipulation of symbolic values to gain influence, U.S. Embassy officials focused on the minutiae of conference organization, tallying their observations in what they called "scorecards," apparently believing that these details could reveal some larger truth about Gaddafi's power. (This may also provide a hint that, in needing to document surface appearances at public events, these officials had very limited contacts in the Libyan state that could have provided them with the deeper understandings they sought.) In one, U.S. Ambassador Gene Cretz commented:

> "That Libya was able to house and feed all attendees was a minor miracle, enabled by the hosts paying hefty sums on hospitality on the eve of the Summit. The pageantry was likely aimed at currying favor with African guests, while providing a not-so-subtle reminder of Libya's oil wealth for countries hesitant to join with al-Qadhafi's aggrandizing vision of unification but equally wary of losing out on Libya's dinar diplomacy." (USET, 2009/7/15)

Ambassador Cretz continued, "summit planning: almost perfect, but not quite" and added further comments in a petty tone that betrayed an unstable combination of both condescension and reluctant envy: "it was clear that Libyan officials sought to promote a Qadhafi-centric dog-and-pony show" (USET, 2009/7/15). Scrutinizing the Libyan government's abilities as if judging the merits of a party-planner, Cretz remarked: "it

---

5. For a detailed log of Obama's promises, as a candidate, to speak to "America's enemies," see On the Issues at <http://www.ontheissues.org/2012/Barack_Obama_Foreign_Policy.htm> and <http://www.ontheissues.org/2007_Stephanopoulos_Dems.htm>. This has been further underscored in 2012 campaign propaganda by the Republican Party—see GOP at <http://gop.com/news/research/the-big-fail-obama-befuddled-by-iran-and-syria/>. The promise and strategy identified and advocated by diplomats such as Nicholas Burns (2008/10/24), was never to come to life under Obama, and Libya was the first to get a clear sense that the U.S. under Obama would not offer any positive change, and indeed, offered much worse.

was clear that neither detail nor substance had featured prominently in Libyan planning....Apartments reserved for delegations...were in various stages of construction and no provision had been made for food, transportation to Sirte...or ground transportation during the Summit...food was difficult to locate," but then that all changed. As Cretz then tediously detailed:

> "Libyan officials apparently decided to open the purse strings to complete all last-minute details. Light shows, electronic signs, and free food met attendant pomp as heads of state arrived in Tripoli. Shuttle jets between Tripoli and Sirte began operations, bringing in planeloads of foreign diplomats and 'traditional African kings'. Foreign workers abounded: hundreds of Turkish and Greek hospitality staff manned kitchens, buffets, temporary coffee tents, and floating hotels. One waiter told Poloff [U.S. Embassy Political Affairs Officer] that he had been notified of his travel to Libya less than 24 hours before getting on a plane to Sirte. Throughout the conference, foreign laborers continued public works projects near delegation lodging sites, including paving sidewalks and building beachfronts." (USET, 2009/7/15)

As if more of such detail was still lacking, another U.S. Embassador, Donald Yamamoto assigned to Addis Ababa, Ethiopia, produced an almost identical cable, the same day, where he grudgingly conceded "Qadhafi pulls it off, barely." Yet even the success in organizing the AU Summit was turned against Gaddafi: "Qadhafi pulled out all the stops—sometimes to the point of hilarity—to make delegates feel welcome" (USEAA, 2009/7/15). While quickly observing the Pan-Africanist slogans painted across Sirte, including "Death to Africa's Enemies" and "One African Currency," Ambassador Yamamoto was particularly taken with the fact that Gaddafi, "provided free lodging, meals, SIM cards, and protocol vehicles to many delegations," and that in the Ouagadougou Conference Complex, "Muzak Christmas songs and Mendelssohn's wedding march played incessantly and loudly" (USEAA, 2009/7/15).

A cable titled, "Libya: Darfur Conference Atmospherics" exemplifies this obsession with party-planning, mixed with envy, a need to cast events in a negative light, followed by a grudging acceptance that things turned out well for Libya, but then finishing with one last snide "insight." Referring to a conference in Sirte and Tripoli in April of 2007, this cable tells us (*briefly*) that while it was a "substantive success," nonetheless,

> "the scheduling challenges posed by a last minute decision by the Leader to fly all delegates to Sirte to meet with him exemplify the capricious environment in which even Libya's most senior diplomats operate. African Affairs

Secretary Ali Treiki pulled out all stops, organizing the conference in Tripoli's most expensive venue, the Corinthia Hotel, and bedecking it with all the trappings (flags, signs, simultaneous translation in three languages etc.), but had to smile his way through an eight hour delay in start time (from 3 p.m. to 11 p.m.) in order to fly all conferees to Sirte and back, with a lengthy delay in Sirt [sic] waiting for the Leader." (USET, 2007/5/4)

The U.S. diplomat admits however that "once the conference actually started, most delegations expressed satisfaction with Libya's role as host." Not to end on a positive note, the cable adds: "the Sirte misadventure and ever-shifting schedule could make many think twice before attending another conference in Libya" (USET, 2007/5/4). This cable creates a comical image of U.S. diplomats sidling up to their African counterparts during conference breaks, asking them in quiet tones about the quality of the breakfast or the bed linens.

Given this abundance of picayune chatter, some readers might find it hard to believe commentators who have written that the WikiLeaks cables show U.S. diplomats "doing diligent and perceptive reporting" (Kinsman, 2011, p. 45), and that they have been "accurate and diligent in their reporting of events overseas" (Byers, 2011). Though perhaps obsessive, U.S. diplomats were nonetheless keenly attuned to the ways that Gaddafi went about accumulating symbolic capital, through displays, rituals and ceremonies, and how this could add to the political çapital he had gained among African heads of state and government. The implication is that his gains were their loss. And they were right.

In chapters three and four we will consider the less symbolic and far more material dimensions and aspects of Gaddafi's Pan-African activism, and the challenge posed to U.S. ambitions on the African continent, as represented by its banking, natural resource interests, and the creation of AFRICOM, which then led the U.S. effort to militarily overthrow Gaddafi.

Sirte's Place in the Development of Libya

Sirte was the place Gaddafi chose to summon ConocoPhillips CEO Jim Mulva for a "browbeating," as recently as February 24, 2008, to get U.S. oil firms to pressure their government into not pursuing further legal action against Libya. Sirte was also the place where Gaddafi "threatened to dramatically reduce Libya's oil production and/or expel U.S. oil and gas companies" if the U.S. continued to threaten asset seizures in relation to the Lockerbie bombing (USET, 2008/3/12). Sirte's own development under the Al-Fateh Revolution serves as a touchstone of the government's policies, Libya's external relations, and the unforgiving resentment of competing regions in Libya. One of the most important development projects that Sirte intersected was the Great Man-made River Project.

The Great Man-made River Project (GMR), initiated in October 1983 on the decision of the General People's Congress, involved an investiment of $3.3 billion U.S. in the construction of a 1,900 kilometre pipeline, that would carry at least two million cubic metres of water per day, and irrigate around 180,000 hectares of land, with distribution to both Benghazi and Sirte (Anderson, 1987, p. 88; Beaumont, Blake & Wagstaff, 1988, pp. 88, 541). Thanks to the the the project, new industrial activities and extensive irrigated agriculture along the Sirte coast now became possible (Beaumont, Blake & Wagstaff, 1988, p. 538). The first phase, which brought freshwater to Benghazi and Sirte, was completed as planned in 1994 (Niblock, 2001, p. 66).

Even though none of the major urban areas was to be deprived of this water, Benghazi, a long-time stronghold of opposition to Gaddafi and lingering support for the overthrown monarch, still remained dissatisfied. One researcher candidly wrote that, "of all the Libyans, the Cyrenaicans, who inhabit eastern Libya, are perhaps the most cynical. They say that Qaddafi dreamt up the Great Man-made River as an excuse to take Cyrenaica's water and irrigate his...home district of Sirte, which has been outfitted with a brand new thirsty city paid for with Cyrenaica's oil" (El-Kikhia, 1997, p. 93).

This regional dissatisfaction was of course duly noted by U.S. Embassy officials in their own documentation. According to the U.S. Embassy, based on a talk with one of their contacts in Benghazi, "Easterners have ...been frustrated that Cyrenaica has not benefited economically under al-Qadhafi's regime to the extent that Tripoli, Sirte and other areas viewed more favorably by the regime have [sic]" (USET, 2008/8/25).

Apart from the GMR itself, Sirte was also a focus for international investment and obvious competition by world powers against each other. In 1987, the Soviet Union began negotiations for the construction of a large nuclear facility in Sirte, to be constructed by Atomenergoeksport, a project that was "discontinued in response to U.S. pressure, Soviet hesitation, and a decline in Libya's oil profits" (Solingen, 2007, p. 217). This was one of the earliest signs of how the development of Sirte would become one focal point of the Libyan conflict with the U.S. as the latter sought to further its economic dominance in Africa. In addition, it's part of a longer story of friendly Libyan relations first with the USSR and then with post-Cold War Russia—relations that continued to keep the U.S. on edge.

In more recent years, Russia, which abstained from supporting UN Security Council Resolution 1973 permitting NATO's military intervention, had continued to invest in Libya, and in Sirte. In 2008, following a visit in April by Russian President Vladimir Putin, Libya inaugurated the Russian Railroad Company's work on "a multi-billion dollar contract to construct a 554-kilometer rail spur between Benghazi and Sirte" (USET, 2008/10/17). In a meeting with the Russian Ambassador to Libya on April 23, 2008 (USET, 2008/4/24), the U.S. Embassy's Chargé d'Affaires tried to ascertain the exact extent of Russian investment there. Russia's Ambassador repeated publicly known details of Russia's 2.2 billion Euro investment in the Sirte to Benghazi rail line mentioned above. Ambassador Koslov told the U.S. diplomat that he anticipated Russia and Libya "would also sign commercial contracts on housing construction in Janzour and Zawiya, electricity line installation, road construction, and possibly an additional section of Libya's planned coastal railroad between Tunisia and Egypt." Moreover, Libya and Russia signed a general agreement on the promotion of investments, a memorandum of understanding on economic cooperation, and three such memoranda on oil and gas exploration between Gazprom and the Libyan authorities. The U.S. CDA's report on his meeting with Kozlov mentioned that, despite press reports, Russian diplomats maintained that no military contracts were signed during Putin's visit to Libya. On the other hand, this might have been deemed by the Russian Ambassador to be confidential military information, and he did tell the Chargé d'Affaires that Russia and Libya signed an agreement on the protection of confidential commercial and military information (USET, 2008/4/24).

The U.S. Embassy generally kept careful watch over foreign investments in Sirte (and across Libya), while noting how U.S. corporations were often suffering exclusion from business opportunities under Gaddafi. The embassy noted plans to build a 15-megawatt combined solar/hydro plant in Sirte, ostensibly to be undertaken by a German firm that was conducting a feasibility study for the project (USET, 2009/6/4). (Germany was the only NATO member to abstain, at the UN, from supporting NATO military intervention.) Other U.S. allies, such as South Korea, also benefited from contracts in Sirte while the U.S. was essentially frozen out. South Korea planned to invest $5 billion U.S. in building a power plant in Sirte, while any U.S. investment was held up in the air (USET, 2006/9/24).

FIGURE 1.9 Vladimir Putin visiting Muammar Gaddafi in Libya on April 16, 2008. (Source: Russian Presidential Press and Information Office via WikiMedia Commons)

FIGURE 1.10 The president of Russian Railways, Vladimir Yakunin (left) and the Secretary of the Libyan General People's Congress sign a contract for the construction of the Sirte-Benghazi railway line in the presence of Vladimir Putin and Muammar Gaddafi on April 17, 2008. (Source: Russian Presidential Press and Information Office via WikiMedia Commons)

China was another state that abstained from supporting the resolution authorizing NATO to intervene in Libya and that also had investments in Sirte. As observed by the U.S. Embassy, the China Railway Construction Corporation started a $1.7-billion project consisting of building a 453-kilometer railway line linking Tripoli with Sirte. Libya, the embassy commented, was "one of China's largest trading partners in Africa, with two-way trade estimated by Libyan officials at more than $2.0 billion during [2007]." Moreover, the embassy pointed out that, "the railway line is part of a major Libyan plan to build a railway network linking it to other African states, including neighboring Maghreb countries" (USET, 2008/12/22).[6] In this instance, Sirte was at the intersection of various lines of international competition for dominance in Africa: the line of competition between the U.S. and China, with the latter spreading its influence far and wide across Africa, and the line of competition between the U.S. and Libya in determining whose continental project would prevail.

The U.S. on the other hand, even with its alleged reconciliation with Libya, either was unable to secure investment opportunities or faced immense difficulties. The U.S. Embassy reported in 2008 on an "unsuccessful year-long bid by U.S. firm Bechtel to build a commercial port in the Libyan city of Sirte," an investment totalling more than $1 billion U.S. It added that, "the fact that an operator with Bechtel's savvy and deep pockets was ultimately unable to secure its contract serves as a cautionary tale for the many U.S. and western companies seeking to enter Libya's booming market" (USET, 2008/7/23). Bechtel did not lose due to a lack of effort: the entire bidding process involved a memorandum of understanding with Libya's Prime Minister, a resolution by Libya's equivalent of a government cabinet, a year's worth of negotiations, and $1 million U.S. in expenses. Yet the contract never came to be. The U.S. Embassy clearly implied that Gaddafi, or those closest to him, must have intervened to prevent Bechtel from gaining a contract.

Bechtel's senior representative, Charles Redman, also a former U.S. Ambassador to Germany, went to Tripoli in July 2007 at the invitation of the Gaddafi Development Foundation (GDF) headed by Saif al-Islam Gaddafi. Redman's approach—that "Bechtel wanted, but did not need, business in Libya and had a record that spoke for itself"—did not sway

---

6. That the U.S. Embassy had to rely on a Reuters article for its report might occasion some interesting speculation of the barriers U.S. diplomats faced in getting information directly from the Libyan government itself.

Saif Gaddafi, who wanted the company to prove itself. In order to prove itself, Bechtel was called upon to partner with the Libyan Economic and Social Development Fund (ESDF) to execute the Sirte Port project (USET, 2008/7/23). This did not eliminate obstacles in Bechtel's way. The company had "increasingly difficult" relations with the General People's Committee for Transportation, manifested in the lack of facilitation of travel visas for Bechtel's representatives. The company also faced political conditions: then Deputy Prime Minister of Libya, Muhammed Siala, "remarked publicly during a visit to Washington that Bechtel would not secure the Sirte port contract if Secretary Rice failed to visit Libya by year's end" (USET, 2008/7/23).

Secretary Condoleeza Rice did in fact visit, but apparently that too was insufficient. It is especially important to note the ire of the U.S. Embassy in this matter with Bechtel, in part because of the influence of Bechtel in the U.S. government. The Embassy noted that the episode of rejecting Bechtel should serve as "a cautionary tale for other U.S. companies considering major investment projects here" (USET, 2008/7/23). It thus also points to one of a number of points of hostile contention that endured in the relationship between Libya and the U.S., and helps us understand why the U.S. government, as always interested in muscling in on countries in order to make space for its corporate allies and benefactors, would have little reason to want to see "the Gaddafi regime" continue in power.

The Bechtel Group, Inc. is the largest contractor in the U.S., specializing particularly in oil, natural gas, and chemicals. It has a long record of winning large government contracts and operates in over 60 countries, bringing in annual revenues in excess of US$11 billion. Bechtel is also a defence contractor with very strong political ties, particularly in the Reagan administration and in the successor Bush administrations of 1988-1992 and 2000-2008—a revolving, if not entirely open door between it and government. Historically, senior personnel have also had ties with the CIA. William Casey, CIA director under Ronald Reagan, worked as a consultant for Bechtel. Bechtel was behind the oil pipeline deal with Saddam Hussein that brought future Secretary of Defense Donald Rumsfeld to Iraq to meet with Hussein, an event from which the famous handshake video emerged. Edwin A. Meese III, former White House Counsel and Attorney General in the Reagan administration, was also investigated by a special prosecutor for improper dealings with Bechtel. Bechtel's former vice president, W. Kenneth Davis, was appointed Deputy Secretary of the U.S. Department of Energy from 1981 to 1983. In addition, Riley Bechtel, the company's CEO, was appointed by George W. Bush to serve on the President's Export Council. George P. Shultz, a former Reagan-appointed Secretary of State, serves as a director at Bechtel. Using his political ties in Washington, Shultz also lobbied for the 2003 invasion of Iraq. Caspar Weinberger, former Secretary of Defense under George H.W. Bush, was vice president and general counsel at Bechtel before his work in government. Daniel Chao, a Bechtel senior vice president, served on the advisory committee of the U.S. Export-Import Bank (Eximbank). Ross J. Connelly served the Bechtel Group for a long time before he became the chief operating officer for the Overseas Private Investment Corporation (OPIC), a major source of funding for U.S. companies overseas. An administrator for the U.S. Agency for International Development (USAID), Andrew Natsios, previously worked with Bechtel as the chairman of the Massachusetts Turnpike Authority. The U.S. Department of Energy's National Renewable Energy Laboratory is operated in part by Bechtel. Finally, General Jack Sheehan was a senior vice president of Bechtel for Europe, Africa, the Middle East, and Southwest Asia, as well as a member of the U.S. Defense Policy Board; Gen. Sheehan was also the Commander-in-Chief of U.S. Atlantic Command, and NATO Supreme Allied Commander. Sheehan is also an "international patron" of the right-wing British thinktank, the Henry Jackson Society. (Baker, 2003/4/18; Chatterjee, 2003/5/22; CorpWatch, 2003; Herbert, 2003/4/14; Juhasz, 2006/8/4; OpenSecrets, 2012; Oppel & Henrqiues, 2003/4/18; RightWeb, 2010; SourceWatch, 2008, 2011; Thomspon, 2004). George Grant, an Associate Fellow of the Henry Jackson Society is now the Assistant Editor for the newly created Libya Herald newspaper and a strident anti-Gaddafi op-ed writer.

If Muammar Gaddafi had been aware of a just a segment of this converging and overlapping network of collaborative interests in which Bechtel nested, he would have had ample reason to step in and stop any possible signing of a contract. This would not just stem from Bechtel's ties to the Reagan administration, Gaddafi's sworn enemy, which he never forgave since the bombing of Tripoli and Sirte in the 1980s (to which we return later). It can also be explained by the fact that Saudi Arabia's Bin Laden family were investors in a Bechtel subsidiary to the tune of $10 million U.S. or more (Mayer, 2003). As Gaddafi was a resolute and consistent enemy of Al Qaeda and Saudi support for Salafist movements, and had been so well before the U.S., these sorts of ties could only have inflamed him. That others in the Libyan government would have advanced Bechtel's bid as far as it went, reveals the kinds of divisions within the government which did not go unnoticed by the U.S. Embassy, as its own cables indicate.

Bechtel was not the only U.S. firm to be impeded from operating in Sirte. Caterpillar, noted for its heavy construction machinery, stood to lose $40 million U.S. from a ban on imports of its machinery, and expected to exit the Libyan market given its refusal to partner with the Economic and Social Development Fund (USET, 2009/8/3a, pars. 1, 7). Caterpillar had negotiated a $30 million U.S. deal with the Russian Railways Company to provide equipment for their railroad construction project along the coast from Sirte to Benghazi (USET, 2009/8/3a). However, Libya's Law Number Six regulating foreign distributors required that they establish distribution facilities in four cities (Tripoli, Benghazi, Sebha, and Sirte), with distinct and unrelated trade agents in each city (USET, 2009/8/3b). U.S. Ambassador Gene Cretz suspected that the obstacles were being raised at the highest levels of the Libyan government (USET, 2009/8/3a).

Fast forward to 2011: just as the Libyan government began to crumble after six months of continuous NATO bombings of its troops and civilian brigades, the U.S. immediately rushed in to secure business opportunities, especially the kinds from which they had been blocked before. As battles raged in Sirte in late September 2011, U.S. Ambassador Gene Cretz returned to Tripoli just a week after those loyal to the Al-Fateh Revolution were beaten back, and he immediately "participated in a State Department conference call with about 150 American companies hoping to do business with Libya." Which kinds of business opportunities most occupied Cretz? Infrastructure. As he told the media, "even in Qaddafi's time they were starting from A to Z in terms of building infrastructure." Cretz added: "If we can get American companies here on a fairly big scale, which we will try to do everything we can to do that, then this will redound to improve the situation in the United States with respect to our own jobs." While "oil is the jewel in the crown of Libyan natural resources," Cretz stated that it was never the "predominant reason" for U.S. intervention— indeed, to say so would neglect all of the other economic, strategic, and military reasons. *The New York Times'* correspondent observed that Cretz's remarks were "a rare nod to the tacit economic stakes in the Libyan conflict for the United States and other Western countries," and that his comments "underlined the American eagerness for a cut of any potential profits" (Kirkpatrick, 2011/9/22).

As the fighting ravaged Sirte, Tayyip Erdogan, Prime Minister of Turkey and a NATO member, also visited Tripoli, "hoping to reap political and

economic dividends from Libya's new rulers." Turkey had contracts totalling around $15 billion U.S. in Libya. As for other leading NATO members
that actively led in the attack on Libya, France and the UK were told by
Libya's NTC that "their support may be repaid in business contracts" (Logan
& Farge, 2011/9/16).

As early as a week before Muammar Gaddafi was murdered in Sirte on
October 20, a delegation of 80 French companies arrived in Tripoli to
meet with the new NTC regime and the new British defence minister,
Philip Hammond, urged British companies to "pack their suitcases" and
head to Tripoli. Western security, construction and infrastructure companies turned the NTC's dependency on and support for NATO into a
competitive advantage, as they spotted profit-making opportunities in
Libya. Such opportunities were just starting to diminish in Afghanistan
and Iraq: "entrepreneurs are abuzz about the business potential of a country with huge needs and the oil to pay for them." "Whilst speculation
continues regarding Qaddafi's killing," Trango Special Projects said on
its Web site, "are you and your business ready to return to Libya?" (Shane,
2011/10/28).

Finally, Mahmoud Jibril's comments deserve mention. Jibril served
first with the National Economic Development Board under Gaddafi from
2007 to 2011, and then joined the NTC and toured as its "Head of
International Affairs" before serving as an interim Prime Minister under
the NTC. He later resigned from the NTC altogether and made some
stunning declarations that few seemed to want to discuss. In one interview, Jibril stated quite plainly: "every foreign power you can think of is
trying to look after its own interests in Libya. No one is excluded. This is
the name of the game. This is politics. Countries have interests in Libya
and everybody is looking out for their own" (Campell, 2011). Far from
being a humanitarian mission to save lives, deeper interests were at work,
according to Jibril himself, someone with intimate familiarity with a wide
range of deals that were struck behind closed doors as NATO bombed
Libya.

Sirte: Reforms, Divisions, and Raised Expectations

Sirte also attracted a lot of attention from U.S. diplomats as the base for
the General People's Congress. If Libyan democracy was a sham and the
people's parliament a mere rubber-stamp mechanism, the U.S. Embassy
cables reveal nonetheless just how seriously the U.S. appreciated the real

workings of Libyan politics. Simplistic caricatures of Gaddafi as some omnipotent tyrant who micro-managed every detail of Libyans' lives may have been deemed suitable propaganda for public consumption in the U.S., but U.S. diplomats in Libya were more concerned with reality as it confronted them. That reality was substantially more complicated and filled with suspense.

The U.S. Embassy clearly kept a close watch on the debates at the General People's Congress, something one would not do if one believed the Congress to be a mere formality of little consequence, undeserving of careful observation. As admitted in one cable, "the results of this year's General People's Congress (Parliament-equivalent), which commenced in Sirte on March 2, will be closely watched for signs that the Libyan leadership remains committed to economic reform and reengagement with the international community" (USET, 2008/3/3). Speaking more widely, U.S. officials acknowledged that "observers will also carefully weigh the expected new government's composition," with especial interest in the factional struggles that had lined up behind either Saif Gaddafi or his brother Muatassim, as well as a keen interest in seeing who the Congress would choose as prime minister, foreign minister, and several other ministers (USET, 2008/3/3).

Since August 2006, when Saif Gaddafi gave a speech at the Youth Forum in Sirte, he had advocated for a new constitution that would abolish the system of Revolutionary Committees and the People's Congress in favour of a Western-inspired system that could have included multiparty elections (Abu Henanah, 2009). His plans, according to the U.S. Embassy, "drew harsh criticism at the time from the Revolutionary Committees and other conservative regime elements," which also indicates the presence of factions, disputes, and struggles within what was otherwise presented to the Western public as a monolithic, totalitarian state (USET, 2008/8/28). In his Youth Forum address in 2007, Saif moderated his language and instead spoke of a "social pact," and in his 2008 address he spoke of, "something which is perhaps called a constitution" (USET, 2008/12/5).

Information on the process of drafting a new constitution for Libya was provided to the U.S. Embassy by Muhammad Tarnesh, the Executive Director of the Human Rights Society of Libya (USET, 2008/12/5). Tarnesh explained that Saif Gaddafi first approached his father in late 2004/early 2005 to argue the need for a constitution that would codify the relationship between individual Libyans and the government. Muammar Gaddafi initially questioned the idea, seeing a constitution as a redundant barrier between the masses and the popular committees, preferring that even the identity of a formal "government" should remain largely undefined. As the late Chris Stevens, then the Chargé d'Affaires at the U.S. Embassy, reported, Libyan officials had told U.S. diplomats that, "we don't have a government here—we have something else [the Jamahiriya system]" (USET, 2008/12/5). Thus while initially critical of the idea, Muammar Gaddafi eventually reconciled himself to the argument that "some political adjustments were necessary to underpin badly needed economic reform," and he then played a role in selecting some of the members of a constitutional committee, in consultation with Saif (USET, 2008/12/5). Muammar Gaddafi also agreed to not include Revolutionary Committee members and former ministers, instead preferring "independent personalities" such as academics and lawyers. The intention was to maximize the credibility of the project and "to mitigate potential criticism that the constitution was just another political ploy to give the existing Jamahiriya system a face-lift" (USET, 2008/12/5).

A twenty-member committee was thus formed in 2007 to draft a constitution that would then go to the General People's Congress for consideration. The committee included in its ranks a half-dozen foreign academics, including professors from the Sorbonne and Cairo University. It had also been advised by the U.S. National Democratic Institute (NDI); Muhammad Tarnesh himself also participated in several of its meetings and knew some of its members well. Moreover, the U.S. Embassy cables cast few doubts on his credibility (USET, 2008/12/5). Muammar Gaddafi chose to obscure his role in supporting the project in order to have maximum room for manoeuvre "to cajole reluctant old guard members into accepting a constitution," thereby indicating a split within the government. Indeed Tarnesh noted that without Muammar Gaddafi's support nothing as politically significant as this project could have continued to exist for as long as it had (USET, 2008/12/5). The draft constitution was then circulated for review in mid-November 2008 (the U.S. Embassy obtained a copy), and was destined for Secretaries of General People's Committees and then the Basic People's Committees. Suggestions for changes to the draft would be reviewed, and the next draft of the constitution would then go to the General People's Congress (USET, 2008/12/5). Ultimately, it was the General People's Congress that rejected the draft constitution.

The U.S. National Democratic Institute, as mentioned above, knew of the nature of the reform process in Libya and eagerly sought to exploit it—indeed, it returned to Libya early in 2011 to capitalize on its contacts with the opposition. The NDI conducted two "political assessments" in Libya in 2006 and 2008 and met with government officials, lawyers, academics and activists (NDI, 2012). The NDI at that time also launched programs outside of Libya, to which it brought Libyan reform activists for training in "new media technology, political advocacy and women's political participation," and to meet and collaborate with like-minded activists from Algeria, Egypt, Morocco and Tunisia (NDI, 2012).

The NDI's activities are significant also because of what they reveal about political freedoms in Libya under Gaddafi, and the reforms that allowed foreign organizations such as it to become involved. In a 2006 report the NDI affirmed that there were political divisions in the governing structures of Libya: on one side was what the NDI called a "reform movement" that favoured liberalizing the economy, improving relations with the West, and openly calling for improved human rights, greater legal transparency, and a new constitution to codify new democratic advances; on the other side, the "conservatives" as the NDI called them, generally took the opposite view, wanting to preserve the status quo (NDI, 2006, p. 8). The NDI found the conservatives to be in the People's Congresses, government ministries, and the Green Book Center, while reformers were to be found in Saif Gaddafi's Development Foundation, universities, the lawyers' association, and the journalists' union. Repeatedly throughout its report, the NDI commented that none of the competing factions was interested in "regime change" (its words), either the end of the Al-Fateh revolution or the overthrow of Gaddafi, interesting comments that reflect back on the NDI's own interests and own way of defining democratic change in Libya (NDI, 2006, pp. 8, 9, 10). It is also interesting to note the degree of political freedom the NDI found in Libya, which provides a jarring contrast to what we can find in most U.S. media reports and op-ed commentaries. For example:

> "NDI met with several high profile lawyers who said that they were free to defend human rights cases in the courts without political intervention. It is well-known that many of Libya's high profile lawyers are also amongst the most vocal supporters of reform to the political system. At the current time the universities are the only forum [though the NDI just mentioned the courts] where freedom of expression is tolerated. Prominent professors are generally free to teach as they wish, even in sensitive matters of political science…. those professors who support change and are bold enough to speak or write about it are generally tolerated by the regime….even the Green Book Center,

representing the heart of Libyan political orthodoxy, holds conferences and debates in which it is possible to hear people expressing views that are critical of the system." (NDI, 2006, p. 9)

As the General People's Congress ended its week-long session in Sirte on March 5, 2009, the Deputy Chief of Mission at the U.S. Embassy, J. Christopher Stevens, filed a report pointing out that one of Muammar Gaddafi's own proposals had been shelved. That proposal involved disbanding government ministries and distributing Libya's oil revenues directly to all of its citizens. In addition, one of Saif Gaddafi's projects was also pushed aside: the Congress did not discuss a new, draft constitution. Other measures adopted by the Congress also limited reforms being urged by Muammar Gaddafi, who was himself publicly critical of the government for "for failing to address the needs of the people" (USET, 2009/3/11; 2008/3/3). Even some key NTC leaders who served in the Jamahiriya, expressed views to U.S. officials in private that were at least ambivalent, rather than strident denunciations of "tyranny." Mahmoud Jibril, who would become interim prime minister and foreign liaison for the NTC, served as Chair of the National Planning Council under Gaddafi and head of the affiliated Economic Development Board, and "was personally wooed back to Libya by Saif al-Islam to help implement reforms recommended in a Monitor Group report developed under the direction of Harvard University's Dr. Michael Porter" (USET, 2008/3/3). As for NTC Chair Mustafa Abdul Jalil, while he served as Minister of Justice under Gaddafi he privately told U.S. diplomats just a year before the revolt that he "maintained that Libyans could 'say anything they wanted' in the forum of the General People's Congress. He insisted that journalists were free to write anything they chose, provided they did not make personal accusations against anyone (i.e., slander)" (USET, 2010/1/27). If any of this describes "tyranny," then tyranny isn't what it used to be.

If there is one thing that all dictators depend upon it is a commanding, if not absolute, control over revenues, and a strong state structure. Yet, here we have the U.S. Embassy telling us that Gaddafi was dispensing with both, and was being stopped from doing so. In addition, a new constitution was to be adopted that, in Saif Gaddafi's hands, promised more Western-style civil liberties that privileged individual rather than collective rights. There can be little reason to doubt that the reform process began in Libya years before the protests of February 2011. On these topics, the international media were largely asleep, and one finds little if any coverage at the time, let alone any mention once the protests started in

2011. Few if any commentators have addressed the possibility that the proposed reforms, the competing projects between different branches of the Libyan government and different members of Gaddafi's family, coupled with the influx of massive new oil wealth and more trade with the West, might have themselves ushered in the fractures that would doom the government.

It was Muammar Gaddafi himself who, in addressing the opening of the 2008 session of the General People's Congress, gave a lengthy speech "in which he directed strong criticism at the government for failing to address the needs of the people" (USET, 2008/3/3). Here the U.S. Embassy is in fact noting that Gaddafi is criticizing "the government" as something that stands separate and apart from him (which is not to say that it was not subject to his leading influence). Gaddafi "decried the failure of the General People's Committees to effectively distribute Libya's oil wealth to its people," adding that "widespread corruption and failed implementation at all levels of government had engendered widespread dissatisfaction with public services, especially education, health, and infrastructure development," thus going counter to the 1969 revolution which had been successful in reclaiming Libya's oil wealth for all of its citizens (USET, 2008/3/17). Gaddafi was quick to note that oil-rich states that failed to fairly distribute oil wealth, risked being overthrown in the near future by their own people. Increased oil prices thus made the cost of the General People's Committees' failure to effectively distribute that wealth all the more untenable (USET, 2008/3/17). Asserting that Gaddafi was "out of touch" with his own people would now seem to be a remarkable statement of misunderstanding (see for example Beeman, 2011/2/23); not even the U.S. Embassy believed that.

U.S. Ambassador Gene Cretz interestingly downplayed the significance of political factors, while keeping a keen eye on political developments since Libya appeared "to be in one of its intermittent periods of intense political foment [sic]" (USET, 2009/2/27). Titling his cable "For Ordinary Libyans, It's the Economy, Stupid," Cretz said that "ordinary Libyans have largely eschewed politics and remained primarily focused on improving their daily standard of living" (USET, 2009/2/27), and he quoted several local sources to support that claim. One was Khaled Nayyed, son of a prominent businessman and a successful importer, who told the Embassy's Chief of Political and Economic Affairs that most Libyans do not really care about politics or political reform: "Do not give us free speech, parties, a constitution or elections—give us the ability to make and freely spend money" (USET, 2009/2/27). This opinion largely coincides with that of the vast majority of Libyans who, post-Gaddafi, care little for multi-party electoral democracy (BBC, 2012/2/15). Willing to forego political reform, another source told a U.S. diplomat, "I don't give a damn about politics" (USET, 2009/2/27, pars. 5, 6). What was a "significant danger," in Cretz's view, "was the increasing disparity between what Libyans saw and wanted to buy and what they could afford" (USET, 2009/2/27). In another cable, Cretz quoted Professor of Comparative Politics and Democratization at Garyounis University, Zahi Mogherbi: "The people see what the rest of the world has and know that the country is wealthy, but they do not see any of the wealth. They wonder where it goes" (USET, 2009/10/26, pars. 2, 3).

The combination of heightened expectations and splits in the ranks of the leadership (USET, 2009/3/9) are classic elements needed for any revolutionary situation—no revolutions, as most political scientists understand, have ever been caused simply by poverty and oppression. Otherwise, there would have been many more revolutions in the world than we have had. None of this is meant to diminish longstanding U.S. interests in effecting regime change in Libya; it is, however, an acknowledgment that short of invasion and occupation, local conditions and forces had to play a significant role, and these interests had to converge.

CHAPTER TWO

Sirte: Touchstone of Imperialism

Sirte: Reagan, Regime Change, Rapprochement(?)

Sirte was in the crosshairs of U.S. bombers well before 2011, going back
more than 30 years. In 1973, Libya made a historic claim to the entire Gulf
of Sirte (or Sidra) as its territorial waters, a claim that was then repeatedly
challenged by the U.S. and that led to multiple military confrontations.
The precursor to the European Union, the European Community, also
protested Libya's enclosure of these waters, with only Burkina Faso and
Syria having recognized Libya's claim from early on (Langford, 1987, p.
140). When Ronald Reagan came to power in the U.S., he used the Gulf
of Sirte dispute as a deliberate point on which to forcefully apply pressure
against Libya. The U.S. sought not to only to isolate Libya diplomatically,
but to find ways of overthrowing Gaddafi (Wright, 1981-1982, p. 13). From
that vantage point, "the Gulf of Sirte was tailor made for the United
States:....Between 1981 and 1989, the two nations skirmished in the Gulf
of Sirte at least four times" (Pollack, 2002, p. 413).

Africa, and in particular the forum provided by the Organization of
African Unity, saw Reagan immediately upon entering office trying to
pressure Libya's neighbours into isolating it. Prior to the OAU summit in
Nairobi in June of 1981, U.S. diplomats,

> "lobbied several African member states to move motions of censure against
> Libya, and to shift the venue of the OAU summit meeting, as well as the
> presidency of the OAU for the year, from Libya to alternative sites in Senegal
> and Niger. A major effort combining economic and military aid, naval port-
> calls, the despatch of military advisers, and diplomatic pressure was focused
> on the Liberian government to persuade it to break relations with Libya, and
> expel the Libyan mission." (Wright, 1981-1982, p. 14)

The U.S. sent two AWACS planes to Egypt to monitor Libya's borders, "in the event of a coup d'etat that was planned for that time within Libya," with a need to coordinate any Egyptian military support that might be sent to aid the rebels (Wright, 1981-1982, p. 15). In 1981, the U.S. shot down two Libyan fighters in the Gulf of Sirte, in what was planned as a deliberate provocation.

American officials began speaking of Gaddafi "in terms that implied their support for his downfall and death" (Wright, 1981-1982, p. 16). For example, when Reagan was asked the day after the Gulf of Sirte incident if he would "not be sorry to see Qaddafi fall," he replied: "diplomacy would have me not answer that question;" General Alexander Haig, Reagan's Secretary of State, referred to Gaddafi as, "a cancer that has to be removed;" then Vice President George H.W. Bush described him as an "egomaniac who would trigger World War III to make headlines;" an alleged moderate, former President Jimmy Carter spoke of Gaddafi as "subhuman," while former President Gerald Ford said Gaddafi was a "bully" and also a "cancer;" and, not to be left out, disgraced former President Richard Nixon said Gaddafi was "more than just a desert rat," but also "an international outlaw," and urged an international response to Gaddafi (Wright, 1981-1982, p. 16). To cancer, subhuman, and rat, we would later add Reagan's famous line that Gaddafi was a "mad dog"—the pattern of utter dehumanization and demonization of Gaddafi was set long before the first NATO bombs started to fall on Libya in March of 2011.

In the 1980s, virtually every terrorist attack and every alleged plan for one was blamed squarely on Libya by the Reagan administration. This included the entirely fabricated "plot" of a Libyan hit team sent to the U.S. to assassinate Reagan, or the unsubstantiated allegations that Libya was behind the Rome and Vienna airport bombings in 1985. U.S. intelligence not only acknowledged failing to find any links and, if anything, their searches took them far from Libya.

In addition to the coup attempt, coordinated with Egyptian military support as noted above, Reagan had the CIA draft a plan by the then deputy director for operations, Max Hugel, in the first two months of his administration. Various proposals were considered, ranging from disinformation and propaganda against Libya, to sabotaging Libyan oil installations, and organizing military and financial support for Libyan dissident groups in Morocco, Egypt, Sudan, and in the U.S. itself; U.S. media churned out dozens of articles and op-eds encouraging the campaign against Gaddafi; and, Tunisian and Saudi officials confirmed privately that they were "told by officials of the Reagan administration that Qaddafi would be eliminated by the end of 1981" (Wright, 1981-1982, p. 16). Among the anti-Gaddafi strategies that were used was the CIA's creation of real and illusionary events with the goal of making Gaddafi believe "that there is a high degree of internal opposition to him in Libya" (Woodward, 1987, p. 481). A number of published accounts have already documented the CIA's and the National Security Council's "obsession" with Libya during Reagan's term, its planning of covert actions and "building a set of escalating tactics designed to eliminate a political opponent defined within the Reagan administration as a threat to U.S. and Western interests." They even went as far as trying to convince Egypt to invade Libya (Perdue, 1989, p. 54; Woodward, 1987, pps. 181-186, 409-410, 419-420).

The Assistant Secretary of State for Africa, Chester Crocker, declared to the Senate Foreign Relations Committee in July 1981 that Libya's diplomacy was a "diplomacy of subversion" (two decades later, this became "dinar diplomacy"), aimed at subversion in Africa and in the Arab world, "a diplomacy of unprecedented obstruction to our own interests and objectives" (Wright, 1981-1982, p. 17). In all of this, Sirte was once again thrust into the centre of direct military conflict with the U.S.

In March and April 1986, the U.S. conducted two military operations in the Gulf of Sirte designed to provoke a Libyan reaction, which the U.S. could then use as justification for bombing Libyan installations. "Operation Attain Document III" (also "Operation Prairie Fire") involving as many as three U.S. aircraft carriers, 23 other warships (other reports say 27), and 250 aircraft, finally drew a Libyan response. Sirte itself became involved when the Libyan surface-to-air missile (SA-5) battery at Sirte launched missiles at U.S. F-14 fighters (Pollack, 2002, p. 416). The U.S. fired upon Libyan naval vessels and the missile base in Sirte.

Like Barack Obama 25 years later, Reagan also did not bother to obtain the consent of Congress for his war operations against Libya, completely ignoring the War Powers Resolution (Tananbau, 1997, p. 472). Then, as now, the U.S.' own principles of democracy and checks and balances were thrown to the curb to make way for an imperial president with a point to prove in smashing Libyan resistance. While Reagan would justify U.S. military actions as "retaliatory," it was instead later disclosed that no matter what the Libyan response might have been, "Reagan had authorised the destruction of the Libyan missile base at Sirte right when he had given his approval for the naval exercises off Libya on March 14," and the

Pentagon itself conceded that there had been "no second round of attacks on U.S. ships before the latter unleashed their renewed attacks on the Libyan missile base and patrol boats" (*Economic and Political Weekly*, 1986, p. 553).

Just as was the case 25 years later, the point of U.S. military action had little to do with supporting international law; rather, the immediate goal was the same in both cases: regime change. As the former British Foreign Secretary, David Owen, put it:

> "An important warning note had been served on the Libyan military—and notice I say Libyan military and not just Colonel Gaddafi—namely, that if they allowed Gaddafi unbridled power and he exercised it contrary to international law, they would face military defeat. That, in my view, is a necessary message to send, for the military elite in any country do not like humiliation and Gaddafi will be controlled or toppled, in my view, not by the masses but by the elite." (Owen, 1987, p. 85)

Moreover, Owen regretted that the U.S. acted alone: "It would have been a far more effective demonstration to Colonel Gaddafi if other NATO nations, including particularly Britain and Italy, had sailed with the U.S. fleet," as that would have emphasized, "collective resolve and action" (1987, p. 85). Owen must have been delighted that his wishes came true, even if not as soon as 1986.

What transpired in the 25 years that followed in supposedly altering Libyan-U.S. relations is a complex story that requires very careful documentation and analysis. It is also a story that largely lies beyond the scope of this chapter and this book, focused as it is primarily on NATO's intervention in 2011, and its consequences, both for Libya and for the domestic politics of NATO member states. U.S. plots against Libya, and multiple coup attempts continued to occur throughout the 1980s and 1990s. International sanctions were also imposed following the passage of UN Security Council Resolutions 748 (adopted on March 31, 1992) and 883 (adopted on November 11, 1993) in response to the alleged role of Libya in the downing of PanAm 103 over Lockerbie, Scotland, in 1988, and an attack on UTA 772 in 1989. Those sanctions, both financial and military, were suspended with the passage of UNSCR 1192 (in 1998), and entirely lifted in 2003 with the passage of UNSCR 1506 (UN, 2003). Libya began to take a different route, cutting ties to guerrilla movements, and facilitating investigations of these attacks, turning over suspects, and then ultimately abandoning plans for the development of "weapons of mass destruction" (WMDs), including nuclear weapons, in the wake of the U.S. invasion of Iraq in 2003.

There was palpable American excitement in Sirte in 2004 as a seven-member delegation from the U.S. House of Representatives led by Republican Curt Weldon, along with representatives from more than a hundred countries, met with Gaddafi. Also in attendance, Senator Joseph Biden, who would later become vice president under Barack Obama. Gaddafi offered a very long explanation of what led to his conclusion, as understood by some of the delegates, that yesterday's enemies would now be Libya's friends. "At first, I was just listening to the speech," said Democrat Susan Davis, "but what he [Gaddafi] was saying was so amazing that I started writing it down so I could report to my constituents. I took 24 pages of notes" (Timmerman, 2004, p. 18). Gaddafi's address to his guests, while called "brutally self-critical," in fact shined part of the light on Libya's allies: Libya had reaped international isolation for the sake of supporting the Irish Republican Army (IRA), the Palestine Liberation Organization (PLO), and the African National Congress (ANC), but now they had each made their own separate peace, leaving Libya behind continuing to fight. Gaddafi asked rhetorically: "Are we more Irish than the Irish? Are we more Palestinian than the Palestinians?...How can [Yasser Arafat] enter the White House and we not improve our relations with the United States?" (Timmerman, 2004, p. 19). In a statement that was easily misinterpreted as a *mea culpa*, Gaddafi underlined the sacrifices that Libya willingly made for others: "No one separated Libya from the world community. Libya voluntarily separated itself from others....No one has imposed sanctions on us or punished us. We have punished ourselves....all these things were done for the sake of others" (Timmerman, 2004, p. 19).

Indeed, Gaddafi was a remarkable and unique exception among the whole range of modern Arab leaders, for being doggedly altruistic, for funding development programs in dozens of needy nations, for supporting national liberation struggles that had nothing to do with Islam or the Arab world, for pursuing an ideology that was original and not simply the product of received tradition or mimesis of exogenous sources, and for making Libya a presence on the world stage in a way that was completely out of proportion with its population size (for example most of the larger Caribbean nations have larger populations). One could be a fierce critic of Gaddafi, and still have the honest capability to recognize these objective realities, or, if preferring to maintain the narrative of demonization, "to give the devil his due."

When Gaddafi turned his attention to Libya's nuclear weapons program, his guests in Sirte claimed to be astonished that he was admitting its existence. Why did he "surrender" this program? Here one needs to pay careful attention to his words. Dismantling the nuclear weapons was "in our own interest and for our own security," and the program was terminated because, "it was a waste of time. It cost too much money," and besides, "if there is any aggression against Libya now, the whole world will come to defend Libya" (Timmerman, 2004, p. 19). This is also the clearest possible statement of Gaddafi's fatal miscalculation, revealing an underlying assumption that, in the end, honour must rule international relations. That says a lot about him, and it also says a lot about NATO states. Few states will ever again call the West's bluff on peaceful reconciliation.

Gaddafi made other practical calculations in this address that might be called his Sirte Declaration II. He clearly hoped to gain U.S. technology. In this respect, he would not throw open the doors to foreign investment, and at most he would allow joint ventures with Libyan firms, thus maintaining Libyan control. As noted above, this ultimately rankled some of the biggest U.S. transnational firms. Gaddafi was going to buy his way into elite circles. Some call it being "in bed with the west," but one might still see this as an alternative route of what Reagan administration officials called a "diplomacy of subversion." Indeed, Obama seems to have understood it in that manner, refusing at every possible instance any state visit with Gaddafi, anywhere (and this is from a person, who as a candidate for the presidency, vowed he would even meet and speak with the U.S.' "enemies").

Congressman Curt Weldon stood in Sirte and exclaimed, "We were part of history tonight. Col. Qaddafi's statements were unequivocal. There were no ifs, ands or buts. It reminds me of the sea change that occurred when the Berlin Wall came down, or when [Boris] Yeltsin stood on top of a tank in front of the Russian White House. As startling as it is to us, we'd better take advantage of it" (Timmerman, 2004, p. 19). Here is another fatal error: few in the U.S., whether in government and even less so in the media, should ever have allowed themselves the false sense of certainty that they had understood Gaddafi as if the latter spoke plainly. The sands shift as the wind blows…there are always "ifs, ands, or buts."

"We'd better take advantage of it," said Weldon of Gaddafi's "openness." Also present, as mentioned before, was Joe Biden, clearly ready to take advantage. "I told Qaddafi there are certain basic rules to playing in the global economy," said Biden in Sirte at a dinner with Libyan officials, "no one will invest in your country without transparency or without stability. To deliver the promise to your people is going to require significant change, not dictated by the United States but by reality" (Timmerman, 2004, p. 19). As a matter of fact, Biden would form part of the administration that would in fact dictate that change, and make regime change a reality. His remarks, typically blunt, were an open threat. Immediately, "observers in the Libyan capital" were quick to point out another "reality" that Gaddafi's apparent openness could be exploited for vulnerability.

> "[Gaddafi] appears to be more worried today about his grip on the country than ever before and is seeking to open it to Western investment to quell popular discontent with his mismanagement of the nation's economy. Streets in Libya's bustling downtown market remain unpaved, telephones work only periodically, and no foreign newspapers are allowed....At the same time, however, Libyan universities are graduating large numbers of well-educated young people with engineering and other degrees who are unable to find work. The potential for social unrest is very real." (Timmerman, 2004, p. 19)

Gaddafi also found ways to take advantage of this "opening," by insisting on Libyan national rights in new but still limited ways. Once again, Sirte would be the stage. On March 2, 2009, Italian Prime Minister Silvio Berlusconi flew into Sirte, along with the diplomatic corps, for the ratification of the Libya-Italy treaty of "friendship and cooperation." As noted by the U.S. Embassy, Belusconi apologized for what it called Italy's "misdeeds" (colonial occupation and the slaughter of at least a third of all Libyans), and noted that Gaddafi raised his arms "in triumph and glee" (USET, 2009/3/11). The treaty committed Italy to pay Libya reparations of $200 million U.S. per year for 25 years for its "wrong-doing" (USET, 2009/3/11). Italy was keen on obtaining preference for its companies in the development projects to be funded by Libya, as well as for Libya to aid it in blocking illegal migration to Italy, which Libya had promised in the past, but as the U.S. Embassy admitted, "they have failed to do in previous iterations of migration agreements" (USET, 2009/3/11). Berlusconi also invited Gaddafi to Italy and to the G8 summit scheduled for July 2009 in L'Aquila, Abruzzo, where Gaddafi would act in his capacity as Chairman of the AU (USET, 2009/3/11).

Sirte became the venue for a series of high-level U.S. delegations that travelled to meet with Gaddafi. In each case, Gaddafi's remarks to his visitors, and even his demeanour, ranged from interest to indifference to recriminations. One of the most persistent themes in nearly all of his discussions was his visceral hostility for Islamic extremists, Wahabis/ Salafists, Saudi Arabia, and especially Al Qaeda. Another persistent theme was Gaddafi's continual expression of what was almost regret: that Libya had opened itself up, dropped its WMD programs, participated in the Lockerbie prosecution, and yet received very little in return. He was especially keen on obtaining military technology. Once again, the view proffered by some that Gaddafi was now "in bed with the West," is at the very least a strange view of romance.[1]

On August 20, 2005, Senator Richard Lugar traveled to Sirte to meet with Gaddafi, accompanied by Tim Pounds (Director for Syria, Lebanon, Egypt, and North Africa at the National Security Council in Washington, DC) and other advisors and officials. Gaddafi made it clear to his visitors that "Libya had not been properly recognized and rewarded for its decisions on WMD," and that the most appropriate rewards would be "defensive weapons to protect the country against the threat of emerging extremist regimes in its neighbors, and the application of nuclear technology for peaceful purposes." He stressed that "the greatest threat to the region came from religious extremism," which he argued was "inextricably linked to the Saudi regime" (USET, 2005/8/31, pars. 1, 8). Lugar, for his part, chose to focus on the sorts of issues the U.S. could exploit in undermining the Libyan government—he expressed his concern about "human rights," the fate of opposition activist Fathi al-Jahmi, and the situation concerning Bulgarian and Palestinian medics detained on charges that they had deliberately infected patients with HIV (USET, 2005/8/31).

In his remarks, Gaddafi made it clear that peaceful relations between Libya and the U.S. would also be of benefit to the U.S.: "No one benefited from confrontation in the past; everyone lost. We need to change our policies for mutual benefit" (USET, 2005/8/31). Gaddafi consistently ham-

---

1. One can find such arguments embedded in a range of electronic media, including many of those who asserted their opposition to NATO's intervention in Libya. A few examples include the now apparently defunct Yansoon blog (Shirien, 2011/8/23), Phyllis Bennis at the Institute for Policy Studies (Democracy Now, 2011/4/19), and Akuetteh (2011/9/22). *Veterans Today*, which supported NATO's intervention, produced an exceptionally bizarre article, that while ostensibly seeking to challenge "conspiracy theories," produced a preposterous and wholly unsupported one of its own: that Gaddafi was actually backed by Israel, and that Israel had armies of African mercenaries which it sent to Libya to defend Gaddafi— which in itself is an interesting convergence of opinion between a Western militarist and some of Gaddafi's most extreme Islamist opponents (see Duff, 2011/3/21).

mered away at the fact that Libya was not benefiting as promised from
dropping its WMD program and that he heard from both North Korea
and Iran that "Libya's experience is a bad example," which meant it was
a good example of why giving up such programs would be pointless. He
noted that Libya had been attacked in the Arab press for being "foolish
for surrendering its power and advantage without any compensation," to
which Gaddafi said, "this is true" (USET, 2005/8/31, pars. 4, 5). Libya, in
fact, continued to remain on the U.S. list of "state sponsors of terrorism."
While Senator Lugar did not promise to do much to remove Libya from
that list, he was keen to get the Libyans to more readily issue visas for U.S.
businessmen (USET, 2005/8/31). Gaddafi also appeared to be ready to play
one power bloc off against the other, as when he told Lugar that he would
like to meet with President George W. Bush "about Africa and 'the new
colonialism from the East' (i.e., growing Chinese and Indian influence in
Africa)" (USET, 2005/8/31). As in many other instances, Gaddafi, as noted
by the U.S. Embassy, focused his concerns on the threats coming from
Wahabist extremists sponsored and encouraged by Saudi Arabia, and
because Syria too was strongly resisting such extremists, the U.S. should
modify its stance towards it, Gaddafi argued.

It is striking to see how all of these themes persisted right into NATO's
attack against Libya in 2011—that the NATO intervention, in other words,
was not an abrupt change of course, but the extension of a continuum of
friction and underlying hostility. Indeed, even U.S. diplomats recognized
that a significant faction of the Libyan government remained critical and
hostile towards any expanded relations with the U.S., let alone "cooperation" (USET, 2009/1/15).

A year later, Congressman Tom Lantos, ranking Democrat on the
House Foreign Relations Committee, made his second trip to Libya in
two years, meeting with Gaddafi in Sirte during August 22-24, 2006.
Lantos' trip coincided with that of another high-ranking congressional
delegate, Senator Arlen Specter, thus combining their meetings. In addition to Gaddafi, most of Libya's highest-ranking officials were present,
including Saif Gaddafi; Abdullah Senussi, Director of Military Intelligence;
Musa Kusa, Director of the External Security Organization; Abdurrahman
Shalgam, Secretary of the General Peoples Committee for Foreign Liaison
and International Cooperation; Ahmed Fatouri, Secretary of American
Affairs; and, Abdelati Obeidi, Secretary for European Affairs. The U.S.
congressmen announced that Libya had been removed from the U.S. list
of sponsors of terrorism, and invited Libya to increase the number of

students it sent to the U.S. from the current level of 150 to 6,000 (USET, 2006/8/31a, pars. 1, 2).

Hearing of the U.S. interest in receiving more Libyan students, Gaddafi noted how the U.S.' chosen ally, Saudi Arabia, had recently witnessed its Grand Mufti declaring that Saudi students should be barred from attending university in the U.S. From there, Gaddafi once again stressed his worry about the spread of Wahabi fundamentalism from Saudi Arabia (USET, 2006/8/31a). This topic rarely seems to have engaged U.S. officials, with this occasion being one of the exceptions. Senator Specter asked Gaddafi how the U.S. could aid Libya in dealing with terrorists. Gaddafi smiled and answered, "on the contrary, you support them; you support the Saudi royal family that funds Wahabi fundamentalists" (USET, 2006/8/31b).

On Libya-U.S. relations, Gaddafi told Specter that Libya "gave up every-thing and got nothing in return" (USET, 2006/8/31b). Gaddafi was about to be instructed on what he would instead get: "democracy." Sitting there in Sirte, future site of NATO's devastation and Gaddafi's murder, Specter commented on the need to bring "democracy" to Libya, telling Gaddafi that "there would be democracy in Libya in the future" (USET, 2006/8/31b). In response, Gaddafi lectured Specter on the fact that Libya was "the sole country that enjoys direct democracy, we hope the U.S. becomes like Libya, it is the ultimate level of democracy where Libyans rule themselves instead of electing officials to represent them." He also told Specter that he hoped the U.S. would one day benefit from Libya's Jamahiriya (state of the masses) system (USET, 2006/8/31b).

It appears that Specter poisoned the meeting for himself, for as soon as he raised the issue of obtaining land in Tripoli to build a new U.S. Embassy compound, Gaddafi retorted: "maybe the Libyans heard the Embassy will be a staging ground for opposition activities and counter-Libyan movements. Maybe the Libyans don't want a big U.S. Embassy" (USET, 2006/8/31b). The U.S. Embassy felt that Gaddafi's comments were offered "half-seriously." But apparently they were not, as Gaddafi con-tinued: "people know that chanceries are for cooperation between states and diplomats shouldn't interfere in internal affairs, but people see U.S. embassies all over the world from other angles." This occasioned a chal-lenge from the U.S. Embassy's CDA. Then Senator Specter, trying to rescue a deal, turned to Suleiman Shihumi (Secretary of Foreign Affairs of the General People's Congress) seeking his support and said a new U.S. chan-cery could help with job creation in Libya and thus also help re-energize its economy. In sharp response to this crass gesture of waving dollars under Libyan noses, Shihumi stated: "we have survived for thirty years without U.S. money and had no problems" (USET, 2006/8/31b). Bowing down before the West is decidedly not what Gaddafi was doing.

We should note how Gaddafi understood the dominant U.S. worldview in a statement he made just a few years before these meetings took place, back in 1999, the same year of the Sirte Declaration:

> "America unfortunately treats us as if the world was the way it used to be. Americans accept that changes have taken place since the end of communism, but not in their treatment of Libya. So in the end, they take a racist and fanatical position, similar to the way Hitler treated the Jews. We feel that America is much like Hitler. We have no explanation for this, except that it is a religious, fanatical, racist position. Some analysts call this a new colonialism. But colonialism is colonialism, and it is always unjust. It is how we were treated by the Italians, Algeria by the French, India by the British. This is imperialism, and we seem to be entering a new imperialist era. The cause of our conflict with America is not that we attacked them. We have never attacked an American target. America started the aggression against us right here in the Gulf of Sirte. When we defended ourselves, they attacked us in these very tents. We were bombed by missiles in our own territorial waters. In 1986 our own children were killed. No one can bring my daughter back to me. Then Lockerbie came along. Now we'd like this chain of events to be over. But America doesn't want to turn the page. We shall, however, show courage and be patient, and America will be the loser." (Quoted in Viorst, 1999, p. 66)

Sirte: MI6 and Early Islamist Attacks against Gaddafi

In early March 1996, as Colonel Gaddafi travelled in a motorcade through the streets of Sirte lined with bystanders, members of the Libyan Islamic Fighting Group (LIFG) attempted to assassinate Gaddafi. They had placed a bomb under what they thought would be Gaddafi's car, except that Gaddafi would always periodically order a convoy to stop so that he could change cars. The bomb thus exploded under the wrong car and killed several bodyguards and innocent civilian bystanders. In the gunbattle that followed, several LIFG militants were killed. The person in charge of the attack, Abd al-Muhaymen, was "a Libyan fundamentalist who had trained and fought in Afghanistan," in support of the mujahideen against Soviet troops, and thus had "access to CIA and British intelligence operatives" who helped to organize the mujahideen. David Shayler, "a renegade MI5" British intelligence officer, claimed that MI6 (MI5's counterpart responsible for foreign operations and counter espionage) was also behind the plot to assassinate Gaddafi and had collaborated with the LIFG (Bright, 2002/11/10; Darwish, 1998; Immigration and Refugee Board of Canada [IRBC], 1998). Two MI6 agents, Richard Bartlett and David Watson, code-named PT16 and PT16B respectively, had overall responsibility for the operation (Bright, 2002/11/10). Credible reports by French intelligence were that the LIFG was at the time affiliated with Al Qaeda and that MI6 paid large amounts of money to what was an Al Qaeda cell (Bright, 2002/11/10). Indeed, the very first Interpol warrant issued for the arrest of Osama Bin Laden, came at the prompting of the government of Libya in March 1998 (Bright, 2002/11/10).

Muammar Gaddafi was steadfast in his condemnation of Islamic fundamentalism, as he was persistent in directly attacking Islamic militants in Libya. Years before Bin Laden became a household name in the West, Libya issued an arrest warrant for his capture. Indeed, as Libya led by Gaddafi fought against Al Qaeda years before it became public enemy number one in the U.S., Western intelligence agencies collaborated with Al Qaeda to kill Gaddafi. The meeting between Western intelligence agencies and Libyan Islamic militants would not be restricted to Sirte and would not just occur in 1996: the collaboration was renewed in the "revolution" of 2011 as NATO prepared to bomb its way toward regime change. Gaddafi's loose remarks that the only people rising up against him in February 2011 were Al Qaeda were partially correct and rooted in precedent. While Gaddafi's notion that his opponents were drug addicts was exaggerated, and sometimes backed up with what Western media mocked as ineffectual displays of caches of ordinary, non-prescription drugs, that notion also had some foundation in fact. Here sometimes even Western media reports would make fleeting, understated mention of rebels "rolling hash joints" as they waited to attack a Gaddafi stronghold in Bani Walid (AP, 2011/9/19). Media such as the AP, while not noting that this conformed with Gaddafi's characterization, failed to raise the most important and immediately pertinent question: how could largely untrained forces, high on hash, be expected to fire heavy weapons anything but indiscriminately and thus endanger civilians?

In 2011, the destruction of Sirte and the destruction of Gaddafi and the Al-Fateh Revolution ended up converging. U.S. plans for the overthrow of Gaddafi did not initially take into account the possibility of the kind of unflagging resistance mounted by the residents of Sirte, which made them nearly invincible and made a mockery of notions of a "popular" and "national" uprising against a "dictator" that allegedly "all Libyans" hated.

Barack Obama and How Empire Revisited Sirte

Since Barack Obama assumed the U.S. presidency, ice crystals once again began to form on the barely thawed U.S. attitude toward Libya. What no cabinet official in Obama's administration apparently wanted to do was to attend any event in Sirte that could symbolize a form of recognition and amicability. It was almost as if they wished to resist anything that could mitigate plans for the eventual destruction of the Al-Fateh Revolution and the defiant independence that marked Libya as led by Gaddafi.

Musa Kusa, Libya's equivalent of a Foreign Affairs Minister, attempted to prod U.S. diplomats to lobby their seniors in Washington to send a high-level U.S. official to Sirte to attend the 40th anniversary celebrations of the 1969 revolt in 2009. Gaddafi had also personally extended an invitation to Barack Obama to attend the summit of the African Union in Sirte in July 2009 "but for some reason he could not come." Kusa hoped for such high-level attendance because, as the U.S. Embassy understood, "it would be very meaningful to Libya and an important signal of the USG [U.S. government] commitment to the bilateral relationship." As several Arab, African and European heads of state had already agreed to participate, "yet another rejection" from the U.S. "would not be well-received or understood" (USET, 2009/8/5). Kusa suggested that at the very least, on the margins of the meeting of the UN General Assembly in 2009, perhaps Gaddafi could meet with Obama (USET, 2009/8/5). That too never happened. When Barack Obama finally made his presence felt in Sirte, it was through a prolonged campaign of steady bombing, the nearest he came to even getting "up close and personal" with the city.

"For generations, the United States of America has played a unique role as an anchor of global security and as an advocate for human freedom," declared Barack Obama on March 28, 2011, in what already sounded as a victory speech only nine days after the first NATO bombs were dropped on Libya (see Obama, 2011/3/28, for this and subsequent quotes). Obama spoke at the National Defense University in Washington, DC, and like his predecessor, George W. Bush, he chose a captive military audience and opened with the customary militarist salute, but with a "humanitarian" veneer. "I want to begin by paying tribute to our men and women in uniform who, once again, have acted with courage, professionalism and patriotism. They have moved with incredible speed and strength. Because of them…countless lives have been saved." Obama indeed made remarks that echoed his predecessor's infamously premature "mission accomplished" speech about Iraq aboard a U.S. aircraft carrier. According to Obama, not only had lives been saved, but what was allegedly the primary objective of NATO's intervention was even then declared to have been achieved: "tonight, I can report that we have stopped Qaddafi's deadly advance." Obama repeated the point later in his speech: "In just one month, the United States has worked with our international partners to mobilize a broad coalition, secure an international mandate to protect civilians, stop an advancing army, prevent a massacre, and establish a no-fly zone with our allies and partners." For emphasis, Obama again stated moments later: "we've accomplished these objectives." And yet again: "I want to be clear: The United States of America has done what we said we would do."

However, Obama was not being clear. He took a new turn in his remarks: "That's not to say that our work is complete." Since he had established how successful the U.S. had been in accomplishing what it declared it had set out to do, the most obvious and immediate question that few media commentators bothered to ask was: then why is the bombing continuing?

Even restricted to a close and critical reading of Obama's narrative alone, the answers to that question take the form of two pairs of themes: "protecting civilians" joined with "Gaddafi has lost legitimacy and must go;" and, "interests and values" joined with the "Arab Spring."

Let's begin with the first pair. Obama claimed in his March 28 speech that, "broadening our military mission to include regime change would be a mistake," adding, "if we tried to overthrow Qaddafi by force, our coalition would splinter." He then reminded his audience about Iraq: "To be blunt, we went down that road in Iraq….regime change there took eight years, thousands of American and Iraqi lives, and nearly a trillion dollars. That is not something we can afford to repeat in Libya." Left at that, one might be forgiven for thinking that Obama was absolutely against regime change, except that is not the case, not even according to his own statements in the very same speech. What Obama was really against was landing an occupation force plus an expensive engagement. Those are his only actual objections to "regime change," and they are not even about regime change as such, but rather nation-building. Obama blurs together regime change and nation-building in his speech, which helps to create an illusion that he was not actually for regime change. In fact, as Obama himself asserted, "I made it clear that Qaddafi had lost the confidence of his people and the legitimacy to lead, and I said that he needed to step down from power." He made it clear, as if he had the authority and the legitimacy to speak for all Libyans and to dictate a new government to them. This type of narrative can only ever be about one goal: regime change. Obama once more stated in his speech: "we continue to pursue the broader goal of a Libya that belongs not to a dictator, but to its people" (i.e., regime change). He added, "there is no question that Libya—and the world—would be better off with Qaddafi out of power. I, along with many other world leaders, have embraced that goal," that goal being regime change. Furthermore, Obama pledged the U.S. would work "with other nations to hasten the day when Qaddafi leaves power": regime change. Obama sent Secretary of State Hillary Clinton to London to confer with allies on "supporting a transition to the future that the Libyan people deserve": regime change. He claimed that he would pursue that goal by non-military means…and yet the bombs continued to drop, and they dropped on Gaddafi's very own living quarters on repeated occasions. That is because regime change was one of the actual, immediate goals to which Obama himself admitted behind this increasingly tired and clumsily woven veil of deliberately foggy speech (likely the hastily negotiated product of multiple committees, agencies, and press advisers targeting disparate audiences). Later Hillary Clinton publicly revealed that the former CDA in Tripoli, Christopher Stevens, was sent back to Libya in the early days of the 2011 "revolution" to covertly work with the insurgents in order to overthrow Gaddafi (Clinton, 2012/9/12).

The "Gaddafi must go" theme can only be understood in conjunction with that of "protecting civilians." In Obama's speech that night, as in all subsequent NATO communiqués and press briefings, anything and everything done to overthrow Gaddafi—including targeting civilian communities that supported Gaddafi—would be justified, however incredibly, as "protecting civilians." This fact appears in Obama's very own remarks: "Qaddafi has not yet stepped down from power, and until he does, Libya will remain dangerous." As Obama said, as of March 27, "NATO decided to take on the additional responsibility of protecting Libyan civilians," an additional responsibility that went beyond the already achieved objectives which Obama led Americans to believe were the sole objectives. Even Noam Chomsky (2012/1/7) succumbed to this logic that there were "two interventions," one to establish a no-fly zone, and the second to prolong the rebels' war against Gaddafi. Chomsky openly supported the first, remarkably without understanding how it led to, justified, and served as the gateway to the second—UN Security Council Resolution 1973 itself listed the no-fly zone and the broader protection of civilians within the same document. Indeed, there was no such thing as "two interventions," except as cover for poor judgment and flawed analyses that took Obama at his word.

The second pair of themes in Obama's speech also reinforce each other. In his March 28 address, Obama never clearly defines what U.S. interests were in Libya. The fact that they should remain unspoken is not an accident or a mere oversight—nothing ever is at this level. Obama was playing a difficult game here. On the one hand, Obama could assert that the war, which his press secretary Jay Carney [Carney, 2011/3/23] and others [York, 2011/3/23] had defined as not a war but merely a "kinetic military action," was one that served U.S. interests, possibly in an effort to quiet "isolationists" and the realpolitik crowd at home at a time of rising anti-war sentiment. On the other hand, by not specifying what those interests actually were, and by coupling his remarks with "humanitarian" concerns, Obama can claim that the U.S. was not motivated by instrumentalist strategies of gain, but rather universal, freedom-loving altruism. In waging war on Libya, the U.S. leadership also engaged in a war on language (Schell, 2011/6/21). Robert Gates, who in early 2011 was still Secretary of Defense, went on NBC's *Meet the Press* and made an effort to explain, however ambiguously: "No. I don't think it's a vital interest for the United States, but we clearly have interests there, and it's a part of the region which is a vital interest for the United States" (NBC, 2011/3/27). Hillary Clinton, on the same program, elaborated on those interests:

> "did Libya attack us? No. They did not attack us. Do they have a very critical role in this region and do they neighbor two countries—you just mentioned one, Egypt, the other Tunisia—that are going through these extraordinary transformations and cannot afford to be destabilized by conflict on their borders? Yes. Do they have a major influence on what goes on in Europe because of everything from oil to immigration?....So, you know, let, let's be fair here. They didn't attack us, but what they were doing and Gadhafi's history and the potential for the disruption and instability was very much in our interests, as Bob said, and seen by our European friends and our Arab partners as very vital to their interests." (NBC, 2011/3/27)

This is where "interest" and controlling the events of the "Arab Spring" merge, according to Gates, Clinton, and Obama. Obama was quite direct in defining U.S. "national interest" as one that encompassed not letting Gaddafi triumph over his armed opposition: "America has an important strategic interest in preventing Qaddafi from overrunning those who oppose him," which takes us back to regime change (Obama, 2011/3/28). This was never a "kinetic humanitarian action." The only lives the U.S. was interested in saving were those of the insurgents, saving them so they could defeat Gaddafi.

Sirte: Toxic to Empire

"They [NATO] are trying to push the country to the brink of a civil war," exclaimed Khaled Kaim, the Deputy Foreign Minister of Libya, "this is the objective of the coalition now, it is not to protect civilians" (Fahim et al., 2011/3/29). Libya of course continued to remain "dangerous" well past the date of Obama's remarks, and, from the U.S. standpoint, this was especially true once they encountered Sirte's near impregnability to insurgent advances. On March 29, 2011, the very next day after Obama gave his speech, the insurgents fighting to overthrow Gaddafi were forced to retreat and found themselves 150 kilometres from Sirte (BBC, 2011/3/29). What Western governments and media had billed as a "popular uprising" now seemed to be particularly dependent upon NATO to make any sort of headway.

The New York Times correspondents reported from the scene that "Hundreds of trucks and cars carrying fighters began streaming away" (Fahim et al., 2011/3/29). The insurgents had only been able to advance to where they had thanks to NATO air cover. When still optimistic about taking Sirte quickly, one insurgent spoke to Reuters about the rapid advance: "This couldn't have happened without NATO, they gave us big support" (Hendawi, 2011/3/28). As much as Obama had tried to blur his strategy to pursue regime change, a "blunt assessment by the American military, which is conducting the bulk of the air campaign against pro-Qaddafi forces," concluded that "insurgent advances would be reversed quickly without continued strikes by coalition warplanes" (Fahim et al., 2011/3/29). As *The New York Times* noted, the "contest" for Sirte raised the question of "how the allies could justify airstrikes if, as seems to be the case, loyalist forces enjoy widespread support in the city and pose no threat to civilians" (Fahim et al., 2011/3/29).

"Sarkozy, where are you?" some rebels shouted, pleading for air strikes against Sirte as their rapid advance turned into "a panicked retreat," and as one journalist concluded, "the rout of the rebels...illustrated how much they rely on international air power" (Lucas, 2011/3/28a). Before that, the insurgents hoped to storm Sirte itself, a stronghold of support for Gaddafi and the Al-Fateh Revolution. As if to underscore their dependency on NATO, some of the insurgents who spoke to the foreign press, such as 27-year-old Mohammed Bujildein, admitted: "if they [pro-government fighters] keep shelling like this, we'll need airstrikes," but nonetheless proclaimed that with international airstrikes, "we'll be in Sirte tomorrow evening" (Lucas, 2011/3/28a). That statement would not be proven true even after several months of sustained NATO airstrikes against Sirte. In the meantime, the alleged "popular uprising" had been vanquished in most of western Libya (without any evidence of the gross, large-scale massacres of whole populations as NATO leaders claimed "would have happened" in Benghazi). In some towns and cities, there never was an uprising (Lucas, 2011/3/28a).

As for NATO "protecting civilians," it had bombed Sirte early in the morning as early as March 27, 2011 "where most civilians are believed to support Gaddafi" (Lucas, 2011/3/28b; Lucas & Al-Shalchi, 2011/3/27; Hendawi, 2011/3/28). That some of those civilians were the intended target of NATO airstrikes is a given. NATO's aim was to demolish any armed forces that opposed the insurgents, and as journalists found within Sirte itself on March 27, as NATO bombed the city for the first time, "it was swarming with soldiers on patrol *and armed civilians*, many of them wearing green bandanas that signaled their support for Gadhafi" (Lucas & Al-Shalchi, 2011/3/27, emphasis added). As the bombing of Sirte reached a crescendo in October 2011, Reuters reported residents of the city telling them, "there are no Gaddafi brigades, they are volunteers inside" (El Gamal, 2011/10/5). *The Telegraph* reported the same, namely that civilians had professed their loyalty to the Brother Leader (Gaddafi) and the city remained "staunchly loyalist," quoting residents as saying that "there is no sign of an internal uprising, the civilian areas are filled with volunteers for Gaddafi" (Sherlock, 2011/9/28). Even months later, it was reported that, "many of those fleeing Sirte said that the stiff defense against revolutionary fighters who have been trying to battle their way into Sirte for three weeks is coming not from Gadhafi's military units but from *residents themselves, volunteering to take up arms*" (Al-Shalchi, 2011/10/4, emphasis added).

Based on quotes from insurgents that were "manning rows of rocket launchers," we were told that "they knew they were fighting civilians, but that Sirte's residents had 'chosen to die'" (Sherlock, 2011/9/28). *Chosen to die?* How this bit of exterminationist logic failed to attract the commentary of impassioned humanitarians whose hearts bled for Benghazi is quite remarkable. By the same logic, Benghazi in March 2011 had also chosen to die. NATO had clearly chosen to "protect" some (armed) "civilians," and not others. This actual failure to protect, and to even do the opposite, became a consistent and definiting feature of the kind of "humanitarianism" represented by NATO's military intervention.

Sirte: Fantasy Land of the Insurgents

Also consistent was the unreliability of the National Transitional Council as a source of information. On March 28, Shamsi Abdul Mullah, a NTC spokesman, claimed that Sirte had been taken at 11:30 pm the night before. Another NTC spokesman apparently felt that a good fabrication is improved with further elaboration: the added claim was that Sirte was found to be "unarmed" and that NTC insurgents "did not encounter much resistance" (Al Jazeera, 2011/3/28). This was even as two Reuters reporters within Sirte itself, reported the exact opposite (Lucas & Al-Shalchi, 2011/3/27). These imaginative claims were dutifully supported by the one international media organization that also consistently reproduced NTC claims with little in the way of questioning: Al Jazeera.

In August, after months of fighting, NTC officials said that they would only need about ten days to capture Sirte (when two more months of the heaviest fighting instead lay ahead), and that their main goal was "liberation not blood" (Stephen & Tiron, 2011/8/28). The only "negotiations" that interested them however were about the terms of Sirte's surrender, yet Gaddafi's chief spokesman, Moussa Ibrahim, reported that Gaddafi wanted to negotiate with the insurgents to form a transitional government (Stephen & Tiron, 2011/8/28). Indeed, at almost every stage of the conflict, Gaddafi reiterated calls for a peaceful transition, which were always rejected out of hand by the foreign-backed opposition, in favour of continued violence.

Even at the start of October, when the onslaught against Sirte was reaching its peak, a "Colonel" Ahmed Bani, speaking for the so-called "Defense Ministry" of the new regime-in-the-making, vowed that opposition forces "will be able to completely dominate Sirte in the next few days"

(Al-Shalchi, 2011/10/5). Weeks of fighting remained. As for "dominance," it seems that the NTC never understood the concept in terms other than total destruction, rather than winning support.

While NATO bombing and insurgent attacks ceased almost immediately after Gaddafi was killed on October 20, 2011, it was reported that officials of Misrata's military council claimed their forces captured Sirte on September 15, more than a month too soon, "after a day of heavy fighting" (Stephen, 2011/9/16). Instead of "heavy fighting," Mohammed Darrat, who was another, more imaginative, spokesman for the rebel administration in Misrata, said that insurgents not only advanced into Sirte, but they had also "met minimal resistance" (McDonnell, 2011/9/16).

Sirte: Allah, Muammar, Libya—and Memory

"The only way for it [Sirte] to fall is through an internal rebellion," said Mustafa Mohammed Abdul Jalil, chairman of the NTC, in August 2011, recognizing the fact that even months after the rebellion had started elsewhere in Libya, Sirte had yet to reject Gaddafi (Fadel, 2011/8/22). Indeed, such a rejection never came. And it still has not.

For weeks during the final NATO/NTC onslaught on Sirte that began in late August 2011, snipers held back the insurgents, "making forecasts of a quick end to the battle for Sirte look premature" (El Gamal & Gaynor, 2011/10/6). NATO spokespersons who lacked historical knowledge and a basic understanding of the contemporary political realities of Libya called the continued resistance of Sirte "surprising" (Gamel & Al-Shaheibi, 2011/10/15). "We will love Gaddafi until death," Sadina Muhammed declared about herself and fellow residents of Sirte (Sheridan, 2011/10/15). "What are they liberating us from? We want Moammar," another Sirte resident shouted, standing in a group. Another warned, "Let me tell you one thing. The people of Sirte are Bedouins and the Bedouin man does not forget to avenge injustice. We will not forget what happened in Sirte. We will not forgive and will not allow anyone from Benghazi or Misrata to enter Sirte again" (Reuters, 2011/10/16).

"Only Allah, Muammar and Libya," a truck driver in Sirte defiantly shouted toward journalists a few days after Gaddafi was killed there. He first told the same reporters that Gaddafi provided jobs and security, while NATO brought only destruction—as for the NTC, he chose to call them "rats" (AP, 2011/10/28). After losing Muammar Gaddafi, leaders of the tribe to which he belonged, the Gaddadfa (or Gaddafiya), threw their support behind his son, Saif al-Islam, who had not yet been captured (Randall, 2011/10/23). Standing over the graves of Gaddafi's mother and other relatives, which had been emptied and desecrated by insurgents, a member of Gaddafi's tribe told a visiting journalist: "Would you forget if someone killed your son unjustly? No you won't forget. People here will never forget. It will be blood feuds" (El Gamal, 2011/11/4). A young girl, resident of Sirte, exclaimed to the same journalist, "We only have four things in life, do you understand me?" and then taking the journalist's pen and notebook wrote, "Allah, Muammar, Libya. And ... that's all." Then she explained that, "we lived in security with Muammar, we never thought we will end up living in a school. Look around you, do you see any food aid from organizations or any officials visiting us? No one" (El Gamal, 2011/11/4). The memory of Gaddafi, now the "Martyr Leader," remained preserved in the photographs that some Sirte residents "tucked secretly among their belongings" (El Gamal, 2011/11/4).

If NATO leaders and the ranks of our op-ed punditry could imagine a turning of the tables as a "success" and as bringing freedom and democracy to Libya, it could only be by refusing to read the words that our own reporters brought back to us, sometimes printed just a few pages away from the triumphalist columns blaring imperial fantasies. Conquering Gaddafi—or more accurately, the millions who rallied behind the Al-Fateh revolution even to the last minutes of its sunset (see Figure 2.1)—was supposed to make

FIGURE 2.1 Green Square, Tripoli on July 1, 2011: a part of the immense crowd that turned out to cheer a speech by Muammar Gaddafi. (Photo courtesy of Mahdi Darius Nazemroaya, all rights reserved. Reproduced with permission.)

us feel good. The words of Sirte's residents should have had us worried about the shallowness of our preferred truths and about the depths of their memories, as they certainly worried the authoritarian regime led by the NTC that followed.

Who Voted With Their Feet?

Of course, not all Western journalists were keen to report on the reality of Sirte's resistance to the NATO-backed rebellion, and their continued loyalty to the Al-Fateh Revolution. In a piece of remarkably cynical and unscrupulous misrepresentation, the editorial board of *The Christian Science Monitor* produced an editorial on the same day that Gaddafi was brutally tortured and murdered, claiming that his end "was made possible only after thousands of civilian supporters in his hometown of Sirte deserted him;" the editorial concluded, "they voted with their feet." Not to rest there, it continued by asserting that even while it is true that many civilians simply fled the fighting (a point which does not detain the editors any further), "both Libya's transitional government and NATO went out of their way to hold their fire and set up a siege that would allow the people to leave." In the editors' eyes, this was "strategic patience" that was "driven by a reverence for life." This, they claimed, was in "stark contrast" to Gaddafi's threat against rebels in Benghazi, "a threat that justified NATO's military intervention" (*Christian Science Monitor*, 2011/10/20).

Let us examine what was behind that alleged "strategic patience." How was the insurgents' and NATO's "reverence for life" put into practice and what were the effects? How did their actual acts of war compare with a mere threat? How also did the editors at a prominent Western newspaper go about counting "votes" in a war zone? (We do not need to point out that once the opposition gained control over Benghazi in February 2011, refugees continued to pour out of that city toward the Egyptian border [Crilly, 2011/3/19; MacSwan, 2011/3/19]. Perhaps they too were voting with their feet. Or do feet only cast votes when they run in *The Christian Science Monitor*'s appointed direction?)

Several media reports did in fact state (with little questioning) that the insurgents laying siege to Sirte allowed civilians to flee. Both NATO and media commentators also took the fact of a city being besieged as not in itself worthy of comment, when if it had been Benghazi that was besieged it would have occasioned hyperbolic moral concern, just as it did with Misrata. After all the siege of Sirte did entail residents being cut off from food, water, electricity, fuel, and medicine (Al-Shalchi, 2011/9/18; BBC, 2011/9/27; El Gamal & Gaynor, 2011/10/5; El Madany, 2011/9/20). These facts did little to perturb the pro-intervention Western commentators and political leaders, and the UN remained entirely mute. Among those reporting that insurgents had given civilians the opportunity to leave (on different dates) were the BBC (2011/10/7), Reuters (2011/10/1; Dziadosz, 2011/9/22), and the Associated Press (Al-Shalchi, 2011/10/5).

While Reuters like others reported that the NTC called a two-day truce on October 1, 2011 to allow civilians to leave, its reporters on the ground also noted that insurgents continued their heavy rocket and mortar fire nonetheless; moreover, the strategy of the insurgents was to respond to precise sniper fire from government troops and brigades in Sirte with the far more indiscriminate and excessive use of rockets and unguided artillery (El Gamal & Logan, 2011/10/1). In another Reuters report on this so-called truce, civilians fleeing Sirte told them that, "they knew nothing of the ceasefire, and that the shooting had not stopped" (Gaynor & El Gamal, 2011/10/2). As for NATO, which *The Christian Science Monitor* also credits for a truce to allow civilians to flee, it did not cease bombing Sirte on either October 1 or October 2, according to its own press releases for those dates (NATO, 2011/10/1, 2011/10/2). Continuing to fight and bombard Sirte is just one way that "strategic patience" and "reverence for life" are disproven. More alarming, however, is the idea that a truce was announced, which potentially drew civilians out from their homes and therefore, with NATO jets continuing their bombings, the risk of civilian casualties increased.

It was also reported that the reason for the NTC's so-called "truces," purportedly to allow civilians to leave Sirte, was in fact a shortage of ammunition for insurgent forces and the NTC's need for time to resupply them. Quoting NTC fighters on the frontline, Reuters reported that the fighters were "unable to defeat forces loyal to deposed leader Muammar Gaddafi in the city of Sirte because the country's new rulers are failing to supply them with enough ammunition." One fighter told the reporter that they had only been able to fire off a single Grad rocket that day (El Madany, 2011/9/20). The reported ammunition shortage was so severe that it would cause NTC forces to stop fighting for up to a week (BBC, 2011/9/22). Yet, once resupplied, NTC fighters immediately resumed their assault on Sirte: "Over the last week, fighters said they wouldn't attack until all the city's civilians were out. In the end, they decided to advance Saturday" (Hubbard & Al-Shalchi, 2011/9/24). Yet the NTC even twisted this to make it seem like continued fighting would in fact aid civilians. However, the only civilians that actually concerned them were those from Misrata, the home town of many of the insurgents, still stuck in Sirte: "they feared many families from Misrata that were stuck in the city were in danger, said a brigade commander, Mohammed al-Sugatri. 'There are lots of people from Misrata who are stuck in the city living in basements. They have no food or water and many of their children are sick so we had no choice but to attack,' he said" (Hubbard & Al-Shalchi, 2011/9/24). Only one news report juxtaposed the announcement of the truce with the NTC ammunition shortage (the real reason for the cessation of fire): "'The only delay at the moment is they are waiting for the residents to clear out,' Busin said today in an interview in Tripoli, the capital. The council's fighters are also running low on ammunition for assault rifles and anti-aircraft guns, and are waiting for new supplies to arrive, he said" (Tuttle & Alexander, 2011/9/27).

At the same time of the supposed truce, NATO again continued to bomb Sirte, with British Tornados attacking targets with Paveway bombs (NATO, 2011/9/27; Tuttle & Alexander, 2011/9/27). As a matter of fact, the illusion of a NTC truce was simply to clear the way for NATO bombing in this instance: "We were ordered to leave downtown Sirte because NATO has a mission to do there. We left after 7:00 pm last night (Saturday)," an insurgent told AFP (2011/9/26). NATO then proceeded to launch a dozen airstrikes in Sirte, according to AFP. In fact, there is no evidence that NATO ever observed any sort of truce in its bombing of Sirte on any of the truce dates mentioned—this notion was entirely fabricated in the romantic narrative of *The Christian Science Monitor*.

The weapons used in the assault on Sirte were also of the most indiscriminate kind, a fact that evinced little moral outrage in the West and relatively little comment from Western human rights NGOs (and when comment was made, it was relatively subdued in tone). Reporters nevertheless did mention that "grad rockets, artillery and tank fire rained down" on what they assumed were these (loosely defined) "Gaddafi positions" (El Gamal & Gaynor, 2011/10/19). "Sustained tank and mortar fire has been targeting Sirte and there are huge columns of smoke across the city," reported the BBC, "with many buildings struck and on fire" (BBC, 2011/10/7). One insurgent commander boastingly confirmed, "we have heavy weapons—Grad launchers, tanks, rockets" (Dziadosz, 2011/9/22). These are unguided munitions that create a great deal of damage around where they strike. To make matters worse, the people firing these munitions were for the most part untrained and therefore less capable of achieving any sort of discriminate precision. Other reporters contradicted the notion that the insurgents wished to exercise care in not harming civilians: "Rebel commanders said they were rethinking their strategy of avoiding the use of heavy weapons in the city centre" (Black & Stephen, 2011/9/18). And "rethink" they did, with lust. The UN Human Rights Council's own International Commission of Inquiry on Libya (UNHRC, 2012) reported that damage caused by the insurgents' use of these heavy weapons "was so widespread as to be clearly indiscriminate in nature" (p. 15), repeating that in the assault on Sirte, "the scale of the destruction there and the nature of the weaponry employed indicated that the attacks were indiscriminate" (p. 16). These are documented war crimes.

The indiscriminate nature of the opposition forces' attacks against Sirte deserve more attention because this fact belies the claim that every attempt at minimizing civilian losses was taken. "All those involved in the fighting have legal obligations to spare civilians by ending immediately the use of indiscriminate weapons like GRAD rockets, and not firing artillery and mortars into residential areas," said Hassiba Hadj Sahraoui, Middle East and North Africa Programme Deputy Director at Amnesty International (AI, 2011/10/3). AI reminded us that "international humanitarian law prohibits the use of weapons that are inherently indiscriminate or which cannot be targeted at military objectives," and noted that the opposition fighters attacking Sirte "have been found to use GRAD rockets, which pose a lethal danger to populated areas because they are unguided" (AI, 2011/10/3). Unfortunately, AI chose to deliberately limit the critical impact of its own admonition first by reminding readers that AI had collected evidence that "Gaddafi's forces" had committed war crimes thoughout the conflict, and second by repeating NATO's claim that "pro-Gaddafi forces" were using civilians as "shields" in Sirte (AI, 2011/10/3), an assertion for which no evidence has ever been produced, least of all by AI. Why AI should even need to produce these criticisms of "Gaddafi forces" (choosing as always to reduce the discussion to Gaddafi) in a report on insurgents' attacks on Sirte, shows just how uncomfortable AI has been in unveiling any kind of wrong doing by the intervention that its own directors supported in February 2011.

Evidence of indiscriminate attacks is obviously clearly etched into the faces of almost all of Sirte's buildings as witnessed on the cover of this book. Beneath that, more facts emerge to show that the opposition forces could not have spared civilians given the way they fought. For one, the insurgents frequently fired on each other without knowing—in one such "friendly fire" incident, the insurgents killed fifteen of their own (Gillette,

2011/10/19). Second, while many of the fighters were feted in the international press for being doctors, students, lawyers, etc., it also meant that many lacked the requisite training in how to use their weapons and would not likely have been able to exercise much care in firing them. Indeed, numerous news videos show insurgent forces letting off long bursts of heavy machine gun fire, sprayed down a street, or insurgents raising their assault rifles over the tops of walls and firing blindly or firing rockets into a city but without any advance spotters on the ground to direct the fire. The lack of knowledge on how to use their weapons often backfired on insurgents. Two Reuters reporters personally witnessed "one fighter blow his own head off and kill a comrade while handling a rocket propelled grenade," and in another incident, "a fighter wounded himself and another fighter after losing control of his machinegun" (Dziadosz & Golovnina, 2011/9/22). In another case, "one fighter nearly shot himself when he fired a celebratory round into the side of the barrel of a captured tank, sending the bullet ricocheting," while another group, "fired a Grad missile into a lamppost during a battle, knocking off the light and sending the rocket crashing to the ground about a hundred meters away from their position." Unreassuringly, the reporter tells us that the insurgents "coordinate" airstrikes with NATO, "whose jets frequently roar overhead" (Dziadosz, 2011/9/22). On the other hand, this same NATO claimed not to have anyone on the ground guiding its targeting (AFP, 2011/12/15), and also boasted of gathering targeting data from Twitter (Norton-Taylor & Hopkins, 2011/6/15; Smith, 2011/6/14). (Such assertions pose a lose-lose situation for NATO propaganda, which was amateurish at best during this campaign: if the claims are correct, they indict NATO targeters for firing with little reliable information on their targets, thus failing to protect civilians; if incorrect, it means that what NATO destroyed, it did so deliberately, knowing that civilians could be killed.)

There is again the issue of the nature of the weapons used in civilian areas by the insurgents, which included tanks, anti-aircraft guns that fire large caliber rounds, and heavy artillery (Gamel & Al-Shaheibi, 2011/10/15). As Abdul Hadi Doghman, commander of the insurgent Dat al-Ramal brigade, told Reuters: "We are going to engage them with tanks and heavy artillery first, after that we will send in the pick-up trucks with anti-aircraft guns, then the infantry" (El Gamal & Gaynor 2011/10/14). Reporters witnessed insurgents using six Russian-built 130-mm cannons away in the desert, firing dozens of shells an hour into Sirte. Ashiq Hussein, a Sirte resident, explained that "the incoming shells from NTC forces were hit-

SIRTE: TOUCHSTONE OF IMPERIALISM 95

ting civilian homes. They are missing their targets and often hit civilian homes" (Sky News, 2011/10/2). Others saw insurgents on a hillside from where "they sent rockets and tank shells raining down on the city" (Sherlock, 2011/9/28). Other Sirte residents reported, "they're shelling constantly. There's indiscriminate fire within individual neighborhoods" (Maclean, 2011/9/29). Finally, when it comes to the act of being indiscriminate and showing little "reverence for life," the question of intent is raised. As one resident fleeing Sirte emphasized, "the rebels from Misrata say they will destroy Sirte because Misrata was destroyed" (El Gamal, 2011/10/5), which would mean being "indiscriminate" by design, done to produce the maximum damage possible (for which there is abundant visual evidence).

The insurgents' "reverence for life" was questioned even by some Western reporters working for anti-Gaddafi media such as the BBC. Wyre Davies reported: "This is almost a scorched earth policy. The pro-Gaddafi fighters defending this city won't surrender, so Sirte is being systematically destroyed, block by block. Fighting is intense, incredibly destructive, and almost mind-numbing" (quoted in O'Connor, 2011/10/19). Reporting live, Davies commented: "When all else fails, blast the heck out of the place you're trying to take—current NTC thinking in Sirte. Intense shelling again today," followed by "Retribution in Sirte. Some NTC fighters deliberately burn houses in Gaddafi's home town."[2] Reporters for *The Telegraph* described Sirte as a "squalid ruin" reminiscent of "the grimmest scenes from Grozny" (quoted in O'Connor, 2011/10/19). The insurgents' alleged "restraint" was questioned by other mainstream Western reporters: "the attacking forces clearly feel no need for restraint in bombarding the Gaddafi loyalists....The revolutionaries have been firing purloined antiaircraft guns and artillery at apartment buildings where pro-Gaddafi snipers have holed up, causing heavy damage" (Sheridan, 2011/10/15).

When NTC fighters allowed civilians to leave, they used the opportunity to search their vehicles to establish whether or not they were "Gaddafi loyalists" (Dziadosz & Golovnina, 2011/9/22). Rather than simply being "allowed" to flee, civilians had to go through checkpoints established by NTC forces, so that even this became part of a military strategy rather than respect for international humanitarian law (Hubbard & Al-Shalchi,

---

2. Wyre Davies made these comments in Twitter: <http://twitter.com/#!/WyreDavies/status/124204478441324544> and <http://twitter.com/#!/WyreDavies/status/125302224401350656/photo/1>

2011/9/24). What some Sirte residents openly told journalists at those checkpoints is very illuminating: "This so-called revolution is not worth it," said Moussa Ahmed, "But we can't say anything now; when we meet the revolutionaries we have to hide our feelings" (Al-Shalchi, 2011/10/4). The reporter found, "a palpable dislike between those fleeing and the fighters searching through their belongings" (Al-Shalchi, 2011/10/4). Other reporters also found that, "NTC fighters manning the checkpoints made no secret of their disdain for the residents of a city which was so privileged under the ousted regime and where loyalty to the ousted Kadhafis ran deep" (Mulholland, 2011/10/4). Others also reported that "the fleeing residents viewed the checkpoints with fear and suspicion, and many remained unsympathetic to the rebel side"—an elderly woman spoke angrily at a checkpoint guard: "Since the 19th [of] March when NATO started bombing we have been living in hell," and her fearful husband asked her to be quiet (Sherlock, 2011/9/28). NTC fighter Mohammed Shahomi, looking at Sirte residents at a checkpoint, told a reporter: "They are all Kadhafi loyalists. You think they are leaving because they believe in the revolution? They are just scared" (Mulholland, 2011/10/4). Apparently Shahomi had not read *The Christian Science Monitor*. There is also some evidence to suggest that those fleeing civilians who were wounded in crossfire may have been detained at the checkpoints. As one NTC fighter said, "we also check for people with bullet injuries, because that means they likely were fighting for Gadhafi" (Al-Shalchi, 2011/10/4).

If *The Christian Science Monitor* misled some of its readers into believing the spin about NTC fighters' patience and reverence for life, the notion that Sirte's residents engaged in an approximation of a rebellion against Gaddafi by "voting with their feet," would prove even less tenable, not to say inexcusably cynical. "It was my sick mother and father who made me get out of Sirte. Look at my father, he is a sick man, how can I take care of him like that. Look at the kids' faces, they had diarrhoea and were sick because of the water and lack of food." He was asked to explain why he left Sirte with his family, but it is interesting to note that the very question itself (a reporter searching for signs of anti-Gaddafi dissent among those fleeing for their lives) and the answer would disappoint any loyal reader of *The Christian Science Monitor* (El Gamal, 2011/10/2). "I am not scared. I am hungry," another fleeing resident said (Logan & El Gamal, 2011/9/30). While reporting on families flowing out of Sirte, others indicated that those fleeing were "unbowed in their deep distrust of the revolutionaries trying to crush this bastion of the old regime," and that if anything, "the fleeing residents were a sign of how resistance to Libya's new rulers remains entrenched" (Al-Shalchi, 2011/10/4). Halima Salem asked, "How can it be that Libyans are doing this to us? Aren't we the same people? I feel bad for our army....They were honorable men with high morals. And now this chaos" (Al-Shalchi, 2011/10/4). "Fear of the NTC fighters" also kept some Sirte residents from leaving (Mulholland, 2011/10/4). Some fled Sirte and then some also returned as well: "We refuse to leave, we don't want to suffer... We would rather die here than leave our houses and suffer" (El Gamal, 2011/10/5). Others "didn't want to leave. Some people are scared of being slaughtered by the rebels" (El Gamal, 2011/10/5).

Even for readers restricted to only reading Western mainstream media reports, *The Christian Science Monitor*'s claims are revealed to be both outlandish and callous. Desperate to finally be seen as the liberators of Arabs, rescuing poor victims with the finest of American exports (human rights), some would understandably feel compelled to exploit the suffering of others (residents fleeing Sirte) and turn that into something worthy of celebration. This is an example of the abduction process at the centre of Western, liberal humanitarianism: it can only function by first directly or indirectly creating the suffering of others, and by then seeing every hand as an outstretched hand, pleading or welcoming. We see (or imagine) helpless others, gobbling morsels of food that we hand them, brown mouths chugging down water from our plastic bottles, and we feel accomplished. Our moral might is reaffirmed by the physical plight of others. Clearly, the humanitarian relation is not a relation between equals. We are not our "brothers' keepers" then, but rather we are more like animal keepers. Bombing for us is really just an animal management technology, and our relationship to the world remains a zoological one.

That the NTC could ever be cast as "revolutionary" is thus also remarkable, and meant to bewilder Western audiences. The NTC found use for NATO, even if just out of cynical, cold, instrumentalist calculation, but the fact remains that they helped to reinforce and revitalize the zoology of imperialism. There is nothing revolutionary about being neo-colonial, and aiding empire. That is not revolution: it is restoration.

War Crimes: Civilians Targeted in NATO Attacks

One of the dominant myths about NATO's military intervention in Libya is that it was intended to "protect civilians," a topic touched upon above, and to which we will return throughout. NATO escalated its bombing of

Sirte at the end of August 2011, as the final assault on the city began. While Gaddafi's government had been removed from Tripoli, and the government's defences began to shrink, U.S. Defense Secretary Leon Panetta said, "I think fighting has to end" for NATO to stop bombing (Mulholland, 2011/10/4). Similarly, French Defence Minister Gerard Longuet said the airstrikes would not cease "until all remaining pockets of resistance are suppressed and the new government asks for them to end" (Lekic, 2011/10/6). UK Prime Minister David Cameron, using words now rendered sinister and macabre, also stated: "We must keep on with the NATO mission until civilians are all protected and until this work is finished" (McDonnell, 2011/9/16). Even after more than 9,600 strike missions and the near complete destruction of Sirte, British Defence Secretary Philip Hammond told BBC radio that NATO would decide when the mission is "complete" and "once we are satisfied that there is no further threat to the Libyan civilians and the Libyans are content, NATO will then arrange to wind up the operation" (Lekic, 2011/10/21). (That Hammond could presume to speak about "no further threat" to civilians, when NATO was the prime threat in government strongholds, and that it could then decide which Libyans could speak as being "content," is a good example of how an amoral vacuum, filled with Orwellian doublespeak, has become institutionalized and normalized in NATO's political leadership.)

Yet all of NATO's stipulated conditions for ceasing operations had been satisfied already by September (NATO, 2011/4/14). Even in going beyond the actual UN resolution authorizing military intervention, Obama only listed the following: "Qaddafi must stop his troops from advancing on Benghazi, [and] pull them back from Ajdabiya, Misrata, and Zawiya"—Sirte was never mentioned (Obama, 2011/3/18). In fact, Sirte was specifically not listed by NATO as one of the places from which Libyan government forces were to have withdrawn, which was also an extra condition imposed by NATO that went beyond anything authorized by the UN. None of the so-called "Gaddafi strongholds" are listed as areas of NATO concern (NATO, 2011/4/14), which is only logical since the Libyan government would pose no threat to its own bastions of support. NATO nonetheless continued to bomb those very cities in the name of "protecting civilians," even months after the conditions listed had been satisified. When NATO and the insurgents it backed then proceeded to target Sirte, Bani Walid, and other strongholds, they in fact created a threat to civilians where none existed before—and there was nobody to protect the residents of Sirte from NATO and their local allies, other than what remained of the so-called "Gaddafi forces."

With what Western media and NATO members claimed was the collapse of the Gaddafi regime, all of NATO's stated objectives had been achieved (NATO, 2011/4/14). Yet, as NATO was bombing Sirte on August 30, 2011, the NATO spokesperson, Roland Lavoie, "appeared to struggle to explain how NATO strikes were protecting civilians at this stage in the conflict. Asked about NATO's assertion that it hit 22 armed vehicles near Sirte, he was unable to say how the vehicles were threatening civilians, or whether they were in motion or parked" (Laub & Schemm, 2011/8/30). Also highly suspect, given that Obama had declared the successful achievement of a no-fly zone back in March, was NATO's claim to be striking radars and anti-aircraft sites in Sirte as late as five months after Obama's declaration, when these would have necessarily been the first sites to be destroyed. Either NATO failed to do what was necessary to declare that a no-fly zone had been imposed (which by itself would be a striking find) or its targets in Sirte were not what NATO claimed them to be (NATO, 2011/8/28, 2011/8/30).

With limited resources and little international concern over the plight of Sirte, two separate international investigations have strikingly documented the exact same war crimes perpetrated by NATO in the bombing of Sirte. In particular, the following action reported by NATO in unremarkable terms became one focus of attention. From NATO's media update concerning its strike sorties on September 15, 2011, we were told: "Key Hits 15 SEPTEMBER: In the vicinity of Sirte: 1 Military Storage Facility, 2 Armed Vehicles, 1 Tank, 4 Multiple Rocket Launchers, 8 Air Missile Systems" (NATO, 2011/9/15). The mention of "2 Armed Vehicles" says nothing of course about civilian deaths, and might seem unremarkable.

First, the Independent Civil Society Mission to Libya, which was established by the Arab Organization for Human Rights (AOHR) in cooperation with the Palestinian Centre for Human Rights (PCHR) and the International Legal Assistance Consortium (ILAC), conducted an investigation in Sirte on November 21, 2011 (see FFM, 2012). The Mission interviewed two principal witnesses in Zone 2, "a western residential area in Sirte which was one of the last holdouts of Gaddafi supporters in the country." These two witnesses reported "a NATO attack which resulted in the death of 57-59 individuals, of whom approximately 47 were civilian." (FFM, 2012, p. 44). The Mission "found these witnesses to be credible, and their report was confirmed by unrelated witnesses" (FFM, 2012, p. 45). According to their reports, on September 15, 2011, insurgents seized control of the western part of Sirte but were subsequently driven out in a counterattack. Two jeeps—the two armed vehicles listed by NATO—which were fitted with weapons and held five combatants each, took a postion on an open road with the beach to one side and houses to the other. Just after sunset, but with some light remaining, NATO aircraft destroyed the two jeeps with one missile each. In an attempt to rescue survivors and retrieve the dead a large crowd of civilians flocked to the scene—witnesses affirmed that the crowd was exclusively civilian. Almost five minutes after the first attack on the jeeps, a third missile was fired at the area killing 47 of the civilians present. The Mission itself observed "three impact craters with blast patterns in the street which were consistent with an air attack from the south" (FFM, 2012, p. 45).

There is little reason to doubt that NATO deliberately committed the attack knowing that civilians would be the ones to die. This strategy, known as "double tapping," is used by the U.S. commonly in drone strikes in Pakistan and Yemen. It targets both rescuers and often mourners at funerals for the victims as well. Moreover, this has been amply documented by the Bureau of Investigative Journalism (BIJ) in a series of damning, not to say repulsive, documentary reports of such attacks, including ones occurring at the time this book was being written (see BIJ, 2012/2/4, 2012/6/4). These attacks on civilians have been legitimated within the Obama administration with the redefinition of "civilian", such that all males of combat age can be redefined as combatants and thus legitimate targets (BIJ, 2012/5/29). These are indisputable war crimes and they also meet most definitions of terrorism. The Independent Civil Society Mission to Libya explained that it was aware "that missiles fired from an aerial platform are typically fired 'eyes-on'. This means that, at the time of firing, NATO forces should have had the target area under visual observation" (FFM, 2012, p. 45). We see similar attacks against unarmed, civilian rescuers tending to the wounded in the now infamous "Collateral Murder" video released via WikiLeaks—the pattern of U.S. forces deliberately attacking civilians is evident and available for all to see.

While NATO Secretary General Anders Fogh Rasmussen asserted, "I can tell you that no target was approved or attacked if we had any evidence or reason to believe that civilians were at risk" (NATO, 2012/3/5), that is precisely what NATO forces did in another case, in the town of Majer, 160 km east of Tripoli on August 8, 2011. This has now been abundantly documented by news media, pro-intervention human rights bodies such as Human Rights Watch (HRW), and a UN Commission of International Inquiry on Libya. In this case, according to HRW, NATO not only struck a farming compound where not a shred of evidence for any military activity was ever found, it then struck a second time as civilian rescuers came to look for survivors.

> "A second strike outside one of the compounds killed and wounded civilians who witnesses said were searching for victims. The infrared system used by the bomb deployed should have indicated to the pilot the presence of many people on the ground. If the pilot was unable to determine that those people were combatants, then the strike should have been canceled or diverted." (Human Rights Watch [HRW], 2012/5/14; see also HRW, 2012, pps. 27-32 and Garlasco, 2012/6/11)

Raji Sourani, head of the Palestinian Centre for Human Rights, who took part in the Mission later stated that, "we have reason to think that there were some war crimes perpetrated" (Shabi, 2012/1/19). Rather than investigate the matter further or call for some accountability from NATO (which absolutely denied that there were any civilian casualties whatsoever), UN Secretary-General Ban Ki-Moon instead adamantly insisted, "Security Council resolution 1973, I believe, was strictly enforced within the limit, within the mandate" (Shabi, 2012/1/19). The very same body that claimed to be outraged by human rights abuses, crimes against humanity, and war crimes when Gaddafi was fully in power, now turned a complete blind eye to the those killed as a result of UNSCR 1973, without any accountability, without apology, and without a moment's pause to understand the extraordinary hypocrisy that would thoroughly discredit all Western concerns for protecting civilians. "Protecting civilians" is an ideological weapon of war.

There was yet another international investigation of the matter by Amnesty International (AI), itself a party to the original intervention in Libya which it called for and supported. AI's investigation took place in January and February 2012, thus roughly two months after the Mission discussed above, with parallel missions and reports by Human Rights Watch, *The New York Times*, and a UN Commission of International Inquiry. One of the locations AI visited was Sirte. AI only documented nine named civilian deaths in Sirte—it is not apparent that the previous Mission sought to name the 47 civilians killed in the September 15, 2011 missile strikes; however AI did acknowledge that, "additional incidents of civilian casualties have been reported to have occurred in circumstances where it has been difficult to distinguish between combatants and civilians. For example, Amnesty International was told by residents in Sirte that on September 15, 2011, NATO strikes killed several members of al-Gaddafi forces in their two vehicles, as well as more than 40 civilians, most of whom had rushed to the scene after the first vehicle was struck" (AI, 2012b, p. 6). There was no apparent attempt by AI to name these civilians. AI thus creates two separate counts—one, that is exceptionally small, and appears more credible because the dead are named, and another, much larger figure, that is mentioned only secondarily and less prominently, and is made to appear less documented. Moreover, AI adds an alibi for NATO forces by noting above "circumstances where it has been difficult to distinguish between combatants and civilians." AI thus does two things: it corroborates the report by the Independent Civil Society Mission to Libya, by reporting the same findings months later without any change; but it also does more to downplay the number and significance of the September 15 NATO attack.

Amnesty International did however document additional civilian deaths in Sirte for other dates, with much more work remaining to be done. AI reported that on September 16, 2011, several airstrikes targeted a large apartment building in Sirte containing roughly ninety apartments and "at least two residents were killed" (AI, 2012b, pps. 13-14; also HRW, 2012, pps. 50-53). NATO does not even list an apartment building as one of its targets, preferring instead to produce a list that NATO hoped would be taken at face value: "Key Hits 16 SEPTEMBER: In the vicinity of Sirte: 5 Command and Control Nodes, 3 Radar Systems, 4 Armed Vehicles, 8 Air Missile Systems" (NATO, 2011/9/16).

In addition, on September 25, 2011, just before dawn, NATO carried out an airstrike against the home of Salem Diyab, in Sirte, killing four children and three women—the apparent target was Mosbah Ahmed Diyab, a Brigadier-General, but "who lived in another area of the city." AI concluded: "If this civilian house was targeted because it was believed that Mosbah Ahmed Diyab was present, NATO should have made sure it had information on the presence of any civilians there. The fact that at least seven civilians were in the home should have been reason enough to cancel or delay the attack out of concern that it would have been disproportionate" (AI, 2012b, p. 15; see also HRW, 2012, pps. 47-50). Unfortunately, some readers of the report might have needed AI to tell them the obvious: if this attack targeted so-called "command and control" and produced multiple civilian deaths, we can expect that other "military" targets listed by NATO could also entail civilian casualties. Once more, NATO misrepresented events by not indicating that it was deliberately targeting civilian structures: "Key Hits 25 SEPTEMBER: In the vicinity of Sirte: 1

command and control node [the Diyab home?], 2 ammunition/vehicle storage facility, 1 radar facility, 1 multiple rocket launcher, 1 military support vehicle, 1 artillery piece, 1 ammunition storage facility" (NATO, 2011/9/25).

The New York Times collaborated with Amnesty International in investigating reports of NATO's civilian casualties in Sirte, and unearthed further accounts, while acknowledging that what they did uncover was not in any way a complete account for all casualties of NATO. "It was the anti-Gaddafi forces who endangered civilians they suspected of having sympathies for the dying government," the Times reported, based on accounts from Sirte residents (Chivers & Schmitt, 2011/12/18). Then they reported the following account, worth quoting in full as it speaks to so many of the actualities of NATO's practice that rendered NATO's humanitarian claims to be largely false:

> "On a recent afternoon, Mahmoud Zarog Massoud, his hand swollen with an infection from a wound, wandered the broken shell of a seven-story apartment building in Surt [Sirte], which was struck in mid-September. His apartment furniture had been blown about by the blast. He approached the kitchen, where, he said, he and his wife had just broken their Ramadan fast when ordnance hit. 'We were not thinking NATO would attack our home,' he said. Judging by the damage and munitions' remains, a bomb with a delayed fuze struck another wing of the building, burrowed into another apartment and exploded, blasting walls outward. Debris flew across the courtyard and through his kitchen's balcony door. His wife, Aisha Abdujodil, was killed, both her arms severed, he said. Bloodstains still marked the floor and walls." (Chivers & Schmitt, 2011/12/18)

NATO, of course, never reported facts such as these when their spokespersons addressed the press. However, when "provided written questions, NATO declined to comment" on its strikes against civilian homes (Chivers & Schmitt, 2011/12/18).

Aside from the international investigations presented above, numerous media reports during the course of fighting in Sirte cited many more cases of civilians killed by NATO strikes. Civilians fleeing Sirte blamed both NATO bombing and NTC shelling for killing civilians and destroying buildings in the city (El Gamal & Logan, 2011/10/1; El Gamal & Gaynor, 2011/10/5). One man affirmed that his 11-year-old son was killed by NATO rockets, and said he knew of similar attacks that to him appeared random (El Gamal & Gaynor, 2011/10/6). Some ended up sleeping in the streets out of fear that their homes could be bombed: "Abdul-Wahab said he had been sleeping in the streets with his family after a NATO airstrike hit a building next to his house, making him fear his home could also be struck" (Logan & El Gamal, 2011/9/30). Another resident reported that NATO struck an apartment building with 12 or 13 bombs: "The whole building with nearly 600 flats is razed to the ground now" (Sky News, 2011/10/2). Others also pointed out that "a lot of civilian buildings were getting hit," and one reported, "two of my neighbours died yesterday in a NATO bomb which hit their home" (Sky News, 2011/10/2). Civilians pouring out of Sirte told other reporters that NATO "hit all kinds of buildings: schools, hospitals;" one man said he had lost six members of his family in the bombings, and angrily declared: "NATO bombing is killing civilians. Where is the United Nations? Where is the Muslim world to stop this genocide of the people of Sirte?" (Coglan, 2011/9/27). One analyst at the Royal United Services Institute in London explained that NATO lacked sufficient intelligence to allow it to pinpoint targets in Sirte without endangering civilians (Pawlak, 2011/9/30). The BBC's Wyre Davies, reporting live from the ground, pointed to NATO airstrikes in Sirte and commented: "Risky strategy with civilians trapped in the city."[3]

"NATO has brought destruction, and the revolution has brought destruction," an angry resident of Sirte told reporters (El Gamal, 2011/10/5). "Paving the way" for the start of the final offensive against Sirte, NATO flew more than 130 strike sorties at the end of August (Crilly & Evans, 2011/8/26). Sirte's residents, trying to defend themselves from an armed takeover, and from the kinds of atrocities insurgents committed in other towns they took, NATO somehow managed to twist even this into a threat: "This is an extremely desperate and dangerous remnant of a former regime and they are obviously trying to disrupt the fact that the Libyan people have started to take responsibility for their own country" (Crilly & Evans, 2011/8/26). In just three days, since insurgents first entered Sirte itself on September 15, 2011, NATO bombed 39 targets including what it claimed were "command centres, vehicles and missile sites;" meanwhile, the insurgents themselves began their attack on the Ouagadougou Conference Centre, site of African Union meetings, actively defended by forces supporting the government (Black & Stephen, 2011/9/18). In a period of three weeks, NATO struck 296 targets in Sirte—and that was before the final month of bombings (Stephen, 2011/9/16). Even the enthusiastically pro-NTC

---

3. Live communication via Twitter: <http://twitter.com/#!/WyreDavies/status/123648340096331776>

Tony Birtley of Al Jazeera (which itself played the lead role in promoting outright falsehoods pushed by the NTC) could not help himself from remarking that Sirte had, "taken such a bombardment in the last 13 days. Nothing could survive in here for very long" (AJE, 2011/10/20).

While there is likely no chance of NATO leaders and officers being held accountable, a proper accounting of what we supported and what the consequences have been is needed. Too many reports, including by the most prominent international human rights agencies, draw a thick distinction between civilian casualties caused by NATO and those caused by the insurgents. Yet the two frequently acted in concert, especially in the last months of the war to overthrow Gaddafi (Libya effectively remained at war past October 2011). The civilian casualties caused by insurgent military actions were facilitated and enabled by NATO's support and cover. Moreover, NATO's civilian casualties go far beyond the immediate victims of its bombings and missile strikes. They should be understood to include all victims that were produced by NATO escalating, widening, and prolonging an armed conflict that seemed certain to come to an end in March 2011, before NATO intervened to support the insurgents.

Liberal Intervention and the Myth of "Protecting Civilians"

The key to understanding "liberal intervention" is that its rhetoric is what is most identifiably liberal about it: individual freedoms, universal human rights, civil liberties, etc. There is otherwise nothing that is liberal about its practice, its intent, the projects it defends, the fog of squalid moral dualism that surrounds it or the Orwellian torture it inflicts upon language. In practice, such intervention is as scandalous in its propagation of atrocities as any other military blitzkrieg under any other name—it commits "shock and awe," but it does not necessarily have the bad sense to parade spokesmen before cameras to celebrate the shock and awe. The bloodlust was kept to a minimum in speeches by NATO leaders during the bombing campaign, and the use of spectacle-making bomb-cam videos was also relatively minimal when compared to previous NATO campaigns or U.S. assaults on Iraq. While the aesthetics of the public performance may not have been as ghoulish as under George W. Bush, the imperial language of authoritative command, of declaring this or that as "unacceptable," or "non-negotiable," and instructing foreign leaders that they "must go" because a U.S. President has decided that they have lost "legitimacy," is exactly the same. As we will see, there were also awful moments of rejoicing in brutal murder—the paradox of cheap façades is that their maintenance costs can prove to be too expensive. Behind the practice of feel-good, look-good "protection of civilians," we find the desire if not the plan to either suppress or annihilate all opposition, civilian or not.

The residents of Sirte would not be forgiven for genuinely supporting the Al-Fateh Revolution and the leadership of Gaddafi. NATO provided both the air support and special forces needed for the insurgents to beat Sirte into submission—in this supposed popular revolution for freedom and democracy, Sirte's residents did not have the option to choose what suited them best. Surrender or die, this is what "democracy" meant when visited on Sirte. The insurgents were allowed to freely move tanks into place to surround and then enter Sirte, yet any attempt by government forces to move as much as a jeep, as we read above, was met with an instantaneous volley of NATO missiles, both against the jeep and against any civilian rescuers. The mere fact of Sirte remaining defiant was in and of itself deemed to be "threatening civilians"—even when it was masses of armed civilians that defended the city. As Craig Murray (former UK diplomat) explained, NATO "in effect declared being in Gadaffi's political camp a capital offence" (Murray, 2011/8/26). He also noted the text of UNSCR 1973, which had the following as the top aims of the Security Council:

> "Acting under Chapter VII of the Charter of the United Nations, [the Security Council]
>
> "1. Demands the immediate establishment of a ceasefire and a complete end to violence and *all attacks against, and abuses of, civilians*;
>
> "2. Stresses the need to intensify efforts to find a solution to the crisis which responds to the legitimate demands of the Libyan people and notes the decisions of the Secretary-General to send his Special Envoy to Libya and of the Peace and Security Council of the African Union to send its ad hoc High-Level Committee to Libya with *the aim of facilitating dialogue to lead to the political reforms necessary to find a peaceful and sustainable solution*." (United Nation's Security Council [UNSC], 2011/3/17, emphasis added)

As for "liberal intervention," Craig Murray's understanding is that it does not even exist and is instead the opposite: "highly selective neo-imperial wars aimed at ensuring [political]... client control of key physical resources" (Murray, 2011/8/26). It does exist, however, not just as the idealistic fantasy-scape populated by the emotions of momentary puritans, but also as imperial warfare that binds to it various neo-colonial underlings.

To say that liberal intervention does not exist is to say one took it too seriously, on its own terms.

"The city of Sirte is the worst affected area in the country," the African Press Organization (APO) reported, speaking of the unexploded ordnance that still littered Sirte months after NATO's campaign formally ended. The work of the International Committee for the Red Cross in trying to remove these explosives still remained (2012/2/16). Clearly, the ICRC, like Médecins Sans Frontières (Doctors Without Borders), Amnesty International, and numerous Western news agencies, was aware that Sirte had been so pulverized that the damage itself had a momentum, continuing well past NATO's pilots return home to heroes' welcomes. What about the UN whose senior officials so actively courted the Libyan opposition and pressed for military intervention? There was Georg Charpentier, the UN Resident and Humanitarian Coordinator for Libya, who spoke of "the liberation of Bani Walid and Sirte in October," and after personally visiting Sirte in January, 2012, celebrated the return of 60 percent of those who fled the city (even while there were no consistent estimates of how many had left). Yet Charpentier's own remarks betrayed what "liberation" UN-style looks like, with his enumeration of just some of Sirte's needs which indicated what had been demolished: "Public infrastructure, housing, education and health facilities need to be rehabilitated, reconstructed and reactivated, intense and focused reconciliation efforts also need to be encouraged" (UN, 2012/1/5).

Occasionally we heard from the "protected civilians" of Sirte once they returned to their homes. There was Aisha, a 52-year-old widow and mother of seven children from Sirte who found herself stuck outside of the city during the fighting with one of her sons. When she finally managed to return home she found that "her house had been completely burned down and her six other children were dead" (APO, 2012/2/16). One will not find such testimonies, even in the speeches of Barack Obama who likes to sprinkle his chilling demands and inopportune triumphalism with occasional ornamental quotes from suitable Libyans. One will not read such facts in any NATO press release either—NATO continues to firmly maintain that there were no confirmed civilian casualties (NATO, 2012/3/5). The problem is not that this is not "liberal intervention," the problem is that it is exactly that.

Let us recall some of what we learned about the consequences of NATO "protecting civilians" in Sirte. The bodies were strewn everywhere. An AFP reporter entering Sirte almost immediately after the climax of fighting found relief workers preparing to bury more than 175 bodies covered with white sheets and spotted another 25 charred bodies nearby (Bastian, 2011/10/23). Another saw more than sixty dead in body bags in a field near where a NATO jet and U.S. predator drone struck at Gaddafi's convoy as it attempted to leave Sirte (Pizzey, 2011/10/23). The Al-Mahari hotel close to the centre of Sirte was found riddled with holes from artillery and small weapons fire while an "overpowering odour" emerged, as the reporter came across "60 corpses…rotting on the lawn. Many of the victims have been killed execution-style, a bullet to the head. Some have been bound hand and foot" (Bastian, 2011/10/23). Just days after NATO ceased its bombings, the International Committee for the Red Cross entered Sirte. The ICRC on its own found 200 corpses during its visit (ICRC, 2011/10/27).

The story of Ibn Sina hospital in Sirte also illustrates the real nature of NATO "protection" and the then NTC-aligned rebels' much touted "reverence for life." To be clear, Ibn Sina hospital served wounded civilians in Sirte and fighters injured in defending the city. There is therefore little logic and no evidence to support any conspiratorial argument that "Gaddafi forces" would target their own hospital; moreover, the documented use of indiscriminate heavy weapons fire pertains almost exclusively to the NTC insurgents, especially in the final six weeks of the assault on Sirte. Médecins Sans Frontières reported that Ibn Sina hospital had suffered grave damage. Barbara Frederick, MSF emergency coordinator, reported: "Ibn Sina Hospital came under fire and was attacked. An explosion destroyed an operating room and most of the windows were damaged. As a result of the fighting over the last few weeks, patients had to be moved into the hallways." The hospital also had neither water nor electricity with obvious implications for surgeries (MSF, 2011/10/19; see also MSF, 2011/10/14). Indeed, medical workers reported that "people wounded in fighting…are dying on the operating table because fuel for the hospital generator has run out." One recounted to Reuters: "I saw a child of 14 die on the operating table because the power went out during the operation" (Gaynor & El Gamal, 2011/10/2). A biochemist at the hospital, Mohammed Shnaq, told journalists: "It's a catastrophe. Patients are dying every day for need of oxygen" (Gaynor & El Gamal, 2011/10/2). Elderly patients were also reported to be dying from severe malnutrition (El Gamal & Logan, 2011/10/1). The Red Cross found only a few doctors left in the hospital, which was "packed with civilians from the neighbourhood, including many women and small children" (El Gamal & Gaynor, 2011/10/6). One estimate was that around 200 patients remained inside the hospital (El Gamal & Logan, 2011/10/1). There were also reports that the insurgents deliberately shelled the hospital in order to prevent a Red Cross team from delivering medical supplies, and that an artillery shell hit the roof of the hospital (O'Connor, 2011/10/19). Another report said that the Red Cross team saw the water tower of the hospital being hit and damaged (El Gamal & Logan, 2011/10/1).

For a Western public long fed a diet of "incubator baby" horror stories from the Iraqi occupation of Kuwait, to endless tales of Syrian government forces deliberately targeting children for massacres and tortures, one must wonder what accounts for the sudden silence when actual children die either at the hands of our forces or indirectly because we bomb one side in a grisly civil war. When it came to protecting civilians at Ibn Sina, NATO was not quite as silent as it should have been: the thuds and explosions of its bombs could be heard all around by people inside the hospital. Where it was silent was on any expression of concern for how its actions threatened Sirte's civilians.

Where were UN officials whose organization did so much to promote foreign military intervention in Libyan affairs? In all fairness, UN aid workers did try to reach Sirte in late September (Logan & El Gamal, 2011/9/30). The problem was that UN aid workers were not permitted to enter Sirte, "for security reasons" (Evans, 2011/9/26). Somebody must have been restricting their movements in particular, especially as journalists were somehow entering Sirte. Those who supposedly claimed the right to protect civilians, with all their reverence for life, were blocking food and medical supplies from reaching the besieged residents of Sirte—this in itself is a war crime. Panos Moumtzis, the UN's humanitarian aid coordinator for Libya, "made no direct comment when asked if there was concern over continuing NATO strikes against populated areas still held by forces loyal to the deposed leader" (Evans, 2011/9/26). He made no comment, even though his own agency was being blocked from upholding the very resolution that the Security Council had passed. Over and over again we have seen how the so-called "responsibility to protect" endorsed by Western interventionists played out in Libya, and Sirte has been the touchstone revealing the truths of Western humanitarianism.

Liberating Sirte: Massacres, Looting, Torture, Racism

The spectacle of an imagined massacre in Benghazi seemed enough to provoke shrill "humanitarian" outcries from Western liberals and large elements of the establishment left, not to mention various human rights

organizations and large parts of the mainstream media supplying the necessary choir of pleas to "do something." This choir was amplified by the calls
of various self-designated "socialists" and "human rights activists" in Egypt,
who by then had captured the media's attention as representatives of the
"Arab Spring." The choir had first been mobilized, and then capitalized
upon by the political leaderships of the dominant NATO member states
with representation in the UN Security Council. Yet the only massacre to
have occurred anywhere near Benghazi was the massacre of innocent black
African migrant workers and black Libyans falsely accused of being "mercenaries," and the massacre of a small, retreating column of government
forces, which was a smaller-scale reenactment of the gruesome "highway
of death" that we saw with the slaughter of Iraqis retreating from Kuwait
in the first Gulf War. The "new Libya" is keen on retribution, revenge, and
hunting down every possible figure that might be associated with Gaddafi.
Yet even after the archives of the national intelligence headquarters had
been thoroughly ransacked by the NTC, it is instructive to note that nobody
has produced a single name of a military officer in command of any part
of an alleged plan for a massacre in Benghazi. No names of military units,
no data on their size and the munitions they were allotted, nor any evidence
at all about an actual campaign to mount a wide-scale slaughter in Benghazi
have been produced. Large campaigns in large state bureaucracies where
word of mouth is an entirely ineffective communication medium necessarily produce large numbers of plans, orders, and logistical reorganization,
and thus documents. It is almost entirely as a religious act of faith, a leap of
the imagination, that one faces demands to believe that a massacre in
Benghazi would have happened.

But what is it about the actual massacres—real, documented massacres—that took place in Sirte that failed to move the same body of
shrieking outrage? Had Benghazi suddenly become untouchable, holy
ground for Western liberals so that all else could be sacrificed for it? Or
is it that, behind the feigned concern for absolute strangers on the other
side of the planet, what really mattered was making use of any weapon,
ideological or military, to overthrow a long-established thorn in the side
of the West? Why did Sirte matter less, when its massacres were not of the
fictive kind?

"We found 53 decomposing bodies, apparently Gaddafi supporters, at
an abandoned hotel in Sirte, and some had their hands bound behind
their backs when they were shot," said Peter Bouckaert, emergencies director at Human Rights Watch. Executing prisoners is a war crime. The

bodies of the 53 were clustered together on the grass in the sea-view gar-
den of the Hotel Mahari in Zone 2 (District 2) of Sirte. The area, according to witnesses interviewed by HRW, was occupied by insurgents from
Misrata, with five brigades taking the trouble to even sign the names of
their units on the walls of the hotel. The blood on the grass beneath the
bodies, as well as bullet holes in the ground, suggest that these prisoners
were shot in that location, and the similar state of decomposition suggested the same time of execution: "some of the bodies had their hands
tied behind their backs with plastic ties. Others had bandages over serious
wounds, suggesting they had been treated for other injuries prior to their
deaths" (HRW, 2011/10/23, 2011/10/24). Amnesty International reported
that the number killed at the Mahari was 65 and that they were found on
the grounds of the hotel on October 23, 2011, which at the time served as
the base for opposition fighters in Sirte.

> "Some of the bodies had their hands tied behind their back and many had
> been shot in the head. Video footage taken by opposition fighters themselves
> on 20 October 2011 shows them hitting, insulting, threatening to kill and spit-
> ting at a group of 29 men in their custody, many of whom were found dead
> on 23 October 2011 at the hotel. One of the opposition fighters is heard saying
> 'take them all and kill them'. Among the 29 men seen in the video in the cus-
> tody of the opposition fighters are civilian residents of Area 2 of Sirte and men
> from other parts of Libya, some of them longtime residents of Sirte and some
> who may have been volunteers with al-Gaddafi forces." (AI, 2012a, p. 39)

Ibrahim Beitelmal, a spokesman for the Misrata military council,
denied these claims but he then produced multiple stories to support his
denials. He said the dead were probably executed by their own comrades
(thus suggesting they were not civilians, and evading the fact that opposition forces controlled the area); then he suggested the executions were
probably done just to "blacken the image" of the insurgents; and then he
said civilians were allowed to leave so those remaining must have been
"hardcore loyalists." This twisted series of justifications seemed to evolve
and mutate before the spokesman could finish a single sentence. However,
a university professor in Sirte, Zarouk Abdullah, put all such claims into
serious doubt when he attested to the killing of his brother, Hisham, a
civilian who stayed behind in Sirte to protect his family only to be arbitrarily rounded up by the insurgents and executed along with others at
the hotel (AP, 2011/10/28).

At another site, HRW found the bodies of another ten people who had
been executed and then dumped in a water reservoir. At a third site, near

where Gaddafi had been captured, HRW found another set of bodies of as many as ten people who had been executed (HRW, 2011/10/23).

As HRW pointed out about war crimes:

"Violence of any kind, and in particular murder, inflicted during an armed conflict on combatants who have laid down their arms or are in detention, is a war crime under the Rome Statute of the International Criminal Court (ICC). The ICC has jurisdiction in Libya for all crimes within its mandate committed since February 15, 2011. Under the court's treaty, criminal liability applies to both those who physically commit the crimes and to senior officials, including those who give the orders and those in a position of command who should have been aware of the abuses but failed to prevent them or to report or prosecute those responsible." (HRW, 2011/10/23)

To date, however, the ICC has issued not a single charge or indictment for anyone in the new regime to hold them accountable for these war crimes, in obvious contravention of its own mission and UNSCR 1973. Once more, the cry to prosecute war crimes has been entirely one-sided and merely a tool for advancing regime change. HRW merely issuing these reminders is a way of politely reproducing a game where those targeted by empire are made accountable for human rights abuses, where the vanquished are tried, and where the victors are issued reminders and pleas for further investigation. For some, this may create an illusion of balance. Instead, it is a form of inoculation.

Days after the capture and murder of Gaddafi, bodies continued to be discovered, up to 500 people including civilians and fighters in just the few days that had transpired in Sirte alone (Milne, 2011/10/26). CBS reported that "nearly 300 bodies, many of them with their hands tied behind their backs and shot in the head, have been collected from across Sirte and buried in a mass grave. It also reported on a graveyard with no names, only numbers, "572 so far and counting" (Pizzey, 2011/10/25).

In that graveyard, CBS was told that most of the dead were "mercenaries" (which typically meant that they were black—either black Libyans, or migrant African workers, presumed to be Gaddafi supporters and summarily apprehended for the colour of their skin). We are told that "local officials freely admit that some were summarily executed," and in the words of insurgent Sheikh Fathie Dariez, "there was no mercy for foreign mercenaries" which suggests that prisoners were executed (Pizzey, 2011/10/25). Ali Tarhouni, the NTC's so-called oil minister, said that considering what the NTC fighters had suffered, "I am amazed at their self-restraint;" while CBS' Allen Pizzey remarked: "the evidence indicates that little restraint was shown" (2011/10/25). The numbers presented above do not include massacre sites elsewhere in Libya, nor the growing mountain of evidence furnished by agencies such as AI and HRW of mass abductions, detention, torture, and murder committed by the forces that NATO backed in the name of protecting civilians.

What is more striking is that even while few have ever produced a total for the number of people allegedly killed by the Libyan government prior to the February 2011 uprising—and there is considerable dispute of how many were killed in the weeks leading up to NATO's intervention—there is no doubt that Libya has not witnessed mass slaughter on such a scale, with atrocities committed by all sides, since the time of Italian colonization. For an international regime that espouses the "responsibility to protect," violence in Libya was far from stopped because of NATO's military campaign: it was vastly increased, and increased to a degree that anything one may believe of Gaddafi's human rights records would pale by comparison.

In addition to massacres of prisoners in Sirte, anti-government militias (wrongly presumed by the media early on as all being "NTC forces") also committed torture. Amnesty International, visiting in January and February 2012, interviewed "scores of victims of torture," in several cities and towns, including Sirte.

> "Detainees told Amnesty International that they had been suspended in contorted positions; beaten for hours with whips, cables, plastic hoses, metal chains and bars, and wooden sticks; and given electric shocks with live wires and taser-like electro-shock weapons. The patterns of injury observed were consistent with their testimonies. Medical reports confirmed the use of torture on several detainees who had died." (AI, 2012a, p. 6)

Formerly host of many international meetings, Sirte—even now that it has been devastated—has become home to some of Libya's newest class of citizens: internal refugees. Thousands of persons from the villages of Tomina and Kararim were barred from returning to their homes by the new authorities in and around Misrata; moreover, their homes in those villages continued to be openly burned and looted into February 2012 (HRW, 2012/2/21). Both villages had been occupied by government forces during the war, and then evacuated, which appears to have led Misrata authorities to engage in guilt by association and thus assume that everyone in those villages was a partisan for the government of Muammar Gaddafi. Residents of the villages relocated to several other locations in

April and May 2011, including Sirte, where they remain stuck. Their properties have effectively been expropriated; they are largely the innocent victims of war who are being punished even further.

Looting was also a defining feature of what many insurgents actually meant by "liberating" Sirte. "Are you coming to liberate the city or to steal from it?" was the rhetorical question posed by a Sirte resident (Randall, 2011/10/23). Starting in Abu Hadi, a centre of the Gaddadfa tribe about 16 kilometres south from downtown Sirte, reporters found that many of the homes had been broken into and looted: "After capturing this hamlet… revolutionary fighters have gone on a vengeance spree, looting and burning homes and making off with gold, furniture and even automobiles" (Al-Shalchi, 2011/10/5). "What's happening in Sirte is revenge, not liberation. When someone comes and takes your personal car and destroys your home, this is not liberation" said Abu Anas, a Sirte resident, on returning home. Many more also accused the insurgents of "demolishing and looting homes, shops and public buildings" (Randall, 2011/10/23). Mohammed, another Sirte resident said to Reuters: "Some revolutionaries passed by us when we were sitting outside the house and told us 'wait, you didn't see anything yet'," (2011/10/16). While NTC forces stated that they were only checking homes for weapons, what Reuters reporters witnessed was starkly different.

> "Reuters reporters saw many of them roaming the streets of Sirte with chairs, tires and computers on the backs of their pickup trucks. Brand new BMW and Toyota cars were seen being driven away by the fighters and being towed outside of the city. One fighter tried to push a white Porsche car up a street as another drove a looted beach buggy nearby. In another incident witnessed by Reuters, a group of fighters fired machine guns at an iron safe in an electronics shop. After 15 minutes of shooting, during which they considered trying a hand grenade, they finally opened it. It was empty." (Reuters, 2011/10/16)

Likewise, reporters from the Associated Press TV, "said they saw trucks loaded with everything from tractors and heavy machinery to rugs, freezers, furniture and other household goods being driven off" by insurgents (BBC, 2011/10/16). More reporters witnessed looting, and recorded testimony from Sirte residents of their homes having been destroyed by insurgents unhappy that they did not find much to loot.

"Liberation" in Sirte took on another set of meanings as both racist attacks by insurgents against black victims and the effects of ethnic cleansing were both felt there. After Misrata insurgents completely depopulated the town of Tawargha (also *Tawergha*), inhabited mostly by black Libyans, a number of the surviving refugees ended up in Sirte before it too was devastated. "It's about the color of the skin. That's why they have problems with Tawargha," said Samia Taher, "a light-skinned Libyan woman born in Illinois" who married into a Tawergha family (Dziadosz, 2011/9/30). Reuters found a group of 135 Tawarghans in Sirte. Finding themselves in the centre of wholesale destruction— "we're in the middle of a battle here in Sirte," as one said—many questioned the values of the so-called "revolution": "All this and you're calling for freedom? What kind of freedom are you seeking?" (Dziadosz, 2011/9/30). Only non-Tawarghans fleeing Sirte were allowed to temporarily settle in Tawargha, which reveals the desire for ethnic cleansing. "To avoid the recurrence of any future problems, we should separate the two groups," said a Misrata man named Saleh as he stood by an apartment block housing non-Tawarghans (Dziadosz, 2011/9/30).

Near Sirte, where fleeing residents sought medical attention, insurgents blocked them and gave priority to fighters from Misrata. Three medical workers told Human Rights Watch, "the de facto director of the makeshift hospital between Sirte and Heisha...told the staff to treat Misrata fighters ahead of everyone else, including ahead of 'Tawerghans, people who are black, civilians from Sirte, Gaddafi soldiers, and women. Basically anyone not from Misrata'" (HRW, 2011/10/30). A physician said that guards blocked a pregnant woman from travelling to a hospital in Misrata. "The rebels call us rats and say we will never go back," he told HRW, consistent with other reports that Tawarghans were essentially blocked from travelling either to Tawargha, Misrata, or even Tripoli (HRW, 2011/10/30). When detained in compounds guarded by insurgent fighters from Misrata, many Tawarghans reported being beaten and tortured (AI, 2012a, p. 19).

Save Benghazi, Slay Sirte: Under Cover of Humanitarian Intervention

"And when Qaddafi and his forces started going city to city, town by town, to brutalize men, women and children, the world refused to stand idly by.

"Faced with the potential of mass atrocities—and a call for help from the Libyan people—the United States and our friends and allies stopped Qaddafi's forces in their tracks. A coalition that included the United States, NATO and Arab nations persevered through the summer to protect Libyan civilians." (Obama, 2011/10/20)

Save Misrata, slay Sirte. Protect Benghazi, pound Sirte—how the label "humanitarian" comes to be applied in such cases defies logic. That is because myth is not designed to be tested by logic. Leaving aside the documented crimes by the insurgents against black Libyans and African migrant workers, the insurgents were also found by Human Rights Watch to have engaged in "looting, arson, and abuse of civilians in [four] recently captured towns in western Libya" (HRW, 2011/7/13). In Benghazi, which the insurgents have held for months now, revenge killings have been reported by *The New York Times* as late as May 2011 (Fahim, 2011/5/10), and by Amnesty International (2011/6/23) in late June 2011, with the insurgents' NTC clearly faulted by AI.

The tables were turned, and Sirte, under the umbrella of foreign intervention, actually became what Western opinion leaders imagined would have befallen Benghazi without foreign intervention. Yet few could be heard invoking the new UN norm, the "responsibility to protect" (R2P). Had NATO really committed itself to simply protecting civilians, NATO would have bombed armed forces on both sides of the conflict, and the result would have been a political stalemate, which the Western interventionists were obviously not prepared to accept. NATO would also have taken greater care not to target civilian infrastructure and civilian rescue workers. This adventure was never about "stopping the killing of civilians;" it was instead about who would get to do so with impunity.

"We destroy in order to save," writes Chris Hedges (2011/9/5), and the bombing of Sirte "mocks the justification for intervention." Hedges adds: "Our intervention, as in Iraq and Afghanistan, has probably claimed more victims than those killed by the former regime. But this intervention, like the others, was never, despite all the high-blown rhetoric surrounding it, about protecting or saving Libyan lives. It was about the domination of oil fields by Western corporations." Hedges, a veteran Middle East correspondent for *The New York Times* turned peace activist, was also one of those who initially supported foreign intervention in Libya. Hedges may now say, "you would think we would have learned in Afghanistan or Iraq. But I guess not," but as he admits, "stopping Gadhafi forces from entering Benghazi six months ago," was something "which I supported." Throughout this debacle, anti-imperialism has been scourged as if it were a threat greater than the West's global military domination, as if anti-imperialism had given us any of the horrors of war witnessed thus far this century. Anti-imperialism was treated in public debate in North America as the province of political lepers: right-wing isolationists and libertarians in the U.S. and Marxists in Latin America. European socialists and columnists for Al Jazeera consistently excoriated the Latin American left for failing to put "democracy" and "human rights" ahead of anti-imperialism. One must wonder where these stalwarts of structurally adjusted, neoliberal socialism now find either democracy or human rights in the ashes of Sirte.

Goal No. 1: Regime Change

Up to this point a catalogue of human rights abuses, atrocities, and war crimes perpetrated against civilians and armed forces that supported the Libyan government has been presented. That catalogue of details is, the reader will agree, already extensive without being comprehensive, and it focuses exclusively on Sirte. When the description is expanded to encompass Benghazi, the mountains of western Libya, and so forth, the reign of terror suffered by civilians both during the war and then after NATO formally ceased operations on October 31, 2011 inescapably makes a lie of claims of Western humanitarian concern in backing and conducting this war. The almost unanimous opinion now is that NATO exceeded the UN mandate in its pursuit of regime change. Moreover, it is regime change that makes the most sense given the evidence and given the historical context of Libya's relations with the West from colonial times to the new imperial present. Nevertheless, the Obama administration and NATO's public faces such as Rasmussen consistently denied that regime change was a goal. Regime change continues to be a violation of international law, just as the assassination of foreign heads of state continues to be prohibited by U.S. law. That both sets of laws could be dismissed reaffirms the realities at work, namely those of a global dictatorship led by an imperial president (Canestaro, 2003; de Zayas, 2012; EO12333, 1981, 2.11; Palmer, 2005/5/1; Payandeh, 2012; UN, 1948a, Art. 2, par. 4).

As early as February 25, 2011, a little over a week after the first street protests against the Libyan government erupted, "President Obama, David Cameron, President Sarkozy of France and Italy's Prime Minister, Silvio Berlusconi, discussed ways to remove the Libyan dictator" (Fletcher & Haynes, 2011/2/25). Then on February 26 Obama publicly declared that Gaddafi had "lost the legitimacy to rule and needs to do what is right for his country by leaving now." He then pronounced that the instability in Libya was an "unusual and extraordinary threat" to U.S. national security and foreign policy—words needed to justify military action (AP, 2011/2/26). Obama repeated this on March 3 (Lee, 2011/3/3). Obama was backed up in a separate statement by Secretary of State Hillary Clinton who declared at the end of February, "Gadhafi has lost the confidence of his people and he should go without further bloodshed and violence. The Libyan people deserve a government that is responsive to their aspirations and that protects their universally recognized human rights" (AP, 2011/2/26). Nicolas Sarkozy had already determined that Gaddafi "must go" and wanted to see the West working to remove him (*Times*, 2011/2/26). As early as February 28 UK Prime Minister David Cameron began working on a proposal for a no-fly zone (MacDonald, 2011/3/1).

In March 2011, prominent NATO leaders again publicly endorsed the overthrow of Gaddafi as their goal. Hillary Clinton told reporters that "Gadhafi has lost the legitimacy to lead, so we believe he must go. We're working with the international community to try to achieve that outcome" (Lucas, 2011/3/28). French Defense Minister Gerard Longuet told France-Inter radio that both the UK and France believed that the NATO campaign "must obtain more" than the end of shooting at civilians (Lucas, 2011/3/28). While the NTC's Mahmoud Shammam, attempted to save face by saying, "we are not asking for any non-Libyan to come and change the regime," it's not clear that NATO was waiting for such an invitation (Lucas, 2011/3/28). If the NTC had genuinely taken a nationalist position, of the kind historically supported by most Libyans, it would have been more careful: inviting NATO to fight is inviting NATO's own agenda, which goes well beyond Libyans' freedom to hold picket signs. In terribly suspicious wording, "a senior U.S. official said the administration had hoped that the Libyan uprising would evolve 'organically,' like those in Tunisia and Egypt, without need for foreign intervention" (Richter, 2011/3/18). This sounds like exactly the kind of statement made when something begins in a fashion that is not "organic" and when events in Libya are evaluated as marked by a potential legitimacy deficit and lack of critical mass. The statement also suggests that if the uprising did not evolve "organically," that the U.S. would then intervene. The U.S. intervened.

By October 2011 official denials about the pursuit of regime change stopped. It was officials within the Obama administration itself who told *The New York Times*, "the killing of Colonel Qaddafi...was one of the three scenarios considered" at a 90-minute meeting on October 19, 2011, just a day before Gaddafi was in fact killed (Landler, 2011/10/24). In addition, French Defense Minister Gerard Longuet stated, "as for Gaddafi...as long as he disappears from the stage, that would be important, but not enough. The NTC wants to capture him, and one can understand that." This is an obvious statement of support for one side, with the aim of overthrowing

Gaddafi (Reuters, 2011/10/6). Finally, on a "surprise" visit to Tripoli (Figs. 2.2, 2.3), where she laid down the general features of a new Libyan government, Hillary Clinton said about Gaddafi: "we hope he can be captured or killed soon, so you don't have to fear him any longer" (AP, 2011/10/19). Two days later, Gaddafi was both captured and murdered. That NATO should cease its mission to "protect civilians" precisely when it had participated in the execution of Gaddafi, whose murder was made possible by NATO's intervention and came about as a result of NATO airstrikes, is a telling chronological fact. NATO's bombings ceased immediately on the same day, and within days the operation as a whole was formally ended. Meanwhile, the new regime continues to threaten civilians seen as pro-Gaddafi with arbitrary detention, abduction, ethnic cleansing, torture, and outright execution.

The quick dispatch of military and other government personnel to Libya, as early as February 2011 itself further substantiates the fact that from very early on Western powers were determined to use the façade of local protests as cover for their overthrowing Gaddafi and the Al-Fateh Revolution. By the end of March, *The New York Times* reported that for "several weeks" CIA operatives had already been working inside Libya, which would mean they were there from mid-February, that is, roughly when the protests began or very soon after. They were then joined inside

FIGURE 2.2 U.S. Secretary of State Hillary Clinton disembarks from a U.S. Air Force transport in Tripoli on October 18, 2011. (Source: U.S. Department of State.)

FIGURE 2.3 U.S. Secretary of State Hillary Clinton greets grateful rebel militia commanders on her arrival in Tripoli on October 18, 2011. (Source: U.S. Department of State.)

Libya by "dozens of British special forces and MI6 intelligence officers" (Mazetti & Schmitt, 2011/3/30). The *NYT* also reported that "several weeks" before (again, around mid-February), President Obama "signed a secret finding authorizing the CIA to provide arms and other support to Libyan rebels" (Mazetti & Schmitt, 2011/3/30), with that "other support" entailing a range of possible "covert actions" (Thomas, 2011/3/30; Reuters, 2011/3/30). USAID had already deployed a team to Libya by early March (DipNote, 2011/3/10; Lee, 2011/3/3).

Then of course there is Mahmoud Jibril, the former interim prime minister of Libya, appointed by the NTC, who served for many of the critical months during NATO's war as the NTC's international ambassador at large. Gaddafi was "killed based on a request by a certain foreign power" that wanted the dictator to be "silent forever," Jibril said in an interview (Krause-Jackson & Alexander, 2011/11/14). Jibril told the reporters that had Gaddafi ever been taken alive, "too many secrets could have been discovered... He [Gaddafi] was the black box of the whole country. He had too many wheelings and dealings with too many leaders in the world. With him, unfortunately, a lot of information is gone." Speaking of Libya, post-NATO, Jibril added: "every foreign power you can think of is trying to look after its own interests in Libya. No one is excluded. This is the name of the game. This is politics. Countries have interests in Libya and everybody is looking out for their own." Jibril also said that Qatar as the "most obvious" example of foreign intervention, given that it trained and supplied rebel fighters with weapons, provided humanitarian aid and at least $100 million in loans, and its jets helped enforce the UN-imposed no-fly zone. Qatar also had hundreds of its own troops on the ground and on the frontlines (Black, 2011/10/26).

Finally, there are the concrete actions designed to achieve regime change, taking us full circle by reintroducing the lawless nature of U.S. efforts to overthrow Gaddafi. NATO repeatedly launched missile strikes and bombings aimed at both Gaddafi, his living quarters, and members of his family, killing one of his sons and three of his grandchildren on May 1, 2011. We are also reminded that, "as early as 1969, as Henry Kissinger revealed in his memoirs, discussions were held within the U.S. government about covert action to assassinate Gaddafi, largely because of his radical Arab nationalism, his interference with U.S.-Saudi control over OPEC oil policies and his closing down of the Pentagon's biggest airbase on the African continent [Wheelus]" (Van Auken, 2011/10/24). As we know from the outset of this chapter, there was a long history of intervention under the Reagan administration designed to overthrow Gaddafi as well as collaboration between the U.K.'s MI6 and Libyan jihadists in trying to kill Gaddafi.

Hunting for Gaddafi in Sirte

"As a matter of policy, NATO does not target individuals." So read the press release from NATO (2011/10/20, p. 2) on the day of Gaddafi's capture and murder after his convoy was first struck by NATO, which acknowledged that it struck 11 "armed vehicles" in Sirte (p. 2). By the end of October NATO had completed a total of 9,634 strike sorties against Libyan targets, out of a total of 26,156 sorties overall as part of what it called "Operation Unified Protector" (p. 2). On other occasions too NATO Secretary-General Anders Fogh Rasmussen would emphasize that Muammar Gaddafi "is not the target of our operation" (Reuters, 2011/10/5; Thomet & Lamloum, 2011/10/31). He claimed it was solely about protecting civilians, and yet everywhere Gaddafi happened to be was automatically cited as in and of itself a threat to civilians. Likewise, Marine Col. David Laplan insisted that NATO's mission was not about hunting down individuals. Yet, at the same time British Defense Secretary Liam Fox was telling reporters that NATO intelligence and reconnaissance assets were being used to try to "hunt down" Gadhafi (Al-Shalchi, 2011/8/25).

The following is NATO's account of its strikes against Gaddafi's convoy. At approximately 8:30 a.m. on October 20, 2011, NATO aircraft,

> "struck 11 armed military vehicles which were part of a larger group of approximately 75 vehicles manoeuvring in the vicinity of Sirte. These vehicles were leaving Sirte at high speed and were attempting to force their way around the outskirts of the city. The vehicles had a substantial amount of mounted weapons and ammunition, posing a significant threat to the local civilian population." (p. 2)

NATO did not elaborate on how exactly a convoy leaving the scene of battle, and fleeing from fire, was posing a threat to the local civilian population, especially since all sources acknowledged the reality that the local population was firmly behind Gaddafi. The assertion makes no sense. NATO claimed that its aircraft attacked in order to "reduce the threat;" "initially, only one vehicle was destroyed, which disrupted the convoy and resulted in many vehicles dispersing and changing direction." Unsatisfied with the results, NATO aircraft attacked again: "a group of approximately

20 vehicles continued at great speed to proceed in a southerly direction, due west of Sirte, and continuing to pose a significant threat. NATO again engaged these vehicles with another air asset. The post strike assessment revealed that approximately 10 pro-Qadhafi vehicles were destroyed or damaged" (p. 2). In coming to that determination, NATO claimed to have not known before the strike that the vehicles were "pro-Gaddafi" (Lekic, 2011/10/21), but that it was determined from a "post-strike assessment," based on "open sources and Allied intelligence." NATO routinely denied having any forces on the ground so it is highly peculiar that it would admit to the fact of Allied intelligence on the ground. This was underscored quickly: "NATO does not divulge specific information on national assets involved in operations" (p. 2). The question arises: if NATO had intelligence operatives on the ground, as it is clearly stating it did, how credible is it that NATO would not have known that the convoy was carrying Gaddafi, considering the constant aerial surveillance?

Let us pause on the claims that NATO did not target individuals, that the Alliance did not seek to assassinate Gaddafi, and furthermore that it did not even know of Gaddafi's whereabouts. In addition to early critical analyses (e.g. Campbell, 2011/10/27; Dembélé, 2011/10/27), the available information we now have strongly suggests that such claims are either false or highly questionable. If we deem NATO's claims to be false, then NATO's determination to advance such claims would have to be the result of a commitment to carry out regime change—in the most brutal, direct, and personalized sense. This is well out of line with the UN mandate, in violation of the UN Charter, and in violation of U.S. law, which would be applicable to U.S. involvement in the operations. It would, however, be in keeping with a decades-long history of U.S. efforts to overthrow Gaddafi. It would also be yet another indictment of the imperial uses to which the idea of "protecting civilians" had lent itself.

First, we know that NATO aircraft had already targeted Gaddafi's home in Sirte:

> "His home, surrounded by a sprawling farm on the edge of Sirte, lies in ruins. The buckled walls and gaping holes in the ceiling are mute testimony to the ferocity of the bombardment of this, the nerve-centre of Gaddafi's eccentric and violent regime. You can wander through the labyrinth of rooms, and down into the network of concrete bunkers under the house, blown open by Nato bombs." (Head, 2012/2/9)

Notwithstanding the BBC correspondent's ironic use of language to describe Gaddafi's regime, while he was in the middle of describing NATO's immense violence, it is clear that NATO knew where Gaddafi's home was, and then proceeded to bomb that home to pieces. No explanation was produced about how the home posed a threat to civilians, in a stronghold of determined support for Gaddafi.

Second, intelligence agencies, journalists, and insurgent commanders, and officials of the new NTC regime had at different points deduced or confirmed Muammar Gaddafi's presence in Sirte during the final weeks of fighting, making it very unlikely that NATO could not have known his whereabouts. As NATO had previously identified top levels of the Libyan government as "command and control," there is no reason to believe it would not have followed Gaddafi's movements with keen interest, even if we take NATO's claims on their own terms. STRATFOR Global Intelligence, a private intelligence and analysis firm, in fact reported as early as August that French intelligence sources knew that Gaddafi had moved to Sirte after he left Tripoli as the insurgents overran defences (Friedman, 2011/8/30). In September, news sources were openly speculating that Gaddafi was likely in Sirte, or his other bastion of staunch support, Bani Walid (BBC, 2011/9/27; Stephen, 2011/9/16). By early October a military spokesman for the NTC regime claimed that Gaddafi's son, Muatassim, was "hiding" in a hospital in Sirte (El Gamal & Gaynor, 2011/10/5). A little later, officials in the new NTC regime claimed that Muatassim had been captured in Sirte; and indeed, if not then true, it would later become a fact (El Gamal & Gaynor, 2011/10/14). As reporters noted before Gaddafi was killed, Zone 2 (District 2) in the northwestern part of Sirte, "had still yet to fall despite overwhelming firepower ranged against it," and "such defiance has led rebel commanders to conclude it must contain high-level regime figures including Muatassim, son of Col. Gaddafi, and perhaps Abu Bakr Yunis, former defence minister" (Farmer & Sherlock, 2011/10/15). What a fascinatingly precise "guess." They were correct, on all three counts.

Whether that information actually came from NATO intelligence or was relayed to them, we are safe in assuming that this was communicated between NATO and the NTC. As Mansour Dao, a member of Gaddafi's clan and his chief guard later confirmed, fighters in Sirte were led by Gaddafi's son, Muatassim, who with 350 men (at most) was able to fend off thousands of insurgents for several weeks (AP, 2011/10/25). Other sources also reported that the NTC rebels deduced from the stiff resistance—

defying two months of attempts to capture Sirte—that this indicated the presence of Muammar Gaddafi himself: "Why else would a sniper try to take on a tank?" asked Jafar Al Sharif, a rebel tank commander (El Gamal & Gaynor, 2011/10/19).

Third, there are credible claims of active U.S. and other NATO involvement in the planning and execution of Gaddafi's murder. We have already noted how Gaddafi's capture and killing occurred less than two days after Hillary Clinton arrived in Tripoli, where she publicly approved of Gaddafi being captured or killed and appeared to be calling for that. Beyond that, however, certain powers with knowledge of U.S. operations affirmed U.S. involvement. Russia's then Prime Minister Vladimir Putin specifically highlighted the role of U.S. drones and Special Forces (Osborn & Spillius, 2011/12/15). After Putin described the televised images of Gaddafi's final moments as "horrible, disgusting scenes," he pointedly stated:

> "Is that democracy? Who did this? Drones, including those of the U.S., struck his motorcade and then commandos, who were not supposed to be there, called for the so-called opposition and militants by the radio, and he was killed without an investigation or trial." (Tkachenko, 2011/12/15)[4]

Yet the response of the Pentagon, which was to immediately dismiss Putin's statement as "ludicrous," is itself a statement that does little to increase the credibility of U.S. official sources. Captain John Kirby, spokesman for U.S. Defense Secretary Leon Panetta, stated that, "the assertion that U.S. special operations forces were involved in the killing of Colonel Gaddafi is ludicrous" (AFP, 2011/12/15). Then going further in his denial he added, "we did not have American boots on the ground in the Libya operation" (Osborn & Spillius, 2011/12/15). It is very curious that the Pentagon should deny the presence of U.S. forces on the ground in Libya when, as detailed in the previous section, the U.S. president assigned the CIA to work in Libya along with British MI6 and special forces. As early as February 2011 small groups of CIA agents were already on the ground, to "gather intelligence for military airstrikes and to contact and vet the beleaguered rebels," joined by more later, as well as by the British SAS,

---

4. Putin made his statement in Russian. There is another translation of his words that read as follows: "They attacked his column. Then using the radio—through the special forces, who should not have been there—they brought in the so-called opposition and fighters, and killed him without court or investigation" (AFP, 2011/12/15).

SBS, and MI6 (Mazetti & Schmitt, 2011/3/30). This is also why NATO denials that its forces could not "confirm" civilian casualties for lack of agents on the ground are entirely false.

Fourth, we have some indication that the U.S. government contracted its own mercenaries (euphemistically called "private security contractors") in Libya based on hacked emails from STRATFOR, which were published by WikiLeaks and others. Here we speak specifically of Jamie F. Smith, former director of Blackwater and currently CEO of another "security firm," SCG International. SCG International was itself contracted to protect NTC members and to train insurgents in Libya (Kelley, 2012/3/20). STRATFOR's Anya Alfano described Smith as a "US Govt security contractor on US Govt assignment in Libya;" and in an internal email dated October 20, 2011, STRATFOR staff exchanged the following:

> "From source in Sirte who took part: He (Gaddafi) was killed while trying to escape via a drainage pipe in Sirte by Misratah brigade. Along with him was his def minister (dead) and his son Muatassim (dead). All the bodies have been taken to city of Misratah." (Al Akhbar, 2012)

Given the growing privatization, subcontracting and outsourcing of U.S. military and intelligence work, which has grown exponentially since September 11, 2001, it is entirely credible and makes perfect sense that intelligence was being gathered by STRATFOR (whose clients include every major U.S. national security agency) and that covert work was being done by SCG International (Al-Saadi, 2012/3/19).

Fifth, official sources themselves detailed how the U.S. was involved in Gaddafi's capture and killing. The day after Gaddafi's murder, Panetta himself admitted: "it was a U.S. drone combined with the other NATO planes that fired on the convoy" that carried Gaddafi (Tkachenko, 2011/12/15). For some, this would be enough to indict the U.S. for being actively involved in Gaddafi's murder. However, we have even more information on the wider scope of U.S. involvement. Confirming much of what has been said thus far, an exposé published by *The Telegraph* (Harding, 2011/10/20) based on intelligence sources detailed the ways that NATO tracked Gaddafi. According to the report, Gaddafi had been under surveillance by NATO forces for a week prior to his killing, after an intelligence breakthrough allowed NATO to pinpoint his location—apparently, Gaddafi made the mistake of breaking his rigid rule of telephone silence on one occasion, using a mobile or satellite phone. A U.S. drone plus an "array of NATO eavesdroping aircraft" had been trained on Gaddafi's location in Sirte, "to ensure he could not escape"—no pretense here of "protecting civilians," his escape was in and of itself something NATO would not permit. Contrary to U.S. and NATO official denials, "MI6 agents and CIA officers on the ground were also providing intelligence and it is believed that Gaddafi was given a code name in the same way that US forces used the name Geronimo during the operation to kill Osama bin Laden" (Harding, 2011/10/20). Indeed, since Gaddafi had left Tripoli in late August 2011, "intelligence services have been searching for Gaddafi across Libya and beyond using agents, special forces and eavesdropping equipment" (Harding, 2011/10/20). French drones and U.S. Predator drones staked out the centre of Sirte for several weeks: "They built up a normal pattern of life picture so that when something unusual happened this morning such as a large group of vehicles gathering together, that came across as highly unusual activity and the decision was taken to follow them and prosecute an attack" (Harding, 2011/10/20). French and U.S. electronic warfare aircraft thus picked up Gaddafi's movements as he attempted to escape. A U.S. Predator drone, flown out of Sicily and controlled via satellite from Creech air force base near Las Vegas, Nevada, "struck the convoy with a number of Hellfire anti-tank missiles," and then moments later French jets "most likely Rafales, swept in, targeting the vehicles with 500lb Paveway bombs or highly accurate £600,000 AASM munitions" (Harding, 2011/10/20).

Another report suggested that more than one Predator drone circled above Sirte, each capable of maintaining flight for 18 hours and each equipped with surveillance and attack capabilities (Farmer, 2011/10/22). Gaddafi's convoy was spotted leaving, and that fact alone, namely that he was leaving, was followed by a command to one of the remote Predator pilots to open fire on Gaddafi's convoy. There is no mention of any supposed threat assessment involving local civilians. NATO AWACs planes over the Mediterranean "took control of the battle and warned two French jets that a loyalist convoy was attempting to leave Sirte" (Farmer, 2011/10/22). Those jets then struck the convoy a second time. As we learned later, the fact that it was "French jets" does not mean that they were flown by the French air force. The source for this was Barack Obama himself: "In fact, American pilots even flew French fighter jets off a French aircraft carrier in the Mediterranean. Allies don't get any closer than that" (Obama, 2011/11/4; see also Miles, 2011/11/4).

In fact, several sources in reports produced by numerous prominent Western news media confirmed that the intelligence and special forces of

NATO member states were on the ground actively hunting for Gaddafi for many weeks throughout the campaign. On the ground, on the day of the attack, what appeared to some journalists as a "wild" and "chaotic" situation, "had, in fact, been foreseen by the British SAS and their special forces allies, who were advising the NTC forces" (Farmer, 2011/10/22). British military sources told *The Sunday Telegraph* that "small teams of SAS soldiers on the ground in Sirte" had warned NTC forces throughout the siege of Sirte to be on the lookout for "fleeing loyalists." Indeed, the much applauded move by the NTC to allow people to flee Sirte only rarely mentioned that it was a slow, controlled exit that served a surveillance function: "Assisted by other special forces—in particular the Qataris, with whom the SAS have a long relationship dating back 20 years—the SAS tried to impress on the Libyans the need to cover all escape routes....the SAS urged the NTC leaders to move their troops to exit points across the city and close their stranglehold" (Farmer, 2011/10/22).

In addition, NATO powers had forces on the ground hunting for Gaddafi many weeks prior to the attack in Sirte. Again *The Telegraph* reported that, "as a £1 million bounty was placed on Gaddafi's head, soldiers from 22 SAS Regiment began guiding rebel soldiers after being ordered in by David Cameron." This came from Defence sources, which also stated that the SAS had been in Libya for several weeks before the date of the report (placing their arrival in early July 2011 at the latest) and that it played "a key role in coordinating the fall of Tripoli" (Harding et al., 2011/8/24). SAS commandos "dressed in Arab civilian clothing" and "carrying the same weapons as the rebels," were ordered to begin hunting for Gaddafi as soon as Tripoli fell (Harding et al., 2011/8/24). British troops on the ground in Libya became somewhat of an open secret in the UK (UKSF News, 2011/10/25), regardless of what Rasmussen said.

British forces in fact were on the ground in Libya as far back as March 2011. One British report was that "hundreds of British special forces troops [SAS, SBS, and SFSG] have been deployed deep inside Libya targeting Colonel Gaddafi's forces." An estimated 350 troops were already engaged in covert operations, with 250 of those on the ground from before the launch of the first air strikes to establish a no-fly zone on March 19, 2011, some as many as a month beforehand (Williams & Shipman, 2011/3/25). That fact would place British covert forces on the ground in Libya just days after the first street protests erupted in February. A little earlier even, another British news report revealed that "hundreds of British SAS soldiers have been operating with rebel groups inside Libya for three

weeks" (Mirror, 2011/3/20). A separate British news report, which came
out earlier still, related the fact that U.S. sources had disclosed that British
SAS commandos had been in Libya already for about ten days (Winnett
& Watt, 2011/3/2), thus placing their presence in Libya from around
February 20, either before or at the very same time as Cameron and
Sarkozy began to call for military intervention in Libya, publicly. In private, they had already taken their steps, and must have made the
decision to send forces and prepare for their expedition even earlier than
that. This suggests the possibility that Western powers were at least waiting for the first opportunity to intervene in Libya to commit regime
change under the cover of a local uprising and without any hesitation to
ponder what if any real threats to civilians there might have been.
Protecting civilians, human rights records, local protests, all worked to
provide the necessary media fig leaves. This is not to suggest that the local
uprising was somehow not authentic and without grounding in long-
brewing local grievances. It is to suggest that while there may not have
been a "conspiracy," something even better undeniably unfolded: a convergence of interests and actors, a surfeit of opportunism, and a seemingly
uninterrupted supply of tactical mistakes, knowledge gaps, and conceit
on Gaddafi's side.

It was not just U.S. and British forces that were on the ground in Libya,
but Qatari troops as well (Black, 2011/10/26). Indeed, Mustafa Abdul Jalil,
head of the NTC, praised Qatar for "having planned the battles that paved
the way for victory" (Black, 2011/10/26), and said the Qataris were "a major
partner in all the battles we fought" (Al Arabiya, 2011/10/26). Qatar, for
its part, officially confirmed the nation had sent troops to Libya. The
Qatari chief-of-staff, Major-General Hamad bin Ali al-Atiya, said: "We
were among them and the numbers of Qataris on the ground were hundreds in every region. Training and communications had been in Qatari
hands. Qatar…supervised the rebels' plans because they are civilians and
did not have enough military experience. We acted as the link between
the rebels and Nato forces" (Al Arabiya, 2011/10/26; Black, 2011/10/26).
Qatar trained Libyan insurgents within Libya itself and back in Doha,
and gave $400 million to the insurgents (Black, 2011/10/26). In the assault
on Tripoli, and even on Gaddafi's own compound, "Qatari special forces
were seen on the frontline" (Black, 2011/10/26). It is interesting to note that
in the videos of the actual capture and killing of Muammar Gaddafi in
Sirte, many viewers have spotted troops dressed unlike any of the Libyan
insurgents and not in Libyan military uniforms, rather they were wearing

U.S.-style helmets and flak jackets, and were right up front and among the insurgents grabbing and beating Gaddafi.[5]

Sixth, Mahmoud Jibril himself, the NTC's former interim prime minister and now a key political leader in Libya whose party won more seats than others in the July 2012 elections, has gone on the record and stated that a "foreign agent," who was "mixed in with the revolutionaries," was responsible for killing Gaddafi. Rami El Obeidi, the former head of foreign intelligence for the NTC, also backed up Jibril, and said the agent who assassinated Gaddafi was French. The accusation is that French president Sarkozy wanted to see Gaddafi terminated, rather than tried, so as to effectively cancel a debt and protect his own reputation. According to these allegations, Sarkozy feared that in any prospective trial Gaddafi might reveal that he had spent millions of dollars in getting Sarkozy elected (see Al Arabiya, 2012/10/1; Blomfield et al., 2012/9/30; Cremonesi, 2012/9/29). [6]

Finally, in making the case that NATO's deliberate and knowing targeting of Gaddafi, which is itself a war crime (Bosco, 2011/10/24), and the ensuing assassination of a captive Gaddafi (also a war crime) was a planned part of U.S.-directed regime change, we have the words of none other than retired U.S. General Wesley Clark. Former commander of NATO's Operation Allied Force in the Kosovo War during his term as the Supreme Allied Commander of NATO from 1997 to 2000, General Clark was also a former candidate for the presidential nomination of the Democratic Party. Moreover, Gen. Clark generally supported the war

---

5. While numerous videos posted to YouTube have been deleted over the past months, at the time of writing two of the surviving ones of relevance here were: "Gaddafi Captured Alive by Qatari Soldiers," uploaded by snapperski on October 21, 2011, at <http://www.youtube.com/watch?v=T2PH2O86NsU> and "Gaddafi Captured Alive and shot dead," uploaded by AljazeeraNewsArabic on October 20, 2011, at <http://www.youtube.com/watch?v=TR6zDYLxDp8>. Other videos that showed the foreign troops in slower motion and in closer detail have either been deleted by YouTube itself, or the accounts that uploaded them have been shut down.
6. However, El Obeidi also implicated Syria, in the act of providing NATO with the number for Gaddafi's satellite phone. We might take these reports with a grain of salt: NATO would not have needed a phone number in order to track the satellite phone communications emanating from Sirte. What is more likely, given that at least two different sources affirm this, is that NATO tracked Gaddafi, set up an ambush, and directed Libyan insurgents to the spot where NATO aircraft had bombed his convoy to a stop. It is also not unlikely that foreign agents were indeed among those capturing Gaddafi.

against Libya. This is what he had to say in a public address on October 3, 2007, at the Commonwealth Club in San Francisco.

> "I came back to the Pentagon about six weeks later [after Afghanistan was attacked in 2001] and I saw the same officer [from the Joint Staff] and I said, 'Why, why haven't we attacked Iraq? Are we still gonna attack Iraq?' [and] he said: 'Aw sir, it's worse than that'. He said…he pulled up a piece of paper off his desk, he said, 'I just got this memo from the Secretary of Defense's office, it says we're gonna attack and destroy the governments in seven countries in five years. We're gonna start with Iraq and then we're gonna move to Syria, Lebanon, *Libya*, Somalia, Sudan, and Iran. I said, Seven countries in five years. I said: 'Is that a classified memo?' He said, 'Yes sir!' I said, 'Well don't show it to me,' he was about to show it to me, 'because I want to talk about it'." (FORA. tv, 2007/10/3, emphasis added)[7]

Celebration at the Safari Club

"We came, we saw, he died!"—a jubilant, laughing U.S. Secretary of State Hillary Clinton triumphantly shouted in front of a reporter, moments after hearing of Gaddafi's death. Ghoulish, chilling, and perverse was this utterly remorseless display of how bloodthirsty U.S. power can be, coming immediately as scenes of Gaddafi's brutal murder were flashed across screens around the world, bloodied, sodomized with a knife, beaten, shot and then put on public display as his body rotted next to Muatassim, only to then be secretly buried in an unmarked grave. (The NTC wanted to control which public reactions to Gaddafi's death could be allowed, clearly fearing that sanguine triumphalism, gory revenge, and inhumane voyeurism might not exhaust all possible options.) "Wow!" Hillary Clinton had breathlessly muttered before cameras, as she checked her Blackberry and read the first news of Gaddafi's capture. She excitedly shared the news with aides and reporters then visibly restrained her joy by admitting that many times before these unconfirmed reports coming from the NTC had been misleading. This was later followed by her imitation of a Roman conqueror. Asked by a reporter if her visit to Tripoli might have had some-

---

7. In another public appearance that was televised, Gen. Clark identified his source as a fellow General. The story, even when told many months apart, remained identical. See "Proof: Libyan invasion was planned more than 10 years ago! General Wesley Clark on DemocrazyNow," uploaded by astarotcito on July 2, 2011, at <http://www.youtube.com/watch?v=pNuIPcVv4hw>.

thing to do with Gaddafi's death, Clinton chuckled and said, "I'm sure it did" (Daly, 2011/10/20).[8]

In a war that saw many role reversals, where Fox News featured numerous reports and commentaries critical of the war while Al Jazeera supported and aided the insurgency, Hillary Clinton might not have expected Chris Wallace, host of *Fox News Sunday*, to ask her if she regretted her gleeful comment now that some legal experts were calling Gaddafi's killing a war crime. Wallace had to ask the question twice. Finally, Clinton replied: "I'm not going to comment on that" (Fox, 2011/10/23).

As a Fox News headline, "Obama Brandishes another Scalp," reminded us, 2011 was a year in which Obama, Nobel Peace Prize laureate, went on an international execution binge (Stirewalt, 2011/10/21). In addition to Gaddafi, the U.S. targeted and murdered American citizens, the cleric Anwar al-Awlaki and his teenage son; then Osama Bin Laden, shot in the face and dumped in the ocean; and, not to mention dozens of victims of drone strikes. With all of the gravitas that does not come from cordially chit-chatting with a welcoming late-night comedian, Obama told Jay Leno of *The Tonight Show* that obviously nobody likes to see someone come to an end like Gaddafi's (that is, apart from his own Secretary of State), but then he celebrated the good news of the murder by saying what a "strong message" it sent to dictators about human rights (*Huffington Post*, 2011/10/25). No comment, however, from any celebrity host in the U.S. news-entertaintment industry about what the public should expect as the rightful outcome for those who command a global dictatorship currently conducting several wars simultaneously across Africa, Asia, and the Middle East, while never being held accountable for war crimes, torture, arbitrary detention, and unlawful executions (even when their own citizens are the target). This is the humanitarian moment in late Western empire, where the gloss of human rights is quickly applied like Revlon and is even more easily smeared.

Sounding like little more than a dull reenactment of Ronald Reagan, Obama pompously intoned: "Today, the government of Libya announced the death of Muammar Qaddafi. This marks the end of a long and

---

8. See: "Hillary Clinton 'Wow' Reacts to Moammar Gadhafi's Capture," uploaded by MrBlue11900 on October 21, 2011, at <http://www.youtube.com/watch?v=lwAiw4QGEFM> and "Hillary Clinton on Gaddafi: We came, we saw, he died," uploaded by FederalJacktube6 on October 20, 2011 at <http://www.youtube.com/watch?feature=player_embedded&v=Fgcd1ghag5Y>.

painful chapter for the people of Libya, who now have the opportunity to determine their own destiny in a new and democratic Libya." However, rest assured, the U.S. would hover over Libya: "But the United States, together with the international community, is committed to the Libyan people. You have won your revolution. And now, we will be a partner as you forge a future that provides dignity, freedom and opportunity." No longer was it necessary to repeat the worn lines from the act of "protecting civilians"—Obama's speech contained not a word of that. Instead, Obama exulted in regime change: the "rebuke" to "Gaddafi's dictatorship," the "revolution" that "broke the regime's back," the "dark shadow" now lifted, making abundantly clear what the desired outcome had been for the U.S. all along, just as Obama had stated from the outset of the intervention, even prior to military action (Obama, 2011/10/20).

Neither imperious pontification nor vain swaggering was exclusively an American performance. "Relieved and very happy" is how German Chancellor Angela Merkel pronounced herself at the news of Gaddafi's death, then moralizing: "Finally the way is free for a political rebirth for peace" (Satter, 2011/10/21). UK Prime Minister David Cameron called Gaddafi's death a chance for a "democratic future" for Libya—except, of course, for those who supported Gaddafi—and then Cameron decided to revive issues that the UK had buried for many years as it sought lucrative business contracts in Libya pre-2011. "I think today is a day to remember all of Colonel Gaddafi's victims," Cameron added, "from those who died in connection with the Pan Am flight over Lockerbie, to Yvonne Fletcher in a London street, and obviously all the victims of IRA terrorism who died through their use of Libyan Semtex" (Farmer & Henderson, 2011/10/20). Suddenly, the "victims" mattered again, but only some: the far greater number of Libyan victims of British bombing merited no mention.

Here we might also remember some of the earlier cheers of vanquish that came from both Cameron and French President Sarkozy as they visited Benghazi in September 2011, as Sirte was being bombed toward ruin. Cameron told the supplicants assembled in Benghazi, "your city was an inspiration to the world" (McDonnell, 2011/9/16)—not being clear about who or what in the world was inspired by Benghazi, other than it being a useful pretext for NATO's bombing. "It's great to be here in free Benghazi and in free Libya," shouted Cameron over the chants of Benghazi's grateful; Sarkozy "beamed" at chants of "One, two, three; Merci Sarkozy!" possibly wishing he could substitute Benghazi for the French voters who soon after ousted him from office. Cameron and Sarkozy then held NTC chairman Mustafa Abdul Jalil's arms aloft "like a victorious boxer" (Logan & Farge, 2011/9/16). About Gaddafi's death, UN Secretary General Ban Ki Moon called it an "historic moment" (BBC, 2011/10/20). The European Union said Gaddafi's killing "marks the end of an era of despotism and repression from which the Libyan people have suffered for too long"—as if there was something about a bloody mob rampage in a city of ruins that should inspire such romantic lyrics (AJE, 2011/10/20). Predictably, NATO Secretary General Anders Fogh Rasmussen called the bombing campaign a "positive story" and "a successful chapter in NATO's history" (Sheridan, 2011/10/15; Thomet & Lamloum, 2011/10/31). Al Jazeera's Tony Birtley, an enthusiast of the NTC whose reports rarely even pretended at impartiality, said while in Sirte itself that Libyans were celebrating the beginning of a "new Libya" and that "this is bringing a form of closure" (AJE, 2011/10/20). Of course one also says this about funerals. Finally, among some of the celebrated Egyptian bloggers and journalists of Egypt we find the self-described "revolutionary socialist" Hossam Hamalawy, who lent his words of support to the Western media in celebrating NATO's overthrow of Gaddafi: "This will signal the death of the idea that Arab leaders are invincible," and, concerning the gory slaughter of Gaddafi, he added, "all this will bring down the red line that we can't get these guys" (Gillette & Gamel, 20110/20). But who is this "we"?

"We have been waiting for this moment for a long time," said Mahmoud Jibril, the NTC-appointed prime minister of the new interim government, adding "Muammar Gaddafi is dead." This was before he expressed buyer's remorse and confessed that foreign powers actively sought to kill Gaddafi. The NTC's Abdel Hafez Ghoga proclaimed Gaddafi's death was "the end of tyranny and dictatorship" and that Gaddafi had "met his fate" (ironically, a few weeks later a mob in Benghazi also set upon Ghoga, and months later regime defectors were still being eliminated). Mahmoud Shammam, the NTC's chief spokesman, called it "the day of real liberation" (Fahim et al. 2011/10/20). Jalil, the NTC's chairman, had earlier said that NATO allies could expect preferential treatment in return for their help in ending Gaddafi's rule: "As a faithful Muslim people, we will appreciate these efforts and they will have priority within a framework of transparency" (Logan & Farge, 2011/9/16). "On behalf of the Libyan people, we express our appreciation and gratitude to the alliance, both the NATO alliance and Arab countries and friends. Thank you for that effort, which achieved victory for us," Jalil said in giving obvious credit to NATO (Thomet & Lamloum, 2011/10/31).

Jalil then went over the top for NATO saying that "it was very accurate in the way that civilians were not affected"—*civilians not affected*—which then allowed Rasmussen, then visiting Jalil, to say that, "on one occasion we publicly declared that we could not exclude the possibility that we might have caused civilian casualties but the follow up investigation couldn't confirm that" (Thomet & Lamloum, 2011/10/31). Except that there never was any NATO investigation. Indeed a game was set by NATO and the NTC where NATO would say it would only investigate civilian casualties at the request of the NTC-appointed interim government "of Libya," which for its part denied any civilian casualties at all. In fact, the cold cynicism of the narrative, its inherent unbelievability directly and vividly confronted by the realities of places like Sirte, succeeded in turning off more people in the opinion-shaping sectors of the international public and making them quieter about endorsing "humanitarian intervention."

One of the few dissenting voices reported by the Western media, in relation to Gaddafi's murder, was that of President Hugo Chávez Frías of Venezuela. He stated: "They murdered him....We will remember (Gaddafi) all our lives as a great fighter, a revolutionary and a martyr" (Satter, 2011/10/21). As a committed anti-imperialist, and someone who directly experienced a U.S.-supported coup using local Venezuelan opposition elements, regardless of his popular victories in free and fair elections, Chávez needs to be heard more in the North American mainstream media.

Even if one believes the worst of Gaddafi, the best that could then be said about what followed in Libya is that one "brutal dictator" had been replaced by thousands of smaller dictators with an apparently bottomless bloodlust and thirst for personal power. The glee would prove to be short-lived, almost immediately. For many there would never be any glee at all, as they were abducted from their homes and streets and found themselves in prison, without charge, subjected to the most heinous torture.

To summarize, for a wide array of reasons, Sirte was central to the story of post-colonial Libya, the seat of the leader of the Al-Fateh Revolution, the focus of international attention, and the climax of NATO's war, which was pursued to effect regime change as part of a broader strategy. Now it is time to examine more closely what that broader strategy was, how it was shaped, and what it aimed to accomplish beyond Gaddafi the person. We have established that "human rights" was neither the reason nor part of the character of NATO's intervention, and that nothing about any regime's record could justify such an assault as NATO's. Later, we will examine the manipulations of "human rights" by Western powers, international organizations, and local political entrepreneurs in search of international sympathy.

CHAPTER THREE

Libyan Pan-Africanism
and Its Discontents

The ultimate purpose of what was AFRICOM's first war, and NATO's rehearsed military expedition, was not in some simplistic sense to simply seize oil, nor in an even more simplistic sense to protect civilians, and not even just regime change in terms of a change of Libyan leadership. What is more credible, and explains a broader range of facts, is that the goal of U.S.-led military intervention was to disrupt an emerging pattern of independence and a network of collaboration within Africa that would facilitate increased African self-reliance. This is at odds with the geostrategic and political economic ambitions of extra-continental powers, namely the United States. As Sirte symbolizes a resurgent Pan-Africanism in the making and a persistent anti-imperialist perspective articulated by Gaddafi, so the termination of NATO's military operations there brought to a bloody end any immediate prospects for greater African independence through new forms of integration.

In previous years, the U.S. Embassy in Tripoli noted the extent to which Africa mattered to Libya when led by Gaddafi. American diplomats noted that his "interest in Africa dates to the late-1980's when it became clear that efforts to position Libya as a leading Arab state were unlikely to succeed." They added that "Libya has significant commercial investments and development projects in sub-Saharan Africa, and has leveraged them as part of its 'dinar diplomacy' approach to managing relations on the continent," further observing that Gaddafi, "is keenly focused on African issues and seems to genuinely aspire to be the founding father of a United States of Africa" (USET, 2009/7/21). The U.S. also observed how in the mid-1970s Libya established the World Islamic Call Society (WICS), "an educational institution mandated to provide Arabic language and religious training to foreign candidates for the Islamic clergy as a means to propagate more moderate iterations of Islam in sub-Saharan Africa and Asia." Also senior Libyan officials often referred to this among other facts as demonstration that "Libya was ahead of the international community in recognizing the dangers of Islamic fundamentalism (invariably described as 'Wahhabism') and moving to actively counter it" (USET, 2009/5/18). Throughout the files published by WikiLeaks, one reads genuine apprehension by the U.S. over Gaddafi's African role, mixed with opportunistic observations on how the U.S. might exploit his role, along with making occasionally derisive comments about Gaddafi.

The African Union, and the Pan-African project as a whole, has suffered immediate consequences from the elimination of Gaddafi. Robert Nolan, an analyst of the African Union, summed up the consequences as follows:

> "In the short term, the AU will lose its most avid financial backer. It is estimated that roughly 15 percent of the AU operating budget provided by member states came from Libya, in addition to Tripoli's covering of dues for a number of smaller African countries in arrears. With a 2010 operating budget of just $200 million, and increasing peacekeeping responsibilities placed on the AU by the international community in places like Sudan and Somalia, the gap in funding is not insignificant. Just this month, for example, the 9,000-strong AU mission tasked with pushing back al-Qaeda linked Islamists known as al-Shabab in Somalia announced a $10 million shortfall for operations. While Gadaffi was often accused of stoking conflicts across the continent (he was linked to dozens of coups and civil wars across Africa over the years), Libya's contribution alone could easily cover the shortfall." (Nolan, 2011/12/5)

As Nolan further described, Libya led by Gaddafi was also a major source of aid and investment in numerous African countries: "Libya invested in infrastructure and agricultural projects, the construction of mosques and hospitals and companies continent-wide. While the exact figure of Gadaffi's Africa investments are not yet known, some estimate the number at $150 billion" (Nolan, 2011/12/5).

Immediately following the overthrow of Gaddafi, AFRICOM very rapidly instituted a number of military missions across Africa, with seemingly little in the way of a unified African front to confront it. In addition, North Africa was destabilized, with the fragmentation of Mali in the wake of NATO's war. AFRICOM now cast itself as the necessary remedy for ensuring the kind of stability that it had destroyed, propelling new military ventures of benefit to the U.S. As journalist Dan Glazebrook put it succinctly and correctly,

> "in taking out Muammar Gaddafi, AFRICOM had actually eliminated the project's fiercest adversary....Gaddafi ended his political life as a dedicated pan-Africanist and, whatever one thought of the man, it is clear that his vision for Africa was very different from that of the subordinate supplier of cheap labour and raw materials that AFRICOM was created to maintain." (Glazebrook, 2012/6/14)

Furthermore, "barely a month after the fall of Tripoli—and in the same month Gaddafi was murdered (October 2011)—the U.S. announced it was sending troops to no less than four more African countries: the Central African Republic, Uganda, South Sudan and the Democratic Republic of Congo." AFRICOM further announced 14 major joint military exercises planned with African states for 2012, an unprecedented number of such exercises (Glazebrook, 2012/5/25-27). Clearly, with Gaddafi out of the way, AFRICOM's ambitions soared as it now saw Africa as an open playing field.

Predictably, a few months after the overthrow of the Libyan government, AFRICOM announced that it had formed a military relationship with the new regime appointed by the NTC, not waiting for an elected government to make this decision (Miles, 2012/6/15). Amazingly, AFRICOM said that it was "still dealing with some of the residual challenges left by the former regime," going on to specify the "residual challenges" as consisting of the presence of Al Qaeda-linked fighters (Miles, 2012/6/15). This is amazing because the government AFRICOM overthrew was a leader in fighting Al Qaeda and associated elements in Libya, for years both before and since the U.S. announced its "war on terror." The fighters that the foreign military intervention enabled, and who fought on the same side, were now being used as an excuse to penetrate Libya further, while introducing the very dangerous possibility of greater armed violence between former militia allies.

For its part, the interim NTC government took an openly anti-African line, only to find itself immediately isolated on the continent when it mattered most. Anti-black racism became the apparent policy of the new NTC regime and the disparate militias that controlled portions of Libya. This met with little in the way of denunciation from "the international community," even as Libya witnessed actual ethnic cleansing and the forced displacement of entire towns for the first time in its modern history.

Africa and the *Green Book*: Getting Past Eurocentrism

Under the assertive heading, "Black People Will Prevail in the World," in the third part of Muammar Gaddafi's *Green Book* addressing "The Social Basis of the Third Universal Theory," we read the following (reproduced in full):

> "The latest age of slavery has been the enslavement of Blacks by White people. The memory of this age will persist in the thinking of Black people until they have vindicated themselves.

> "This tragic and historic event, the resulting bitter feeling, and the yearning or the vindication of a whole race, constitute a psychological motivation of Black people to vengeance and triumph that cannot be disregarded. In addition, the inevitable cycle of social history, which includes the Yellow people's domination of the world when it marched from Asia, and the White people's carrying out a wide-ranging colonialist movement covering all the continents of the world, is now giving way to the re-emergence of Black people.

> "Black people are now in a very backward social situation, but such backwardness works to bring about their numerical superiority because their low standard of living has shielded them from methods of birth control and family planning. Also, their old social traditions place no limit on marriages, leading to their accelerated growth. The population of other races has decreased because of birth control, restrictions on marriage, and constant occupation in work, unlike the Blacks, who tend to be less obsessive about work in a climate which is continuously hot." (Gaddafi, 1975, pps. 45-46)

With the start of Western calls for military intervention in Libya, and especially when Benghazi was captured by the opposition, more Western media commentators than ever started to write about the *Green Book*. They jeered and sneered all the way, using the opportunity for hasty, crass commentaries that seemed designed to prove that Gaddafi was a demonic idiot, a prematurely hatched hybrid offspring of stupidity and insanity. (For examples see BBC, 2011/4/29, and Roberts, 2011/3/2; the latter is roundly condemned by readers who will not easily be fooled.) In doing so, they missed opportunities for careful analysis, understanding, and a means of illuminating key historical and cultural issues for their readers. Yet, in producing mocking vilification such writers also helped justify the violent overthrow of Gaddafi—he deserved it, for being so "crazy."

In earlier years, with war not on the horizon, media commentaries on the *Green Book* were more measured, with *The New York Times* characterizing it as "a mottled mix of pan-Arabism, mystical Islam, socialism, anti-Zionism and anti-Americanism" (Krauss, 1991/3/17). It thus avoided any cheap psychoanalysis or sloppy, Eurocentric literary criticism that missed the many wise points in the book. Moreover, the likes of Britain's BBC and Andrew Roberts (Fellow of the Royal Society of Literature) conveniently missed every opportunity to subject the ideology and propaganda of the Benghazi rebels to the same scrutiny, that is, until it was too late and they heard that the World War II graves of British soldiers in Benghazi had been smashed and desecrated by "Islamists"—not once, but twice (*Sunday Mail*, 2012/3/5; *Calgary Herald*, 2012/3/9; Reuters, 2012/6/16).[1] Also too late was any critical commentary following the near assassination of the UK Ambassador in Benghazi (BBC, 2012/6/11), just days before the second attack on the British war graves.

Gaddafi's writing above should, in my opinion, be treated as an anthropological document, a perspective on the human condition, which is of ethnographic value for being the product of a key historical actor. In this frame of mind, the key points to note are that the document was written in 1975, thus offering a very early preview of the roots of Gaddafi's reorientation and eventual alignment with Pan-Africanism, away from Pan-Arabism. It is also a contradictory piece, perhaps paradoxical, as it ranges from a kind of monumental respect for what Gaddafi saw as the eventual triumph of black Africans, to a massaged repetition of some of the gross stereotypes that have characterized black people as promiscuous and lazy, equally blaming culture ("old social traditions") and nature (the "hot" environment). Interestingly, he does not mention imperialism and neocolonialism at all as having anything to do with that imposed and

---

1. The commentary in the *Sunday Mail* (2012/3/5) is especially caustic, in ways that were previously reserved for speaking about Gaddafi, but now with some remorse: "The cemetery had remained inviolate through all the long years of enmity between Britain and the Gaddafi regime. But things are different in the new Libya." Then the paper's editors proceeded to draw several "uncomfortable conclusions"—again, too late—such as: "Libya after the fall of Gaddafi is a lawless and ungovernable place where horrible actions can be done with impunity by those who have enough guns. The second is that there is no gratitude among many of those we have helped. The third is that those who warned that we did not know–or care enough–who we were aiding have now been vindicated in the most spectacular and gruesome way.... our leaders, and our media, should cease to be so simple-mindedly enthusiastic about endorsing every revolutionary movement that appears in the Arab world. Tyrants are bad, but their opponents are not necessarily any better." Indeed, sobriety that came too late to the pages of the UK corporate media.

enforced "backwardness." Yet, even Gaddafi's limited presentation above was double-edged: Africans' social "backwardness" worked to ensure their "numerical superiority," which will eventually help them to prevail. This is a "numbers count" view of history, simple but not entirely invalid. Gaddafi thus attempts, roughly at first, to balance power with poverty, and to see the power in poverty. Seeing poverty across Africa, and seeing the promise of power coming out of that poverty, Gaddafi thus perhaps intuitively perceived who Libya's future partners ought to be.

Mandela and Gaddafi: Moral Pan-Africanism

"I have also invited Brother Leader Gaddafi to this country [South Africa]. And I do that because our moral authority dictates that we should not abandon those who helped us in the darkest hour in the history of this country. Not only did they [Libya] support us in return, they gave us the resources for us to conduct our struggle, and to win. And those South Africans who have berated me, for being loyal to our friends, literally they can go and throw themselves into a pool."[2]

These words were spoken by then South African President Nelson Mandela as he stood next to visiting U.S. President Bill Clinton in late March 1998. Clinton had criticized Mandela's meeting with Gaddafi. As Bill Clinton had also broached the subject of a UN-led peacekeeping force for Africa, Mandela responded directly and sharply: "I certainly would never put my troops under somebody who does not belong to Africa" (Ross, 1998/3/27).[3]

The public relationship between Nelson Mandela and Muammar Gaddafi was a very close and warm one, and began from very early. After serving 27 years in prison under the South Africa's apartheid regime, and merely three months after his release from jail, Mandela travelled to Libya as the leader of the African National Congress (ANC) on May 18, 1990. In an interview given to journalists at the airport in Tripoli, Nelson Mandela declared:

---

2. Text transcribed from <http://www.youtube.com/watch?v=wEoK4KGMO54>
3. In 1994, a draft foreign policy plan of the ANC, soon to form the government, established South African opposition to a U.S.-led "New World Order," and explicitly criticized the UN for being undemocratic as well as condemning the work of international development agencies in continuing to keep Africa in poverty (AP, 1994/2/19).

"My delegation and I are overjoyed with the invitation from the Brother Guide to visit the Great Popular and Socialist Arab Libyan Jamahiriya. I have been waiting impatiently ever since we received the invitation.... I would like to remind you that the first time I came here, in 1962, the country was in a very different state of affairs. One could not but be struck by the sights of poverty from the moment of arrival....with all of its usual corollaries: hunger, illness, lack of housing and of health-care facilities, etc. Anger and revolt could be read in those days on the faces of everyone....

"Since then, things have changed considerably. During our stay in prison, we read and heard a great deal about the changes which have come about in this country and about the blossoming of the economy which has been experienced here. There is prosperity and progress everywhere here today which we were able to see even before the airplane touched ground. It is thus with great pleasure that we have come on a visit in the Jamahiriya, impatient to meet our brother, the Guide Qadhafi." (Mathaba, 2012/3/31)

Mandela's observations are confirmed as it is an established fact that Libya's population, which grew to six times its size in the time Gaddafi was in power, had achieved enormous social, economic, and health gains—a fact acknowledged in even some Western media. When Gaddafi seized power, life expectancy was 51 years. Under his regime it increased to 74. Literacy grew to 95 percent for men, 78 percent for women, and the per capita income increased to $16,300 U.S. (Pugliese, 2012/2/17). Even now, the U.S. State Department's webpage on Libya[4] still points to a Library of Congress Country Study[5] on Libya that features some of the Gaddafi government's many social welfare achievements over the years in the areas of medical care,[6] public housing,[7] and education.[8] According to the United Nations Development Program, Libya is the only continental African nation to rank "high" in the UNDP's Human Development Index (see UNDP, 2009, p. 171). In a rare piece, a BBC reporter also recognized such achievements:

"Women in Libya are free to work and to dress as they like, subject to family constraints. Life expectancy is in the seventies. And per capita income—while not as high as could be expected given Libya's oil wealth and relatively small population of 6.5m—is estimated at $12,000 (£9,000), according to the World

4. U.S. Department of State's Libya page: <http://www.state.gov/p/nea/ci/ly/>.
5. A Country Study: Libya—Library of Congress Call Number DT215 .L533 1988. Available online at: <http://lcweb2.loc.gov/frd/cs/lytoc.html>.
6. <http://lcweb2.loc.gov/cgi-bin/query/r?frd/cstdy:@field(DOCID+ly0068)>.
7. <http://lcweb2.loc.gov/cgi-bin/query/r?frd/cstdy:@field(DOCID+ly0069)>.
8. <http://lcweb2.loc.gov/cgi-bin/query/r?frd/cstdy:@field(DOCID+ly0070)>.

Bank. Illiteracy has been almost wiped out, as has homelessness—a chronic problem in the pre-Gaddafi era, where corrugated iron shacks dotted many urban centres around the country." (Hussein, 2011)

"We consider ourselves comrades in arms," Mandela said in thanks to Gaddafi. "You have given military training to South Africans who wanted to obtain their liberation through armed struggle," Mandela said after hugging Gaddafi outside his tent. He added, "your readiness to provide us with the facilities of forming an army of liberation indicated your commitment to the fight for peace and human rights in the world." Taken to see the ruins of Gaddafi's compound in Tripoli, bombed by the U.S. in previous years, Mandela condemned the bombing and insisted on seeing every room in the building (UPI, 1990/5/19). On criticisms of his visit to Libya, Mandela incisively replied:

"No country can claim to be the policeman of the world and no state can dictate to another what it should do. Those that yesterday were friends of our enemies have the gall today to tell me not to visit my brother Gaddafi. They are advising us to be ungrateful and forget our friends of the past." (Quoriana, 2011/7/18)

Mandela was also awarded Libya's International Gaddafi Prize for Human Rights. In response, Mandela said:

"I was deeply touched by this Prize insofar as it represents further support for the struggle taking place in South Africa, to the ANC and to the combat of the people of South Africa. This Prize, which was awarded to us by the Guide of the Libyan Revolution, has been of utmost importance in that it has encouraged the combat or the liberation of South Africa, and it has confirmed the support of the Jamahiriya for our struggle." (Mathaba, 2012/3/31)

Mandela's words went very deep in thanking Libya and thanking Gaddafi personally, and considering what a popular icon of the struggle for freedom Mandela became even in the West, it is easy to see why few were reminded of his words during the war in 2011.

"We are extremely grateful to have been invited to visit your country. History has thus given us the opportunity to make your acquaintance and to express the solidarity and support of the people of South Africa to the Arab Libyan people. Allow me, too, to express our deepest gratitude for the limitless aid which the Glorious Revolution of Al Fatah has not ceased to bring in support of the fight to the people of South Africa.

"On many occasions, you have taken a firm stand against all forms of injustice and oppression, and you have given military support to the South African people in their struggle for freedom and self-determination....Our situation is identical to that of all peoples who are in struggle. Just as we, you are convinced that armed struggle is the only effective way to recover freedom, as can be seen in your commitment to the service of the most elementary of human rights throughout the world, and most notably in South Africa." (Mathaba, 2012/3/31)

Gaddafi thanked Mandela in return, and said:

"Who would ever have said that, one day, the opportunity for us to meet would become a reality. We would like you to know that we are constantly celebrating your fight and that of the South African people and that we salute your courage during all of those long years you spent in detention in the prisons of apartheid. Not a single day has passed without our having thought of you and of your sufferings." (Mathaba, 2012/3/31)

Then in late October 1997, having just visited a month earlier on his way to the Commonwealth Heads of Government conference, Mandela returned to Libya. It was five years after the UN imposed sanctions on Libya, and Mandela made the trip against U.S. objections. What's more, he was forced to travel over land from Tunisia as not even passenger planes were allowed to land in Libya. Along the way, Mandela was greeted by giant banners: "Mandela's visit to Libya is a devastating blow to America." This was Mandela's first trip to Libya as President of South Africa. The South African Department of Foreign Affairs (DFA) issued a statement on the trip, underlining that "Libya is a country which was very supportive of the South African liberation movements during the struggle against apartheid" (DFA, 1997).[9]

"My brother leader, my brother leader, how nice to see you," Mandela told Gaddafi as he hugged and kissed Gaddafi on each cheek. Indeed, it was rare to not see the two holding hands for long stretches of time when meeting, joyful and relaxed in a manner that conveyed a reunion between long lost brothers.[10] In response to U.S. criticisms of the visit (see Muhammad, 1997/11/4), Mandela had these powerful words to offer:

---

9. The same point is made prominently on the website of the South African government's Department of International Relations and Cooperation: "Unofficial relations between South Africa and the Great People's Socialist Libyan Arab Jamahiriya are of long standing and go back to the days of the struggle against apartheid." See <http://www.dfa.gov.za/foreign/bilateral/libya.html>.
10. As just one example, offering uninterrupted raw footage, see: <http://www.youtube.com/watch?v=G7-g4cdSb7M>

"Those who say I should not be here are without morals. I am not going to join them in their lack of morality. This man [Gaddafi] helped us at a time when we were all alone, when those who say we should not come here were helping the enemy (South Africa's white government)." (*NYT*, 1997/10/23; Reuters, 1997/10/22-23)

Thousands of Libyans lined the streets to greet Mandela on October 22, 1997. Gaddafi hailed Mandela not just as a South African leader but as a symbol of hope to all peoples of the world (CNN, 1997/10/22, 1997/10/21). Libyans gathered outside Gaddafi's compound, as Mandela toured it once more, chanting: "Mandela, our hope for Africa!" (*LATimes*, 1997/10/23). Mandela urged an end to international sanctions: "We cannot be unmoved by the plight of our African brothers and sisters" (*LATimes*, 1997/10/23).

Mandela made another trip to Libya at the end of 1998. This time the purpose was to establish a South African diplomatic mission, with diplomatic relations having been established in 1994 (DFA, 2002).

In 1999 Gaddafi, on his very first trip outside of Libya since UN sanctions were lifted, visited Mandela in South Africa, as Mandela's last official visitor at the end of his presidency. The end of the sanctions largely resulted from the efforts of Mandela in convincing Gaddafi to release the two suspects wanted by the UK and the U.S. for the PanAm 103 bombing over Lockerbie. Mandela praised Gaddafi for his efforts in seeking a peaceful solution to the conflict in the Democratic Republic of Congo. Gaddafi in return bestowed the Libyan Decoration of Steadfastness on Mandela in appreciation of his "unlimited courage and prolonged steadfastness" (BBC, 1999/6/13). Through rain and rough seas, Gaddafi travelled to Robben Island, where Mandela had been imprisoned for 18 years, and in Mandela's former cell he raised his fist and praised Mandela as a hero (BBC, 1999/6/14).

Once more, Mandela had very direct and profound words to offer in a speech welcoming Gaddafi on June 13, 1999, about those who would criticize their relationship and presume to offer other paths for Africa: "Those who dedicate themselves to causes affecting the lives of millions ought to have a clear understanding of history. They should plan their actions with a sense of their impact on those for whom they believe they act." Speaking of the "controversy" around Gaddafi's visit, Mandela added: "The relationship between our two selves and between Libya and democratic South Africa has not been without controversy and therefore some special significance in world affairs. As a responsible member of the international community of nations, South Africa would never defy predominant international opinion deliberately and merely for effect (…) In a world where the strong may seek to impose upon the more vulnerable." Mandela continued, "and where particular nations or groups of nations may still seek to decide the fate of the planet," it is in such a world that there is a need for "respect for multilateralism, moderation of public discourse and a patient search for compromise." Turning to Gaddafi, he added: "When we dismissed criticism of our friendship with yourself, My Brother Leader, and of the relationship between South Africa and Libya, it was precisely in defence of those values." Mandela was clearly directing a moral critique against imperial condemnations of their reunion: "There must be a kernel of morality also to international behaviour….the amorality which decrees that might is right can not be the basis on which the world conducts itself in the next century." Then Mandela landed a heavy blow:

> "It was pure expediency to call on democratic South Africa to turn its back on Libya and Qaddafi, who had assisted us in obtaining democracy at a time when those who now made that call were the friends of the enemies of democracy in South Africa.

> "Had we heeded those demands, we would have betrayed the very values and attitudes that allowed us as a nation to have adversaries sitting down and negotiating in a spirit of compromise. It would have meant denying that the South African experience could be a model and example for international behaviour."

Mandela then added: "We look forward with joy and anticipation to the full re-entry of Libya into the affairs of our continent and the world" (Mandela, 1999).

The moral order of solidarity, reciprocity, and obligation, and most of all a shared history of struggle against colonial rule and imperial domination, are what we see articulated in this potent combination of the personal and the institutional in Libyan-South African ties, and in the relationship between Gaddafi and Mandela. To some extent it also accounts for the distinct South African perspective on the war against Libya, but this will be dealt with in the final chapter.

Libya, Gaddafi, and Pan-Africanism:
Anti-imperialism after Pan-Arabism

"Had we heeded Nkrumah's advice in 1963," Gaddafi told leaders at an African Union summit in Sirte, "Africa would now be like the United

States of America or at least close to it. But we did not heed his advice, and even worse we ridiculed those predictions. So we are still standing in the same place we were in 1963" (Gaddafi, 2005, p. 31).

Here was Gaddafi then, picking up the mantle of the famous Pan-Africanist and socialist, the late Kwame Nkrumah of Ghana, while speaking to the developmentalist ambitions of his counterparts and ideals of material achievement about which Gaddafi himself was sometimes personally ambivalent. Gaddafi was in a hurry to make up for lost years: "Some of the [African] Union's institutions have yet to be established, namely the African Central Bank, the African Monetary Fund and the Court of Justice. Now we should put an end to this and assume our historical responsibilities." As if addressing those worried that Libya might be taking on too great a role, Gaddafi added, "if any country has voluntarily offered to host those institutions and was not able to do it, they should give way to any other member state to host an institution which has yet to be established" (Gaddafi, 2005, p. 31). The African Monetary Fund had been planned as far back as 1980 in fact (UNECA, 1983).

An African Central Bank, the Africa Investment Bank, and the African Monetary Fund would be institutions that would directly challenge the hegemony of the World Bank and International Monetary Fund (AU, 2012). The founding of an African Court of Justice would render entities such as the International Criminal Court (ICC) even less relevant than they are currently, thereby supplanting institutions that were poorly attuned to local values, traditions, and understandings. Obama's Secretary of State, Hillary Clinton, appeared to be most concerned by the latter development, especially when at a recent African Union summit in Sirte in July 1-3, 2009, Africa's leaders decided not to cooperate with the ICC. In an urgent cable marked "secret" and not for foreign eyes, Clinton asked all U.S. diplomatic posts to inform her on how the AU "arrived at this decision despite the opposition of member states at the Summit." She could only cite two dissenting states, Ghana and Botswana, both pro-U.S., and even then all she could say is that they were "distancing themselves from this decision" (Clinton, 2009/7/17). Clinton wanted to know if the AU resolution was binding, how many states had representatives present at the summit, whether Gaddafi was alone in presenting the resolution—thus highlighting his role as its sponsor. She further asked if there were any objections, who opposed it, and what chances there were of the resolution being ratified, and if it needed any ratification. Given the prominent role hastily given to the ICC during the foreign intervention in Libya

in 2011, at the urging of Hillary Clinton and others, and whose indictments were one-sided and focused solely on Gaddafi and his closest officials, it is significant and not merely coincidental that Clinton was so
concerned about where the AU stood on the ICC at this summit in 2009.
It also shows the kind of grinding friction that existed between the U.S.
and Libya with its Pan-Africanist role. That role would better explain
eventual U.S. military intervention—led by its Africa Command—than
the mass media portrait of a sudden explosion of U.S. concern about
human rights in Libya, where Americans could not "stand idly by" as if
Libyans' rights suddenly moved them to the very core of their being.

Gaddafi spoke directly at the 2005 AU summit about the question of
sovereignty and self-defence from foreign intervention. He reminded atten-
dees that as stated in Article 3, Section B, of the AU's Constitutive Act, "the
objectives of the Union include safeguarding its integrity and independence. We put this in the statute and the people ratified it." Then he asked:
"But what does this mean? What have we done to defend the sovereignty
of the member states and their integrity and independence?" He answered,
"we are in need of a means of defence. We promulgated the Security and
Defence Charter and it was a great achievement but this should not be only
on paper, there should be a mechanism for its implementation" (Gaddafi,
2005, p. 31). From there Gaddafi raised the issue of the African Peace and
Security Council, the constitution of African peacekeeping forces and
decisions about their deployment, the need for a common defence minister, and the implementation of the Joint Security and Defense Charter
(Gaddafi, 2005, p. 31). Gaddafi realized that there was disquiet among
member states of the AU about surrendering their individual sovereignty
to AU institutions, and he thus turned the tables on their logic.

> "We do not accept diminished sovereignty and interference in our internal
> affairs from others, not even for the sake of the unity of Africa. But our
> national sovereignty is violated and threatened by the lack of African unity.
> That is why we agree to compromise our sovereignty to foreign powers and
> we accept this as a matter of fact. But when we talk about compromising any
> part of our collective sovereignty for the sake of the African Union, we say
> 'no, we will not compromise our sovereignty'. So, we have sovereignty without
> unity." (Gaddafi, 2005, p. 33)

Collective action in relation to the "huge markets and great blocs" such
as China, Japan, NAFTA, and the European Union were high on Gaddafi's
Pan-Africanist economic agenda as well. He cautioned against small states
negotiating on their own with the giant economic blocs, as was and is

currently the situation. He called for the creation of one African market and for a common Minister for Foreign Trade, adding, "we are a big consumer and producer market but who represents it now? We are doing that individually. There is a need to express ourselves collectively" (Gaddafi, 2005, p. 31). The ultimate and immediate aim was that of "creating an integrated economy and a unified monetary zone" (Gaddafi, 2005, p. 32). Citing Nkrumah, Gaddafi emphasized, "Nkrumah says there is no chance for an independent African country today to follow an independent path of economic development. Those of us who have tried to do that were destroyed and forced to return to the framework of the old colonial rule" (Gaddafi, 2005, p. 32).

Still on the economic front, Gaddafi said that as Africans, "we have to adapt our lives in a way that is different in terms of social and economic matters," but this did not mean rejecting all cooperation with the international community. However, "such cooperation should be based on mutual benefit and respect. We are being subjected to a double-faced phenomenon which is benign on the surface and malicious underneath" (Gaddafi, 2005, p. 33). Gaddafi criticized foreign aid to Africa:

> "there is an attempt to promote proposals aimed at extending aid for Africa. But when aid is linked to humiliating conditions, we don't want humiliation.... If the aid is conditional and leads to compromises, we do not need it. If the aid is connected to intervention about particular cultural practices like circumcision, then we don't need this aid." (Gaddafi, 2005, p. 33)

Furthermore, at the AU Summit in Sirte in 1999, a decision was made to engage Africa's creditors for the "the total cancellation of Africa's external debt" (Melber, 2001, p. 5).

Gaddafi was also keenly aware of Western powers' hunger for African natural resources, and African weakness in defending a claim to a share in their own wealth.

> "They are the ones who need Africa—they need its wealth. Fifty per cent of the world's gold reserves are in Africa, a quarter of the world's uranium resources are in Africa, and 95% of the world's diamonds are in Africa. A third of chrome is also in Africa, as is cobalt. Sixty-five per cent of the world's production of cocoa is in Africa. Africa has 25,000 km of rivers. Africa is rich in unexploited natural resources, but we were [and still are] forced to sell these resources cheaply to get hard currency. And this must stop." (Gaddafi, 2005, p. 33)

In very prescient statements, Gaddafi linked all of these issues of economic and political sovereignty and self-defence to the prospects of both foreign intervention and the overthrow of revolutionary regimes. Gaddafi thus quoted Nkrumah's words: "I [Nkrumah] warned in Addis Ababa that unless we unite as soon as possible under one government, there will be incidents over borders and our people in their desperate attempt for a better standard of living will rebel against the revolutionary authority" (Gaddafi, 2005, p. 32). To this Gaddafi added:

"This is exactly what happened. All revolutionary authorities were overthrown. We have problems over borders. If we made one step forward, the enemies made several steps; and our weakness is growing and widening and benefiting our enemies. Subsequently conditions in Africa will be conducive to the neocolonialists. This is what Nkrumah said." (Gaddafi, 2005, p. 32)

Again citing Nkrumah, Gaddafi articulated the Pan-Africanist vision: "Our proposals since 1963 contain one voice for Africa, a single currency, an African monetary zone, an African central bank, a continental communication system. These are the words of Nkrumah in 1963" (Gaddafi, 2005, p. 32).

A few years after the 1999 AU founding summit in Sirte, and other high-level ventures between Gaddafi and his African partners, we saw Gaddafi crowned as the "King of Kings" of Africa. The title was bestowed on him at a meeting of more than two hundred traditional African rulers in Benghazi. At the meeting Gaddafi urged the assembled chiefs and sheikhs to join his campaign for African unity: "We want an African military to defend Africa, we want a single African currency, we want one African passport to travel within Africa" (BBC, 2008/8/29). Gaddafi wanted the traditional leaders to create a grass-roots movement to create pressure from the bottom up on building African unity, what became known as the Forum for African Traditional Leaders (FATL).[11]

---

11. Following Gaddafi's overthrow, the Asantehene, Otumfuo Osei Tutu II, was nominated to replace Gaddafi, as the next chairman of the Kings and Sultans of Africa Forum. The decision was taken at a meeting in Nairobi in October 2011. The forum was created by Gaddafi, "with the sole goal of pushing for Africa unity, leading to the formation of United States of Africa," and Gaddafi was the first and life chairman of the group. The Forum, with traditional leaders such as King Monogo of Congo Brazzavile, Queen Best of Uganda, Kin Chikaya of Congo, King Bagidi of Benin and King Agokoli, Tokoli, took the decision at a crisis meeting. Some members of the Ghana National House of Chiefs also were active members of the Forum, which usually meets on the symbolically important date of September 9 each year (Awuah, 2011/12/13).

The BBC quoted Tanzanian Sheikh Abdilmajid who said, "the people believe in the chiefs and kings more than they believe in their governments" (BBC, 2008/8/29). U.S. diplomats took note of course, even reproducing the BBC's quote (without attribution) in one of its cables. The U.S. Embassy in Tripoli appeared pleased to report that Gaddafi's "campaign to create a 'United States of Africa' under his leadership was dealt another blow" when a meeting planned in Kampala, Uganda, with two hundred traditional leaders was cancelled by the Ugandan government on the grounds that such leaders were "banned" from entering a political debate—a restriction on "democracy" that occasioned no comment from U.S. diplomats (USET, 2009/1/21). The U.S. Embassy rightly saw this as an effort by Gaddafi (and the traditional leaders, it must be added) to "additional, bottom-up political pressure on African governments to support his dream of a united Africa." It should be noted how U.S. diplomats personalized and reduced the campaign to one man: Gaddafi (USET, 2009/1/21).

With the "King of Kings" title, the U.S. Embassy in Libya worried that Gaddafi had gained more political capital than the U.S. diplomats felt he deserved. Speaking of Gaddafi's entrance to the AU summit on February 2, 2009, when he was elected as Chairman, the U.S. Embassy pointed out that he entered the convention accompanied by "a retinue of tribal kings," adding that this was "an attempt to frame him as the popular choice of ordinary Africans" (an attempt by whom is unclear) (USET, 2009/2/11). Casting doubt on whether Gaddafi was chosen as AU Chairman by consensus, the U.S. Embassy further chose to frame Gaddafi as a threat to democracy: it said that Gaddafi gave a speech, "in which he said that Africa remained predominantly tribal and therefore ill-suited to multi-party democracy." Though this view is not without merits and was long advocated by some political scientists and anthropologists, the U.S. Embassy nonetheless added that this "did little to assuage concern that the AU had chosen a dictator as its chairman during a period in which it has endeavored to promote democratic governance" (without specifying whose "concern" this was) (USET, 2009/2/11). The U.S. Embassy's cable contains much in the way of snide and sneering commentary, mocking Gaddafi for "humbly" accepting his new title, and using quotes when speaking of "African" populations in the Caribbean and South America invited by Gaddafi to somehow join a new, united Africa.

At the AU summit in Ethiopia in July 2009, the U.S. Embassy in Addis Ababa noted how one of the more than one hundred "traditional kings" invited to the summit "showered praises on the Libyan Leader," and that

Gaddafi "returned the favour" by telling the conference that "traditional monarchs are the 'true voice' of Africa that should be heeded," and that he "disparaged outside influences on the continent." In a statement both wry and erroneous, the U.S. Embassy mocked Gaddafi's title saying that he "calls himself the 'King of Kings'" (USEAA, 2009/7/15).

Keenly aware of how Gaddafi was gaining both symbolic and political capital, the U.S. Embassy in Tripoli noted that the 1999 Sirte Declaration is "touted here" as the genesis of the AU and a "platform for the future 'United States of Africa',", adding that "domestic propaganda" celebrated Gaddafi as "the father and guide of closer integration on the continent" (USET, 2008/10/2). Gaddafi, another U.S. cable remarked, "views himself as a man of particular historical importance," as if this were a question merely of self-image rather than historical fact, which all of the U.S. concern seemed to affirm (USET, 2009/7/21). Gaddafi also "prides himself on Libya's humanitarian activities on the continent, which are primarily focused on improving conditions for women and children," noted another cable (USET, 2009/5/18)—a major departure from the recent rhetoric about Gaddafi as a "brutal dictator." While previously appearing to snicker at Gaddafi's alleged sense of self-importance, the same U.S. diplomats appreciated the fact that, "the Leader is open to an international solution for Darfur," and that during her visit to Libya then U.S. Secretary of State Condoleeza Rice told Gaddafi that, "the U.S. wants to cooperate with Libya to secure peace in Africa and particularly in Sudan" (USET, 2008/10/2). Elsewhere, they noted with pleasure that Gaddafi, "has expressed willingness to assist U.S. efforts in Darfur, Somalia, and in ending the Chad-Sudan conflict" (USET, 2009/7/21).

As the U.S. Embassy itself reported, Gaddafi "seeks symbolic gains as much as he does substantive ones." With his election in 2009 to the chairmanship of the AU, Gaddafi would have "a high-profile platform from which he can trumpet his vision of Africa and rail against Western interference on the continent," while also serving "as confirmation of his regional importance" (USET, 2009/4/17). That this should concern the U.S. is logical: symbolic capital can be converted into political capital, and is a measure of Libya's "soft power" precisely at a time when the U.S. was dramatically losing support and legitimacy internationally.

The other dimension of Libya's power that worried the U.S. was Libya's seeming ability to convert real capital (aid, investment, lavish spending) into much needed political capital and increased legitimacy. In this regard, U.S. Ambassador Gene Cretz frequently wrote about Libya's "dinar diplomacy" and "the power of its purse." Here too Gaddafi's summit "pageantry" was scrutinized by U.S. diplomats who saw it, correctly, as a means of "currying favour with African guests, while providing a not-so-subtle reminder of Libya's oil wealth." At an AU Summit held in Libya in 2009, the U.S. Embassy remarked on how "African delegations were well cared for—ministers and heads of state were housed in expansive villas," while foreign observers "lived in a much more Spartan manner, on foam beds in public housing flats" (USET, 2009/7/15).

The U.S. looked for ways to manipulate the symbolism of Gaddafi's successes in 2009—a critical year as Ambassador Cretz frequently repeated across his many cables. (2009 was the 40th anniversary of the officers' revolt against King Idris, the 10th anniversary of the Sirte Declaration, the election of Gaddafi as AU Chairman, with Libya taking up a seat on the UN Security Council, and Ali Treiki—Libya's top diplomat on Africa—becoming the Secretary General of the UN General Assembly.) Cretz commented that Gaddafi "needs his AU chairmanship to be seen as a success," and that this would be "a potentially useful opening" or a "potentially useful lever" for "increased engagement." Indeed, Cretz recommended that the U.S. should be "crafting programs that give Libya a symbolic leadership role," as this would reduce the chance that Gaddafi, "will play the spoiler"—specifically regarding the presence of AFRICOM (USET, 2009/5/18; 2009/2/11).

The battleground for legitimacy and influence was Africa. Gaddafi outwitted and outmaneuvered the U.S. in this field for many years. At the final summit of the Organization of African Unity in Sirte in 1999, which gave birth to the African Union in 2002, and in which Gaddafi presented his vision of a United States of Africa, there was also a large military display and "Gaddafi assured African heads of state that the Libyan military equipment on display was at the disposal of all African countries to defend them against enemy attacks" (Solomon & Swart, 2005, pps. 473, 479). At the AU's extraordinary summit, called for by Gaddafi, that took place on February 27, 2004, in Sirte, African leaders "agreed to a common security policy that will effectively give the African Union authority to intervene in border wars and internal conflicts" (Solomon & Swart, 2005, p. 481). This was Libyan symbolic capital converted into political capital—a *United States of Africa* sounded more and more like a banner message to imperial power: *United States (USA) out of Africa*.

Prior to the formation of the AU, Gaddafi had already been active on the continent in spreading his message of anti-imperialism. In May 1997,

FIGURE 3.1 Muammar Gaddafi, in a famously long speech at the 64th session of the UN General Assembly in New York on September 23, 2009, tears into the violations of the UN Charter by the great powers and the inconsistencies and contradictions of the UN system. (Source: courtesy of the United Nations, photograph by Mark Garten.)

speaking at a mass congregation for the Muslim New Year in the central mosque in Niger's capital Niamey, Gaddafi "urged Muslims to obey God's word rather than that of the UN Security Council, which was allegedly controlled by anti-Islamic Christian colonialists." In Nigeria he was reported to have sought to mobilize millions of Muslims to do battle against the U.S. and Europe, and the Nigerian ruler, General Sani Abacha, at a state banquet in Kano awarded Gaddafi Nigeria's highest medal of honour (Solomon & Swart, 2005, p. 476). Similarly, in his relations with Uganda, Gaddafi was awarded the Order of Katonga, Uganda's highest military honour in 2004, after bestowing a similar honour on Yoweri Museveni in 1988 in Libya (Samora, 2011/4/12).

As some have noted, one of the striking features of the 1999 Sirte summit "is the apparent deference shown to Gaddafi." In their 2001 statement, the assembled leaders paid tribute to "Brother Muammar Al Gaddafi, Leader of the Great Al Fatah Revolution, for his role and efforts as the son of Africa" and reaffirmed their confidence in his "determined efforts, aimed at realizing Africa's collective vision for unity, co-operation, development, peace and security on the African continent" (Solomon & Swart, 2005, p. 479).

Gaddafi's turn toward Africa was arguably a turn away from the Arab world. On many occasions Gaddafi had sought a political union of Libya with other Arab nations, signing agreements with Egypt, Tunisia, Syria, Chad, Morocco, Algeria, and Sudan, in 1972, 1974, 1980, 1981, 1984, 1987, and 1990 respectively. All of these efforts were failures. Thus in 1998 Gaddafi declared that "the Arab world is finished" and that "Africans and not Arabs were Libya's real supporters" (Solomon & Swart, 2005, p. 479). In March 1999, Gaddafi went as far as to exclaim: "I have no time to lose talking with Arabs, I now talk Pan-Africanism and African Unity!" (Solomon & Swart, 2005, p. 479). In the "new" Libya, post-Gaddafi, this position has been almost completely reversed, as discussed later.

The turn toward Africa was also a direct challenge to European efforts to shore up continental neo-colonialism, with both the UK and France still expediting troops to "hot spots" consisting of their former colonies. Nikolas Sarkozy's Union for the Mediterranean (UfM) unsuccessfully tried to peel away North African nations from the rest of the African continent, and realign them politically and financially with the European Union, a structure that ideologically was to be both "supranational and anti-national" and mirrored NATO partnership agreements with select North African states (Laughland, 2008/3/12). While still in existence, the UfM has largely been irrelevant and unsuccessful, from at least 2005 onwards.

Libyan Aid and Investment in Africa

There is substantial interest and disagreement about the extent of Libyan financial support to African nations while Gaddafi remained in power. While the figure of $150 billion in investments in Africa is a widely reported figure, it has come under dispute, along with the details of Libyan financial support for the African Union as an organization. For his part the AU Commission Chairman, Jean Ping, looking forward to improved relations with the U.S.[12] and Libya's NTC, immediately sought to downplay Gaddafi's influence after his overthrow, telling the foreign media:

> "He set up a fund of $5 billion, which is not negligible. But we must not forget that the vast wealth of Libya…$150 billion was invested in Europe. If the new authorities and the Libyan people want to complain that their money was invested outside the country, the first beneficiaries were Westerners." (Lamloum, 2012/1/16)

Ping added that Libya had not paid its dues to the AU for 2010 and 2011 (unsurprisingly, since a war ravaged Libya in 2011), and that it was not exceptional in paying 15 percent of the AU's budget as the same share was

---

12. Jean Ping can hardly be considered a reliable friend of Gaddafi. Ping is Gabonese, and Gabon voted for military intervention at the UN, in violation of the AU charter. Ping was a former Minister of Foreign Affairs for Gabon, and held various ministerial portfolios throughout his career, and is obviously well connected to Gabon's political leadership. In the next chapter more is presented on the controversy surrounding Ping, and his unseating at the AU.

paid by Algeria, Nigeria, South Africa, and Egypt (Lamloum, 2012/1/16). Ping's comments were previously affirmed by one very hostile anti-Gaddafi writer who asserted that for all of Gaddafi's "invective against the west," the Libyan foreign investment agency (LAFICO) had $6 billion in investments in Italy alone, compared with $800 million in Africa in 2002 (Pelham, 2002, p. 19). One question is whether this is correct. If so, and even if so, the fact remains that such figures leave out direct aid. While we cannot promise a new set of definitive sums, using a range of sources we can piece together the larger picture of Libyan financial support for African nations of a commercial, developmental, or political nature, and apart from support for rebel movements. Answers to these questions may shed some light on at least some of the West's motivations for unseating Gaddafi.

That Libya invested heavily in Europe and the U.S. caused some to believe in the simple image of Libya as being in bed with the West, a notion largely dispelled thus far in this book. We can complicate the analogy a little more: Libya was buying the West's bed—not all of it, of course, but a large piece at precisely the same time that Western economies began to sink. The real threat of Libya led by Gaddafi, free of sanctions, and buying up parts of major Western corporations, was that Gaddafi was not being subordinated to Western hegemony, rather he was buying it. Gaddafi was also buying and ensuring access, making it more difficult to sideline Libya's corporations, short of sweeping sanctions. Gaddafi, long the outsider, was suddenly very much an insider, a financially strong shareholder without debt and with lots of money to spend. The problem, as U.S. diplomatic cables constantly suggest, is that Gaddafi the "new friend" remained Gaddafi the anti-imperialist troublemaker guided by suspicious intentions. Rather than fawning over his Western guests, Gaddafi sometimes showed a kind of disinterest in high-level visitors from the U.S., clearly marking his personal priorities in not-so-subtle ways. The Deputy Chief of Mission at the U.S. Embassy, Joan Polaschik, provided a detailed description of how Gaddafi "greeted" the visit of Senators John McCain, Joe Lieberman, and Lindsey Graham.

> "[the] meeting with Qadhafi took place so late in the evening (nearly 11 pm) because the Leader had been fasting and usually takes a nap after breaking his fast. The Libyan officials told us that Qadhafi often fasts on Mondays and Thursdays and is doing so now, in the run up to the holy month of Ramadan. Qadhafi appeared as if he had been roused from a deep slumber for the meeting. He showed up with rumpled hair and puffy eyes, and was casually dressed

158

SLOUCHING TOWARDS SIRTE

in a short-sleeved shirt patterned with the continent of Africa, wrinkled pants and slip-on shoes." (USET. 2009/8/19)

There were several institutional vehicles for Libya's commercial investments across Africa. The Libyan Investment Authority (LIA) was established in August 2006 by the General Peoples Congress. The LIA included the assets of the Libyan Arab Foreign Investment Company (LAFICO), the Libyan African Investment Portfolio (LAP), and Oilinvest Company. The Libyan African Investment Portfolio (LAP) had $5.2 billion U.S. in capital and was created by the Libyan government in February 2006. Its significant holdings included: OiLibya, Afriqiyah Airways, Sahel-Saharan Investment and Trade Bank (BISC), LAP Green Network, Libyan Arab African Investment Trade Company, and the Libyan African Portfolio (Suisse) SA. The Libyan Arab Foreign Investment Company (LAFICO), which was founded in 1981 and was controlled by the Central Bank of Libya, was an investment management firm that focused on industrial, commercial, agricultural, tourism, and real estate sectors, with around $1.8 billion in capital (SWF, 2011). Other parts of the LIA operating in Africa were the Libyan Arab African Investment Company (LAICO), and Tamoil, whose African operations ran under the OiLibya brand (Samora, 2011/4/12). Among its many projects, Libya funded the construction of 23 hotel resorts in 15 different countries, as well as oil refineries, banks and telecommunications networks across Africa (Bruguière, 2011/11/22). Overall, by 2002 the LIA had "accumulated or extended investments in at least 31 countries throughout Africa." Some of the largest investments were in "the Zambian telecommunications firm Zamtel ($394 million) and in oil storage and pipeline infrastructure linking Moanda to Matadi in the Democratic Republic of the Congo (around $300 million)," on top of many smaller investment projects and subsidized oil exports (STRATFOR, 2011/3/14).

LAICO owns, manages, and/or constructed several hotels and resorts across Africa, specifically in Burkina Faso, Congo, Gambia, Guinea, Kenya, Mali (2), Tanzania, Tunisia (3), and Uganda.[13] OiLibya had over 1,260 gas stations across Africa and serviced 36 airports by 2009, operating in 19 African countries.[14] OiLibya marketed itself as a brand for Africa:

13. See <http://www.laicohotels.com/>
14. See <http://www.oilibya.com/>, <http://www.oilibya.com/index.php?Id=6&lang=en>, <http://www.oilibya.com/index.php?Id=15&lang=en>.

"As a key player in the African energy industry OiLibya's core values are firmly rooted in Africa. Our presence in [19] African countries makes us a leading member of the societies where we operate, contributing to their economic and social development, and therefore to that of the continent as a whole.... Loyal to its African character, OiLibya strives to be a responsible African group operating in accordance with certain key African values: ethics; integrity; honesty and equity. We work constantly for the betterment and prosperity of Africa as a whole."[15]

The Libyan African Investment Portfolio (LAP) was chaired by Bashir Saleh Bashir, who in a 2007 interview with *African Business* outlined his background: "I joined the revolution from its beginnings, helping to co-ordinate the movement's activities in the south of Libya. After the success of the revolution I was made an ambassador to the Central African Republic and afterwards served as ambassador to Tanzania and then Algeria," and he added, "I have a passion for Africa and I want to help my leader to achieve his vision for Africa, especially his vision for working towards a United States of Africa." The magazine described Bashir as "a man who is steering much of Libya's oil wealth in developing Africa's economic renaissance" (Williams, 2007). We are told that the LAP alone had $5 billion U.S. in funds, which it invested across Africa in numerous economic sectors: banking, aviation, oil refining and distribution, real estate development, communications, and agriculture, having committed already $3 billion by 2007 (Williams, 2007). Bashir spoke at length about agriculture and communications. He explained that one of the LAP's mandates was to focus on adding value to Africa's exports, the absence of which had long been a serious capital drain that benefited Western nations since Africa was colonized. Speaking of Liberia, he noted: "Liberia is a major producer of rubber, but are there any factories producing rubber products in Liberia? Are there any factories for adding value to raw materials in Liberia? There are not; there is not even a small factory producing balls or rubber toys for Liberian children. All Liberia produces is raw materials for export" (Williams, 2007). He gave similar examples, citing the Ivory Coast and cocoa, and Kenya and coffee. Bashir explained: "If we could follow this philosophy of added value, Africa would require less assistance from the West" (Williams, 2007). The added fact is that Europe and the U.S. would also be losing out on the value-added process

---

15. From <http://www.oilibya.com/index.php?Id=75&lang=en>.

and the profits generated from keeping Africa as an exporter of unprocessed cash crops and raw materials.

The LAP was also a partner in a joint venture with Russia's power plant builder, Technopromexport to build power plants in Africa. The joint venture, Laptechno-Power, involved building and operating power plants in at least five African countries besides Libya as well: Algeria, Egypt, Ghana, Namibia, and Uganda. The LAP managed $6.73 billion U.S. in funds for this project alone (USET, 2008/12/22).

The LAP's chairman also spoke about a new satellite that Libya would launch in December 2007, "which holds the potential to transform communications in Africa. Its footprint will cover the whole of Africa providing connections for all the countries of the continent and carrying data, voice and internet communications as well as educational services and facilitating African telecommunication systems" (Williams, 2007). LAP Green Networks, the digital telecommunications arm of the LAP, also invested nearly $1 billion in telecommunication companies across Africa, operating mainly mobile telephone and Internet businesses (Khisa, 2012/6/4).

Libya's leadership in gaining a satellite for Africa also represented a significant blow to Western business interests. In 1992, 45 African nations established RASCOM (Regional African Satellite Communication Organization) so that Africans would have their own satellite and thus cut the exorbitant costs of communication on the continent:

> "This was a time when phone calls to and from Africa were the most expensive in the world because of the annual US$500 million fee pocketed by Europe for the use of its satellites like Intelsat for phone conversations, including those within the same country. African satellite only cost a one time payment of US$400 million and the continent no longer had to pay a US$500 million annual lease." (Pougala, 2011/4/20a)

In July 2007, the LAP acquired a 61 percent stake in RASCOM (STRATFOR, 2011/3/14). For 14 years the World Bank, IMF, and a host of Western nations had floated ideas about supporting African satellite communications, which resulted in no action. Libya instead stepped up and it alone paid $300 million U.S. for the satellite, with the African Development Bank adding another $50 million U.S., and the West African Development Bank a further $27 million U.S. (Pougala, 2011/4/20a). Thus, Africa obtained its first satellite on December 26, 2007. As Cameroonian Jean-Paul Pougala put it:

"Gaddafi's Libya cost the West, not just depriving it of US$500 million per year but the billions of dollars in debt and interest that the initial loan would generate for years to come and in an exponential manner, thereby helping maintain an occult system in order to plunder the continent." (Pougala, 2011/4/20a)

When the UN authorized intervention in Libya it imposed an asset freeze on both the LIA and the LAP, and without any explanation continued that freeze well past six months after NATO's bombing campaign ceased (Barigaba & Khisa, 2012/2/18; Lederer, 2012/3/12; Nebehay, 2012/2/16). The more than $30 billion U.S. frozen by the Obama administration belonged to the Libyan Central Bank. Those funds were earmarked as the Libyan contribution to three projects: the African Investment Bank, to be headquartered in Libya; the African Monetary Fund (AMF), to be headquartered in Yaoundé, which was to have been launched in 2011 as NATO began its war against Libya (Mimboé, 2010/12/16), and was to have a $42 billion U.S. capital fund; and the African Central Bank, to be based in Abuja, Nigeria, and which was planned to print an African currency (Pougala, 2011/4/20b; see also Africa Bulletin, 2010/12/15, Xinhua, 2010/1/31). With Algeria contributing $16 billion U.S. and Libya $10 billion U.S., together they would have thus been contributing 62 percent of the AMF's capital (Pougala, 2011/4/20d).

The AMF in particular represented a direct challenge to the IMF, which according to Pougala (2011/4/20b) had less than half as much capital for Africa, and which piled all sorts of conditionalities that forced African nations into privatization. "No surprise then," wrote Pougala, that in December 2010 "the Africans unanimously rejected attempts by Western countries to join the African Monetary Fund, saying it was open only to African nations" (Pougala, 2011/4/20b). According to a document published by the African Union:

"Many African experts support the idea of creating the AMF, on the grounds that programs supported by the IMF have not solved the balance of payments problems of the African countries in a lasting manner. In their view, these programs have tended to rely too much on 'adjustment' without providing the 'financial resources' needed to promote growth and reduce poverty." (AU, n.d., p. 1)

Despite regime change in Libya, the AU is still working on fulfilling plans for creating the AMF, planned to be launched soon as final arrangements have been completed and await signing by AU member states (Anuforo, 2012/3/1).

In addition to large investment plans that took Africa as a whole as their focus, Libya also invested heavily in bilateral relations, both with states and with kingdoms within them. "Entire hospitals and mosques" bear Muammar Gaddafi's name across the continent as a result of Libya's aid and investments (Malone, 2011/11/11).

Uganda in particular received a great deal of investment and aid while Gaddafi was in power, totalling at least $375 million U.S. by some estimates (Samora, 2011/4/12). Libya invested in Uganda's "agriculture, hotel, health, infrastructure, construction, food and finance sector" through the LAP, with the results being that Libya owned 49 percent of the National Housing and Construction Corporation, with additional shares worth $21.1 million U.S. in developing the housing projects at Lubowa housing estate along Entebbe Road and Naalya housing estate (Tripoli Post, 2012/1/2). Libya also had an interest in the Uganda Coffee Development Authority, following a 2007 joint venture agreement that involved the construction of an $11-million U.S. soluble coffee plant, thus adding value to Uganda's coffee exports (Tripoli Post, 2012/1/2). Libya also owned shares in Tropical Bank, House of Dawda, Uganda Pharmaceuticals, Uganda Telecom (owning a 51 percent share [Bariyo, 2012/3/7]) and Lake Victoria Hotel Entebbe (Tripoli Post, 2012/1/2). Other Libyan-owned companies in Uganda included Tamoil East Africa, which was in the process of extending Kenya's Mombasa-Eldoret pipeline to Uganda (Bariyo, 2012/3/7).

Beyond business ventures, Libya also provided extensive aid. Libya reportedly spent unspecified "millions of dollars" in renovating the palace of Toro King Oyo Nyimba at Fort Portal, and paid for the education of the young king at a prestigious school in London; in the Kingdom of Buganda, Libya provided financial support to Prince Kassim Nakibinge (Samora, 2011/4/12). In March 2008, Gaddafi travelled to Kampala to open the Gaddafi Mosque, the second largest mosque in Africa, able to accommodate 15,000, with a promise to finance its refurbishment and maintenance for ten years—unlikely to continue now (Samora, 2011/4/12). Also at the end of 2008, Libya's World Islamic Call Society (WICS) launched the Islamic University in Uganda,[16] which has already graduated over ten thousand students (USET, 2008/12/22). Generally, the WICS focused on Sub-Saharan Africa, educating would-be Imams, "who are given comprehensive scholarships to pursue undergraduate and graduate-level studies

---

16. See the University's website at <http://www.iuiu.ac.ug/>.

FIGURE 3.2 The Gaddafi Mosque in Kampala, Uganda. (Source: Uganda Picks, photographer unknown.)

in liberal arts and Islamic studies at its well-appointed campus in Tripoli" (USET, 2008/6/9).

In the case of Liberia, even with the pro-U.S. President Ellen-Johnson Sirleaf in office, Libya's relationship with the country flourished. Gaddafi and Johnson-Sirleaf visited each other several times and developed close ties. In 2009 according to U.S. reports, "a series of Libyan investments in Liberia valued at $45 million was announced on February 8" (which the U.S. speculated was behind Liberia's "seemingly unenthusiastic" acceptance of Libya as Chair of the AU, with as little sense as this makes other than as an expression of wishful thinking) (USET, 2009/2/11). One LAP-funded project in Liberia involved the establishment of a $15 million U.S. rubber processing plant, thus adding value to Liberia's exports. Libya also renovated dozens of schools affected by Liberia's civil war, provided hundreds of scholarships to Liberian students, and installed large power generators to bring electricity back to Monrovia (Samora, 2011/4/12). The major project funded in Liberia by the LAP is one that goes far toward guaranteeing food security, involving a "$30 million concession for large-scale commercial rice production…the first large scale domestic rice program in a country that imports over 55% of all its rice" (USEM, 2009/12/22). As the U.S. Embassy in Monrovia itself affirmed, after the U.S. ambassador there personally went to witness the first harvest in Lofa County, "improved rice production is key to Liberia's food security" (USEM, 2009/12/22). Dependence on previously imported rice, as the U.S. Embassy noted, subjected impoverished Liberians to drastic price increases in times of food crises as occurred in 2008. This resulted in dependence on foreign loans, and worse: "the scarcity of rice was blamed for the country's political unrest in 1979, which led to 25 years of instability" (USEM, 2009/12/22).

In Mali, LAICO's investments include the Laico L'Amitie and Laico El Farouk hotels in Bamako, along with a stake in the National Tobacco Company (SONATAM), and a 96 percent stake in the Banque Commerciale du Sahel, which Libya capitalized with $30 million U.S. Libya has also provided "technical assistance in the agricultural sector, helping combat locust plagues and providing food aid to northern Mali" (STRATFOR, 2011/3/14).

In support of Mauritania, Libya cancelled $100 million U.S. of Mauritanian debt and provided $50 million U.S. for the construction of a hospital and the University of Al-Fateh. Libya's ADA also provided 26 tons of food and tents for flood victims in 2009, and $1 million U.S. to fund the construction of schools in six regions of Mauritania in 2010. Going back to 1972, Libya has held a majority stake in Chinguitty Bank, as a shared investment with the Mauritanian government (STRATFOR, 2011/3/14).

In Niger, Libya donated 260 tons of food aid in 2008 through the Libyan Foundation for Aid and Development in Africa (ADA). In 2010 the ADA agreed to provide $100 million U.S. to capitalize a Nigerien development fund. Otherwise Libya also had extensive investments in Niger, including 51 percent ownership of the Société nigerienne des telecommunications (SONITEL) and SahelCom, both formerly state-owned telecoms. LAICO also invested in real estate and construction, focusing on an "administrative, commercial and residential complex in Niamey and other agricultural and land holdings." Moreover, Libya agreed in 2008 to build a $155-million U.S. trans-Saharan railway through Niger, though by 2011 work had yet to begin (STRATFOR, 2011/3/14).

In the Central African Republic, Libya constructed a luxury hotel in Bangui through the Laico Hotel Group. Libya also holds a 50 percent stake in the Compagnie centrafricaine de mines (COCAMINES) (STRATFOR, 2011/3/14).

In Chad the five-star Kempinski Libya Hotel in N'djamena and the Chari commercial bank are both owned by LAICO, and a stretch of villas were also constructed by Libya (Bruguière, 2011/11/22). The Libyan Foreign Investment Company-Chad (fully owned by LAICO), invested in a bottled water factory, a textiles business, the hotel mentioned above, and an administrative center in N'djamena. The Banque commerciale du Chari was equally co-owned by the governments of Chad and Libya, with Libya providing $12.5 million U.S. in seed capital to the bank (STRATFOR, 2011/3/14). Projects that remain incomplete, due to the overthrow of Gaddafi, are the construction of an Islamic centre on 50,000 hectares of land set aside by the government of Chad (Bruguière, 2011/11/22). There was also a $90-million telecommunications deal in place with Chad (Malone, 2011/11/11).

In Burkina Faso, Libya's LAICO wholly owns the Société pour l'investissement et commerce (SALIC), which has "an administrative, commercial and residential complex and a five-star hotel in Ouagadougou's new Ouaga 2000 district." Along with the state in Burkina Faso, Libya has equal co-ownership of the Banque commerciale du Burkina, one of five major commercial banks in the country. Burkina Faso's agrarian economy, with limited foreign investment apart from Libya's, was also dependent on Libyan oil supplies (STRATFOR, 2011/3/14).

In Gambia, Libya donated tractors and gave Gambian President Yahya Jammeh aid and huge herds of camels (Malone, 2011/11/11).

With respect to Guinea, Libya cancelled a debt of $24 million U.S. owed to it. Gaddafi also promised to supply Guinea with hydrocarbons, buses and tractors, and announced plans for the construction of a five-star hotel to be financed by Libya in the capital, Conakry. From 2012, Gaddafi had promised to make thirty scholarships available to Guinean students—a promise now unlikely to be respected. Libya was the first country to give financial and material aid to Guinea after the military junta led by Captain Moussa Dadis Camara took power on December 23, 2008, and Gaddafi was the first foreign leader to travel to Guinea in 2009 after the military took control following the death of President Lansana Konte (PANA, 2011/2/6).

In Zambia, LAP Green Networks owns a 75 percent stake in the telephone company, Zamtel, purchased for $257 million in June 2010 (Reuters, 2012/1/7b). As the NTC gained power, however, Zambia nationalized the

Libyan share claiming that it had been sold illegally, leading the NTC into one of its first disputes with an African state that had been a beneficiary of Libyan investment under Gaddafi. It is still not clear what if any compensation Zambia will pay to LAP Green Networks (Malakata, 2012/3/20; Reuters, 2012/1/31).

Zimbabwe has also been a major recipient of Libyan aid. Until 2003, Libya had provided up to $500 million U.S. in oil subsidies and loans. Libya's ADA also donated tractors and fuel to Zimbabwe in 2008. Libya also has a 14 percent stake (valued at $15 million U.S.) in CBZ Bank. LAICO has also invested in Rainbow Tourism Group, Zimbabwe's second-largest hotel company (STRATFOR, 2011/3/14).

In Tanzania, Libya's North Africa Investment Trading Company invested in the Bahari Beach Hotel, purchasing it under Tanzania's privatization arrangement. The Libyan company invested about $5.8 million U.S., and created 160 jobs created for Tanzanians, according to the Minister of State in the Prime Minister's Office (Investment and Empowerment), Dr Mary Nagu (Tarimo, 2012/2/4).

Finally, in North Africa, in Egypt alone, Libya had increased its investments to $10 billion U.S., with 236 Libyan companies operating in Egypt. In addition, Libya planned to construct a natural gas pipeline that would allow Egypt greater ease in exporting to Europe. Moreover, free trade and industrial zones between Egypt and Libya were planned. Also, a joint oil refinery was to be set up in West Alexandria with Libyan financing and it was to refine Libyan oil. The two countries also planned joint food security ventures in Sudan and Uganda, with plans for growing wheat, barley, and rice. Trade between Egypt and Libya was expected to reach around $2 billion U.S. per annum. Similarly outstanding was the fact that Libya had also invested up to $5 billion U.S. in Morocco alone (AEDI, 2008).

Another important fact to note about the Libyan relationship with Egypt in recent years is that as many as two million Egyptians went to Libya to find work, a country that had one-twelfth of the population of Egypt. Official sources put the number at between 330,000 and 1.5 million Egyptians working in Libya before the war, which accounted for annual remittances to Egypt between $19.5 and $33 million U.S. (IOM, 2011). Of those Egyptians, at least 28 percent were illiterate, and 85 percent were of rural origins (IOM, 2011). Where U.S. media like to speak of people who "vote with their feet," it is interesting that this fact would not have led them to conclude that a great many people had voted their approval for Libya under Gaddafi.

The Security Dimension of Libyan Pan-Africanism

Security, and constituent elements such as territorial integrity, self-deter-mination, food and fuel security, and non-aggression between neighbours and within states, was vitally important to the African Union and its found-ing principles. The AU as a body was itself instituted because "many African countries recognized the necessity of combating the adverse consequences of globalization and the African continent's continued marginalization in international affairs" (Adi & Sherwood, 2003, fn. 1, p. xi). At the founding summit of the AU in Sirte, Gaddafi likewise warned Africa to "beware of recolonisation which might come in different forms" (Moonga, 2001, p. 10). Tragic it was then that in the war against Libya the AU provided very little in the way of a shield and did not adhere to its own principles. Moreover, contrary to the racial myths of big, black, African mercenary bogeymen flooding into Libya to fight for Gaddafi, the fact is that despite all the aid and investment, and years of supporting other struggles, Gaddafi and his government saw no such reciprocity. How all of this unfolded would have confirmed for some U.S. analysts that, in the end, there was little to fear from a revitalized AU. Nonetheless, the U.S. had to remain watchful regarding the chances of an alternative power bloc forming that could pro-vide even friction or any impediment that would raise the costs of U.S. penetration of the continent. Nor could the U.S., France, and the UK afford to see allies that they had cultivated, if not installed in power, being slowly pulled from their orbits by Libya, China, and other powers.

Since Africa had suffered direct colonial rule, and then intervention in the form of mercenaries and foreign-funded guerrilla armies, it is not surprising that the AU should have developed some very robust policies, such as the Common African Defence and Security Policy (CADSP). This policy stipulated that "any attack against an African country is considered as an attack against the Continent as a whole," which nearly replicated NATO's own Article 5 (AU, 2004a, p. 4; Touray, 2005, p. 643). The AU thus specified that, "each African country's defence is inextricably linked to that of other African countries, as well as that of other regions and, by the same token, that of the African continent as a whole" (AU, 2004b, p. 3). The AU would itself have the right "to intervene in any member state in the event of war crimes, genocide and crime against humanity to restore peace and stability" (Touray, 2005, p. 643).

Common defence was an integral element of pan-Africanist ideals for many decades. That Gaddafi pushed so hard for this led some to recognize that "fundamentally, it appears that of all the African leaders, Gaddafi, has taken up the Pan-African mantle of Nkrumah" (Biney, 2008, p. 148). Gaddafi sought to have the AU develop a single African army and greater powers of intervention by Africans to maintain peace within African states. Gaddafi seemed to achieve some progress in this regard, in that AU leaders approved "Nkrumah's brainchild" in instituting an African Standby Force by 2010. This resembled Nkrumah's call in 1960 for an African High Command and many similar calls that since then have been made and rejected or neglected. At the Fifth Summit of the AU held in Libya in July 2005, Gaddafi called for a system to be put in place that would be responsible for the defence of the entire continent, calling also for a single Minister of Defence to implement the AU's joint security and defence charter as stated in Article 3 of the AU's Constitutive Assembly. Gaddafi then criticized the former OAU for achieving little during its almost forty years of existence and he cited Nkrumah's address at the founding of the OAU in 1963, noting that Nkrumah had predicted that artificial borders would create conflicts. He also criticized those who thought that a "United States of Africa" was being rushed: "We have been moving gradually for 100 years" (Biney, 2008, p. 149).

At the AU Summit in Libya in 2009, Gaddafi elaborated on the common defence theme further, and the U.S. was paying attention. According to the U.S. Embassy, Gaddafi described two types of conflicts that should be the concern of the AU. One was "state-to-state belligerence and internal conflicts such as coups and rebellions," which Gaddafi blamed on "European colonial powers for drawing arbitrary lines across the continent." The formation of a union should help to diminish this. The other type of conflict consisted of internal conflicts, a subject on which the U.S. characterized Gaddafi as being "coy." Gaddafi maintained that, "from a legal standpoint, international bodies and third-party states had no right to interfere in the internal problems of another state." The role of the AU should instead be "to mediate between opposing factions in an effort to bring peace. However, if internal conflict were to be intensified by exogenous forces (he provided the example of oil-thirsty foreign governments in Sudan), then the AU had a duty to intervene in a protective capacity." Had Gaddafi's vision been fulfilled, NATO's war against Libya would either have been forestalled or opposed by an entire continent, militarily. Jean Ping, Chairperson of the AU Peace and Security Commission, "three times thanked Libya for its work to bring Peace and Security issues to the fore" (USET, 2009/9/8).

The U.S. was eager to see Gaddafi fail in attaining his vision of a supranational African Authority and maintained a close watch on the process of establishing such an Authority (USET, 2009/4/9). In one cable, the U.S. Ambassador in Tripoli scoffed at reports of Gaddafi making progress in convincing African delegates of the need for such an authority, and while barely aware that such an agreement had even been secured, he quickly derided the ability of AU member states to bring it into being if it had been (USET, 2009/7/15). In another cable, however, written on the very same day, but this time by the U.S. Ambassador to Ethiopia who was also in attendance at the AU Summit in Libya, rather different comments were made. The AU delegates had indeed agreed to replace the AU Commission with the AU Authority, and had not rejected Gaddafi's call for the establishment of an African Defence Council under that Authority (USEAA, 2009/7/15). What is most telling of all here is the repeatedly implied desire of U.S. diplomats to see Gaddafi fail. U.S. diplomats tried to convince themselves that Gaddafi would indeed fail, stating that the Libyan government "lacks the human and institutional capacity to successfully manage a concerted effort to unify Africa, an effort that most other African leaders oppose in any event" (USET, 2009/2/11)—momentarily downplaying the success of Libya's "dinar diplomacy" in ultimately getting things done.

U.S. diplomats seemed confused (see USET, 2009/2/11). On the one hand, they criticized the power and influence of Libya's "heavy-handed (and deep-pocketed) tactics." On the other hand, all they saw at times seemed to be "rhetoric and grand gestures" and policies that were "short on deliverables and implementation," even contrary to evidence (USET, 2009/2/11). U.S. diplomats were trying to get some fix on Libya's power but found themselves caught in the hinges of their own crudely crafted analyses. Unfortunately, that could have escalated anxiety in Washington.

However, there was another prospect for failure that U.S. diplomats found interesting: an internal source of opposition to Libya's further integration with the African continent. This would eventually bear fruit for the U.S. Their embassy reported this to Washington:

"More vexing for ordinary Libyans is that al-Qadhafi's ambitious Africa policy—a common army, a common currency, and a common passport—seems to represent another foreign policy adventure that is long on spectacle and short on feasibility, but which is *likely to divert more financial resources away from improving their lot.* The fact that al-Qadhafi's election [as AU Chairman] coincides with slumping oil prices and an attendant re-calibration of the national budget (to include ratcheting back popular infrastructure development initiatives) makes *the tension between domestic and foreign policy equities* an even bigger problem for the regime." (USET, 2009/2/11, emphasis added)

Again, U.S. diplomats saw failure looming as "internal political and economic reforms" (admitting, at least, that there were reforms), rendered the Libyan government "ill-equipped to actively promote and implement a unified African government" (USET, 2009/2/11). Elaborating further, they wrote that Gaddafi's goals for a united Africa as listed above "are at odds with some of Libya's domestic interests" and could "complicate relations with EU member states." Any move toward the creation of a single African currency, the Afro (as Gaddafi named it), "would saddle the Libyan economy with debts and inflationary pressures of countries bereft of the mineral wealth and massive foreign trade surpluses Libya enjoys," and this would be "unpopular and impractical." A common passport and customs zone would also pose "political and diplomatic challenges." Finally, and this spoke to long-festering identity issues that would come to the fore during the 2011 war, "despite al-Qadhafi's fascination with Africa, the majority of Libyans self-identify as Arabs" (USET, 2009/2/11).

The creation of a single passport, as proposed by Gaddafi, also represented a threat to both Libyans seeking easier access to Europe, and to European states trying to block the flow of African immigrants. As the U.S. Embassy noted: "Europeans, sensitive to the fact that tens of thousands of illegal migrants who make landfall in Europe each year depart from Libyan shores, will bristle at the potential for still greater numbers of sub-Saharan Africans to travel more easily to jumping-off points along Libya's littoral" (USET, 2009/2/11).

Increased African security and cooperation seemed to elevate U.S. and European perceptions of their own increased insecurity. Looking for avenues that would either make Gaddafi stumble and fail in achieving greater African cooperation, or for means of cajoling Gaddafi into suddenly becoming a useful partner for the U.S., marked the multitude of cables from U.S. diplomats. What threw a wrench into some of their plans and hopes was something somewhat smaller than the AU, which Libya founded and led: the Community of Sahel-Saharan States (CEN-SAD).

CEN-SAD: A Victory for Libya

The Community of Sahel-Saharan States was in many ways the vanguard in the formation of the African Union. It was established on February 4, 1998, in Tripoli, during a gathering organized by Muammar Gaddafi that brought together the heads of state of Mali, Chad, Niger, Sudan, and a representative of the President of Burkina Faso. The primary objectives of the organization were regional development, free trade and free movement of persons among member states, enhanced telecommunications, and a common security policy. CEN-SAD was headquartered in Tripoli. The Central African Republic and Eritrea joined CEN-SAD during the First Summit of the organization held in Sirte in April 1999. Senegal, Djibouti and Gambia joined during the N'djamena Summit in February 2000. Also in 2000, CEN-SAD became a regional economic community and attained observer status at the UN General Assembly. By 2005, the organization had grown to include 23 member states, over half as many members as the AU. In 1999, Libya funded and launched the Sahel-Saharan Bank for Investment and Commerce (BSIC) with 250 million Euros to support regional development initiatives and it also set up the Fund for Assistance and Support to Women, Children and Youths. By 2006, the CEN-SAD General Secretariat was being funded by a budget of $7.6 million U.S. with another $1.8 million U.S. devoted to the CEN-SAD Economic, Social and Cultural Council. For CEN-SAD member states, Libya funded an additional $9.3 million for food security programs administered by the UN's Food and Agricultural Organization. Muammar Gaddafi underscored that CEN-SAD "was behind the establishment of the African Union, is its pyramidal base, cornerstone and driving force" (CEN-SAD, n.d; 2003a, Art. 17; 2006a, Art. 14; 2006b, Art. 28).

CEN-SAD, under Gaddafi's leadership, opposed "foreign interference in African judicial problems" and condemned "uncontrollable foreign forces" that sought any pretext for creating a "lasting establishment in our continent and our countries" (CEN-SAD, 2006, Arts. 18, 20). The organization also sought to develop its own mechanisms for common security and conflict prevention (CEN-SAD, 2003a, Art. 26). The guiding principles can be found in the Niamey Declaration of March 15, 2003 (CEN-SAD, 2003b). The failure to attain greater leadership within the AU, which the U.S. Embassy apparently wished for and relished whenever Gaddafi faced any setback, was all made irrelevant by the unquestioned dominance of Libya in CEN-SAD. Indeed, in a January 26, 2009 consultative meeting of

CEN-SAD ministers it was with the unanimous support of all present that Libya was backed for the chairmanship of the AU. U.S. diplomats had to reluctantly suspend their disbelief (USET, 2009/1/29).

Even more troubling for the U.S. was CEN-SAD's position on AFRICOM. On November 21, 2007, CEN-SAD issued a statement from its Tripoli headquarters "categorically rejecting" AFRICOM and any foreign military presence in any CEN-SAD member state, which backed a similar statement made by the then South African Minister of Defence. The U.S. took note of the fact that CEN-SAD's membership covered "roughly half of Africa's territory and population." A U.S. diplomat remarked that this opposition to AFRICOM "echoes" long-standing Libyan objections and Gaddafi's "anti-foreign rhetoric." About CEN-SAD itself, the U.S. saw it as a "Libyan-led political coordination mechanism operating in parallel to the African Union," deliberately choosing to misrepresent it in diplomatic cables as a "Libyan organization" (USET, 2007/11/27).

The ascendance the U.S. feared Libya would gain in the AU was an ascendance it had already achieved with CEN-SAD. The "sour grapes" attitude of U.S. diplomats is again quite telling. It is also strikingly different from the few statements written by those diplomats on Libya's so-called "human rights record," which hardly occasioned any semblance of emotion or personal investment by the U.S. diplomats who wrote the cables.

By the middle of 2012, CEN-SAD did not even own its own domain name, cen-sad.org having gone up for public acquisition. Some international organizations, such as the AU and UNECA, have maintained bits and pieces of the CEN-SAD website which has otherwise vanished from the Web. Any discussion of the role of CEN-SAD, post-Gaddafi, has also vanished. U.S. diplomats now have something to cheer.

Against Africans: Roots of Racist Revolt within Libya

Almost from the date of the signing of the Sirte Declaration in 1999, Libya became the scene of a divide between the leadership and the public, between ideals and policies, between commitments and violations, between invitation and rejection, and broadly between Pan-Africanism and Libyan anti-black racism. Ugly acts of discrimination, persecution, and even outright butchery against migrant African workers occurred well before 2011. The riots of 2000 which were especially intense in Zawiya, Tripoli, and Benghazi, are a case in point.

Fractures were present within the state, signs of impending divisions that in 2011 would become outright defections, and were coupled with blundering on Gaddafi's part as he tried to scare Europe into providing Libya with payment for effectively acting as its border patrol agent. It was the kind of mess that invites all sorts of hasty and lopsided interpretations, some less sober than others. Few would wish to make the careless assertion that "Gaddafi was a racist," yet without a doubt more could have been done to better educate Libyans against racism and xenophobia, and to enforce protection of migrant workers and asylum-seekers. It seemed as if Muammar Gaddafi had become solely an internationalist, a version of the "foreign policy president," who overstretched himself beyond Libya and beyond what ordinary Arab Libyans would tolerate as they saw their country rapidly realigned with a world few of them understood or respected. The important point is that the developments around 2000 would be significant for the unfolding of the war in Libya in 2011, and for what came after Gaddafi was overthrown. As discussed at the end of chapter 4, post-Gaddafi Libya was a reign of terror for black Libyans and black African migrant workers like they had never seen before (and they had seen plenty in Libya before). The events of 2000 would also tell us something about Western "humanitarianism" and the "responsibility to protect." The overwhelming European silence in 2000 was particularly striking.

In an article that *The Economist* titled "Pogrom" provided the following account of events in Libya in September 2000. It reads like a first draft of events that would occur in 2011.

"Planeloads of bodies, dead and alive, flew back to West Africa from Tripoli this week….Emeka Nwanko, a 26-year-old Nigerian welder, was one of hundreds of thousands of black victims of the Libyan mob. He fled as gangs trashed his workshop. His friend was blinded, as Libyan gangs wielding machetes roamed the African townships. Bodies were hacked and dumped on motorways. A Chadian diplomat was lynched and Niger's embassy put to the torch….Some of Libya's indigenous 1m [million] black citizens were mistaken for migrants, and dragged from taxis. In parts of Benghazi, blacks were barred from public transport and hospitals. Pitched battles erupted in Zawiya, a town near Tripoli that is ringed with migrant shantytowns. Diplomats said that at least 150 people were killed, 16 of them Libyans….Anti-black violence had been simmering for months, fired by an economic crisis. Colonel Qaddafi heads Africa's richest state in terms of income per person. This year oil will earn him $11 billion. But Libyans, feeding their families on monthly salaries of $170, see the money squandered on foreign adventures, the latest of which is the colonel's pan-Africa policy. As billions flowed out in aid, and visa-less migrants flowed in, Libyans feared they were being turned into a minority in their own land. Church attendance soared in this Muslim state....A history of racism fanned the flames. Libyans were slave-trading until the 1930s and, under Italian colonial rule, they saw themselves as Mediterranean, calling Africans *chocalatinos*. Black-bashing has become a popular afternoon sport for Libya's unemployed youths. The rumour that a Nigerian had raped a Libyan girl in Zawiya was enough to spark a spree of ethnic cleansing....In their rampage on migrant workers, the Libyan mob spared Arabs, including the 750,000 Egyptians." (*The Economist*, 2000/10/12)

"Ironically," as Gaddafi was "spearheading the vision of a United States of Africa for the sake of the African people, Libya itself was the scene of violent xenophobic attacks in September 2000 by Libyans against African migrant workers" (Solomon & Swart, 2005, p. 481). The targets were all black, nationals from Sudan, Nigeria, Chad, the Gambia, Burkina Faso, and Ghana. As noted above, at the time the Libyan economy had to deal with the presence of 1.5 million foreign workers, while 200,000 Libyans were unemployed (Solomon & Swart, 2005, p. 481). Gaddafi struck many of his compatriots as adding fuel to the economic fire when, "in an effort to confirm his strong policies on Africa," he "dropped visa restrictions on Africans, many of whom were working illegally in the country," and as analysts pointed out:

> "Few of their leader's policies irritate Libyans more than Gaddafi's fervent 'Africanization' of Libya; Tripolitans curse the opening of the borders, which has turned them into a minority in their own capital. This serves as yet another manifestation of the almost 'one-man show' that is Libyan foreign policy, in which it is patently clear that very little if any consultation takes places between the Colonel and his public on foreign affairs, where decisions are almost certainly made by decree, as opposed to participative democracy." (Solomon & Swart, 2005, pp. 481-482)

Writing with caustic sarcasm, one journalist editorialized about what this meant in terms of popular support in Libya for Pan-Africanism: "Libyans armed with machetes showed their support by launching pogroms on black African migrants, and sending hundreds of thousands fleeing from the oil state" (Pelham, 2002, p. 19). Other reports also noted, "Libyans resent the money the immigrants make...and perceive these outsiders as beneficiaries of Gaddafi's support for African union," with hostilities erupting just as Gaddafi had been touring the continent to promote the formation of a United States of Africa (Bald, 2000).

Libya under Gaddafi may have been an excellent financial patron of Pan-Africanism, with imaginative political vision and energetic determination by Gaddafi to establish and develop various new institutions at the regional and continental level, but as long as such ugliness simmered at home Libya could not for long manage any leading role in the African Union. Until domestic racism had been addressed, a problem that can take generations to be resolved, Libyan Pan-Africanism would have always been powered by a battery with a short lifespan. From that point of view, the rise to leadership of the African Union of states such as South Africa, with majority black populations and histories of fighting against white racist rule, may place the AU in firmer hands—perhaps less able or willing to achieve great feats in a flash, but better able to sustain their engagement and commitment for the long-term.

On another front, the events of 2000 were also significant as a dry run for what exploded in 2011. Violence that scapegoats Africans and blames them for all of the most important local problems is clearly not new in Libya, and there is little justification for treating the post-February 2011 violence as some sort of aberration. Those who knew Libya well should have predicted it. Instead what passed as "expertise" in our mainstream and allegedly alternative media, whether CNN or Democracy Now! respectively, were loving appraisals of the events of 2011 as a cry for democracy, another romantic tale of "the people" against "the dictator," supposedly triggered by the arrest of a human rights lawyer. Absent from the media experts' vocabulary were concepts such as power, hegemony, dominance, nationalism, and racism. These were the sources of the gross atrocities perpetrated by Libya's "fighters for democracy," so adored by white liberal imperialists and Euro-American establishment leftists alike, who colluded with racism without as much as a blink. Let's go back then to 2000—it is not so far back in time that it can justify being forgotten as easily as it has been.

In Libya in 2000, according to Boukari Houda, the deputy information secretary, there were 1.4 million black Libyans out of a total population of 5.4 million—with an additional 2.5 million African immigrants living in Libya (*New African*, 2000, p. 12). "It was not easy, because being a black man [in Libya], you can't live there simply," said George Auther, 26, who returned to Ghana in October 2000 after spending two years in Libya as a builder's apprentice. "You can't move around freely," he explained, "the problem is, the Libyans don't like blacks" (Simmons, 2000/12/16). Kwame

Amponsah, 22, another Ghanaian who fled Libya that year felt that Gaddafi had "a good idea, but his people don't like blacks, and they don't think they are Africans because of their skin color" (Simmons, 2000/12/16). Seed Bafo, 23, who worked as a taxi driver in Libya before fleeing to his native Ghana in November 2000, recounted what life was like: "Even small boys would throw stones at us. They would cover their noses when we walked by. They called us monkeys." Bafo, who also worked as a builder's apprentice—many worked in construction—said that once on a bus he was beaten up by youths and thrown off (Simmons, 2000/12/16). Ahmad, a Sudanese asylum seeker in Italy, described conditions he experienced in Libya from 1992-2003: "I can't count the number of times I was beaten up on the street by Libyans....The people in cars try to run you down. There are always insults on the street. You live in fear. I just concentrated on getting home safely from work every day." This is just brief testimony among masses in what reads like an absolute horror story of victimization by both ordinary Libyans and the police (HRW, 2006, p. 1).

Hostility towards black migrant workers in Libya endured. In 2009 *The New York Times* reported, "many people in Tripoli said they resented the presence of so many illegal workers." The paper quoted young Libyans: "We don't like them," said Moustafa Saleh, 28, "who is unemployed, echoing a popular sentiment," and added, "they smuggle themselves through the desert, and the way they deal with us is not good." Paul Oknonghou, 28, a Nigerian, told the *Times*: "They call us animals and slaves" (Slackman, 2009/3/22).

The Libyan government itself helped to ignite the riots by ordering a crackdown against "illegal immigrants" in September 2000,[17] which for too many Libyans was interpreted as a green light to openly persecute black people. Gaddafi was clearly caught within the hinges of his own duality—a no borders Pan-Africanist, then confronted with numerous Africans who could not make a living in their home countries and saw Libya either as a destination in itself or as a bridge to Europe. Gaddafi had articulated a welcoming policy at the September 1999 summit of the OAU, at which the Sirte Declaration was signed. Declaring his Pan-Africanism, Gaddafi, "expressed Libya's intention to welcome immigrants of African

---

17. There is some dispute about what the actual catalyst was for the start of the riots, many stories blaming one seemingly trivial event or another. Not trivial are the disputes over the numbers of Africans murdered, which can range from around 50 to several hundred or more.

origin, while continuing such a policy for Arab immigrants. Africans with passports could freely enter Libya, he said, and could stay without visas for three months with easier access to residency and work permits than other foreigners" (HRW, 2006, p. 14). Libya at the time also depended heavily on foreign workers for its economic growth, particularly in agriculture and construction.

Libya was also caught within the hinges of an expanding and contracting oil market as well as international sanctions, which played a role in creating the material conditions for some Libyans' discontent with African migrants. A report published by the United Nations Development Program explained this situation in some detail:

"It is also important to note that Libya had pursued an open-door policy towards migrants for several decades. During the 1970s and 1980s, the economic boom that followed the discovery of oil attracted many migrants from neighbouring countries like Sudan. In the 1990s, when the air and arms embargo imposed on Libya by the UN Security Council isolated the country more than ever from the West, Gaddafi opened Libya to the rest of Africa. Frustrated by the so-called uncooperativeness of Arab states, and in a radical shift in foreign policy, he recast himself as an African leader inviting Sub-Saharan Africans to seek employment in the country in the spirit of PanAfrican solidarity. Previously the destination point for mostly North African migrants, a major surge took place in trans-Saharan migration to Libya. The country became a major destination country with some one million migrants entering its borders during that decade. Migrants filled up positions in the informal and labour-intensive construction sectors doing menial jobs that citizens did not want to perform. The welcome mat extended to African migrants was already wearing thin by the mid-1990s when the Libyan economy had shrunk, partly due to sanctions, and inflation levels were extraordinarily high. Unemployment rates for citizens reached as high as 30 percent." (Crush & Ramachandran, 2009, p. 38)

Using the removal of sanctions as an incentive, the European Union exerted some pressure on Libya to cooperate with it in intercepting African migrants before they reached EU states. More than mere coincidence, on the very same day (October 11, 2004) that the EU lifted economic sanctions and the arms embargo imposed on Libya since 1992, "the Council of the European Union agreed to embark on a policy of engagement with Libya on migration matters, and decided to send a technical mission there 'to examine arrangements for combating illegal migration'" (HRW, 2006, pps. 93-94).

It is also the case that Libya tried to seek more productive, socially just means of tackling the flow of illegal immigration, a point acknowledged by Human Rights Watch: "the Libyan government has focused on tackling the root causes of forced displacement and economic migration." Hadi Khamis, the head of Libya's deportation camps, said: "We want cooperation with the EU to help development in the countries of origin." The General People's Congress in 2004 called for an AU-EU joint summit, to be hosted by Libya, with the objective of providing means for a "settled and dignified life" in migrants' home countries—but by 2006 such a summit had yet to take place. On its own, Libya committed itself to spending up to $4 billion U.S. over ten years on development in the countries that produced the most migrants, as well as providing humanitarian aid, such as when in October 2004 Libya sent eight truckloads of aid to refugee camps in Chad, added to aid with food programs in Burkina Faso, Niger, Mali, and Sudan (HRW, 2006, p. 99).

There was also no shortage of official resentment in Libya about becoming Europe's coastguard, which suggests that it did so in part due to the pressure of wanting sanctions long in place to be removed as quickly as possible, as noted above. The resentment also involved the large drain on resources that the EU expected Libya to undertake in order to control migration, with Italian contributions offered to Libya representing a small fraction of the costs involved. Libyan officials told Human Rights Watch in 2005 that the EU offered "only €9 million to stop illegal immigration, which they considered laughably small compared to the scale of the problem" (HRW, 2006, pps. 98-99).

This resentment appears to be what was behind the infamous remarks made by Gaddafi in August and again in November of 2010. It appears to be a clumsy and counterproductive attempt to use what Gaddafi perceived as Europeans' racial hysteria against them, by using terms they would understand, in order to get Europe to pay its share of the costs of policing the sea lanes leading to European shores. Gaddafi thereby gave a whole new meaning to "blackmail" when he declared in Rome: "Tomorrow Europe might no longer be European and even black as there are millions who want to come in. We don't know if Europe will remain an advanced and united continent or if it will be destroyed, as happened with the barbarian invasions" (Squires, 2010/8/31). Others reported Gaddafi as also saying that Europe "could turn into Africa," and asking, "what will be the reaction of the white and Christian Europeans faced with this influx of starving and ignorant Africans?" (BBC, 2010/8/31). Years before making these cringe-worthy remarks, Gaddafi had "sent the EU a list of military equipment it needed to police its borders against illegal immigrants," and the total cost of the equipment was "much more than the €5 billion" Gaddafi asked for in Rome, according to sources within the European Union Commission (Camilleri, 2010/9/1). Not having succeeded in Rome, Gaddafi appeared to show even poorer judgment by repeating his remarks in November 2010 during an AU-EU Summit in Tripoli. There he said, "we should stop this illegal immigration. If we don't, Europe will become black, it will be overcome by people with different religions, it will change….North Africa is the link and Europe is the destination….We are the gate and you should listen to us if you want to preserve Europe" (Micallef, 2010/11/30).

Apparently trying to terrify Europeans with the prospects of hordes of African zombies was not entirely off the mark: Italian political parties did after all complain about Gaddafi's remarks which they condemned as black-mail (Squires, 2010/8/31), meaning that there really was such a fright and Gaddafi's choice of words really did make an impact. Their reactions would thus confirm what Gaddafi suspected. Unfortunately for Gaddafi, the European desire to hang on to €5 billion was stronger than their fear. Also unfortunate for Gaddafi is the possibility that many African leaders could have interpreted his comments as showing the true face behind the man with all the cash and talk who steals the limelight, or they could have seen his effort as a poor tactic that reinforced pernicious racial stereotypes.

It is remarkable that at the time the Western press, and especially European political leaders' reactions, appeared to be muted with none calling the remarks "racist." For example, an editorial in the *Times of Malta* (2010/12/9) simply referred to Gaddafi employing "colourful language," and that he even used that language in November in front of "many of the leaders of the 'black' countries of origin from which many illegal immigrants arrive." Western diplomats in Libya saw the comments as an example of Libyan use of "soft power," designed to give Gaddafi "leverage in keeping African and European leaders listening and their doors open," Europe would fear that Libya would act as an usher for migrants wishing to travel there, and impoverished African nations worried about the return of maybe hundreds of thousands of their nationals as a weight on their fragile economies (Slackman, 2009/3/22).

Given the extent to which Western commentary about the Libyan human rights record became shrill when regime change was in the offing and "responsibility to protect" became the chorus line for foreign military

intervention, it is even more noteworthy that an apparent European consensus existed in maintaining a convenient racial blind spot when matters
turned to the treatment of African migrants in Libya by the police and
immigration authorities, which by all accounts was awful even before
2011. For example, when in June 2010 Libya shut down the office of the
UN High Commission for Refugees in Tripoli (BBC, 2010/6/8), the EU's
response was "muted," saying it was "regrettable but understandable." The
EU's ambassador to Libya, Adrianus Koetsenruijter, simply commented
that, "there's a certain fear in the country that with the presence of the
UNHCR, more refugees are being attracted to Libya…thereby causing a
bigger problem in the country" (Jawad, 2010/6/17). Indeed, just days after
Libya shut down the UNHCR office, the EU signed a $60 million U.S. deal
with Libya that would partly finance tighter border controls. The "mood
among European diplomats," the BBC noted, was a "far cry" from the
days "when they sniped at Libya…for its failure to adopt Western-styled
democracy and human rights values" (Jawad, 2010/6/17). This too was a
preview of Western "humanitarian" concerns in 2011, which almost always
discounted black African migrant workers and refugees from being
humans worthy of "human rights" protections. This was despite a slew of
damning reports from both the UN Committee for the Elimination of
Racial Discrimination, and groups such as Human Rights Watch (see for
example: CERD, 1997/4/23, 1998/3/24, 1998/3/30, 2003/6/18, 2004/3/12;
HRW, 2006).

Nor was Libya singled out as a violator of the rights of African migrants.
Italy, as "the country most affected by migration from Libya," was found
to have "most egregiously flouted international laws intended to protect
migrants, asylum seekers and refugees." The Italian government went as
far as denying Human Rights Watch access to the main detention centre
for people coming from Libya, on the island of Lampedusa, where eyewit-
nesses had reported "unhygienic facilities, overcrowding and physical abuse
by guards against detainees" (HRW, 2006, p. 5). Once again, where Africans
were concerned, the notion of "protection" was entirely dismissed, then,
as it would be again in 2011, which is not to let the Libyan government off
its own hook. This is truly astonishing, as one could easily make the argument that both black Libyans and African migrant workers have suffered
human rights violations over the past decade to a degree and of a nature
experienced by no other persons or group of persons in Libya.

The attacks on Africans in Libya in 2000 also demonstrated splits in
the Libyan government that it might otherwise have kept secret so as not

to expose its vulnerabilities. It was reported in the Nigerian press that, "gangs of Libyan youth were allowed free rein to attack settlements populated by black Africans, both in large cities like Tripoli and Benghazi and outlying villages," and that "Libyan police either participated in these attacks or looked the other way" (Bald, 2000). There is no evidence, however, that Gaddafi sanctioned the indiscriminate violence or that he ordered security forces to turn a blind eye to the commission of atrocities. Indeed, in apologizing for the violence against Ghanaians in a publicly broadcast radio address to Jerry Rawlings, then President of Ghana, Gaddafi claimed that "hidden hostile hands" were behind the widespread attacks—furthermore, Gaddafi fired two of his ministers, including the Justice Minister (*New African*, 2000, p. 12; ICFTU, 2000/10/12). Rather than implying a foreign conspiracy, the way some readers interpreted it (Johnson, 2000/10/28), Gaddafi specifically said in his radio address that internal enemies were trying to thwart his plans for Libya's closer integration with the African continent (*New African*, 2000, p. 12). Gaddafi had the kind of intimate knowledge of his fellow Libyans that comes with ruling for 42 years.

The race riots of 2000 show further evidence of a split within the regime, with some of the voices in government that denounced the presence of Africans later becoming the same voices we would hear from within the NTC in 2011. Gaddafi attempted to publicly "distance himself from the ethnic attacks," and he "blamed the violence on enemies of African unity determined to scuttle his project" of creating a United Sates of Africa (Johnson, 2000/10/28). In interviews, Africans fleeing from the attacks said that, "they were carried out by gangs of youths with the complicity if not direct involvement of state forces" (Johnson, 2000/10/28), which suggests that at least a significant segment within the state structure had decided to permit the spiraling violence. One example of elements within the regime backing the violence could be found in the comments made by the Chargé d'Affaires at the Libyan Embassy in Abuja, Nigeria. The Nigerian press reported him to have said, "good riddance to bad rubbish," that more Africans hiding in Libya would be "fished out," and that Nigerians were to blame for rising crime: "some of them who can't get a job, get involved in drug peddling, prostitution and armed robbery, which our society does not like" (Johnson, 2000/10/28). Higher up in the Libyan government, serving as the Secretary of the General People's Committee of Libya (GPCO) for Economy, Trade, and Investment, one Ali Abd-al-Aziz al-Isawi stated this about the African presence: "it is a burden. They are a burden on health care, they spread disease, crime. They are illegal" (Slackman, 2009/3/22). Re-enter Ali Abd-al-Aziz al-Isawi in 2011: he defected from his diplomatic post in India and joined the NTC as its third-ranked member[18] responsible for foreign affairs and international liaison (until he was booted when the NTC turned on him and tried to blame him for the murder of another high-level defector, General Younes). As a regime defector, in his new role in the NTC, al-Isawi promptly turned to denigrating and scapegoating migrant black Africans as "mercenaries" who were killing Libyans: "They [the mercenaries] are from Africa, and speak French and other languages....People say they are black Africans and they don't speak Arabic. They are doing terrible things, going to houses and killing women and children" (Smith, 2011/2/22).

Those who have studied nationalism will know that both the instrumental objectification of otherness and the primordialism of ethnic belonging can be powerful strategies and resources used by ethnic elites in mobilizing supporters. That within the ranks of opponents to Gaddafi there was this agenda of scraping off the stain of "Black Africa" seems convincing given what happened in 2000, 2011, and the convergence of local interests with the U.S. in limiting if not eliminating Libya's role as a leader in Africa.

Post-Gaddafi: Closing Libya's Door on Africa

The newly implanted NTC, having claimed office as NATO completed its bombing campaign against Libya, made its stance on African migrants in Libya and Libya's position on the continent very clear. To sum up, the new regime would reinforce the worst and undo the best of the past.

NTC Chairman Mustafa Abdul Jalil claimed that, as the former Justice Minister under Gaddafi, he had witnessed first-hand that "40 per cent of criminals [in Libya] are Africans, who invade Libya though its southern borders, passing through it, greedily wishing to live in Europe." As Amnesty International commented, "such claims were especially irresponsible in the climate of insecurity and fear of attack by alGaddafi forces that existed among the population in opposition-held areas, fed existing

18. No longer listed as a ranking member of the NTC, al-Isawi's membership and position can be seen on this archived page of the NTC website from March 10, 2011: <http://web.archive.org/web/20110310094316/http://ntclibya.org/english/council-members/>.

racism and xenophobia in Libya and signalled that abuses against foreign nationals would be tolerated by the NTC" (AI, 2011, p. 83). Not to let matters rest there, Jalil went even further, promising to "close the borders in front of these Africans" (AI, 2011, p. 89).

Libya under the NTC would therefore continue to mete out harsh treatment to African refugees, asylum-seekers, and migrant workers, who "will continue to suffer discrimination and abuse in Libya, and be perceived as unwelcome guests" (AI, 2011, p. 89). In another development that Amnesty International called "worrying," Italy signed a memorandum of understanding with the NTC on June 17, 2011, months before Gaddafi was deposed, just to show what weighed on the minds of Italian leaders, besides oil. Both Italy and Libya under the NTC reconfirmed their commitment to joint management of "the migration phenomenon" through the implementation of existing co-operation agreements on "illegal migration." As Amnesty and others documented over many years the "implementation of these very same agreements resulted in grave human rights violations, including the forcible removal through 'push-back' operations conducted at sea, of foreign nationals to Libya, where they faced arrest, torture and detention in appalling conditions" (AI, 2011, p. 89). Readers are invited to please take note: this agreement was signed at the height of a war billed as a humanitarian intervention whose sole mission and mandate was to "protect civilians."

As if walking in a groove left by Gaddafi in Rome, as late as May 12, 2012 the appointed Libyan Minister of Foreign Affairs, Ashour bin Khayyal, met with his counterpart in Rome, Foreign Minister Giulio Terzi. At a joint news conference Khayyal dutifully raised the African alarm for his Italian patrons: "For the moment, the situation is not too bad but we have had indications that it could worsen. African immigrants have arrived at the Egyptian-Libyan border. The numbers are not that big, but they could increase and that is why we are giving this warning." In response, Terzi was predictable: Italy and the EU would have to step up monitoring and security operations (Reuters, 2012/5/12).

Where Libyan investments in Africa were concerned, even before any election could take place the NTC decided that "we have a general view to review all investments in the Arab world, the African continent and elsewhere," as Jalil said at a news conference. Jalil added, "there are some countries where investment will increase and others where projects will stop. There are investments that are worthy of developing and there may be investments that would be better for the Libyan people for them to be closed." The only African country Jalil named that would see increased and diverse investments was Sudan (Reuters, 2012/1/7a). The NTC also announced "it would also be looking at telecommunications investments across the continent, which could see many Libyan investments withdrawn" (ITNews Africa, 2012/1/13).

In Tripoli, a dozen African diplomats told Reuters in interviews that they already sensed a clear shift in Libyan priorities with Gaddafi gone. "Many feel frozen out by Libya's interim rulers, the National Transitional Council (NTC)," and, "some suspect the new government is even going to want some of Gaddafi's gifts back." One of the diplomats told Reuters that Gaddafi "made us feel important. But there aren't so many of us being invited to sit and break bread with NTC leaders. They think that we sided with Gaddafi" (Malone, 2011/11/11). "It wasn't all cynical," another African ambassador told Reuters, "he did a lot of good for African countries... There was little racism in him, unlike some other Arabs, who treat us like slaves when we come here looking for work" (Malone, 2011/11/11).

There has also been a noticeable disparity in the treatment of Western versus African diplomats in Tripoli, under the NTC: "Western diplomats have become more visible in Tripoli, shuttling back and forth between the two luxury hotels where most meetings with NTC officials take place." One correspondent noted, some of the Western diplomats "even wear wristbands in the revolutionary colors, their drivers flashing the 'V' for victory sign at checkpoints run by NTC forces" (Malone, 2011/11/11). It is certainly easy to spot which is now the "in" crowd in Tripoli, and which one is ostracized and threatened: "African diplomats are more rarely seen out and about in a capital where fellow non-Arab Africans can risk arrest, and worse, as suspected pro-Gaddafi mercenaries" (Malone, 2011/11/11). Indeed, there have been grim reports of assaults on African diplomats. The foreign missions of Ghana, Lesotho, Kenya, Congo Brazzaville the Democratic Republic of Congo have been attacked, some on multiple occasions. Ironically, even though Ghana under pro-U.S. President John Atta Mills was quick to recognize the NTC, its ambassador in Tripoli and his wife had their residence attacked by armed gunmen, twice. Ambassador Kodjo Hodari-Okae narrated harrowing ordeals suffered in Tripoli, and that the police, the NTC, and the Libyan Ministry of Foreign Affairs had done absolutely nothing to protect African diplomats such as himself. Despite promises to guarantee their safety, nothing had materialized. The Ghanaian ambassador moved into a hotel instead (Ablordeppey, 2012/4/10). Some Ghanaians felt that the ambassador got what he deserved, for failing to report back on the horrendous atrocities carried out against Ghanaian and other African citizens in Libya at the hands of the militias, while rushing to legitimize and praise the NTC.[19]

FIGURE 3.3 Benghazi residents hold Italian, British, French, American, Qatari and Libyan rebel flags outside the city's main courthouse on April 13, 2011, as a sign of gratitude and support for Western intervention. (Source: Al Jazeera Creative Commons Repository via Wikimedia Commons.)

For the time being it seems as if the era of Libyan Pan-Africanism, thanks to the dual motor forces of racism and NATO bombs, has come to a close.

19. See <http://www.ghanaweb.com/GhanaHomePage/NewsArchive/artikel.php?ID=235990>.

CHAPTER FOUR

A War against Africa:
AFRICOM, NATO, and Racism

"Africa's future is up to Africans," Barack Obama told an audience in Accra, Ghana in 2009, as if this were a concession to a reality that no U.S. president had understood before, or instead a gift of the future bestowed by Obama. However, Obama himself did not believe his own words.

The U.S. military's Africa Command (AFRICOM) was first conceived and put into operation under George W. Bush, and began operations on October 1, 2007. It officially became an independent command on October 1, 2008, but it really only began to take off under Obama, in spite of widespread protest from the African-American community in the U.S., and in spite of even wider protest across Africa itself. Africa's future would only be up to those Africans selected and backed by the U.S. While supposedly conceding that Africa would be making its own choices, Obama in his Accra speech pointedly set out the terms for Africans' future: "History is on the side of these brave Africans, not with those who use coups or change constitutions to stay in power. Africa doesn't need strongmen, it needs strong institutions." Having explained "history" to Africans, Obama proceeded with double-talk, on one side saying that, "the essential truth of democracy is that each nation determines its own destiny," but then adding that when it comes to "genocide" or "terrorists," these are "global security challenges, and they demand a global response." So Africans could have self-determination until the U.S. decided otherwise and reinterpreted local events as either terrorism or, as in the case of Libya in February 2011, genocide. In the usual fog emanating from the president's mouth, he asserted that AFRICOM would not establish "a foothold on the continent," when it already has one: a large base at Camp Lemmonier in Djibouti. Obama's speech, while neither visionary nor rhetorically clever, was at least a clear testament to the extent and content of U.S. "sincerity" (see Obama, 2009/7/11).

FIGURE 4.1 A billboard in Cape Coast, Ghana featuring the late Ghanaian President, John Atta Mills, and U.S. President Barack Obama. (Source: Monocletophat123, Wikimedia Commons.)

FIGURE 4.2 A discarded wrapper of "Obama Biscuits" found on Kokrobite beach, Ghana, November 2009. (Source: Annabel Symington, Creative Commons.)

AFRICOM: Militarizing U.S. Relations with Africa, and Gaddafi's Defiance

For years prior to the creation and launch of AFRICOM, U.S. military, political, and corporate leaders had identified Africa as a zone of risk that stood in the way of new opportunities for capital accumulation, and for challenging the rise of competing powers. Libya stood astride both risk and opportunity, which put it in an extremely dangerous location at the worst time.

Africa as a zone of risk, cast as a source of looming threats, has been one of the central tenets of U.S. policy statements, refurbishing the colonial "Dark Continent" narrative. Three officers writing in an article in *Military Review,* featured on AFRICOM's own website, offer a clear example of the U.S. perception of Africa as a problem to be solved. First, they offer a telling comparison that starkly casts Africans as outnumbering white people: "by 2050, there may be two Africans for every European" (Garrett et al., 2010, p. 16). The comparison has no analytic merit (one could just as easily compare the number of Africans and Fijians), and it therefore finds its only meaning in lingering white racial hysteria. Second, they create a picture of failure: "violent competition for natural resources, low levels of economic development, and inconsistent governance have unfortunately made Africa a world leader in humanitarian crises, failed states, and deadly conflict" (Garrett et al., 2010, p. 17). Africa is thus once more the "heart of darkness." Third, they construct Africa as a zone that needs to be patrolled, laws enforced, in other words tamed and civilized.

> "Africa hosts more United Nations (UN) peacekeeping missions than any other continent and employs the majority of UN field personnel. Eight of 19 current UN peace support missions employ 69,951 of the 95,419 UN troops, police, and observers in Africa. One hundred and sixteen countries contribute military, police, and civilian observers to UN peacekeeping operations in Africa, underscoring a high level of international interest in security and stability in the continent. The frailty of African security institutions, multifaceted economic partnerships, compelling humanitarian needs, and resource development potential make Africa a vital region for the international community and a complex environment for U.S. operations." (Garrett et al., 2010, p. 17)

Speaking more recently, but with the same line of thought, AFRICOM's commander, General Carter Ham, told a Congressional committee that

FIGURE 4.3 U.S. General Carter F. Ham, Commander of U.S. Africa Command (AFRICOM), March 9, 2011. (Source: U.S. Africa Command, Wikimedia Commons.)

2012 would be a "dynamic" year for Africa, "with 20 national elections" and noted that "Africa accounts for 14 of the world's 20 weakest states in Foreign Policy's 2011 'Failed States Index'" (Ham, 2012, p. 3). (That there is an actual "index" for something defined so arbitrarily also merits considerable critique.)

Opportunities for U.S. expansion have been at the forefront of planning for AFRICOM, which as an idea began to be articulated for a decade prior to its establishment. The plan to establish such a program came as a result of "of a 10-year thought process within the U.S. government" that saw the "growing strategic importance of Africa" (Garrett et al., 2010, p. 18). In fact, the idea first took shape in the plans of lobbyists for the oil industry, joined by a select group of members of Congress, and military officers who issued a white paper titled, "African Oil: A Priority for U.S. National Security and African Development" in 2002. The group called itself the African Oil Policy Initiative Group (AOPIG), and included two members of the House Africa Subcommittee (Malik Chaka, Alyssa Jorgenson); Don Norland, former U.S. ambassador to Chad; Lt. Col. Karen Kwiatkowski of the U.S. Air Force and tied to the Department of Defense's Africa Policy unit; and, several representatives of energy lobbying firms and energy companies. Their white paper (AOPIG, 2002) was submitted to Congress and the Bush Administration on May 23, 2002 (Crawley, 2002/5/23). Virtually all of their recommendations were followed, in many cases in the same form and even with the same language.

Recommendations made by AOPIG (2002) included that "Congress and the Administration should declare the Gulf of Guinea an area of 'Vital

Interest' to the U.S." (p. 2). AOPIG emphasized that the U.S. was "on the verge of an historic, strategic alignment with West Africa," given the following facts:

"With projections of over 2.5 million barrels a day in African oil to the American market by 2015, the ambitious goals of the Bush administration's national energy policy for major diversification of oil supply are within reach. The shift in global energy patterns characterized by massive new production levels in Russia, the Caspian Basin, South America, and West Africa, is contributing to America's reevaluation of its global alliance system. Within this context, AOPIG believes that West Africa is being projected onto center stage in global affairs." (p. 6)

As the media noted, bolstering AOPIG's argument, Africa was producing four million barrels per day in 2000, which was more than Iran, Venezuela, or Mexico, and that Sub-Saharan Africa was already the source of 16 percent of U.S. oil imports, as much as from Saudi Arabia. The National Intelligence Council estimated that by 2015 Sub-Saharan Africa would account for 25 percent of U.S. oil imports, thereby surpassing the entire Persian Gulf (Crawley, 2002/5/23). The removal of sanctions on Libya in 2003 greatly accelerated attainment of that goal, and vastly increased the potential supply of oil to the U.S., as Libya alone exports almost half as much as the four million barrels per day noted above.

AOPIG tightly linked military and economic goals, weaving the two in and out of each other throughout their report: "A new and vigorous focus on U.S.-military cooperation in sub-Saharan Africa, to include design of a sub-unified command structure which could produce significant dividends in the protection of U.S. investments" (2002, p. 6). Regarding a declaration of the Gulf of Guinea as a "vital interest" for "U.S. national security calculations," AOPIG, virtually colonizing the region as a domain of U.S. policy, pointed out that:

"The Gulf of Guinea, as part of the Atlantic oil-bearing basin, surpasses the Persian Gulf in oil supplies to the U.S. by 2:1; moreover, it maintains significant deposits of critically important strategic minerals including chromium, uranium, cobalt, titanium, diamonds, gold, bauxite, phosphate and copper. The region is also characterized by underdeveloped hydrological, agricultural and fisheries resources." (2002, p. 15)

Moreover, besides oil and strategic minerals (more on this below), AOPIG identified both China and, significantly, Libya as adversaries that required a U.S. challenge:

"Failure to address the issue of focusing and maximizing U.S. diplomatic and military command organization will be perceived by many in Africa as a device of cultivated neglect by the world's only superpower, and could therefore act as an inadvertent incentive for U.S. rivals such as China, adversaries such as Libya, and terrorist organizations like Al-Qaeda to secure political, diplomatic, and economic presence in parts of Africa. Such threat possibility from such actors exposes U.S. personnel and assets to heightened dangers and diminished opportunities." (2002, p. 15)

The AOPIG report specifically called for "examination and creation of a new regional unified or sub-unified command" (2002, p. 16). It argued that the U.S. needed a military command that solely focused on Africa, "and the lack of a dedicated regional unified or sub-unified command to safeguard rapidly growing American involvement in sub-Saharan Africa is a stark omission that may needlessly raise the risk to U.S. interests in Africa in coming years" (2002, p. 15). Creating such a unified and focused military command oriented toward Africa "would send a powerful signal of long-term U.S. commitment to regional stability and development" (2002, p. 16; see also Lobe, 2007/2/1).

In addition to Libya, the Obama administration has made public its anxiety over the spreading influence in Africa of an ascendant China. At the start of an eleven-day tour of Africa in August 2012, Hillary Clinton took a "swipe" with a "veiled attack" on China, implying that only the U.S. was interested in "democracy" and "human rights," while unnamed others were merely interested in exploiting resources. However, as even Western media noted, China's role is broader than what Clinton described. It was China that built the headquarters of the African Union in Addis Ababa at a cost of $200 million U.S., with a 20-storey tower overlooking a giant round hall that can seat nearly three thousand people (AMT/MF, 2012/1/28). The headquarters were inaugurated on January 28, 2012. In July 2012, China doubled its credit line to Africa, to $20 billion U.S. (Smith, 2012/8/1). China also surpassed the U.S. as Africa's largest trading partner in 2009, with Africa supplying China a third of its imports. Africa is second only to the Middle East when it comes to China's oil imports (Gearan, 2012/8/1). China-Africa trade grew from $6 billion U.S. in 1999 to more than $90 billion U.S. in 2009, and has recently topped $100 billion U.S. (Rice, 2011/2/6).

Meanwhile, the U.S. "does not have the kind of finances available to mount splashy new economic initiatives in Africa," as explained by Jennifer Cooke, head of the Africa program at the Centre for Strategic and International Studies in Washington (Smith, 2012/8/1). Not surprisingly, when speaking of the challenges posed by China's economic rise, Hillary Clinton asked Australian Prime Minister Kevin Rudd in 2009, "How do you deal toughly with your banker?" (Clinton, 2009/3/28). As for charges of a "new colonialism" coming from China, as if China was an invader in a zone that "naturally" belongs to Europeans and Americans, a Chinese trader in Kenya had some interesting comments:

> "Western countries also buy oil, and have mines around the world. People don't talk about 'grabbing', or 'new colonialism' there. So why is it different for Chinese? We are not sending our armies to places and saying: 'Now sell us this!' If you can't compete with us, you find an excuse. It's like two children fighting, and the losing one crying to his parent about funny tricks." (Rice, 2011/2/6)

FIGURE 4.4 The headquarters of the African Union in Addis Ababa, Ethiopia, built by China. (Source: African Union Commission.)

Strategic minerals, of critical concern in the AOPIG report, are a significant focus of U.S. interests in Africa, in addition to oil. The war against Libya may not have been a grab for its oil in any simplistic sense, but controlling access to its oil is terribly critical to U.S. policy. As David Harvey explained, regarding the Middle East, "whoever controls the Middle East controls the global oil spigot and whoever controls the global oil spigot can control the global economy, at least for the near future" (Harvey, 2003, p. 19). The same is true for Africa of course. More than just controlling access, when it comes to strategic minerals the U.S. has an absolute imperative to secure African sources for the U.S.'s own needs. As Harry Magdoff outlined in detail: "The Defence Department operates with a list of strategic and critical materials as a guide to the stockpiling program. These are the materials which are assumed to be critical to the war potential of [the U.S.] and where supply difficulties can be anticipated" (2003, pps. 54-55). In particular we must note that, "for more than half of its strategic materials, 80% to 100% of the supply to the U.S. depends on foreign imports" (Magdoff, 2003, p. 55). Of the critical materials needed to produce just one item, the jet engine, U.S. import dependence is at 100 percent for three of the six critical minerals. Mozambique alone produces 18 percent of the supply of columbium; South Africa produces 31 percent of the supply of chromium, and Zimbabwe produces another 19 percent; the Democratic Republic of Congo produces 60 percent of the supply of cobalt, Zambia produces 11 percent, and Morocco produces 13 percent (Magdoff, 2003, pps. 56-57).

A deep and far-reaching U.S. involvement across a very wide range of social, political, and economic spheres characterizes the new U.S. push into Africa, capped by the development of military relationships. Just as "whole of government" and "full spectrum" approaches to occupation, counterinsurgency, and nation-building have characterized U.S. doctrine in Afghanistan and Iraq, some of the same doctrinal notions are being applied to Africa. Using the approved terms, AFRICOM's mission is described by U.S. military writers as consisting of "diplomacy, development, defence" (Garrett et al., 2010, p. 18).

For a clearer understanding that does not use window-dressing terminology chosen by military elites writing for military elites, we could describe AFRICOM's mission as *infiltrate*, *enlist*, and *expropriate*. It is striking to see the range of areas of activity in which AFRICOM seeks to be inserted: from health, food security, disease, disaster relief, women, youth, security, and elections, to issues of "governance." That in many ways this mirrors the work of the African Union is not a coincidence. At this level, little is ever just a coincidence. Indeed, one of the primary objectives of AFRICOM is to work indirectly, and to use local and regional institutions as its levers of power. As Anthony Holmes, the Deputy AFRICOM commander for civilian-military activities explained, "by and large our approach is what we call '*by, with and through*'," which involves "developing partnerships for extended periods of time," in order to develop African military capacities for dealing with a given "problem" precisely "so we don't have to do it." Holmes further pointed out: "we work with the African Union, [and] we work with the regional economic commissions to develop their peace and security architecture and to promote the cooperation of African countries among themselves" (Kramer, 2012/7/13). Such recent statements fit in deliberately with older plans: the 2010 National Security Strategy makes it very clear, on repeated occasions, that the U.S. cannot afford to take on every "challenge" alone, and that it must work cooperatively, essentially by enlisting other regional organizations. The African Union is one of those mentioned (White House, 2010, pps. 46, 48).

To gain a measure of just how much Libya was doing by itself on the African continent, one can compare it with all of the intended expenditures of the U.S., above and beyond AFRICOM. When sums are added up, U.S. financial commitments under Obama—read generously—barely rival the lowest estimated commitments by Libya ($5 billion U.S.): the U.S. committed no more than $6.3 billion U.S. in total, and a lot of that is not even for Africans. Over one-third of that amount is designed to support U.S. companies' exports to Africa, and to support U.S. corporate investments. Furthermore, that total consists of maximum amounts that could be allotted, not that actually have been (White House, 2012a).

A comparison of the U.S.' and China's investments reveals a striking picture. U.S.-funded news sources put Chinese investment in Africa at $13 billion U.S., wrongly quoting and understating Chinese government sources. Others quote Jia Qinglin, Chairman of the National Committee of the Chinese People's Political Consultative Conference (CPPCC), who puts China's involvement in Africa at $150 billion U.S with more than 2,000 companies working throughout the continent (see Radio Free Europe, 2012/1/29, versus AMT/MF, 2012/1/28). In terms of military spending, the U.S. provided $262 million U.S. to African militaries in 2011 (White House, 2012). Yet that is less than the U.S. spent on its own AFRICOM: "U.S. Africa command received $274 million in Fiscal Year 2010. The Obama administration has requested $298 million for the command for Fiscal Year 2011" (AFRICOM, 2012/5/24). Even when it comes to acting "indirectly," the U.S.' spending priorities clearly privilege U.S. recipients first. However, one has to read "indirect" with some skepticism in the first place.

Given U.S. strategy in Africa, as outlined from those at the highest levels of government, it is far from certain what they mean by working "indirectly" and keeping a "light footprint." According to Obama himself, in announcing a new "U.S. Strategy toward Sub-Saharan Africa" in mid-June 2012 (White House, 2012b), the U.S. would be penetrating African affairs even further. One tactic is to train African "agents of change" and create political ties between them and the U.S.

"Through the President's Young African Leaders Initiative, we are providing the tools to support leadership development, promote entrepreneurship, and connect young leaders with one another, and with the United States. These capable individuals are already changing the continent for the better, and their ideas and ingenuity will shape the trajectory of Africa's progress for years to come." (Harris, 2012/6/14; White House, 2012b, p. 1)

The Young African Leaders Initiative, designed to implant a rising layer of technocrats and politicians with which the U.S. can more comfortably deal, "has so far included more than 2,000 programs for young leaders across sub-Saharan Africa" (White House, 2012a). This would seem to be a very direct form of intervention—but perhaps U.S. officials say "indirect" when what they actually mean is insidious.

U.S. strategy is also very clearly aimed at benefiting and promoting U.S. corporate interests in Africa. Obama emphasized that in working to expand "sub-Saharan Africa's capacity to access and benefit from global markets, promote regional integration, and strengthen economic governance," U.S. corporations, "can and should play a role in this process" (Harris, 2012/6/14). In the formal U.S. Strategy document mentioned above, the U.S. commits itself to "expanding opportunities for U.S. trade and investment" in Sub-Saharan Africa (White House, 2012b, pps. 1-2). Moreover, U.S. strategy aims to ensure that African resources flow in the "right" direction. In a conference in 2008, Vice Admiral Robert Moeller declared that AFRICOM was about preserving "the free flow of natural resources from Africa to the global market" (Glazebrook, 2012/6/14). Preceding AFRICOM, with the signing into law of the African Growth and Opportunity Act (AGOA) on May 18, 2000, the U.S. aimed to create incentives for African nations to "open their economies" (AGOA, 2000; U.S. Congress, 2000). The law was passed when Bill Clinton was president, and has been renewed and amplified by every president since. As a result of instituting AGOA, in just the first year total U.S. trade with Sub-Saharan Africa rose by 17 percent; U.S. imports exceeded $11.5 billion U.S.; and, some countries boosted their exports to the U.S. by over 100 percent (Bush, 2001). As George W. Bush stated, "across the continent, African governments are reforming their economies and their governments in order to take advantage of AGOA." To that he added the Trade for African Development and Enterprise Program with $15 million U.S. in initial funding, designed to "establish regional hubs for global competitiveness that will help African businesses take advantage of AGOA" (Bush, 2001).

Direct military intervention was also spelled out as a key element of Obama's strategy, in addition to U.S. corporate insertion and the training of African leaders. As Obama indicated in his 2010 Strategy document, "the United States will not stand idly by when leaders threaten the credibility of democratic processes" (Harris, 2012/6/14). At greater length, the Strategy states:

> "Our message to those who would derail the democratic process is clear and unequivocal: the United States will not stand idly by when actors threaten legitimately elected governments or manipulate the fairness and integrity of democratic processes, and we will stand in steady partnership with those who are committed to the principles of equality, justice, and the rule of law." (White House, 2012b, p. 1)

The U.S. under Obama was thus more concerned about rule of law in other peoples' homes than in the U.S., where no complete investigations or prosecutions of Bush administration officials have been initiated for authorizing torture, nor has any action been taken on the use of proxy torture in Iraq.

It is therefore clear that well in advance of U.S. intervention in Libya in 2011, the U.S. had committed itself formally to direct military intervention in the political affairs of African states to ensure "democracy." The U.S. even furnished itself with what would become the official, legitimating trope of military intervention: "we will not stand idly by" (see Obama, 2011/3/28). In addition to "protecting democracy," the other self-justification was created under the banner of "preventing atrocities." Officially, AFRICOM thus states that its mission is to "be prepared, as part of a whole of government approach, to help protect Africans from mass atrocities," and "when directed, provide military support to humanitarian assistance efforts" (AFRICOM, 2011).

Statements of humanitarian concern and fealty to other peoples' democracies aside, U.S. strategy documents clearly attest to the fact that U.S. economic interests come first, and that AFRICOM was created to promote and protect those interests, first and foremost. As Vice Admiral Robert Moeller stated frankly, "Let there be no mistake. AFRICOM's job is to protect American lives and promote American interests. That is what nations and militaries do" (Moeller, 2010/7/21). Ensuring "U.S. access to and through Africa" in support of unspecified "global requirements" is one of the intentions (AFRICOM, 2011). In its formal, public mission statement, AFRICOM states the following:

> "U.S. Africa Command protects and defends the national security interests of the United States by strengthening the defense capabilities of African states and regional organizations and, when directed, conducts military operations, in order to deter and defeat transnational threats and to provide a security environment conducive to good governance and development." (AFRICOM, 2012/5/24)

By "good governance" we can understand from U.S. practice that this means regimes that are supportive of U.S. policy and that model their political systems in some fashion on the American one. "Development" can include privatization, free trade, and increased U.S. investment. Even a seemingly arid mission statement contains within it some of the key prongs of U.S. interest and intended intervention in Africa, especially by means of a military command. Building up a network of secret intelligence operations across Africa, with an array of small air bases and numerous flights by drones and other aircraft, is another feature of the growing military presence in Africa (Kramer, 2012/7/13; Turse, 2012/7/12). AFRICOM's promoters may claim the command to be "indirect" and collaborative with civilian agencies, however the fact remains that as General Ham, AFRICOM's commander clearly stated, "that does not mean we simply wait for others to ask for our support. I expect our Command to actively seek and propose innovative and imaginative approaches through which we may apply the considerable military capability of the United States to its best advantage" (Ham, 2011; see also Campbell, 2011/3/31).

Libyan Defiance

The original intention, as stated by George W. Bush himself, was for AFRICOM to be headquartered in Africa itself: "We will also work closely with our African partners to determine an appropriate location for the new command in Africa" (Bush, 2007). Numerous statements from AFRICOM have since tried to downplay that original plan, modifying it with rhetorical wordplay to sound like anything from just a passing idea to simply an option among others. The fact of the matter is that AFRICOM could not be headquartered in Africa due to widespread rejection from governments across the continent, and most notably... Libya (USET, 2009/2/11).

In Tripoli, the U.S. Embassy continued to speculate on what it clearly hoped for, namely failure by Libya to develop a strong and united African Union, even while ignoring what Gaddafi had already achieved with the Community of Sahel-Saharan States (CEN-SAD). On the other hand, betraying its level of concern that Gaddafi might be successful, Ambassador Cretz recommended to his superiors in Washington that there might have been ways for AFRICOM "to quietly gain traction in Libya," and that would be by showing "appropriate deference" to Libya. Otherwise, Gaddafi would "likely continue his public opposition to an expanded role for the command, to include a physical presence, on the continent." Cretz rec-

FIGURE 4.5 Mocking anti-imperialism: On November 26, 2011, U.S. Ambassador to Libya, Gene Cretz, stands by the iconic statue of a fist crushing a U.S. fighter jet, long a feature of Muammar Gaddafi's compound in Tripoli. The statue was stolen and relocated to Misrata by militias who thoroughly defaced it. (Source: U.S. Embassy Tripoli.)

ommended "allowing" Libya to retain "symbolic leadership" in African affairs, and thereby leveraging Libyan support for U.S. initiatives in Sudan, Somalia, and Chad (USET, 2009/2/11).

In a cable from Ambassador Gene Cretz to General William "Kip" Ward in 2009 (USET, 2009/5/18), who was then commander of AFRICOM and was scheduled to visit Gaddafi in Libya, Cretz underscores U.S. fears of Libyan impediments to AFRICOM: "Your meeting with Muammar al-Qadhafi will afford a key opportunity to engage at the strategic level, explain U.S. Africa Command's mission and potentially mitigate possible Libyan obstruction of the Command's efforts on the continent." Nonetheless, Cretz admitted Gaddafi was "unlikely to become a vocal supporter of U.S. Africa Command," but perhaps the U.S. could work to secure his "tacit acquiescence." Cretz also pointed out to Ward that when then Secretary of State Condoleeza Rice visited Libya in September 2008 (Figure 4.6), Gaddafi "warned that U.S. military intervention on the continent concerned Africans and could encourage popular support for terrorism." He added quite diplomatically that he would be "greatly comforted" if AFRICOM continued to be headquartered in Europe, as it has been (see also Rice, 2008/9/6).

During a visit to Washington, Libyan National Security Adviser Muatassim Gaddafi, contrary to premature U.S. enthusiasm about expected Libyan concessions (USET, 2009/4/17), dismissed the U.S.' Trans-Sahara Counter-Terrorism Partnership (TSCTP). He also "reiterated Libya's aversion to membership" in the TSCTP, and he told this directly to Hillary Clinton and to deputies of the National Security Council, CIA, Defense, and Homeland Security (Figure 4.7). Muatassim Gaddafi added that the "Tripoli-based Community of Sahel-Saharan States (CEN-SAD) and the North Africa Standby Force (NASF) obviated TSCTP's mission." On another occasion, Muatassim Gaddafi also criticized Obama for a meeting in September 2009 with African heads of state, but only those from Sub-Saharan Africa, which he called a racist move and one that discriminated against Libya: "We see it aimed at us because we are the head of the African Union" (USET, 2009/11/2). Libya should have been invited as well, he argued. In response, Ambassador Cretz could only say that "Sub-Saharan Africa" is "a term used by the entire international community," but that the "logic" was lost on Muatassim for he answered that, "Africa is not divided; it is a single continent," in which case the logic was lost on Cretz (USET, 2009/11/2).

Clearly, the U.S. was not seeking to simply duplicate efforts: it wanted to either supplant or appropriate what Libya had built and the Gaddafis would not simply roll over. Also, as Cretz reported, "in a meeting of CEN-SAD intelligence chiefs in Tripoli earlier this week, Libya's new External Security Organization Director decried as latter-day colonialism Western attempts to 'interfere' in African security and intelligence affairs and argued that Africans could and should undertake counter-terrorism and intelligence efforts themselves" (USET, 2009/5/18). When one just considers AFRICOM's stated mission alone, these statements from Libya could only cause alarm.

Gaddafi is "keenly focused on African issues," Cretz told Ward, "and credible reporting suggests that he genuinely aspires to be the founding

FIGURE 4.6 U.S. Secretary of State Condoleezza Rice shakes hands with Libyan Foreign Minister equivalent Abd Arrahman Shalgam in September 2008. Muatassim Gaddafi is in the upper right, and Musa Kusa is in the centre. (Source: Michael Gross, U.S. Department of State.)

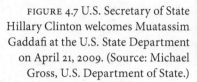

FIGURE 4.7 U.S. Secretary of State
Hillary Clinton welcomes Muatassim
Gaddafi at the U.S. State Department
on April 21, 2009. (Source: Michael
Gross, U.S. Department of State.)

father of a United States of Africa." He reminded Ward that Gaddafi, "will
be suspicious of U.S. Africa Command's potential ulterior motives and
wary of how those could complicate his own efforts to strengthen his
leadership role on the continent" (USET, 2009/5/18).

The U.S. ambassador made a point of relating to General Ward an out-
line of Gaddafi's strong anti-imperialist stance and what it meant for
AFRICOM. Ambassador Cretz remarked that Gaddafi "excoriates European states for having colonized Africa and strongly argues against external interference in internal African affairs," and that indeed Gaddafi
almost has a "neuralgic issue" when it comes to "the presence of non-
African military elements in Libya or elsewhere on the continent." Ward
was reminded that Libya under Gaddafi still took great pride in the expul-
sion of U.S. and British forces from Wheelus and al-Adem airbases,
respectively. The only way Ward might make Gaddafi budge, Cretz suggested, was by taking a very weak line of engaging Libya on peacekeeping
efforts that Libya already supported (USET, 2009/5/18).

General Ward twice travelled to Libya in 2009. Ward met with Muatassim
Gaddafi on his first visit March 10-11, 2009, as recounted in a cable classed
"Secret" from which the following details were extracted (USET, 2009/3/18).
Muatassim Gaddafi clearly expressed Libya's "concerns" about AFRICOM's
mission, including plans for U.S. military bases on the African continent.
Ward made reassurances that the U.S. intent was not to establish military
bases on the African continent and that it would remain headquartered in
Germany. (The U.S. military routinely distinguishes between bases and
smaller installations—so the reassurance may not have counted for much
if Muatassim Gaddafi took all types of U.S. military presence as constitut-
ing "bases.") Not satisfied with the careful U.S. play on words, Muatassim
Gaddafi responded by speaking of the U.S. bases in southern Morocco and
the Gulf of Guinea. Ward denied there were any "bases" in those countries,

but then said that AFRICOM "had set up a training facility in Morocco under TSCTP..., and was assisting GoG [Gulf of Guinea] countries, at their request, under the Gulf of Guinea Africa Partnership Station, with training related to securing their territorial waters." This would have satisfied Muatassim that these were in fact bases in the ordinary sense of the word, just not in the Pentagon's *milspeak*. Muatassim Gaddafi once again also complained that Libya lacked a bilateral security relationship with the U.S., and that by disarming itself by relinquishing its advanced weapons programs, Libya had become vulnerable and remained uncompensated. As for the "success" of this meeting, Ambassador Cretz wrote that the government of Libya "continues to espouse a rejectionist public line—'Africans reject AFRICOM'—characterizing the Command as a vehicle for the United States to promote neo-colonial policies on the continent" (see also USET, 2009/7/21).

General Ward then finally met with Muammar Gaddafi himself on his second trip to Libya on May 21, 2009. The following details come from a cable classed "Secret" and written by Ambassador Cretz (USET, 2009/5/26). Cretz's cable bore the very misleading title, "Al-Qadhafi: No Longer Reluctant to Engage with AFRICOM." The contents of the cable tell the opposite story. Immediately we read that Gaddafi, "told visiting Commander of U.S. Africa Command General William Ward that *Libya supported the establishment of common African institutions*, such as an *African Ministry of Defense*, and *expressed hope that the Obama administration would not pursue a policy of military intervention in Africa*, as he felt *a U.S. military presence on the continent could be a trigger for terrorism*" (emphasis added). Gaddafi also told Ward that, at most, Libya might cooperate with AFRICOM in the fields of "counter-terrorism and counter-piracy," if anything because the latter was already a firm part of Libyan policy and Libya had a long head start on the U.S. in fighting Al Qaeda. Moreover, such "cooperation," might afford Libya leverage in its request for purchases of U.S. military equipment, which Libyan officials made repeatedly (and were denied). Indeed, Gaddafi was constantly looking for reassurances from the U.S. that its intentions toward Libya and the African Union were positive and productive. As a measure of such assurance Libya sought both U.S. weaponry and a commitment to a peace agreement or defensive alliance, thereby getting the U.S. to commit itself to not attacking Libya.[20]

---

20. While not exhaustive, the following is a list of the cables which raise these issues in a prominent manner: USET, 2008/5/8, 2008/12/31, 2009/3/5, 2009/3/18, 2009/4/17, 2009/5/18, 2009/7/21, 2009/8/19, 2009/10/12, 2009/11/2, 2009/12/14, 2009/2/18, 2009/5/3.

Gaddafi also spoke with Ward about China's influence in Africa, clearly understanding that Ward would be interested. Gaddafi characterized "the Chinese approach as soft, the U.S. as hard," and predicted that, "China would prevail because it does not interfere in internal affairs." Gaddafi then criticized "what he said was a U.S. tendency to place military bases near energy sources, observing that if the U.S. did this in the Gulf of Guinea, it would spark terrorism."

In response, Ward apparently "professed" respect for African sovereignty, to which Gaddafi immediately responded by questioning the presence of the U.S. military base in Djibouti. As for cooperating on "counter-piracy," Gaddafi specified what he meant: that an agreement should be reached whereby foreign powers would stop invading Somali waters and looting Somalia of its resources. This being said, one must wonder if either Cretz or Ward could understand Gaddafi's wry wit in concluding the meeting by telling Ward that "he [Gaddafi] could deal with 'the new America without reservation', now that the United States was governed by 'a new spirit of change'."

All of this paints a picture of the U.S. leadership as being worried about Libya's influence, and looking for ways to minimize Gaddafi's leadership. His murder on October 20, 2011, as a result of NATO airstrike and allied forces on the ground, was a most brutal way of assuaging the U.S.

FIGURE 4.8 General Carter F. Ham, AFRICOM commander, speaks on March 24, 2011, to Sailors and Marines aboard amphibious assault ship USS Kearsarge as part of Joint Task Force Odyssey Dawn, established to provide operational and tactical command and control of U.S. military forces in the Mediterranean during the war against Libya. (U.S. Navy photo by Mass Communication Specialist 3rd Class Scott Pittman. Wikimedia Commons.)

FIGURE 4.9 The guided-missile destroyer, USS Barry, launches a Tomahawk missile on March 19, 2011, as part of AFRICOM's Operation Odyssey Dawn, one of approximately 110 cruise missiles fired from U.S. and British ships and submarines against Libya. Most were fired in the middle of the night. (U.S. Navy photo by Interior Communications Electrician Fireman Roderick Eubanks. Wikimedia Commons.)

AFRICOM Overthrows an Opponent, Creating Opportunity for the U.S.

The aftermath of the U.S.-led overthrow of Gaddafi is quite instructive about the nature and urgency of U.S. intentions regarding AFRICOM and Libya. A steady escalation in military engagement is evidence of this.

In December 2011, with the same speed that European and U.S. oil companies rushed to Benghazi to shore up existing contracts or secure new ones, AFRICOM was equally uninterested in waiting for Libya's new "democracy" to take hold before negotiating terms for its own, more permanent insertion. AFRICOM's General Ham announced: "We're looking for ways in which we can be helpful. They [the new Libyan regime] have to find some way to form a national army" (Michaels, 2011/12/7). The plan was for the U.S. to play a role in rebuilding Libya's army, first by training a new generation of officers, since they had largely liquidated the Libyan army that stood in the way of U.S. designs. A few months later, in February 2012, Ham revealed that as soon as NATO's "Operation Unified Protector" officially ended on October 31, 2011, AFRICOM established a joint task force to "command and control post conflict U.S. operations related to Libya." This was called "Joint Task Force Odyssey Guard" and was led by U.S. Army Africa, and by Ham's own admission involved U.S. forces on the ground to reopen the U.S. Embassy and control unguarded Libyan munitions (Ham, 2012, p. 20). In addition, the "Critical Intelligence,

Surveillance and Reconnaissance (ISR) assets" based in Sigonella, Italy, and Souda Bay, Greece, which were used in AFRICOM's Operation Odyssey Dawn and NATO's Operation Unified Protector, continue to be used to conduct surveillance over Libya and neighbouring states (Ham, 2012, p. 20). In March 2012, Ham then revealed that AFRICOM would also be part of developing Libya's border security forces, with training and equipment (Murray, 2012/3/31). This came just weeks after Bani Walid, a bastion of support for Gaddafi, effectively liberated itself from the control of the NTC and its supporting militias and remained that way since. Moreover it was speculated that this was due to a flow of arms coming across the border. Beyond the border security infrastructure, Ham also revealed that AFRICOM and Libya had formed a formal military-to-military relationship, with all this taking place before anything like a legitimate, elected government was even planned to take hold.

> "Libya in general is part of AFRICOM's sphere, and I [Gen. Ham] think the Libyan government really welcomes the idea of a robust military to military relationship with the U.S. They appreciate the value added having a strong relationship with the U.S., so we are just in the very initial phases now of figuring out what that means." (Murray, 2012/3/31)

General Ham credited the war against Libya as itself laying the foundation for AFRICOM in Libya:

> "It's had a very significant effect. The conduct of military operations in Libya did afford now the opportunity to establish a military to military relationship with Libya, which did not previously exist. And we found the Libyans very understanding of the need to establish security across the country and also to contribute to regional stability. And we're seeking to establish what I would call a normal military to military relationship with Libya." (Ham, 2012/3/9)

Note the direction of action implied by Ham's choice of words: the Libyans were found to be very understanding, and "we're seeking to establish." Libya's "transitional" regime was merely on the receiving end of AFRICOM's plans. What a monumental change this was from Libya under Gaddafi.

Apart from border security, surveillance, training, and a formalized military relationship, AFRICOM also decided that it would be the agency to decide on the role of women in the "new Libya." As outlined in the "United States National Action Plan on Women, Peace, and Security," in Libya AFRICOM is "engaging with our international and Libyan partners to ensure that women play an equal role in rebuilding their country's government and civil society institutions" (White House, 2011, p. 24). U.S.

military commanders had long experience with Afghanistan, in using women as a lever of intervention and gender as a front line against "Muslim extremists," and this would be one effective and efficient way to have such forces make themselves more apparent.

In fact, the instability that AFRICOM and NATO created in Libya, and the degree to which they facilitated Islamist forces that Gaddafi had long fought, provided a new source of "opportunity" for AFRICOM to justify its presence in Libya. "There is a real concern in Libya," Ham suddenly decided, after the U.S. media ridiculed Gaddafi's claims that he was fighting Al Qaeda in Benghazi: "we see some worrying indicators that al-Qaeda and others are seeking to establish a presence in Libya" (Ham, 2012/6/26). Thus in June 2012, Ham also pinpointed the "many militia" who fought "very bravely and effectively during the revolution" but who now needed to be brought under control. Hence, the U.S. appointed a defence attaché, and General Ham himself travelled to Tripoli "a number of times," while Libyan officials were brought to AFRICOM's headquarters in Germany. Ham also indicated that some U.S. "assistance," likely in the form of "not a large military presence," would be established in Libya (Ham, 2012/6/26). In addition, Ham also announced in June that the U.S. established an "Office of Security Cooperation" at the U.S. Embassy in Tripoli "that can help coordinate security assistance, international military education and training and other security cooperation." Ham cheerfully added, "we're moving in the right direction." This means that as time passes after this book has been published, the reader can expect even more developments with AFRICOM's insertion into Libya. Finally, Ham added: "It is probably not going to be very often where Africa Command goes to the more kinetic, the more offensive operations in Africa, but nonetheless, we have to be ready to do that if the president requires that of us" (Miles, 2012/6/15).

AFRICOM's insertion into Libya came on the basis of the most fundamentally anti-African processes, namely the launch of a racist war that targeted non-Arab Africans.

The Racist War: Racist Rebels and Racist Humanitarians

Racial fear and xenophobia were at the very crux of the first public calls for Western military intervention, and were the basis for the first utterance of the need for a "no-fly zone." The campaign to incite and spread this fear, to convince international audiences that Africans were a threat, and to justify mass killings and arbitrary detentions of African migrants and black

Libyans, was both deliberate, coordinated, and almost certainly premeditated. Racial fear was combined with fictitious reports of the role of airports
to justify the idea of a no-fly zone, which would serve as the gateway for a
broader and prolonged foreign military intervention. NATO political leaders that sought military intervention (for many more reasons of their own)
latched onto these calls and reinforced the prejudice that underpinned them.

The myth of the "African mercenary" was useful for the Libyan opposition, the NTC and the militias, to insist that this was a war between
"Gaddafi and the Libyan people," as if he had no domestic support at all.
This misrepresentation is colossal, betraying their own fears and insecur-
ities post-Gaddafi. It is a fabrication of the kind that prompts the question:
what opinion do the producers of the myth have of the intellectual capacity
of the audience? As Patrick Cockburn explained, the insurgents' "explanation for the large pro-Gaddafi forces was that they were all mercenaries,
mostly from black Africa, whose only motive was money" (2011/8/28).

Popular discourse was thus infantilized, and reduced to cartoonish caricatures of evil dictators and romantic rebels who could do no wrong. The
myth has been useful, however, for cementing the intended rupture
between "the new Libya" and Pan-Africanism, thus realigning Libya with
Europe and the "modern world," which some in the opposition so explicitly
craved. Indeed, certain people found that "some Libyan rebels seem to
regard the war against Gadhafi as tantamount to a battle against black
people" (Ghosh, 2011/8/31). Amnesty International declared that the new
interim NTC regime has "made matters worse," in that, "they have ignited
public anger by tapping into an existing xenophobia with very dire consequences for many guest workers" (Ghosh, 2011/8/31). Yet, while "genocide"
was quickly proffered by some as the way to characterize the suppression
of the revolt by the government, a term especially popular within the small
circle of Western liberal imperialists whose banner is the "responsibility to
protect," the term "genocide" was never used by those same people, nor by
the UN or Western leaders, to describe actual facts on the ground that
involved "ignited public anger" in a "battle against black people." If this
was "humanitarianism," it could only be so by disqualifying Africans as
members of humanity. The actual practice of intervention did just that.

Airports and African Mercenaries: Origin of the No-Fly Zone

The former Libyan deputy ambassador to the United Nations, Ibrahim
Dabbashi, who defected to the NTC, alleged that Gaddafi was employing

"African mercenaries" to protect the regime (Perry, 2011). This is how *TIME* supported his claims, apart from sanguine mockery of Gaddafi's Pan-Africanism as mere megalomania:

> "The nationalities of the soldiers are not known, though some *unconfirmed reports* indicate some soldiers *may be* French-speaking. The numbers of soldiers is also *unknown*, although *witnesses* in Libya *claim* to have seen several planes land at different *airports across the country* and disgorge hundreds of fighters—an intervention of sufficient size to suggest a foreign government's complicity in their departure for Libya, if not actual support." (Perry, 2011, emphasis added)

In this manner we repeatedly found the link between racial fear of mean African bogeymen swamping Libya like zombies, and airports; and hence the calls for a no-fly zone, which were originally tied to "protecting" Libyan civilians from incoming black mercenaries. Only subsequently were justifications for a no-fly zone widened to include suppression of Gaddafi's air force and targeting his ground forces.

The coupling of fear of African (read "black") mercenaries and the use of airports was affirmed by others in the mainstream Western media. Abdel Bari Zouay, claiming to be an eyewitness, told the media just days after the first street protests began against the government:

> "We call on the United Nations and all those who have a conscience to help the city [of] Ajdabiya. The regime has sent African forces into the city but we are here waiting in the square of the martyrs. Everyone here is ready to defend the city against the mercenaries. We've discovered that these African mercenaries are going to land at Zouitina airport. I can assure you that everybody here is ready to fight against these traitors and African mercenaries." (EuroNews, 2011/2/19)

That this narrative was repeated so often (and never with even an iota of evidence or corroboration) and almost in time with the start of the very street protests, suggests that it was carefully chosen by the rebel leadership before the uprising began in mid-February 2011.

When challenged on their assertions by a lack of evidence, NTC officials always remained silent. For example, a spokesman for the NTC had alleged that a whole army of 3,500 fighters from Chad was responsible for the slaughter of "thousands" of opposition fighters and their withdrawal from frontline cities between Benghazi and Tripoli in late March 2011. This was an attempted explanation for the dramatic reversal in rebel fortunes before NATO bombings began to have a more severe effect

(Deutsche Presse-Agentur, 2011/3/31). However, actual and rare footage obtained from Al Jazeera, taken from within the ranks of a Libyan column and showing government forces moving through one such frontline area, shows absolutely no evidence of this Chadian army or of any apparent mercenaries (AlJazeeraEnglish, 2011/4/9). In one of the rarest instances that the NTC/rebel narrative was questioned, *The New York Times'* David Kirkpatrick (2011/3/21) noted that "the rebels feel no loyalty to the truth in shaping their propaganda, claiming nonexistent battlefield victories, asserting they were still fighting in a key city days after it fell to Qaddafi forces, and making vastly inflated claims of his barbaric behavior."

To help explain one of the bases for creating the African mercenary myth, Issaka Souare, a senior researcher at the Institute for Security Studies in Johannesburg, told *The Christian Science Monitor* that, "there seems to be this idea that if people are supporting Qaddafi, it must be mercenaries from sub-Saharan Africa, because it could not be the work of Libyans. It must be these savage Africans" (MacDougall, 2011/3/6). Nonetheless, in cynical editorializing *The Christian Science Monitor* tried to blame the attacks on Sub-Saharan Africans on Gaddafi's Pan-Africanism, as if support for African integration and aid to African nations could explain or even justify the emerging pogrom in Libya. This was just one of many "passes" that the rebels got from the Western press in an act of open collusion with a racist agenda.

Further building a link between Sub-Saharan Africa, mercenaries, and Pan-Africanism as a triple threat against innocent Arab Libyans, the U.S. media continued to produce articles that justified the opposition's narrative with little or no question. In response to a delegation from the African Union seeking to pursue a peaceful resolution that would end the violence, *TIME* magazine, reaffirming the role of anti-African sentiment, reported: "Benghazi residents are equally suspicious of the Union, having watched Gaddafi hand over their oil wealth to their poorer neighbors rather than invest it in modernizing their country. 'All these countries are good for is taking our money,' lamented Khalid al-Atti, 28" (Sotloff, 2011/4/12). In this case, both Western media and the opposition in Libya used racial fear to somehow disqualify the AU from playing the kind of role to which it was entitled by international law.

Social Media: Racial Hysteria Supporting Foreign Intervention

Anti-African xenophobia and racial fear mongering were also popularized as part of the social media folklore that publicized and promoted NATO and the Libyan opposition's agenda to Western audiences. Twitter, among other social network sites, was one of the most fertile grounds for the international (re)production of myths of savage African mercenaries in ways that brought to mind the manner in which Twitter was used to spread misinformation at the time of the June 2009 Iran election protests (Forte, 2009/6/17). The problem is not that the site is an outlet for creative imaginations, but rather that some of the mainstream media use Twitter as a source for their reports in the absence of correspondents on the ground. A writer for Britain's *Independent* newspaper observed that "foreign media outlets have had to rely mostly on unverified reports posted on social network websites and on phone calls from Libyans terrified of Gaddafi's 'savage African mercenaries who are going door-to-door raping our women and attacking our children'." He also spoke of "a Twitter user based in Saudi Arabia" who "wrote how Gaddafi is 'ordering african (sic) mercenaries to break into homes in Benghazi to RAPE (sic) Libyan women in order to detract (sic) men protesters!'" (Mumisa, 2011/2/24). Mumisa further noted that "Al-Jazeera TV has based most of its news coverage of bands of marauding savage Africans on information posted via tweeter [sic], facebook [sic], and other social networks," adding the very serious observation that "by giving credence to potentially dangerous and unverified reports and rumours posted on social networks without taking into consideration the racial context of Libyan society, Al-Jazeera and other foreign media outlets are complicit in the latest vilification and scapegoating of Libya's Black minorities and its African migrant workers" (Mumisa, 2011/2/24).

One of the changes in international humanitarian law to have come out of the West's claims about the genocide in Rwanda was the role of the media and incitement in helping to spread false rumours that aid in encouraging violence with a genocidal aim (Benesch, 2004; Ghanea, 2011; Harvard Law Review, 2003; Timmerman, 2006). It is arguable that the violence against black Libyans and African migrant workers had such an aim, as the clear intention, both in speech and in violent attacks, was to eliminate their presence in Libya, to marginalize them politically and socially, and to displace entire populations. What makes the role of media so important, and these include Al Jazeera, widely watched in the Arab world and a favourite with the Libyan opposition, and mainstream news-papers in the U.S. and Europe whose reports helped to influence UN debates, is that they may have helped to justify the violence and reinforce the hysteria that was created to support it. This point continues to be ignored in current debates about the war in Libya. It is a point that will come up again in the discussion of Amnesty International in chapter 5.

Twitter provided a window into how the expatriate Libyan opposition and supportive journalists went about constructing a narrative attacking migrant Africans in an effort to delegitimize and unseat Gaddafi. In online epithets Gaddafi in turn was also racialized as a black African just as he was in murals in Benghazi. One of the pro-rebel Twitter users shared with me his derision of Gaddafi's hair ("his kinky Afro") and his look of a "superior baboon." The mass of passive repeaters ("retweeters"), who comprised diverse individuals and some journalists, helped from early on to inseminate the fear of "African terror": the fear of so-called "Afro-mercs" landing at the nearest airport and fanning out to murder Libyans.

The myth was useful to the NTC and the medley of rebels, as it pos-sessed a structure that made it cohere and appeal on a very basic level. 1) all vs. one—"the Libyan people" fantasized as "united against the dicta-tor," so that Gaddafi's only support must have been foreign and Other; 2) the defiling of women—African mercenaries specifically targeting Libyan women; 3) local vs. foreign—proud nationals combating savage intruders; and, 4) Arab vs. African—with the real identity and future of Libya posited as one that turned away from Africa. Some of the tweeted statements are classics of colonial racial propaganda, especially when they revolve around protecting local Libyan women, a useful trope also in both classic and contemporary imperial narratives. What follows is just a brief sample of the kinds of images and misinformation peddled through Twitter. They were aided by journalists such as Mona El-Tahawy, an omni-present U.S.-based Egyptian pundit of the "Arab Spring" who appealed to corporate media and voiced support for Western military intervention, and Al Jazeera's Dima Khatib who used her position in Caracas also to attack the Latin American left for not supporting the rebels in Benghazi, whom she idolized.

One of the prominent sources of the fear-mongering was "LibyanThinker," whose Twitter account was established on February 16, 2011, just as the first street protests started in Libya. It is very telling that this anonymous person claiming to be in Canada had set up an account just to back the opposition, and did so by helping to build the anti-African agenda. The timing, obvious coordination and preplanned scripting, and the account's operation from a base outside Libya are cause for concern.

> LibyanThinker: "URGENT!!! From contact in the Army: So far, 1300 African Mercenaries have arrived in #Libya to date. Cant' the World hear our cries???" Sat. Feb. 19, 2011

> LibyanThinker: "NEW! #Gaddafi has given the African Mercenaries full freedom in raping Libyan women. #Libya." Sat. Feb. 19 2011

The next message was directed to all readers of #Libya news on Twitter, and Al Jazeera English, merely three days after the protest had begun, and long before any alleged threat of a final massacre in Benghazi late in March. In the aftermath, and in the hands of advocates of the "responsibility to protect," this chronology is usually forgotten or whitewashed. The original calls for NATO intervention had nothing to do with stopping any threatened massacre by government forces against Benghazi, fanciful as that was, but rather began as a means to halt these "African mercenaries":

> LibyanThinker: "A massacre against the civilians is going on in #Libya. The international community & UN must intervene to stop the massacre @ AJEnglish." Fri. Feb. 18, 2011

Like some horror movies seek to deliberately increase their impact by claiming they are "based on a true story," a story is made to sound true if one adds "according to witnesses." A key ingredient to all folklore is the tool, "some people say."

> LibyanThinker: "URGENT!!! African Mercenaries danced around and desecrated the bodies of #Benghazi martyrs according to witnesses #Libya#feb17." Thu. Feb. 17, 2011

Similarly, one can try to boost the credibility of an item by merely asserting that its veracity has been "confirmed"—by whom or how, it is never specified:

> LibyanThinker: "Mercenaries operating in #Libya have been confirmed to be #French speaking Africans from CHAD. #feb17#Tripoli #Benghazi." Thu. Feb. 17, 2011

Reinforcing the racial myth, and doing so for a foreign audience (most Libyan soldiers would not have been in Twitter, and most would not read English) were messages such as this:

Tripolitanian: "I URGE THE LIBYAN ARMY TO SIDE WITH THE LIBYAN PEOPLE – don't let these African mercs kill your family! #Libya #Feb17." Sat. Feb. 19 2011

Adding their cold expertise to the frenzy were the ever–shrill Mona El-Tahawy and Dima Khatib. The former, El-Tahawy, is the self-appointed diva of the Arab Spring's revolution in "social media," who does not even try to pretend below that there was a verifiable source. The latter serves her Qatari employers at Al Jazeera, which the Emir of Qatar used again as his personal foreign policy tool, backing Qatar's military intervention in Libya under NATO.

Monaeltahawy: "2 mercenaries caught Bayda. From Chad, claimed 2 b part of Khamees [Qaddafi's son] Military Unit. Said were promised $12,000/ #Libyan killed." Sat. Feb. 19, 2011

Dima_Khatib: "Witness tells AlJazeera.net: a plane full of mercenaries leaves Harare Airport in Zimbabwe headed to #Libya #feb17." Sat. Feb. 19 2011

Falsely claiming "confirmation," another key element of the strategy was to direct messages to the Western media, the one below focusing on CNN and Al Jazeera. The hope was that one of these would at least repeat "there are reports today," which could then in turn be used to suggest that "respected" media were the authoritative sources of the "information."

AliLePointe: "100% CONFIRMED: MERCENARIES IN BADYHA MASSA-CRING PEOPLE! @AJELive@andersoncooper @CNNBRK@CNN @ Cyrenaican #feb17 #libya." Sat. Feb. 19, 2011

This one, in a claim that would later be echoed by Obama and other NATO leaders, asserted that all of Benghazi, a city of nearly 700,000 people, was the target of total annihilation.

AliLePointe: "CONFIRMED: QADDAFI'S PAID AFRICAN MERCENARIES ARE IN BENGHAZI ATTEMPTING TO KILL EVERYBODY. #libya #feb17." Fri. Feb. 18, 2011

"Protect the women!" The classic and time-tested shriek of racist hysteria, whether among European settlers in Africa or among whites in the southern U.S., made an ugly revival and was likely to resonate with certain Western readers.

AliLePointe: "Mercenaries in #Benghazi #Libya going in homes and attacking women while men are in the streets Spread the word PROTECT OUR WOMEN! #feb17." Fri. Feb. 18, 2011

The message was reaffirmed by the so-called "Libyan Youth Movement." Of course there was no need for them to explain how if "the men" were out "guarding," that these "mercenaries" were able to enter their homes to "intimidate" women:

ShababLibya: "more messages being received now of mercenaries entering homes in benghazi... intimidating women while men out guarding #Libya #Feb17." Fri. Feb. 18, 2011

ShababLibya: "again from fellow tweeter: mercenaries are entering homes of libyans while males are out#Libya #Feb17 (as expected city is now lawless)." Fri. Feb. 18, 2011

Here is an interesting admission of either a mass slaughter of African migrants, or the murder of captives:

AliLePointe: "Contact in Jdabiya: the mercenaries we didnt kick out we killed Dont be scared for us, we did the same in #Benghazi #Libya #feb17 mash'Allah." Fri. Feb. 18, 2011

Going back to the very start of the February 17 protests (some protests actually began before schedule on February 15, but February 17, 2011 was the intended and actual mass rallying of protesters in Benghazi), it can be seen that the "African mercenary" myth and simultaneous call for foreign intervention were planted from day one:

ShababLibya: "according to @almanaralibya confirmed African Mercenaries in Western Libya also, the world must investigate this immediately #Libya #Feb17." Thu. Feb. 17, 2011

ShababLibya: "Confirmed, Mercenaries killing protesters across Libya DO NOT speak Libyan, and are from subsaharan Africa speaking french #Libya#Feb17." Thu. Feb. 17, 2011

AlmanaraMedia: "Latest News - All People Of Bayda have gone out to support the Protesters after they heard foreign mercenaries are in the city." Thu. Feb. 17, 2011

AlmanaraMedia: "URGENT: Gaddafi uses African mercenaries to kill the demonstrators from the sons of the Libyan people." Thu. Feb. 17, 2011

AliLePointe: "African mercenaries now in #Benghazi #Libya sources in Libya say they're chasing and killing people with knives and swords. We only fear God." Thu. Feb. 17, 2011

And finally, an example of how the narrative was also oriented against Pan-Africanism:

IbnOmar2005: "People of #Libya to #Gaddafi: leave! leave to (subsaharan) Africa since you love them so much! (referring to mercenaries killing libyans)." Fri. Feb. 18, 2011

In short, Afro-mercs desecrating bodies, wildly dancing, raping women, breaking into homes, these Africans are the only (paid) supporters of Gaddafi, they just landed at a nearby airport, they don't speak Arabic (or "Libyan") so they are mercs, the international community needs to act. This set of tall tales was spun and recounted by most of the mainstream media, and then used by political leaders in NATO states to justify military intervention. Understanding that calls for "humanitarian intervention" and invocations of the "responsibility to protect" were first premised on these foundations tells us a great deal about the role of racial prejudice and propaganda in mobilizing public opinion in the West and organizing international relations.

As the line between mainstream media and social media was crossed, even those heralded as the authorities of confirming and debunking reports, such as NPR's "social media senior strategist," Andy Carvin, played little or no role in countering the racist hysteria. Similarly, Carvin failed to be the first to expose the "Gay Girl in Damascus" hoax (a supposed Syrian lesbian dissident, who turned out to be an American man in the UK). When Andy Carvin was confronted with a swirl of allegations of jets and helicopters firing on protesters (none of which was correct), and of African mercenaries raping and killing Libyans, all he could offer was that "it's just really tough to put together what's true and what's not" and "it seems pretty clear from the Libyans who have been tweeting there, they're scared to death right now." Later he added, "they're clearly scared for their lives and the lives of their families." This comes dangerously close to adding credibility to the rumours, more useful for organizing a chorus of Western tears rather than clarifying matters. Carvin's much vaunted "method" is to start his confirmation process by approaching people he already "knows" (presumably none have ever lied), and he claims to "know" people in each nation that formed part of the so-called "Arab Spring." Carvin acknowledges that the Libyans he "knows" are "some people in the Libyan expat community here in the U.S. and they've been helping me piece together online context on who's who" and "so far they've been fairly reliable." He does not bother to reflect both on the serious bias he was thus admitting into his process and the expatriates' awful record of propaganda as displayed by just a few examples above (see Carvin, 2011/2/21). In the absence of real journalism, we were thus handed an inferior substitute, "Twitter journalism," which served the propaganda goals used to support NATO military intervention.

Beyond Twitter, photographs alleging to show proof positive of African mercenaries were widely reproduced. In one case, we were shown a photograph of Libyan soldiers sitting in jeeps,[21] and since some of them seem to be black, the instant assumption was that they must be mercenaries, as if Libya's population did not already consist of more than a million black Libyans as well as naturalized African citizens. With the same idea, but even less photographic integrity, another image shot from a great distance with the subjects in the shadows, claims to show African mercenaries (since they are "dark").[22] Yet the soldiers are wearing helmets, and are photographed from above, so even if light were added we could still not see their faces. Then there was the foreign ID document, from the Republic of Guinea. This one had the added claim that it was obtained after its owner was killed. Yet all it shows is that the holder is a citizen of an African nation south of the Sahara and not that he was in any way employed as a "mercenary." So if anything this could also be used as evidence of a racially motivated atrocity against an innocent civilian.[23] Another photograph of a so-called "African mercenary" who had been killed[24] was actually a copy of a photograph on Flickr that was taken on January 9, 2006, and is thus not in any way connected with the events of 2011.[25] In addition, the latter photograph may also have been altered, according to one analyst who reviewed and critiqued many of these same photographs and the allegations behind them (Miles, 2011/2/20).

Videos posted online were often used by the mainstream media as "proof" of the presence of "African mercenaries" (without a single one showing them shooting at civilians). Regarding one of the videos made by the opposition to show the capture of a supposed "foreign African mercenary," a black Libyan viewer, Fazzani, recognized one of the captives, as a fellow Libyan. "I am very sorry to see these clips. One of the guys in the scene is black Libyan 'not from other African countries'. His

---

21. At the time of writing, this photograph remained available at: <http://yfrog.com/h24lotoj>.

22. See <http://yfrog.com/hsjkbdaj>.

23. See <http://yfrog.com/h352suxj>.

24. See <http://yfrog.com/h3ztivxj>.

25. See the photograph by Ibrahim Al Agouri at: <http://www.flickr.com/photos/a7fadhomar/5461624996/>.

family lives in EL Mansoura village in Elwadi shatty district. about 200 KM from Borack Ashhati. (Borack AL Shatty is about 700KM south of Tripoli). I have not got permission to put his name here. Hope his family will see this and they will clarify." Nonetheless, France24 spread the allegations of African mercenaries without question (France24, 2011/2/21). *The New York Times* also repeated claims that "groups of mercenaries appeared, in yellow construction hats, to fight the protesters" (Worth, 2011/3/30).

The "yellow construction helmet" motif became one of the most bizarre elements in Western media reports. It would be laughable were it not tragic for the fact that they were referring to construction workers, since the Libyan construction industry had become dependent on imported African workers. Thus the reference is to actual innocent civilians who were being targeted for murder. How Western reports could agree on a "yellow construction helmet" being the recognizable uniform of the international mercenary is simply astonishing. Indeed, these "mercenaries" in safety hats appeared in one video to be wielding nothing more than pieces of wood, rods and two-by-fours from a construction site. But, for the UK's *Mirror*, that was damning enough: "In bizarre scenes, plain-clothed security men—wearing bright yellow construction helmets so they could identify each other—charged demonstrators" (*Mirror*, 2011/2/21). The writers knew that this was "bizarre," but rather than reflect on the absurdity of their reproduction of these tales and the incredulity that they provoke, they ascribe the "bizarre" to the Libyan government.

In an instant classic of cable news media, posted on YouTube,[26] CNN and others showed some of these "yellow hat" mercenaries at work (except that we also see uniformed security forces, and that did not receive any comment). Why was the video so effective and why was it replayed on the major cable news networks? Because it was highly suggestive and had certain dramatic effects, such as incessant and very shrill screams from the women taking the video, who moved their cell phone cameras around rapidly, creating a sense of extreme chaos and alarm. None of the corporate news anchors ever questioned the obvious problems with the video: 1) it was very short and there is no context: no before, no after, no sense of what led to what we see. What if instead these African workers were trying to defend themselves, and security forces had come to their rescue?

---

26. Not likely to be permanent, at the time of writing a copy of the video had been found at: <http://www.youtube.com/watch?v=BziVTiifPDI>.

This is just as likely an explanation, especially as the video shows the workers fleeing, not attacking; 2) another woman's hand and cell phone often intrude in the view, blocking scenes of the action; we never got to see her video on YouTube, just the one from the camera she blocked; 3) where was the massacre that these Africans were supposedly committing? Indeed, where were the protesters? Instead all we heard were the screams of the women high up on a balcony, as they video recorded the scene. In short, the video was meretricious nonsense.

In yet another widely reproduced video used by the mainstream media,[27] the "men in yellow hats" are neither black nor engaged in violence. The video, much of which was recorded from behind large bars and a palm tree, is equally without context, merely showing the men directing traffic. Then a scene of chaos comes on with the men running down the street, followed by nothing, and an absence of any violence against any supposed demonstrators, who in any case make no appearance in the video. With all the cell phones and cameras deployed, videos uploaded to YouTube and photographs disseminated via social media, it is important to note that what were also completely absent were any records of Libyan jets or helicopters firing on protesters. Not one single instance was photographed or recorded. Considering that this too was used as an early justification for a no-fly zone, the absence of evidence and abundance of belief is staggering.

Finally, another prominent video which was replayed in parts across different social media and mainstream media (Al Arabiya, 2011/2/19), featured a gruesome image of a dead, stiff, partly mutilated Libyan soldier being carried around on the street, dragged, and put on public display, while men in sandals stand around the body idly smoking and chatting.[28] The repeated assertion was that the dead man was a mercenary. He was black. No more evidence than that was provided, and apparently no more was needed.

In a unique first-hand report, published by *The Los Angeles Times* (see Zucchino, 2011/3/24), the following confrontation is presented, involving a Ghanaian construction worker held captive in Benghazi and paraded for the cameras (which is a violation of the Geneva Convention).

"One young man from Ghana bolted from the prisoners queue. He shouted in English at an American reporter: 'I'm not a soldier! I work for a construction company in Benghazi! They took me from my house...' A guard shoved

27. See <http://www.youtube.com/watch?v=cHvH8OZFa9k>.
28. See <http://www.youtube.com/watch?v=V9OZJ4WvTJU&bpctr=1344883497>.

the prisoner back toward the cells. 'Go back inside!' he ordered. The guard turned to the reporter and said: 'He lies. He's a mercenary'....'These are the people who came to kill us,' said Col. Ahmed Omar Bani, a military spokesman for the [National Transitional] council, gazing on the detainees with contempt. Asked whether some of the accused might indeed be foreign construction workers, Bani replied: 'We are not in paradise here. Do you think they're going to admit they are mercenaries? We know they are, of course'."

A mercenary indeed: he was black, and probably had a yellow safety helmet. Rebel "justice" thus consisted of "guilty of being black," and one was automatically guilty of crimes until proven innocent. This, then, was a lynch mob, and few in the media, let alone in the councils of the UN, wished to pay any attention to that fact. Intervention on the side of the rebels, as well as moral and political support from them, even from ordinary Twitter users, would thus serve to uphold and defend the lynching. Intervention on one side did not stop attacks on civilians: it multiplied them and made sure that racist violence took a firm and lasting hold. When we in the Western audience were shown these videos and photos, it was because we were the intended audience. Most Libyans did not have Internet access, in normal times, and only about five percent of the minority that did used Twitter. The overwhelming majority of messages, even when supposed Libyans were communicating with other supposed Libyans, were in English. If we were the intended audience it means that the expectation was that we would understand and share in the racial fear, and instinctively recoil at the sight of a running or angry black man. The added assumption is that we would also cry out for our militaries to take action, in the name of "human rights."

Mainstream Media: Disseminating and Inciting Racial Fear

Starting on February 17, 2011, the intended date for the uprising against the government, Al Jazeera picked up and ran with many of the allegations that "African mercenaries" were at work in "massacring" Libyans. On February 18 Al Jazeera broadcast a report that featured someone in Benghazi speaking by telephone who asserted (without any actual evidence provided) that African invaders were killing civilians. In addition, that speaker asked in an impassioned voice: "Where is Obama? Where is the rest of the world?" (AlJazeeraEnglish, 2011/2/18). From the outset, deliberate spreading of rumours, racial scapegoating, and calling for foreign intervention fused immediately. It is doubtful that something

repeated so widely and frequently by disparate actors was merely a coincidence. What is also important to note is that at this starting point, "protecting civilians" specifically meant protecting Arab Libyans against black
Africans. The racist war had thus begun.

Al Jazeera circulated rumour as if it were fact, as in its "Libya Live
Blog" for February 17 (AJE, 2011/2/17). Here are some sample entries dealing with "African mercenaries." They also come from defecting Libyan
diplomats situated in Washington DC, coupled again with very early calls
for U.S. intervention.

"12:01am: Online reports say Darnah city now under attack from 'mercenaries'.

"10:25pm: More on the resignation of the two diplomats from the embassy in
Washington DC. Counsels Saleh Ali Al Majbari and Jumaa Faris denounced
Gaddafi, saying he 'bears responsibility for genocide against the Libyan people
in which he has used mercenaries'.

"They said they had nothing to do with the events and they no longer represent Gaddafi's regime—but that they represent the Libyan people. The pair
also called on Barack Obama to 'work urgently with the international community to press for an immediate cessation of the massacres of the Libyan
people', and they are asking the United Nations to impose a no-fly zone on
Libya to prevent the arrival of mercenaries to Libya.

"9:46pm: Confirmed—Ali al-Essawi, ambassador to India, has resigned. He
has accused the government of deploying foreign mercenaries against Libyan
citizens. We're hoping to get him live on Al Jazeera English. You can watch
our TV feed by clicking here.

"10:00 pm: As fresh violence grips Libya—there are claims that some of
those cracking down on anti-government demonstrators are foreign
mercenaries.

It is worth repeating that in addition to the basic pattern already identified, this was a group of defecting Libyan diplomats, based in Washington
DC (the two above), one in New York (the ambassador to the UN), and
one in India. None of these individuals were on the ground in Libya, and
yet they insisted that they knew that foreign mercenaries were being used,
and specifically called for U.S. intervention, with three of the four diplomats placed in the U.S., and the other who joined the NTC as one of its
top-ranking members (al-Essawi or al-Isawi elsewhere in this book).
Simultaneously, a media blitz was conducted across both international
cable news and social media, in the latter case with numerous anonymous accounts that had no history prior to February 17, 2011. Those accused

of thinking in terms of conspiracy are probably among the few actually thinking through this interesting chain of seeming "coincidences."

It would be untrue to say that Al Jazeera had spoken only about "African mercenaries" and completely neglected how opposition forces targeted African migrants living and working as unarmed, noncombatant civilians. In one report—in fact, it's the only such report for several months—we heard its correspondent say: "What we are looking at here, is the ugly face of the revolution" (AlJazeeraEnglish, 2011/3/1). As Yoshie Furuhashi argued effectively: "Al Jazeera reports on this 'ugly face' as if the channel had nothing to do with its emergence, chalking it up to 'racism' that 'when law and order break down...can rise to the surface'. However, it is none other than Al Jazeera (together with Western corporate media) that, by conveying Libyan rebel testimonies without independently verifying their accuracy, has been spreading the very rumors that it now pretends to deplore." Furuhashi adds, "if Al Jazeera now sees an ugly face in Libya, it is only looking at the face of a monster for whose birth it served as chief midwife" (Furuhashi, 2011/3/2). When several months later Al Jazeera tried, however ambiguously, to show some interest again in the plight of African migrants (AJE, 2011/8/29), it did so only when the Associated Press (AP, 2011/8/29), Channel 4 (2011/8/28), and others started to make a much larger issue of rebel racism than ever before—examples of "post-war skepticism," that could now be aired safely (Hart, 2011/8/24).

Like Qatar's Al Jazeera, Saudi Arabia's Al Arabiya produced much the same, and both nations equally supported the overthrow of Gaddafi. In a report posted on February 19, Al Arabiya stated in a matter-of-fact manner:

> "Libya recruited hundreds of mercenaries from Sub-Saharan Africa...[a] witness told Al Arabiya from the eastern city of Benghazi on Sunday. The witnesses said protesters in Benghazi caught some 'African mercenaries' who spoke French and who admitted that they were ordered by Muammar Gaddafi's son, Khamis Gaddafi, to fire live ammunition at demonstrators. The witnesses, who refused to be named for security reasons, added that they saw four airplanes carrying 'African mercenaries' land in Benina International Airport near the city of Benghazi, the second largest city in the country." (Al Arabiya, 2011/2/19)

The report then quotes, not a source on the ground, but "UK-based Libyan website www.jeel-libya.net (Libya's generation)" and says that it "reported" that "a number of airplanes carrying 'African mercenaries' had landed in Mitiga military airport, 11 km east of the capital Tripoli, and they were dressed in Libyan army uniform." Airports, blacks, mercenaries—repeated over and over again, in conjunction with the very first calls for a no-fly zone, and all this within one to three days after the first street protests in Libya.

TIME magazine for its part breathlessly recited almost all of the allegations stemming from racial hysteria in one swift paragraph, whose primary source is "YouTube and other websites" (Perry, 2011). Wildest of them all, *The Telegraph* "reported" scores of civilians jumping from bridges in Benghazi, fleeing "battle-hardened mercenaries" and quoted local "officials" regarding "tanks full of mercenaries" firing heavy weapons at protesters (Ramdani, 2011/2/20). Of course, *The Telegraph* had "no choice" but to quote unidentified sources with an axe to grind against the government, as its correspondent relayed all these truths from her base, not in Benghazi, but Cairo. UK Foreign Secretary William Hague, picking up on the story on cue, dutifully denounced the *reported* violence as "horrifying." Mission accomplished. Even when expressing some doubts about unconfirmed speculation, the *Guardian* did its own heavy lifting in circulating the rumours and accusations, by dressing them with expert opinion that was suggestive of the possibility of "African mercenaries" being used to quell protests (Smith, 2011/2/22).

The New York Times also received special attention in a critical exposé by Fairness and Accuracy in Reporting (FAIR), on the issue of racism and the media dissemination of the African mercenary myth. This was prompted by a confession from *The New York Times* itself, that the rebels had spread a "racist mantra" among other baseless accusations against Gaddafi:

> "Still, the rebels have offered their own far-fetched claims, like mass rapes by loyalist troops issued tablets of Viagra. Although the rebels have not offered credible proof, that claim is nonetheless the basis of an investigation by the International Criminal Court.

> "And there is the mantra, with racist overtones, that the Gadhafi government is using African mercenaries, which rebels repeat as fact over and over. There have been no confirmed cases of that; supposedly there are many African prisoners of war being held in Benghazi, but conveniently journalists are not allowed to see them. There are, however, African guest workers, poorly paid migrant labor, many of whom, unarmed, have been labeled mercenaries." (Kirkpatrick & Nordland, 2011/8/23)

However, as FAIR noted, that "racist mantra" made a regular appearance in the columns of *The New York Times* itself, as well as other prominent U.S. newspapers such as *The Washington Post*. Indeed, FAIR cited articles co-authored by Kirkpatrick himself to help make its point (see Kirkpatrick & El-Naggar, 2011/2/21; Faheem & Kirkpatrick, 2011/2/22, 2011/2/23):

"From February 22:

By Monday night, witnesses said, the streets of Tripoli were thick with special forces loyal to Colonel Gadhafi as well as mercenaries. Roving the streets in trucks, they shot freely as planes dropped what witnesses described as "small bombs" and helicopters fired on protesters....Two residents said planes had been landing for 10 days ferrying mercenaries from African countries to an air base in Tripoli. The mercenaries had done much of the shooting, which began Sunday night, they said. Some forces were using particularly lethal, hollow-point bullets, they said.

"February 23:

Witnesses said groups of heavily armed militiamen and mercenaries from other African countries cruised the streets in pickup trucks, spraying crowds with machine-gun fire.

"February 24:

Distrustful of even his own generals, Colonel Gadhafi has for years quietly built up this ruthless and loyal force. It is made up of special brigades headed by his sons, segments of the military loyal to his native tribe and its allies, and legions of African mercenaries he has helped train and equip. Many are believed to have fought elsewhere, in places like Sudan, but he has now called them back."

The "African mercenary" myth proved to be one of the most vicious and tenacious of all the myths that served to rationalize the war. Apart from the media mentioned above, many more casually reproduced allegations of an African mercenary presence—just on the basis of skin colour alone in some cases, thereby echoing the racism of insurgents who did the same. Newspapers such as *The Boston Globe* uncritically and unquestioningly show photographs of black victims[29] or black detainees[30] with the immediate assertion that they must be mercenaries,

---

29. See <http://www.boston.com/bigpicture/2011/08/libya_the_fight_continues. html#photo6>.

30. See <http://www.boston.com/bigpicture/2011/08/libya_the_fight_continues. html#photo12>.

SLOUCHING TOWARDS SIRTE

despite the absence of any evidence—that is, apart from the colour of their skin. We were frequently treated to casual assertions that Gaddafi is "known to have" recruited Africans from other nations in the past, without even bothering to find out if those found dead are black Libyans (for example, Graff, 2011/8/25).

Early Reports of Atrocities: Filed and Ignored

In the early weeks of the Libyan conflict, some reports were filed that did indicate that a campaign of deadly persecution against black Libyans and African migrants was underway, with some context provided as well. Some examples are provided below. One example was that of Hussein Zachariah, a welder from Ghana who worked for a Turkish construction company in Benghazi for three years before the conflict began, told the press that he was "often verbally abused on the street and had stones thrown at him;" "They say a lot of things about you. They call you a slave." He also claimed that his friend was "accused of being a mercenary fighter and that he witnessed him being severely beaten by 'protesters' on the street" (MacDougall, 2011/3/6). This act of violence by those billed by Western media as innocent, peaceful protesters passed without comment.

A Turkish oilfield worker who fled Libya and then spoke to the BBC, said: "We left behind our friends from Chad. We left behind their bodies. We had 70 or 80 people from Chad working for our company. They cut them dead with pruning shears and axes, attacking them, saying you're providing troops for Gadhafi. The Sudanese, the Chadians were massacred. We saw it ourselves" (Quist-Arcton, 2011/2/25). The *Los Angeles Times* published one of the very rare early reports of the victimization of African migrant workers.

> "'I am a worker, not a fighter. They took me from my house and [raped] my wife,' he said, gesturing with his hands. Before he could say much more, a pair of guards told him to shut up and hustled him through the steel doors of a cell block, which quickly slammed behind them. Several reporters protested and the man was eventually brought back out. He spoke in broken, heavily accented English and it was hard to hear and understand him amid the scrum of scribes pushing closer. He said his name was Alfusainey Kambi, and again professed innocence before being confronted by an opposition official, who produced two Gambian passports. One was old and tattered and the other new. And for some reason, the official said the documents were proof

positive that Kambi was a Kadafi operative....All I know [says the *LA Times* reporter] is that the Geneva Convention explicitly prohibits prisoners of war from being paraded and questioned before cameras of any kind. But that's exactly what happened today. The whole incident just gave me a really bad vibe, and thank God it finally ended....our interpreter, a Libyan national, asked [*LA Times* reporter David] Zucchino: "So what do you think? Should we just go ahead and kill them?" (Sinco, 2011/3/23)

Mary Fitzgerald, correspondent for *The Irish Times* in Tripoli, reported the following:

"In eastern Libya...I visited several facilities where suspected mercenaries were held. The men came from countries including Chad, Niger, Mali and Sudan. Some said they were innocent labourers who happened to be in the wrong place at the wrong time; others claimed they had been tricked into fighting for Gadafy.

"In Baida, where a number of alleged mercenaries were said to have been hanged in front of the courthouse just after the town fell to the rebels, I saw graffiti which referred to *abeed*, the Arabic word for slaves, which can be used as a derogatory term for black people.

"In the rebel stronghold of Benghazi, I saw fighters bring a pick-up truck full of black men, their hands bound, to the seafront opposition headquarters one night. A hostile crowd milled around before they were driven off to a detention centre." (Fitzgerald, 2011/8/31)

In more numerous instances, reports were made in passing, usually contained within a couple of sentences, or a paragraph at most, buried within larger articles excoriating the "Gaddafi forces." The mainstream media coverage was predominantly framed within a regime change mentality, and careful not to admit too many contrary bits that might unravel their narrative, virtually indistinguishable as it was from that of NATO headquarters or the U.S. State Department. Aside from other forms of militarization, the Libyan war also helped to further cement the militarization of the media by aligning it more closely with the perspectives of a belligerent party to the conflict.

Rebel Bravado: Admissions of Mass Lynching

Some of these reports of "African mercenaries" could be read in other ways, however, for purposes contrary to those of the original authors. They could even indict their actions as crimes against humanity. This can occur when one realizes that, given the absence of any evidence of actual mercenaries, virtually all of the rebels' targets were in fact innocent civilians. Alarms should have sounded among those who profess devotion to human rights when reports such as the following were published. As quoted by *The Guardian* (Black & Bowcott, 2011/2/18), Amer Saad, a political activist from Derna, told Al Jazeera:

> "The protesters in al-Bayda have been able to seize control of the military airbase in the city and have *executed* 50 African mercenaries and two Libyan conspirators. Even in Derna today, a number of conspirators were *executed*. They were locked up in the holding cells of a police station because they resisted, and some died burning inside the building." (emphasis added)

The problem here is that the activist is admitting to crimes against humanity, and at the very least war crimes. Even if the captives were mercenaries, and incontrovertibly so, their execution as prisoners is a crime under international law, and here is one of the opposition members providing testimony. To date, bodies such as the International Criminal Court have simply turned a blind eye to such reports. Except that the eye in question is only blind when convenient, and when the targets were African migrant workers, it was convenient.

Now compare the number above—50 executed—with the grand total of all protesters killed in the first three days of the protests, which according to Human Rights Watch was no more than 24. Therefore, at this same point in the uprisings, the opposition had murdered more Africans than the government had killed members of the opposition. International intervention came down against the government. If this is the logic of "humanitarian intervention," then it is not logical at all and it invites us not to take humanitarianism seriously.

As early as March 2011, Human Rights Watch described what it saw as "a concerted campaign in which thousands of men have been driven from their homes in eastern Libya and beaten or arrested" (Zucchino, 2011/3/24). By then the rebels had captured an unspecified number of migrant African men (Zucchino, 2011/3/24), and we did not learn what became of them. Events such as these did manage to get past the reporting blockade. The *Globe and Mail* reported that on both February 18, 2011, in Al Bayda, and February 23, 2011, in Darna, mobs attacked and lynched "darker-skinned" soldiers (Smith, 2011/4/1). Moreover, Peter Bouckaert, emergencies director at Human Rights Watch, spoke of public mass executions by the opposition. In fact, "darker-skinned" soldiers, taken captive, were treated very differently from their "lighter-skinned" counterparts, according to local doctors speaking of "reprisal" killings that began as early February 17, at the start of the protests (Smith, 2011/4/1). It should be added that the concept of "reprisal" only makes sense if the Libyan protesters had actually been first attacked by those they lynched. Furthermore, the government of Chad publicly complained that dozens of Chadians in rebel-controlled areas had been accused of being mercenaries and were executed. In an official statement, the Chadian government said that it was "calling on international coalition forces involved in Libya and international human rights organization to stop these abuses against Chadians and other migrant Africa workers" (Reuters, 2011/4/3).

In addition, Human Rights Watch had earlier already concluded that there was no evidence of mercenaries anywhere in eastern Libya where these killings of Africans had predominantly occurred (RNW, 2011/3/2). But this didn't stop Kenneth Roth, Executive Director of Human Rights Watch, from speaking out in support of foreign military intervention against the Libyan government as an enactment of the "responsibility to protect" doctrine and citing Gaddafi as "the perfect villain" (Roth, 2011/3/19). Roth said all of this, in spite of what his organization had itself uncovered about the targeted killing of blacks, which outnumbered the killing of protesters as discussed above, and which received no mention at all in Roth's approval of UNSCR 1973.

After the Fall of Tripoli: Ethnic Cleansing by the Insurgents

The racist targeting and killing of black Libyans and migrant African workers continued through the entirety of NATO's military campaign. They seemed to increase once Tripoli fell to insurgent militias and have continued to the present time of writing. In Tripoli, as the insurgents took over, journalists discovered various scenes of sheer horror.

In one case, reporters came across a mass of "rotting bodies of 30 men, almost all black and many handcuffed, slaughtered as they lay on stretchers and even in an ambulance in central Tripoli" (Cockburn, 2011/8/28). Sengupta's visit produced this graphic account, and some admissions:

"The killings were pitiless.

"They had taken place at a makeshift hospital, in a tent marked clearly with the symbols of the Islamic Crescent. Some of the dead were on stretchers, attached to intravenous drips. Some were on the back of an ambulance that had been shot at. A few were on the ground, seemingly attempting to crawl to safety when the bullets came.

"Around 30 men lay decomposing in the heat. Many of them had their hands tied behind their back, either with plastic handcuffs or ropes. One had a scarf stuffed into his mouth. *Almost all of the victims were black men.* Their bodies had been dumped near the scene of two of the fierce battles between rebel and regime forces in Tripoli.

"'*Come and see. These are blacks, Africans, hired by Gaddafi, mercenaries,*' shouted Ahmed Bin Sabri, lifting the tent flap to show the body of one dead patient, his grey T-shirt stained dark red with blood, the saline pipe running into his arm black with flies. Why had an injured man receiving treatment been executed? Mr Sabri, more a camp follower than a fighter, shrugged. It was seemingly incomprehensible to him that anything wrong had been done." (Sengupta, 2011/8/27)

Not too far away, the BBC and its reporter, John Simpson, even in showing the gruesome images from inside the abandoned Abu Salim hospital where hundreds of bodies were found, did not remark on the fact that almost all of the victims shown were black. Simpson then wondered aloud about who might have killed them (BBC, 2011/8/26). This was the Abu Salim hospital in a regime stronghold that fell, where victims who for months had been targeted for the colour of their skin lay dead. Certainly, the evidence is only circumstantial, but now one has to wonder aloud about a reporter who wants us to believe that he remained unmolested by circumstance.

In another case at another site, Alex Thomson, reporting for Britain's Channel 4 news, travelled to Salaheddin and arrived near the base of the deposed government's Khamis brigade. What he found was a mass of 53 people who had been killed five days earlier. He also found the insurgents forcibly gathering any migrant African men they could find, instantly declaring them to be Gaddafi's fighters. "This is a bad time to be a black man in Libya," Thomson stated in his report (Channel 4, 2011/8/28).

When concern from Western NGOs, human rights groups, and governments focused on the citizens of Misrata who were daily getting pounded by government forces, little to no attention was being paid to what some of those same citizens were doing to their black Libyan neighbours. The first reports that Misrata insurgents had engaged in ethnic cleansing against black Libyans in Tawargha (Tawergha) started to appear in June 2011. More than a year later, the town adjoining Misrata remains entirely depopulated, looted, and in a process of gradual physical destruction. Misrata residents have sworn that they never will allow the Tawarghans back. They have become internal refugees in Libya, living in squalid open-air camps, subject to nightly raids, constant rape, and even shootings that have killed children.

Why was there no international outcry over this? What happened to the "responsibility to protect"? How did NATO's intervention facilitate and empower the culprits behind the eradication of Tawargha? Did the Libyan government led by Gaddafi have no right whatsoever to protect Tawarghans and to fight the insurgents? If not, why do other governments have this right, and indeed, how is it that the U.S. and NATO directly engage in counterinsurgency in Afghanistan, presumably in support of the Afghan government, if there is no such right? Had the perpetrators of the crimes been black, and their victims white, would the reactions of Western officials been the same? How did they react when Zimbabweans forcibly retook their lands from the small, white settler minority? These are the sorts of questions that were routinely ignored, never asked even in the "authoritative" commentary that dominated in a war that did great violence to much more than bodies. This war did violence even to the capacity of some to reason, and of others to produce a credible and logical policy that could legitimately win the approval of their own citizenry.

In June 2011 some of the first reports began to appear about the devastation of Tawargha (see Dagher, 2011/6/21, and commentary from Black Star News [BSN], 2011/6/21). The insurgents, calling themselves "the brigade for purging slaves, black skin," vowed that in the "new Libya" black people from Tawargha would be barred from health care and schooling in nearby Misrata (Kamara, 2011/8/26), from which black Libyans were expelled by the insurgents by August (Ford, 2011/8/17). When Andrew Gilligan of *The Sunday Telegraph* visited Tawargha, he found an utterly depopulated town, with none of the inhabitants (mostly black Libyans) visible, and their homes thoroughly looted and vandalized. The town was said to have between 10,000 and 30,000 inhabitants, widely varying across reports. Abdul el-Mutalib Fatateth, the officer in charge of the rebel garrison in the town, told Gilligan: "We gave them thirty days to leave. We said if they didn't go, they would be conquered and imprisoned. Every single one of them has left, and we will never allow them to come back" (2011/9/11). Gilligan reported from his tour of the town, "we saw large numbers of houses, and virtually every shop, systematically vandalized, looted or set on fire." He noted the "racist undercurrent" and confirmed that the Misrata brigade had indeed painted the slogan at the entrance to the town about purging black slaves and black skin (2011/9/11). Another rebel commander declared to Gilligan: "Tawergha no longer exists" (Gilligan, 2011/9/11). The fall of

Tawargha was, as Glen Ford (2011/8/17) appropriately put it, "an event only racists could celebrate, a triumph of hate and Euro-American arms and money over an enclave of dark-skinned Libyans descended from Africans once sold in the town's slave market." After Sirte, whose population was at least allowed to continue living in the city (in ruins), Tawargha suffered a fate like no other town in Libya, including smaller towns in the Nafusa mountains that were ransacked and burned by insurgents during the summer months of 2011 (HRW, 2011/7/13).

Summing up the situation in Libya in August 2011, Fred Abrahams (2011/8/24) detailed the racist-motivated abuses by the insurgents, without going back to discuss how his organization's support for intervention on one side of the conflict created the conditions for such attacks. For this reason and others, HRW is politically compromised.

> "Dark-skinned Libyans and sub-Saharan Africans face particular risks because rebel forces and other armed groups have often considered them pro-Gadhafi mercenaries from other African countries. We've seen violent attacks and killings of these people in areas where the National Transitional Council took control." (Abrahams, 2011/8/24)

Nonetheless, in what appeared to be a complete abandonment of reflexive awareness, Abrahams still wrote the article cited with a sanguine tone that lusted for even more regime change: "Take note President Bashar al-Assad of Syria."

In August 2011, Amnesty International (2011/8/25) reported on the disproportionate detention of black Africans in rebel-controlled Zawiya, as well as the targeting of unarmed, African migrant farm workers:

> "Detention officials in Az-Zawiya said that about a third of all those detained are 'foreign mercenaries' including nationals from Chad, Niger and Sudan.
>
> "When Amnesty International delegates spoke to several of the detainees however, they said that they were migrant workers. They said that they had been taken at gunpoint from their homes, work-places and the street on account of their skin colour.
>
> "None wore military uniforms. Several told Amnesty International that they feared for their lives as they had been threatened by their captors and several guards and told them that they would be 'eliminated or else sentenced to death'.
>
> "Five relatives from Chad, including a minor, told Amnesty International that on 19 August they were driving to a farm outside of Az-Zawiya to collect some produce when they were stopped by a group of armed men, some in military fatigues.

"The armed men assumed that the five were mercenaries and handed them over to detention officials despite assurances by their Libyan driver that they were migrant workers.

"A 24 year-old man from Niger who has been living and working in Libya for the past five years, told Amnesty International that he was taken from home by three armed men on 20 August.

"He said that he was handcuffed, beaten, and put in the boot of the car. He said: 'I am not at all involved in this conflict. All I wanted was to make a living. But because of my skin colour, I find myself here, in detention. Who knows what will happen to me now?'

In Tripoli, fighters for the new regime abducted thousands of black Libyans and African migrant workers, seizing anyone on the street who was black, and detaining hundreds in a stadium on the accusation of being mercenaries (Hubbard, 2011/9/1). Reports continue to mount, with other human rights groups finding evidence of the insurgents targeting African migrant workers (AP, 2011/8/29). Even the routinely ambivalent chair of the African Union, Jean Ping, came out and stated:

"NTC seems to confuse black people with mercenaries. All blacks are mercenaries. If you do that, it means (that the) one-third of the population of Libya, which is black, is also mercenaries. They are killing people, normal workers, mistreating them." (AP, 2011/8/29)

An Amnesty International (2011/8/31) delegation also personally witnessed the abuse and abduction of injured black patients in the Central Tripoli Hospital on August 29 by the rebels:

"An Amnesty delegation visiting the Central Tripoli Hospital on Monday witnessed three *thuwwar* revolutionaries (as the opposition fighters are commonly known) dragging a black patient from the western town of Tawargha from his bed and detaining him. The men were in civilian clothing.

"The *thuwwar* said the man would be taken to Misratah for questioning, arguing that interrogators in Tripoli 'let killers free'. Two other black Libyans receiving treatment in the hospital for gunshot wounds were warned by the anti-Gaddafi forces that 'their turn was coming'."

Amnesty International's Diana El Tahawy also observed that, "what we are seeing in western Libya is a very similar pattern to what we have seen in Benghazi and Misurata after those cities fell to the rebels." Amnesty found around three hundred people, mostly migrant Africans accused of being *mortazaga* (mercenaries), in detention in Zawiyah, twenty miles west of Tripoli, since the rebels took over (Van Langendonck, 2011/8/29).

In September 2011, Amnesty International continued to report that insurgent militias behind the NTC takeover had committed war crimes (2011/9/12). The war crimes involved racist violence against civilians: "when Al-Bayda, Benghazi, Derna, Misratah and other cities first fell under the control of the NTC in February, anti-Gaddafi forces carried out house raids, killings and other violent attacks against suspected mercenaries, either sub-Saharan Africans or black Libyans" (2011/9/12). The organization documented the abuse of prisoners, executions, and forced disappearances. It also noted that between a third and a half of all prisoners in Tripoli and al-Zawiya were either black Libyans or African migrant workers, further pointing out "that widespread rumours that al-Gaddafi forces used large numbers of sub-Saharan African mercenaries in February had been significantly exaggerated" (2011/9/12; also see 2011, pps. 9, 12, 79, 81-86). Amnesty International also documented the lynching (its term) of prisoners in rebel-controlled zones, with the emphasis of the brutality being against black Libyan soldiers (2011, p. 71).

In fact, the rumours that Amnesty alluded to above, concerning "Gaddafi forces" using large numbers of Sub-Saharan African mercenaries, were more than just significantly "exaggerated." They were entirely false. Adding to a stream of reports from Human Rights Watch and various newspaper accounts, no evidence was ever found of any foreign African fighters being employed by the government to fight the insurgents, not even as much as an interview with a "mercenary." Although the insurgents' militias will claim that those they abducted, tortured, and then put on display had "confessed" to their crimes, not one has been convicted. The last word on the subject came in March 2012 with the publication of the UN Human Rights Council's *Report of the International Commission of Inquiry on Libya*. After the mountains of rumours, allegations, and supposed videos and photos, the UNHRC came up with only a single, brief paragraph on "mercenaries."

"The Commission established that an organised group of Sudanese fighters were brought in by the Qadhafi government specifically to fight the *thuwar*. *The Commission has not found that these fighters were promised or paid material compensation* substantially in excess of that promised or paid to local Qadhafi forces, *a requirement for these individuals or groups to fall within the definition of a 'mercenary'* under the United Nations Convention against Mercenaries or under Organization of African Unity (OAU) Convention on Mercenarism. The Commission also determined that there were fighters within the Qadhafi forces who, though of foreign descent, were *born in Libya or resident there.* They would also *fall outside the definition of mercenaries."* (UNHRC, 2012, p. 17 emphasis added)

From the vantage point of the insurgents' militias and NTC, this would be the most "generous" treatment their allegations would ever get in any credible, independent report. None of those captured, identified as "French-speaking," nor any of those persons from West Africa, were ever mercenaries. The only ones who could have been mistaken as such were Sudanese, but ironically there were few mentions if any from the insurgents themselves about Sudanese—not that "the group" of Sudanese were mercenaries by the definition used under international law. Given that Libya shares a border with Sudan, used for regular traffic of goods and persons, it's not even clear that airports would have been needed, and whether these persons were not already in Libya pre-2011. In other words, with the UNHCR report we can continue to observe that at no point has any credible, independent investigation ever found any evidence of African mercenaries.

Amnesty International itself accused EU member states and NATO of doing little more than "paying lip-service" to human rights, and cites this as an "international failure" to protect (2011, p. 87). None of this is meant to whitewash the sins of both the deposed government of Libya and ordinary Arab Libyans against African migrants and refugees, both years prior to the rebellion and in the early stages of the rebellion (see AI, 2011, pps. 79-80). It is significant and noteworthy, however, that even with all of Gaddafi's supposed "mercurial" ambiguity, it was the insurgents that black Libyans and African migrants always feared, as the insurgent militias were the only ones targeting black people.

Who Cares About African Migrants or Black Libyans?

"Who cares about African migrants in Libya?" migration researcher Hein de Haas asked; "why is nobody concerned about the plight of sub-Saharan African migrants in Libya?" (2011/2/21). He offered an accurate prediction in February 2011: "there is a huge danger that there will soon be a day of reckoning for African migrants, and the arbitrary violence has possibly started already." Similarly, Saad Jabbar (Deputy Director, North Africa Center at Cambridge University) told NPR: "I tell you, these people, because of their skin, they will be slaughtered in Libya," fearing that what will come is "a genocide against anyone who has black skin and who doesn't speak perfect Arabic" (Quist-Acton, 2011/2/25). Other experts interviewed also suggested that, "a violent backlash by anti-Gaddafi forces in Libya who link black skin with the regime could lead to a massive genocide once the long-time leader is ousted" (Russeau, 2011/3/21).

Apart from exceptions such as the *Los Angeles Times*, one had to go to African news media to get a different perspective on events in Libya. An Ethiopian news site found that most Ethiopians living in eastern Libya—the insurgent stronghold—were "hiding in their houses because it is dangerous for blacks to come out because they are considered by most Libyans as mercenaries." The news site spoke of those "dragged from their apartments beaten up and showed [sic] to the world as mercenaries. We also heard many Ethiopians killed by angry mob in Benghazi" (Asfaw, 2011). An article in the *Somaliland Press* (2011/2/23) told us that, "in areas where forces loyal to Libyan leader Muammar Qaddafi has been forced out, many angry mobs are targeting black Africans after reports that the government was using 'African mercenaries' to repress the revolt was transmitted by Western media." In that same report, the chief spokesperson for the UN High Commission for Refugees reveals: "One journalist passed information to us from Somalis in Tripoli who said they were being hunted on suspicion of being mercenaries." The UNHCR's only concern here was that people seeking to leave Libya should not face any obstacles in doing so. A while later, the Office of the High Commissioner for Human Rights (OHCHR) produced a mild statement of concern for the fate of migrant workers in Libya from African nations south of the Sahara, without any calls for active intervention on their behalf (OHCHR, 2011/4/8).

When Hillary Clinton along with others in the U.S. government speak of "private security contractors," they mean what the rest of us would ordinarily call mercenaries. But when Clinton finally used the word "mercenaries" (Quinn, 2011/2/28) she was, consciously or not, speaking in racial code: she was referring to black Africans with this label. It has now become impossible for advocates of the "responsibility to protect" (R2P) and closely related liberal imperialist ideals to be taken seriously. Throughout the war in Libya, they diligently ignored the reports of atrocities against black civilians in Libya, even as they laboured at characterizing the government's actions as "genocide" and that only its violence needed to be stopped. Thus of the 24 "human rights groups" that jointly invoked R2P and called for foreign military intervention (UN Watch, 2011/2/21a), not one had mentioned, even once, the plight of black Libyans and African migrant workers targeted and killed by the Libyan opposition because of the colour of their skin and/or their national origin. Instead, for the most part the Western mainstream media, NGOs, and "human rights groups" supposedly informed us that the Libyan opposition consisted of "academics, lawyers, businessmen, professionals." Using this membership list of an elite class, they could create the perception that "we" may "know" something about what such people stand for, because they sound "middle class" like many of "us." We are essentially members of the same professional club, and share the same universal aspirations of our class. However, that was also a way of getting the audience to think white: the opposition, polished as it was, was not like the "rag tag" black mercenaries. The Africans were bearers of evil; the Libyan Arab opposition consisted of respectable people, representing the forces of progress, and they alone were entitled to "human rights."

CHAPTER FIVE

Humanitarianism
and the Invention of Emergency

Military intervention is a way of imposing compliance and conformity, when those who intervene have failed to convince the object of intervention of its duty to succumb to commands. To say that this intervention can then be "humanitarian" is to speak the language of the liberal ideology that has dominated the world system since the so-called end of the Cold War. Humanitarianism—and its correlate of protection—speaks the language of "civilization" (democracy, human rights, free enterprise) and opposes itself to "savagery" (dictatorship, terrorism, command economies). Humanitarianism is thus built on a mode of categorizing the world, of producing the kinds of nomenclatures that are pre-determined to justify the ambitions and fears of the dominant powers. The mythology of Western humanitarianism—great at producing symbols and ideals, almost never realized as actual facts on the ground—is one that promises salvation (liberation, protection, democratization). This is always brought by the West as the self-appointed messiah that has the might to determine which is the "right" side of history: "Here we go again. The cheering crowds. The deposed dictator. The encomiums to freedom and liberty. The American military as savior" (Hedges, 2011/9/5).

Western liberalism's multiple myths of humanitarianism, which include the benevolent spread of democracy, the protection of innocent civilians, the benign building of nations, and the liberation of peoples suffering under dictators, are myths that fabricate a world where there are rightful actors and those acted upon. There are those whose legitimacy is never in question, and those whose legitimacy is always contingent on the good wishes of those in the dominant part of the world system. A basic division prevails between good and evil—this is where we need demons and angels—and the good among us must "do something," while the "evil ones" say we must do nothing. These myths prescribe pragmatic action and moral sanction (or economic sanctions). The actions prescribed by myth promise the creation of a new world order. Bombing fulfills the role of a rite of passage, carrying a society from crisis, through war, and then reintegration into the world system as a newly fashioned object—something that is reborn.

"Arab Spring," which implies rebirth, can be made to fit this narrative construction, if bombing is what the interventionists see as necessary to make the flowers bloom. Seen in this framework, it makes sense that former U.S. Secretary of State Condoleeza Rice should refer to the 2006 Israeli bombing of Lebanon as "the growing—the birth pangs of a new Middle East" (Rice, 2006/7/21). Likewise, with reference to Libya, a Reuters article celebrates "the birth pangs of the world's newest democracy" (Maclean, 2011/9/14) This peculiar phrasing is further echoed by neoconservative scholar Fouad Ajami (2011/8/31): "the birth pangs of the new Libya." Intervention myths are apparently the new creation myths of our time.

We need a close look at how these myths were applied to Libya, beyond what has already been established in the previous chapters.

"Genocide Prevention"

On February 21, 2011, just a few days after the street protests began, the very quick to defect Libyan deputy Permanent Representative to the UN, Ibrahim Dabbashi, stated: "We are expecting a real genocide in Tripoli. The airplanes are still bringing mercenaries to the airports" (Taki, 2011/2/21). This was quite clever: a myth that is composed of myths. With that statement he linked three key myths together: the role of airports (hence the need for that gateway drug of military intervention known as the "no-fly zone"); the role of "mercenaries" (Africans flying in, see chapter 4); and the expectation of "genocide" (geared toward the language of the UN's doctrine of the Responsibility to Protect and the need to "prevent" genocide).

Dabbashi was not alone in making these assertions. Among others like him, Soliman Bouchuiguir, president of the Libyan League for Human Rights, told Reuters on March 14 that if "Gaddafi's forces" reached Benghazi, "there will be a real bloodbath, a massacre like we saw in

Rwanda." This is just another way of referencing "genocide," not actual, but expected (Abbas, 2011/3/14). That is not the only time we would be deliberately reminded of Rwanda. Out came Lt. General Roméo Dallaire, the much-worshipped Canadian force commander of the U.N. peacekeeping mission for Rwanda in 1994, currently an appointed-for-life senator in the Canadian Parliament and co-director of the *Will to Intervene* project at Concordia University in Montreal. In a precipitous sprint to judgment (i.e., "let's hope it's not too late"), Dallaire, not only made repeated references to Rwanda when trying to explain Libya, but he also spoke of Gaddafi as "employing genocidal threats to 'cleanse Libya house by house'" (Dallaire & Bernstein, 2011/3/18). Everywhere is Rwanda for the humanitarian imperialist, which makes one want to know what really happened there in 1994. It is especially present for the one who had no time to listen to Gaddafi's speech in its entirety. The famous speech of February 23, 2011 lasted more than one hour and was not translated live apart from a few minutes at a time, and the full translation and transcript were never made available by the media.[1] This is one instance where selective attention[2] to Gaddafi's suggested rhetorical excess was taken all too seriously, when on other occasions the powers that be were instead quick to dismiss it. U.S. State Department spokesman, Mark Toner waved away Gaddafi's alleged threats against Europe by saying that Gaddafi is "someone who's given to overblown rhetoric" (Sawer, 2011/7/2).

How very calm was Clinton's spokesman by contrast on that occasion. And how very convenient, because it was a very different reaction as seen as early as February 23, 2011, when President Obama declared that he had instructed his administration to come up with a "full range of options" to take against Gaddafi (Branigin, Sheridan, & Lynch, 2011/2/23). And as early as February 25, 2011, NATO Secretary General Anders Fogh Rasmussen ominously indicated the first signs of a NATO move on Libya.

---

1. One individual claims to have produced a transcript of the full speech, which appears to contain many errors and lines that are almost incomprehensible, which suggests he may be unfamiliar with Libyan dialect. It can be found here: <https://docs.google.com/document/d/10dy50LJY2QL7k2VuwKonUpSgCUX-_9ATQ-134Xka9fs/edit?hl=en&pli=1#>.

2. Other attempts were made to underscore that Gaddafi's speeches in response to the protests and uprising emphasized themes of national self-determination, revolution, and dignity, and railed against those collaborating with imperialists, rather than any threat to wipe out his own people. See <http://www.youtube.com/watch?v=MNH9Y0K-duo>.

In one message in Twitter, he stated, "I have called for an emergency meeting in the North Atlantic Council today to discuss Libya,"[3] and in another, "the situation in Libya is of great concern. NATO can act as an enabler and coordinator if and when member states will take action."[4] Rasmussen further indicated that NATO would be "prepared for any eventuality," after NATO met to discuss Libya (NATO, 2011/2/25). These statements came just a single day after Rasmussen said, "NATO as such has no plans to intervene" (NATO, 2011/2/21; see also 2011/2/24). But they came with the added caution that while Rasmussen did "not consider the situation in Libya a direct threat to NATO or NATO Allies...of course, there may be negative repercussions" (NATO, 2011/2/24).

"Genocide," unlike the careless way it was used by those quoted above, has a well established international legal definition, as seen repeatedly in the UN's 1948 Convention on the Prevention and Punishment of the Crime of Genocide, where genocide involves the persecution of a "a national, ethnical, racial or religious group" (UN, 1948, Art. 2). Not all violence is "genocidal." Internecine violence is not genocide. Genocide is neither just "lots of violence" nor violence against undifferentiated civilians. What Dabbashi, Dallaire, and others failed to do was to identify the persecuted national, ethnic, racial or religious group, and how it differed in those terms from those allegedly committing the genocide. They really ought to know better (and they do), one as a UN ambassador and the other as a much-exalted expert and lecturer on genocide. This suggests that their use of the "genocide" label was motivated by something other than a worry of genocide: in Dabbashi's case, it was the use of a convenient action-trigger, a message that was probably conveyed after he had first coordinated with others in the U.S. In Dallaire's case, it was likely a prejudice against Gaddafi, a willingness to believe that the worst case scenario was real, plus ignorance of Libya, and a resolute fixation on Rwanda as the frame of reference. In both cases, they helped to turn a legal concept into a fear and then a myth.

Foreign military intervention did, however, enable the actual genocidal violence that was routinely sidelined in the mass media and was discussed at the UN only once regime change either had occurred fully, or was close to doing so. That was the horrific violence against black African migrants

---

3. See Rasmussen's message in Twitter at <https://twitter.com/andersfoghr/status/41034955039588352>.
4. See: <https://twitter.com/andersfoghr/status/41037040686600192>.

and black Libyans, singled out solely on the basis of their skin colour, and persecuted as such, which fits the definition of genocide much better than violence against protesters. That violence, which could be justifiably quali-fied as "genocide," proceeded without impediment, without apology and until recently without much notice. That is the type of massacre that the white, Western world, and those who dominate the "conversation" about Libya missed (and not by accident). Otherwise, I might agree with Chomsky: "As for the term 'genocide,' perhaps the most honorable course would be to expunge it from the vocabulary until the day, if it ever comes, when honesty and integrity can become an 'emerging norm'" (Chomsky, 2010).

"Gaddafi is Bombing His Own People"

For insurance purposes, two lies are better than one. If one has a primary lie, an auxiliary lie as a failsafe mechanism can come in handy. Opposition activists and defected Libyan diplomats had already asserted that airports were being used to ferry in African mercenaries. That was the first reason for which a no-fly zone was called. However, a second reason was added very quickly, making the no-fly zone an idea that took off not just at the UN but with a whole spate of normally anti-war intellectuals. These included Noam Chomsky, who supported the no-fly zone intervention and the rebellion as "wonderful" and "liberation" (Chomsky, 2012/1/7; Glazebrook, 2011/11/24), and Chris Hedges, who supported the no-fly zone, demonizing Gaddafi as "insane as he appears and as dangerous," but else-where disingenuously commenting, "you would think we would have learned in Afghanistan or Iraq. But I guess not" (Hedges, 2011/9/5). That second reason was that the Libyan government (or "Gaddafi") was allegedly using the air force to fire on and bomb protesters. "Gaddafi is killing his own people," became the refrain, a distinct phrasing that was already tried and tested in the demonization of Saddam Hussein. The model was provided by the George W. Bush administration as it ratcheted up the war rhetoric prior to invading Iraq in 2003 (on March 19, also the date of the first bombing of Libya in 2011).

Thus on February 21, when the first alarmist "warnings" about "geno-cide" were being made by the Libyan opposition, both Al Jazeera (2011/2/21) and the BBC claimed that Gaddafi had deployed his air force against pro-testers. As the BBC "reported": "Witnesses say warplanes have fired on protesters in the city" (2011/2/21). Yet, on March 1, in a Pentagon press conference, when asked: "Do you see any evidence that he [Gaddafi] actually has fired on his own people from the air? There were reports of it, but do you have independent confirmation? If so, to what extent?" U.S. Secretary of Defense Robert Gates replied, "We've seen the press reports, but we have no confirmation of that." Backing him up was Admiral Mullen: "That's correct. We've seen no confirmation whatsoever" (U.S. Department of Defense, 2011/3/1).

In fact, claims that Gaddafi also used helicopters and anti-aircraft guns against unarmed protesters are totally unfounded, a pure fabrication based on fake claims (Cockburn, 2011/6/24). This is important since it was Gaddafi's domination of Libyan air space that foreign interventionists wanted to nullify, and therefore myths of atrocities perpetrated from the air took on added value as providing an entry point for foreign military intervention that went far beyond any mandate to "protect civilians."

"Save Benghazi"

Benghazi became somewhat of a "holy city" in the international discourse dominated by leaders of the European Union and NATO. Benghazi was the one city on earth that could rebel and not be touched by government. It was like sacred ground. Tripoli? Sirte? Sabha? Those could be sacrificed, as we all looked on, without a hint of protest from any of the otherwise vociferous human rights quarters. This was true even as we began to get the first reports of the first mass slaughters in Tripoli as the insurgents entered the city (BBC, 2011/8/27, 2011/8/31).

"If we waited one more day," Barack Obama said in his March 28, 2011 address, "Benghazi, a city nearly the size of Charlotte, could suffer a massacre that would have reverberated across the region and stained the conscience of the world" (Obama, 2011/3/28). In a joint letter, Obama with UK Prime Minister David Cameron and French President Nicolas Sarkozy asserted: "By responding immediately, our countries halted the advance of Gaddafi's forces. The bloodbath that he had promised to inflict on the citizens of the besieged city of Benghazi has been prevented. Tens of thousands of lives have been protected" (Obama, Cameron, & Sarkozy, 2011/4/14).

Yet, French jets bombed a retreating column (IOL, 2011/3/19; also see Figure 5.1), but what we saw was a very short column of 14 tanks, 20 armoured personnel carriers, some trucks and ambulances. That column clearly could have neither destroyed nor occupied Benghazi, a city of

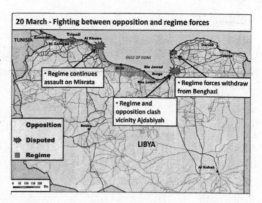

FIGURE 5.1 Map from a March 20, 2011, U.S. Department of Defense briefing showing fighting between rebel and government forces in Libya, and the withdrawal of Gaddafi's forces from Benghazi. (Source: U.S. Department of Defense via Wikimedia Commons.)

nearly 700,000 people (EuroNews, 2011/3/20; Reuters, 2011/3/20). The rebels' media centre in Benghazi in fact proclaimed that they had halted the advance of government armour, and that they had pushed "Gaddafi's forces" out of Benghazi (IOL, 2011/3/19). There was no hint that they were ever in any trouble of being overrun, let alone that they faced the prospect of mass extermination.

To date no evidence has been furnished that shows Benghazi would have witnessed the loss of "tens of thousands" of lives as proclaimed by Obama, Cameron, and Sarkozy. Professor Alan J. Kuperman criticized this proposition from early on:

> "The best evidence that Khadafy did not plan genocide in Benghazi is that he did not perpetrate it in the other cities he had recaptured either fully or partially—including Zawiya, Misurata, and Ajdabiya, which together have a population greater than Benghazi....Khadafy's acts were a far cry from Rwanda, Darfur, Congo, Bosnia, and other killing fields....Despite ubiquitous cellphones equipped with cameras and video, there is no graphic evidence of deliberate massacre....Nor did Khadafy ever threaten civilian massacre in Benghazi, as Obama alleged. The 'no mercy' warning, of March 17, targeted rebels only, as reported by The New York Times, which noted that Libya's leader promised amnesty for those 'who throw their weapons away'. Khadafy even offered the rebels an escape route and open border to Egypt, to avoid a fight 'to the bitter end'." (Kuperman, 2011/4/14)

In the case of Misrata, which was targeted far more ferociously than Benghazi—a reality that was not ended by NATO's military intervention, but rather prolonged—Kuperman also disputes the idea that the government's violence constituted "genocide." At the time of writing in April 2011, he noted that there had been 257 deaths, but that Misrata's population was

400,000. More importantly, of the 949 wounded, he found that just under three percent were women, and therefore the violence targeted men in a ratio that suggests the targeting could not be of an indiscriminate nature, aimed at simply wiping out Misrata (Kuperman 2011/4/14).

With reference to the "threatened" massacre or genocide in Benghazi, it is important to note that, even nearly a year after Gaddafi was overthrown, and the files of his intelligence ministry ransacked, and former officials in his regime were either captured or had defected, not a single document or testimony was ever presented to show that orders were given, troops allotted, munitions distributed, officers put in charge, and plans drawn up for what would have been a massive military operation. We do not have so much as just the name of the officer who would have been put in charge of such an operation. Surely if he existed, he would have been named a wanted man by the NTC. Instead there was absolutely nothing, except a demand for belief: foreign policy and human rights activism, like religion, were conducted on the basis of faith alone.

In fact, during the uprising in Benghazi, Amnesty International found that no more than 110 people had been killed during the protests (including pro-government people), with another 59 to 64 in Baida (Cockburn, 2011/6/24). This is still lower than the 232 persons killed in Cairo during the January protests in Egypt, according to Human Rights Watch (Laub & Al-Shalchi, 2011/2/7). Large-scale massacres in a city did occur, however, but in Tripoli, as the rebels entered and began to "wreak revenge," at the start of a months-long reign of terror (Cockburn, 2011/8/28).

Saving Benghazi is an idea that encapsulated a series of myths propagated to justify the international militarization of the Libyan conflict, aided by major news media in the West. The dominant characterization was that the protests in Libya were peaceful, and met by brutal and lethal force, which then escalated the conflict into military action. As Hillary Clinton pontificated, "When the Libyan people sought to realize their democratic aspirations, they were met by extreme violence from their own government" (U.S. Department of State, 2011/3/24). In line with the State Department, CNN's Ben Wedeman told viewers, "It appears that the policy of Moammar Gadhafi is similar to that of Attila the Hun or Genghis Khan simply slaughtering his opponents where he can....given what we've seen so far from Moammar Gadhafi and his willingness, for instance, to use the air force against peaceful protesters" (CNN, 2011/2/25). Thus CNN added to its earlier postings about helicopters being used to shoot demonstrators, a claim similarly made by Saudi Arabia's Al Arabiya, which went as far as "reporting" that fighter jets were used, or even more bizarre claims that Libyan Mirage jets were conducting bombing runs in Tripoli itself, and yet somehow managed to be recorded by absolutely no one (CNN, 2011/2/19; Al Arabiya, 2011/2/21; Chowdhury, 2011/2/23). Other Western news media made equally extraordinary claims, reporting from Cairo rather than Libya itself, such as *The Telegraph's* Nick Meo who "reported" that, "artillery and helicopter gunships were used against crowds of demonstrators," adding to the myth that aircraft were used against protesters (Meo, 2011/2/20). In addition, some media relied upon partisan "human rights" groups, none of which reported from Libya itself, but were usually small, foreign-based operations. One example was Agence France Presse whose sources for claims of demonstrators killed by government forces included Libya Watch as well as Libya Al-Youm, both based in London along with "Human Rights Solidarity," which was also not reporting from Libya but from its base in Geneva (AFP, 2011/2/16).

Yet there were indications from those who actually reported from the scene of the protests and from interviews with demonstrators that the picture was more complicated than that of peaceful, unarmed protesters brutally slaughtered by government forces. One correspondent revealed that, "In the neighborhoods of the capital that have staged major peaceful protests against Colonel Qaddafi, many have volunteered—speaking on the condition of anonymity—that their demonstrations were nonviolent mainly because they could not obtain weapons fast enough. Even one religious leader associated with Sufism—a traditionally pacifist sect something like the Islamic equivalent of the Quakers—lamented his own tribe's lack of guns for the fight" (Kirkpatrick, 2011/3/21). Others reported that protesters torched police stations, broke into the compounds of security services, attacked government offices, torched vehicles, and called for the overthrow of the government (BBC, 2011/2/16; Black, 2011/2/17; Cowell, 2011/2/16). Meanwhile, in response to the violence, government forces were reported as using tear gas, water cannons, and rubber bullets—very similar to methods frequently used in Western nations against far more peaceful protests that lack the element of sedition (BBC, 2011/2/16). Ali Hashem, who reported from Libya for Al Jazeera and who traveled with the rebels, later revealed:

> "Actually, in Libya, the beginning of the revolution and the real start of the revolution is when the rebels, or, let's say, the activists, at that time, occupied the barracks in Benghazi, and they went inside and took all the weapons. And

then it started. Then everyone had weapons and everyone was kind of, you know, fighting from that time." (Hashem & Jay, 2012/3/21)[5]

In rare instances, the dominant media briefly quoted the kinds of experts that they respect, such as Andrew McGregor of the Jamestown Foundation and director of Aberfoyle International Security, who argued that "this wasn't a peaceful revolution of the masses against a government that had no public support," adding, "this revolt never really had the strength to succeed. There was this feeling among the rebels that all we have to do is show up. But you should take a couple of years to get it organized first" (Basu, 2011/6/29).

This leads to important recognition of the fact that without a considerable degree of popular support the Libyan government could not have lasted as long as it did, driving the rebel forces into retreat and then into a prolonged stalemate that lasted several months. The opposition relied on several prosthetic devices to make up for their neglect of political footwork within Libya, those devices being primarily local violence plus reliance on internationalized violence delivered by NATO. This lack of a necessary political groundwork not only revealed itself in the way that "solidarity" was demanded of Western activists, with the appeal going to their governments and militaries, but in the obvious lack of local legitimacy marking the weak government that followed Gaddafi's overthrow and the proliferation of violent militias that often fought each other.

The UN and the Right to Speak for Libya

"The International Federation for Human Rights said in a statement Monday that at least 300 to 400 people had been killed since Feb. 15, citing the Libyan League for Human Rights, which is a member of the federation": NBC made this report without any question just a week into the uprising (2011/2/22). The same Libyan League for Human Rights (LLHR) claimed that the "Libyan regime is apparently using mercenaries from Chad, Niger, Zimbabwe and some former henchmen of the former dictator Charles Taylor" (FIDH, 2011/2/21). Never did they advance evidence, and never were they proven correct, quite the contrary. It might not have been important, apart from being another example of media bias, if it

---

5. Hashem resigned in protest at Al Jazeera's heavily slanted agenda and the excessive degree to which the Qatari regime, which deployed forces against Libya and funded the rebels, was taking control of the news reporting agenda.

were not for the fact that these were the kinds of voices and statements that were allowed to dominate the "discussion" of Libya at the United Nations in the early days and weeks of the uprising.

Julien Teil, a remarkable independent documentary journalist in France and author of the video documentary project titled "The Humanitarian War,"[6] wrote an overview in French of what his investigations had uncovered, as shown in his documentaries. As he explained, his work makes it possible to further understand "how international law and justice works, but mostly how its basic principles can be bypassed." The resolutions passed against Libya were based on various allegations, he noted, "notably on the statement claiming that Gaddafi had led jet attacks on his own people and engaged in violent repression against the uprising, killing more than 6,000 civilians." These allegations, as Teil found, "were spread before they could have been verified." Yet it was on the basis of such claims that the Libyan government was suspended from the United Nations Human Rights Council, before even being referred to the United Nations Security Council, thereby preventing the Libyan government from countering any of the allegations, or at least demanding that proof be submitted. One of the main sources for the claim that Gaddafi was killing his own people, as Teil pointed out, was the Libyan League for Human Rights (LLHR), an organization linked to the International Federation of Human Rights (the FIDH). On February 21, 2011, the Secretary General of the LLHR, Dr. Soliman Bouchuiguir, initiated a petition in collaboration with UN Watch, a right wing and pro-Israel NGO, and the National Endowment for Democracy (NED). The petition was signed by more than seventy NGOs (UN Watch, 2011/2/21b). A few days later, on February 25, Bouchuiguir went to the U.N. Human Rights Council in order to expose the allegations concerning "the crimes of Gaddafi's government." In July 2011 Teil went to Geneva to interview Bouchuiguir. Soliman Bouchuguir was then the new Libyan ambassador to Switzerland, and he confirmed to Teil both his ties to the opposition NTC and the fact that the numbers presented at the UN were arbitrarily generated (see Teil, 2011).

Bouchuiguir presented allegations at the UN Human Rights Council, claiming 6,000 had been killed, and 3,000 in Tripoli alone (RT, 2011/12/2). When asked by Teil how he arrived at those figures, Bouchuiguir responded: "I got that information from the Libyan Prime Minister, of the other side! That is Mr. Mahmoud of the Warfallah Tribe of the National Transitional

---

6. "The Humanitarian War" at: <http://www.laguerrehumanitaire.fr/english>.

Council, was the one who gave me these numbers." Pressed by Teil to provide evidence of the number of those killed by government forces, Bouchuguir plainly said: "There is no evidence."[7]

The man referred to by Bouchuguir was Mahmoud Jibril, the second-ranked member of the NTC. In addition, Bouchuguir also confirmed that the LLHR and the opposition NTC shared an overlap in membership, with at least one senior representative of the LLHR also being a member of the NTC until March 2011. Further on, he notes that several ministers of the new NTC interim government were also members of the Libyan League for Human Rights, specifically Mahmoud Shammam (the media minister) and Ali Tarhouni (the oil minister), and in fact continued to be members.[8]

Bouchuguir was careful to note the sequence of events in his interview with Teil: all of the NGOs that signed the UN Watch petition were acquainted with one another, and it was the UN Human Rights Council that brought them to Geneva to present their case. That was when they signed the petition.[9] In his presentation at the UNHRC, Bouchuguir further added the allegation that the Libyan government was using planes to bomb its own people, and using indiscriminate violence against all civilians. Bouchuguir's testimony also ended up "informing" the International Criminal Court's indictment of Muammar Gaddafi, Saif al-Islam Gaddafi, and Abdullah Senussi.

The UN Human Rights Council essentially stacked the deck against Libya. It did not allow the Libyan government to represent itself, since it suspended its membership, which is itself a highly questionable move. Yet the Council allowed a "human rights" group tied to a belligerent party to do all the speaking. Moreover, it took that group's claims at face value, without demanding evidence, and without questioning the allegations. It then advanced its report to the UN Security Council.

In addition to being suspended from the Human Rights Council, Libya was barred from appointing a new Permanent Ambassador to the UN to replace its staff that defected to the opposition (AP, 2011/4/27). This is extraordinary if not outrageous, for the UN as an organization was now effectively engaging in an advance form of regime change. It was admit-

---

7. See the interview at http://www.youtube.com/watch?v=MmahzMfw6T4. The response noted comes at around the 5 minute mark.

8. Also at <http://www.youtube.com/watch?v=MmahzMfw6T4> around the 6:40 mark.

9. See the interview at <http://www.youtube.com/watch?v=j4evwAMIh4Y>.

tedly under pressure from the U.S. who refused to issue a visa to Libya's new choice, Ali Treki, one of its most senior diplomats.[10] The Libyan staff that defected—Ambassador Abdurrahman Mohamed Shalgham and his Deputy, Ibrahim Dabbashi—did in fact lose their accreditation, but were given "courtesy passes" by the UN that allowed them "to enter the Security Council visiting room and to deliver anti-Gaddafi statements in the halls of the United Nations" (Lynch, 2011/3/31; Avni, 2011/3/30).

To get around the visa blockade, the Libyan government advanced a replacement in the person of former Nicaraguan Foreign Minister Miguel D'Escoto Brockman, a priest who served in Nicaragua's revolutionary Sandinista government and who years later was also the Secretary General of the UN's General Assembly. On March 31, 2011, D'Escoto was scheduled to make a briefing on Libya at the UN. He was promptly blocked by Susan Rice, U.S. Ambassador to the UN, who argued that D'Escoto was on a tourist visa (not a diplomatic visa) and that it could be "reviewed" —as in revoked—if he tried to speak for Libya or any other country (Lauria, 2011/4/1).[11] In response, D'Escoto said that the UN had become "a lethal weapon of the Empire," referring to the U.S. which was clearly abusing its role as host of the UN in New York (*Prensa Latina*, 2011/3/31). D'Escoto rightly criticized UN Secretary General Ban Ki-moon, accusing him of betraying the UN Charter, while not ruling out coordination between the UN Secretary General and the U.S. to prevent former Libyan Foreign Minister Ali Treki from the entering the U.S. (*Prensa Latina*, 2011/3/31). Meanwhile, at the U.S. mission at the UN, President Obama himself "warmly greeted" defected ambassador Shalgham (Watson & Roth, 2011/3/31). As early as March, the U.S. had shutdown the Libyan Embassy in Washington, DC, ordered its diplomats out, and handed the Libyan embassy over to the NTC by early August 2011 (Labott & Dougherty, 2011/8/2).

Amnesty International versus Libya

On February 23, 2011, mere days into the uprising and well before it had a chance to ascertain, corroborate or confirm any facts on the ground,

---

10. See this BBC live blog at <http://news.bbc.co.uk/2/hi/africa/9414812.stm>.
11. See the coverage by Inner City Press at <http://www.youtube.com/watch?v=PgV_Dc1002w> and see its related write-up at <http://www.innercitypress.com/libya-5descoto033111.html>.

Amnesty International began launching public accusations against Libya, the African Union, and the UN Security Council for failing to take action (AI, 2011/2/23). Even more stunning, given what was described in the previous chapter, was Amnesty's reinforcement of the "African mercenary" myth that justified and provided cover for the lethal targeting of innocent black African migrants and black Libyans.

> "Amnesty International also criticized the response of the African Union to the unfolding crisis, which has seen hundreds killed and persistent reports of mercenaries being brought in from African countries by the Libyan leader to violently suppress the protests against him.
>
> " 'It is outrageous that the African Union Peace and Security Council has not even met to discuss the emergency taking place in one of its own member states,' said Salil Shetty.
>
> "Amnesty International called on the African Union to ensure that its member states, particularly those bordering Libya, are not complicit in human rights abuses in Libya." (AI, 2011/2/23)

Amnesty, in making such specific accusations (echoing the Libyan opposition), in calling for an assets freeze and arms embargo and more actions with each passing day, was essentially representing one side of the conflict, namely the insurgents, adopting their representational strategies, and calling for measures that would benefit them. Amnesty thus effectively made itself a party to the conflict.

Yet Amnesty International showed an amazing ability to speak with two voices, or at least, through two faces. This was captured very vividly in a short documentary by Julien Teil, in his interview with Genevieve Garrigos, president of Amnesty International France, on the subject of Amnesty repeating the allegations of "Gaddafi forces" employing "African mercenaries" (see GlobalResearchTV, 2012/1/12). Garrigos spoke on France24 on February 22, 2011, and clearly said that on February 18 and 19 Amnesty had received "information" that the Libyan government had sent in "foreign mercenaries" to fight against the protesters in order to "accelerate the oppressive process." In this she echoed Dr. Soliman Bouchuiguir and his presentation at the UN Human Rights Council as the representative of the Libyan League for Human Rights, which, as noted above, had overlapping membership with the opposition, and soon to be crowned, National Transitional Council. Within five months, Garrigos took an entirely different position, seemingly forgetting her very own assertions of supposed fact in February 2011. Speaking to Teil, she noted how since the beginning there were "rumours" of "mercenaries" that came from the "anti-Gaddafi forces," as if speaking as an observer. Garrigos further noted that the accusations were against "dark-coloured people or black people," who could also have been Libyans. Garrigos then added: "Today we have to admit that we have no evidence Gaddafi employed mercenary forces," later continuing, "we have no sign nor evidence to corroborate these rumours." She repeated that Amnesty's investigators never found any "mercenaries," agreeing with Teil's characterization of their existence as a "legend" spread by the mass media.

One could very easily argue that Amnesty International made errors in judgment, which it willingly corrected on the basis of the work of its own researchers who contradicted the organization's initial statements. The reader will have noted that throughout this book Amnesty International has been quoted liberally and continues to be, precisely because of its investigators' on-the-ground fact checking and reporting. However, one might also ask if the organization's purposes are not also advanced by making the accusations that justified war and Western support for the insurgents, and then being on the other end to pick up the pieces. It thus benefited twice, which is a boon for an organization that needs to assert its relevance through higher visibility in order to attract donations, maintain budgets, pay for staff, and so forth. The latter observation is not without merit.

Francis A. Boyle, a professor of International Law at the University of Illinois at Urbana-Champaign, and a former board member of Amnesty International-USA, pointed out the following in an interview.

"Amnesty International is primarily motivated not by human rights but by publicity. Second comes money. Third comes getting more members. Fourth, internal turf battles. And then finally, human rights, genuine human rights concerns. To be sure, if you are dealing with a human rights situation in a country that is at odds with the United States or Britain, it gets an awful lot of attention, resources, man and womanpower, publicity, you name it, they can throw whatever they want at that. But if it's dealing with violations of human rights by the United States, Britain, Israel, then it's like pulling teeth to get them to really do something on the situation. They might, very reluctantly and after an enormous amount of internal fighting and battles and pressures, you name it.... You'll see a pretty good coincidence of the enemies that Amnesty International goes after and the interests of both the United States and British governments. Let's take an older example—apartheid in South Africa under the former criminal regime in South Africa. Amnesty International refused adamantly to condemn apartheid in South Africa. Despite my best efforts while I was on the board, and other board members, they would not do it. They are the only human rights organization in the entire world to have refused to condemn apartheid in South Africa. Now they can give you some cock-and-bull theory about why they wouldn't do this. But the bottom line was that the biggest supporter, economic and political supporter of the criminal apartheid regime in South Africa was the British government, followed by the United States government. And so no matter how hard we tried, no matter what we did, they would not condemn apartheid in South Africa. Now I just mention that as one among many examples." (Boyle & Bernstein, 2002)

Just as in Libya, in the lead up to the first war against Iraq in 1991, Amnesty International chose sensationalism first, endorsing the infamous, fabricated stories of Iraqi troops dashing babies from incubators to the floors of hospitals in Kuwait. Amnesty International-UK was hell bent on publishing the report of incubator babies, placing it, "on the fast track, they were ramming it through. They didn't care" (Boyle & Bernstein, 2002). As Boyle pointed out, Amnesty simply refused to acknowledge any error, with dire consequences for Iraq: "They then put the report out, and you know what a terrible impact that had in terms of war propaganda. Of the six votes in the United States Senate that passed the resolution to go to war, several of those senators said that they were influenced by the Amnesty report" (Boyle & Bernstein, 2002).

If there seems to be just a coincidence between the states that Amnesty International prefers to investigate and criticize, and those that are chosen as enemies by the U.S. and UK, it might be a by-product of the revolving door between Amnesty International-USA and the U.S. State Department. Or it might be indicative of an amicable relationship that such an exchange of personnel can occur. In November 2011, Amnesty International-USA announced that it had selected Suzanne Nossel as its new Executive Director (AI, 2011/11/17). From August 2009 to November 2011, Suzanne Nossel was the U.S. State Department's Deputy Assistant Secretary for the Bureau of International Organization Affairs.[12] As Amnesty further pointed out, in her capacity as Deputy Assistant Secretary under Hillary Clinton, "Nossel played a leading role in U.S. engagement at the U.N. Human Rights Council, including the initiation of human rights resolutions on Iran, Syria, Libya, Cote d'Ivoire." Moreover, she had previously served as the Chief Operating Officer of Human Rights Watch, which

---

12. Nossel's archived profile page on the State Department website is available here: <http://web.archive.org/web/20110102101739/http://www.state.gov/p/io/132179.htm>.

shows the spread of the network of connections, overlaps and conver-
gences between elements of the government-human rights consortium.
Last but not least, Nossel also worked for a business consultancy, McKinsey
and Co. In her new capacity at Amnesty-USA, Nossel has taken to writing columns pushing for regime change in Syria. She appears to have little
concern for the "human rights" outcome of a fractured state and escalating civil war, while absolutely gloating about the treatment Libya received
at the UN (Nossel, 2012/2/10).

"Viagra-fueled Mass Rape"

It appears that those reporting the war crimes and other human rights
violations of the "Gaddafi forces" were not satisfied that they were sufficient in number or were awful enough. What was needed was the inven-
tion of a whole new set of hard-to-believe stories, such as the stories of
Libyan government troops, with erections powered by Viagra, going on
a rape spree. Perhaps it was peddled because it's the kind of story that
"captures the imagination of traumatized publics," a story that even the
most severely anti-Gaddafi U.S. newspapers judged a "hoax" (Murphy,
2011/6/13). This story was taken so seriously that some people started writing to Pfizer to get it to stop selling Viagra to Libya, since its product was
allegedly being used as a "weapon of war."

People who otherwise should know better set out to deliberately mis-
inform the international public with crassly phallo-centric illusions. The
press that critically judged its own failings for showing so much credulity
in the first place did little to reflect on the meaning of press freedom and
the use of private media to disseminate propaganda at a time when their
states were at war in demolishing another state. Nor did any international
band of journalists "without borders" or committee to protect journalists,
ever come out and criticize their own for such an egregious betrayal of
their profession's lofty goals.

The Viagra story was first disseminated, unsurprisingly, by Al Jazeera
(2011/3/28) in collaboration with its rebel partners who were favoured by
the Qatari regime that also funds Al Jazeera. Having a somber-voiced,
earnest-looking young British woman do the reporting added some pol-
ish to a story that should have invited mass ridicule. Instead, the story
was then redistributed by almost all other major Western news media (see
Iqbal, 2011/6/8, for some examples of sensationalist reporting, from the
BBC and AP).

Luis Moreno-Ocampo, Chief Prosecutor of the International Criminal Court, appeared before the international media to say that there was "information" (Bowcott, 2011/6/9) that Gaddafi distributed Viagra to his troops (AFP, 2011/6/8) in order "to enhance the possibility to rape" (Zirulnick, 2011/6/9), and that Gaddafi ordered the rape of hundreds of women (BBC, 2011/6/8). Moreno-Ocampo insisted, "We are getting information that Qaddafi himself decided to rape" (Varner, 2011/6/8) and that "we have information that there was a policy to rape in Libya those who were against the government" (Cockburn, 2011/6/24). Reaching a climax of vulgar innuendo, Ocampo exclaimed that Viagra is "like a machete" and that "Viagra is a tool of massive rape" (CNN, 2011/5/17).

In a startling declaration to the UN Security Council, U.S. Ambassador Susan Rice also asserted that Gaddafi was supplying his troops with Viagra to encourage mass rape (MacAskill, 2011/4/29). She offered no evidence whatsoever to back up her claim. Indeed, U.S. military and intelligence sources flatly contradicted Rice, telling NBC News that "there is no evidence that Libyan military forces are being given Viagra and engaging in systematic rape against women in rebel areas" (NBC, 2011/4/29). Rice is a liberal interventionist who was one of those to persuade Obama to intervene in Libya. She used this myth because it helped her make the case at the UN that there was no "moral equivalence" between Gaddafi's human rights abuses and those of the insurgents.

U.S. Secretary of State Hillary Clinton also declared that, "Gadhafi's security forces and other groups in the region are trying to divide the people by using violence against women and rape as tools of war, and the United States condemns this in the strongest possible terms." She added that she was "deeply concerned" by these reports of "wide-scale rape" (Sidner, 2011/6/17). While issuing no such condemnation of the insurgents' lynching of black victims, neither Clinton nor Rice have yet retracted their unfounded rape allegations.

By June 10, 2011, Cherif Bassiouni, who was then leading a UN rights inquiry into the situation in Libya, suggested that the Viagra and mass rape claim was part of a "massive hysteria" (AFP, 2011/6/10). Indeed, both sides in the war made the same allegations against each other. Bassiouni also told the press of a case of "a woman who claimed to have sent out 70,000 questionnaires and received 60,000 responses, of which 259 reported sexual abuse" (AFP, 2011/6/10). However, while his teams asked for those questionnaires they never received them: "But she's going around the world telling everybody about it…so now she got that information to

Ocampo and Ocampo is convinced that here we have a potential 259 women who have responded to the fact that they have been sexually abused," Bassiouni said (AFP, 2011/6/10). He also pointed out that it "did not appear to be credible that the woman was able to send out 70,000 questionnaires in March when the postal service was not functioning" (AFP, 2011/6/10). In fact, Bassiouni's team "uncovered only four alleged cases" of rape and sexual abuse. "Can we draw a conclusion that there is a systematic policy of rape? In my opinion we can't" (Nebehay, 2011/6/10). In addition to the UN, Amnesty International's Donatella Rovera said in an interview with the French daily *Libération* that Amnesty had "not found cases of rape….Not only have we not met any victims, but we have not even met any persons who have met victims. As for the boxes of Viagra that Gaddafi is supposed to have had distributed, they were found intact near tanks that were completely burnt out" (Perrin, 2011/6/22).

However, this did not stop some news manufacturers from trying to maintain the rape claims, in modified form. The BBC went on to add another layer just a few days after Bassiouni's revelations poured justified scorn on the ICC and the media: the BBC now claimed that rape victims in Libya faced "honour killings" (Harter, 2011/6/14). This was news to the few Libyans I know, who never heard of honour killings in their country. The scholarly literature turns up little or nothing on this phenomenon in Libya. The honour killings myth served a useful purpose for keeping the mass rape claim on life support just a little longer: it suggests that women would not come forward and give evidence, out of shame, and fear of being killed by their families. Also just a few days after Bassiouni spoke, Libyan insurgents, in collaboration with CNN (Sidner, 2011/6/17), made a last-ditch effort to save the rape allegations: they presented a cell phone with a rape video on it, claiming it belonged to a government soldier. The men shown in the video, however, were in civilian clothes. There is no evidence of Viagra anywhere in the video. There was no date on the video and we have no idea who recorded it or where. Those presenting the cell phone claimed that many other videos existed, but they were conveniently being destroyed to preserve the "honour" of the victims.

Finally, in March 2012, the UN Human Rights Council's commission of inquiry into war crimes in Libya did not even mention the Viagra allegations in its sections on sexual violence and rape, and even went as far as concluding that it was impossible to say there was any systematic policy of sexual violence against the civilian population.

"The Commission found that sexual violence occurred in Libya and played a significant role in provoking fear in various communities. The Commission established that sexual torture was used as a means to extract information from and to humiliate detainees. The Commission did not find evidence to substantiate claims of a widespread or a systematic attack, or any overall policy of sexual violence against a civilian population." (UNHRC, 2012, p. 14)

The ICC's Luis Moreno-Ocampo, not willing to let a bad joke die, felt nonetheless he needed to get the last word. He repeated more allegations, but again without any evidence, just a promise of evidence, an assertion that evidence exists, even though such evidence had been shared with no one, neither the UNHRC nor the ICC itself. Having spoken to the new Libyan general prosecutor in charge of a system of justice which Ocampo's own ICC had found incapable of holding a fair trial, Ocampo insisted: "he has a very good case....He has witnesses, interceptions, documents; apparently he has a lot of evidence" and this apparently included cases of rape (AFP, 2012/4/21). As others have suggested, Ocampo may have been keen to direct attention to sexual violence in Libya in order to dignify his own record, or perhaps deflect attention away from it. He was the subject of an internal complaint from the ICC's own media spokesman detailing Ocampo's "sexual misconduct" involving his attempt to force himself on a female South African journalist. In retaliation, Ocampo sacked the ICC media spokesman without due process, a decision which ended up costing the ICC £20,000 in moral damages as well as compensatory damages approaching £100,000 (Rozenberg, 2008/9/14).

Both undignified and vulgar, the Viagra-rape accusations showed the atrociously low level to which international discourse controlled by the powerful, and the hypocritical, could sink. More importantly, it demonstrates how the discourse of rights has been enlisted in the service of making war.

"Protecting Civilians"

Having falsely asserted that Libyan civilians faced impending "genocide" at the hands of the Libyan government, it became easier for Western powers to invoke the UN's 2005 doctrine of the Responsibility to Protect (R2P) (UN, 2005, p. 30; UN, 2009). Meanwhile, it is not at all clear that by the time the UN Security Council passed Resolution 1973 (UN, 2011; UNSC, 2011/3/17) that the violence in Libya had even reached the levels seen in Egypt, Syria, and Yemen. The most common refrain used against critics of the selectivity of this supposed "humanitarian interventionism" is that just because the West cannot intervene everywhere does not mean it should not have intervened in Libya. Perhaps, but that still does not explain why Libya was the chosen target. This is a vital point because some of the earliest critiques of R2P voiced at the UN raised the issue of selectivity, of who gets to decide, and why some crises where civilians are targeted (say, Gaza) are essentially ignored, while others receive maximum concern. Did in fact R2P serve as the new fig leaf for hegemonic geopolitics (see Chomsky, 2009)?

Moreover the Security Council manifestly failed to live up to the stipulations of its own resolution, specifically article 2 of UNSCR 1973 which first stressed the need to use diplomacy to find peaceful solutions. The bombing began a mere two days after the resolution was passed. A UN Special Envoy to Libya was to be appointed but his mission existed only on paper. Article 5 granted to the League of Arab States a special role in maintaining peace and security "in the region," and thus denied the African Union its rightful role. Anti-war U.S. Congressman, Dennis Kucinich, also revealed that he received reports that when a peaceful settlement in Libya was finally at hand, it was deliberately "scuttled by State Department officials": "Given that the department of state seems to have taken a singular role in launching the US into this war, it is more than disconcerting to hear that the same agency has played a role in frustrating a resolution to this conflict" (Kucinich, 2011/8/21).

UN Secretary General Ban Ki-moon made a statement that also ran counter to the role of the UN, and to his role within it, when he publicly spoke up in defence of the U.S. and NATO against critics of the war. He declared, "Security Council resolution 1973, I believe, was strictly enforced within the limit, within the mandate. This military operation done by the NATO forces was strictly within (resolution) 1973. I believe this is what we have seen, and there should be no misunderstanding on that" (Charbonneau, 2011/12/14). Russia's ambassador to the UN, Vitaly Churkin, rightly responded that the UN leadership "should not throw its weight around when issues of such importance are being debated within the Security Council. Only the Security Council can be the judge of whether its resolutions have been faithfully implemented" (Witcher, 2011/12/19).

By invoking R2P, the myth that was created for the international audience was that foreign military intervention in Libya was purely guided by humanitarian concerns, and solely with the intent of protecting civilians.

To make the myth work, one has to willfully ignore at least three key realities.

One of these realities is the new scramble for Africa, where Chinese interests are seen as competing with the West for access to resources and political influence. AFRICOM and a range of other U.S. government initiatives are meant to counter this phenomenon, as identified by senior U.S. officials (Christensen & Swan, 2008/6/4; Moraff, 2007/9/19). Gaddafi challenged AFRICOM's intent to establish military bases in Africa (see Rice, 2008/9/6). In a cable marked "secret" released by WikiLeaks, we learned that about AFRICOM the Libyan government "argued that any foreign military presence, regardless of mission, on the African continent would constitute unacceptable latter-day colonialism and would present an attractive target for al-Qaeda" (USET, 2008/8/29). AFRICOM was then later directly involved in leading the Libya intervention as part of "Operation Odyssey Dawn," preceding its aggressive role with a humanitarian one (AFRICOM, 2011/3/5; Skinner, 2011/3/30; Stevenson, 2011/5/9). I agree with Horace Campbell (2011/3/31) and the argument that, "U.S. involvement in the Libyan bombing is being turned into a public relations ploy for AFRICOM" and an "opportunity to give AFRICOM credibility under the facade of the Libyan intervention" (2011/3/24). In addition, Gaddafi's power and influence on the continent had also been increasing, through aid, investment, and a range of projects designed to lessen African dependency on the West and to challenge Western multilateral institutions by building African unity. He thus became a rival to U.S. interests.

Secondly, the anxiety of Western oil interests over Gaddafi's "resource nationalism" must be recognized, even if it was not the sole motive for the intervention (Mufson, 2011/6/10). Gaddafi seemingly threatened to take back what oil companies had gained (USET, 2007/11/15). That anxiety is now clearly manifest in the European corporate rush into Libya to scoop up the spoils of victory (see: Borger & Macalister, 2011/9/1; Shabi, 2011/8/25; Taylor, 2011/8/24; Tong, 2011/8/22; Upstream, 2011). But one must also recognize the apprehension over what Gaddafi was doing with those oil revenues in supporting greater African economic independence, his purchasing access into the central avenues of Western power, and the memory of his historically backing national liberation movements that challenged Western hegemony.

Thirdly, Washington's fear that the U.S. was losing a grip on the course of the so-called "Arab revolution" should be acknowledged (Wall Street

Journal, 2011/4/4). In particular, U.S. strategy became one of steering events toward the preservation of hierarchies in allied states which were critical to the U.S. either for their oil resources (Saudi Arabia), their provision of military bases (Bahrain), or their subservience to U.S. "counter-terrorism" strategy (Yemen). At the same time it encouraged rebellion in "adversary" states, especially those with friendly or close ties to Iran (Libya, Syria), while controlling rebellion and maintaining military dominance in others (Egypt). What first struck some of the more hopeful analysts as a grand act of regional decolonization has turned out to be the exact opposite. However, it is also a situation that continues to create blowback for the U.S., as evidenced in Libya itself, in that some of those the U.S. backed, enabled and fortified, have turned their sights on U.S. targets.

If one can dismiss each of these three key realities, then the idea that the war against Libya was a purely humanitarian war might begin to take on some credibility. However, a significant problem would remain, and that is the issue of "protecting civilians." Here we are faced with documented cases where NATO not only willfully failed to protect civilians in Libya, but it even deliberately and knowingly targeted them in a manner that constitutes terrorism by most official definitions used by Western governments. (See chapter 2 for key instances in Sirte).

Concerning the targeting of civilians, NATO admitted to deliberately targeting Libya's state television, killing three civilian reporters, in a move condemned by international journalist federations as a direct violation of a 2006 Security Council resolution banning attacks on journalists (AP, 2011/8/5; Kirkpatrick, 2011/7/30; UN, 2006). NATO routinely insisted that it carried out "precise" attacks, and in admitting no errors, one can only deduce that when it struck the state television building it did so knowing there were civilians present. A U.S. Apache helicopter, in a repeat of the infamous killings shown in the Collateral Murder video, gunned down civilians in the central square of Zawiya, killing the brother of the information minister among others (CNN, 2011/8/19). Taking a fairly liberal notion of what constitutes "command and control facilities," NATO also targeted a civilian residential space resulting in the deaths of some of Gaddafi's family members, including three grandchildren (Verkaik, 2011/5/1). As if to protect the myth of "protecting civilians" and the unconscionable contradiction of a "war for human rights," the major news media often kept silent about civilian deaths caused by NATO bombardments (FAIR, 2011/8/18). R2P was invisible when it came to protecting civilians targeted by NATO.

In terms of the failure to protect civilians, in a manner that is actually an international criminal offense, numerous reports revealed how NATO ships ignored the distress calls of refugee boats in the Mediterranean that were fleeing Libya. In May 2011, 61 African refugees died on a single vessel (Shenker, 2011/5/8), despite making contact with vessels belonging to NATO member states. In a repeat of the situation, dozens died in early August 2011 on another vessel (Simpson, 2011/8/5). In fact, on NATO's watch at least 1,500 refugees fleeing Libya died at sea during the war (Schwarz, 2011/8/13). They were mostly Africans from south of the Sahara, and they died in multiples of the death toll suffered by Benghazi residents during the protests. R2P was utterly absent for these people (see AI, 2011, p. 87).

In abdicating its assumed role in "protecting civilians," NATO interestingly also adopted the peculiar terminological twist that for Libya was designed to absolve the insurgents of any role in perpetrating crimes against civilians. Throughout the war, spokespersons for NATO and for the U.S. and European governments consistently portrayed all of the actions of "Gaddafi's forces" as "threatening civilians." They did so even when those forces were engaged in either defensive actions or combat against armed opponents, or were merely parked in a location. By protecting the insurgents, in the same breath as they spoke of protecting civilians, NATO clearly intended for us to see Gaddafi's armed opponents as mere civilians. In contrast, in Afghanistan, where NATO and the U.S. fund, train, and arm the Karzai regime in attacking "his own people" (like they do in Pakistan), the armed opponents are consistently labelled "terrorists" or "insurgents." And even if the majority of them are civilians who have never served in any official standing army, NATO does not call them "civilians" as it did in Libya. They are insurgents in Afghanistan, and their deaths at the hands of NATO are listed separately from the tallies for civilian casualties. By some twist of logic, in Libya, armed fighters were treated by NATO as civilians, as long as they were backed by NATO. In response to the announcement of the UN Security Council voting for military intervention, a volunteer translator for Western reporters in Tripoli made this key observation: "Civilians holding guns, and you want to protect them? It's a joke. We are the civilians. What about us?" (Richter, 2011/3/18).

NATO also provided a shield for the insurgents in Libya to victimize unarmed civilians in areas they came to occupy. There was no hint of any "responsibility to protect" in these cases. NATO assisted the rebels in starving Tripoli of supplies, subjecting its civilian population to a siege that deprived them of water, food, medicine, and fuel (Kirkpatrick, 2011/6/24). When Gaddafi was accused of doing this to Misrata, the international media were quick to cite this as a war crime (Stephen, 2011/6/18).

The refugee crisis in Libya, rather than being resolved by NATO's intervention, was instead exacerbated with more Libyans becoming internal refugees themselves as they fled from frontline cities such as Misrata, Sirte, and other towns and cities. Something of the real nature of Western "humanitarian" concern for protecting civilians was also manifested at an early pre-intervention stage by the Canadian government, with (dis) respect to foreign national refugees seeking to leave Libya. A Canadian government official explained how a Canadian plane could leave Libya empty when tens of thousands were seeking to flee: "there were no other citizens from *like-minded countries* who needed the flight" (Canadian Press, 2011/2/25, emphasis added).

The Alternative to Intervention?

The first question that was put to those who opposed NATO's military intervention in Libya, was typically in the form of, "do you want to see innocent Libyans being massacred by their own government?" This question was always flawed, not least of all because it was the first question but also because it begged only one acceptable answer. Similar questions were, "why do you oppose intervention, do you support the dictator?" or "how can we stand by while the opposition gets slaughtered?" They all shared the same flaws.

The core flaws with these arguments, posing as questions, are first: foreign military intervention could never and would never result in the cessation of violence suffered by Libyans. Second, it was not up to us in the West to choose a leader for Libya or determine on our own who stood as a "legitimate representative;" by endorsing one or another we would be justifying violence on the ground regardless. Third, standing by the rebels and standing against violence against civilians were never one and the same thing. If we get beyond the myth-making and the cloud of self-serving allegations, we are left with the realization that Benghazi was not going to be massacred. Some rebels who would not flee or surrender would certainly have been killed, just as certainly as they have been since NATO intervened, and just as certainly as many more Libyans have been killed than would have been the case had the revolt been defeated in March 2011.

The interventionists were instead satisfied with a prolonged war, which reanimated one of the belligerent parties as it was heading to certain defeat. If it was all meant to save lives, then it was a manifest failure: many more died, and continue to die even now, all to make the case that we "saved lives." Certainly some lives were saved, of particular individuals favoured by NATO, but at the cost of many more. Had Gaddafi won, would there not have been a wave of revenge killings? Possibly, however as soon as the insurgents gained ground in the Nafusa mountains, in Tripoli, in Sabha, and in Sirte, we immediately always saw their revenge killing, and few in the West were heard to cry out. Even with Gaddafi not winning, it's not clear that revenge killings from those who supported his mission have not also occurred against militias and members of the new government. Is this less repugnant to the humanitarians? To endorse NATO as the protector of civilians defies logic. In terms of the "responsibility to protect" civilians, NATO has either refused to do what it was mandated to do, or it has ignored that responsibility, or it has done the opposite.

None of the options would have come without a death toll. Those who advocated foreign military intervention enticed their audience with claims that military action that would last "days, not weeks" (Tapper, Khan, & Raddatz, 2011/3/18), and later "weeks, not months" (Keaten, 2011/3/24). They could thus portray the intervention as one that would, at the end of the day, save more lives than would be otherwise be lost because the war would be won quickly. Instead, NATO's bombing campaign lasted a full eight months, and the violence on the ground that preceded it in fact continued off and on well past Libya's elections in July 2012. In fact, NATO's aerial campaign against Libya lasted twice as long as it did in Kosovo, even if slightly fewer attack missions were flown against Libya. NATO's latest figures showed that 26,323 sorties had flown, including 9,658 attack sorties, over a period of 204 days (NATO, 2011/10/23), while in NATO's Kosovo war, which lasted 78 days, the total number of NATO sorties flown was 38,004, which included 10,484 attack sorties (PBS, 2000).

Before March 19, 2011, when military intervention by the West formally began, it seemed clear that there was a greater chance of the Libyan government achieving victory, and thus shortening the armed conflict, than there was of the rebellion achieving the same. Non-intervention would have been, ultimately, the most humanitarian of all of the options, but that is only if actually saving lives had indeed been the primary concern. It should be clear by now however that saving lives was not the primary concern. It is which side terminated more lives of the other side that counted the most. The decision to intervene was therefore political, not humanitarian: it was about turning the tables, not putting an end to conflict, at least not until Western states got the outcome they wanted in political terms.

The Libya intervention was touted as a success, by NATO itself, by the supporters of the intervention, and by happy members of the R2P advocacy crowd. Yes, the no-fly zone was successfully implemented: the Libyan Air Force never challenged it. However, the other measures of success failed to materialize with any of the promised rapidity, or simply never happened. These included: 1) significant government or military defections to the side of the insurgents; 2) an ability by the insurgents to advance without the support of what is ultimately the world's biggest air force (an ability they never achieved); and, 3) popular uprisings against the Gaddafi regime across Libya (which did not happen).

Instead, from early on we witnessed: 1) determined NATO involvement as a partisan to the conflict, where "protecting civilians" clearly meant protecting the insurgents and aiding their military advance; 2) an expansion of the expected duration of the military intervention; 3) a rise in the fighting between government forces and insurgents; 4) mounting human rights abuses committed against African migrants and black Libyans; and, 5) an increased outflow of hundreds of thousands of refugees from towns at the centre of the increased hostilities. Ultimately, Gaddafi was indeed displaced from the centre of power, but the high cost should give rise to sobriety rather than cheerful pronouncements.

So when "humanitarianism" and the cherished tenets of liberal imperialism failed to sway opponents of the war, those in the loosely defined European and American "left" who championed war as perhaps its loudest boosters, turned to the issue of "solidarity." What solidarity? Exactly what about the insurgents either inspired or demanded solidarity? That they hated Gaddafi? Until February 2011 most of the Western public barely mentioned Gaddafi in a conversation. Since the 1990s, he had become something like "old news," even the butt of late-night comedy shows. Few protested when their political leaders, and defence contractors, were the ones to coddle Gaddafi. If hating Gaddafi was the signal virtue of the insurgents, then when did it start to matter to us outsiders and why? A new generation had grown up since PanAm 103. Indeed, the new generation had to be taught about Gaddafi's old alleged transgressions, lest this generation realize that its two-minute hate had little to fall back on. Gaddafi also faced several armed uprisings and coup attempts before—

and in the West there was no public clamour for his head when he crushed them.

Solidarity is exactly the sort of thing that one should never have to demand, and never demand as an automatic, immediate response from complete strangers. Real solidarity is built with communication, exchange, reciprocity, mutual knowledge and trust. Those instructing us on solidarity could not even tell us who these rebels were, as they did not know themselves. Solidarity comes from earnest and transparent political practice, and not from taking morality hostage and engaging in emotional blackmail, while condemning those who would raise questions. It is only when you wish to produce hysteria that you resort to histrionics.

The demand for a NATO-led operation, under the guise of "solidarity," was a validation and legitimation of both that organization, and in a time when budgets for education, health, public works, and programs for the poor are all being slashed across the West, they helped to validate the need for maintaining heavy military spending or for revising cuts to such spending.[13] But then this was an indication of the kind of "solidarity" that figures in the NTC had built within Libya itself—partial, fragmented, and elitist—as evidenced even after the July elections, which produced a government without authority, that stood by and even withdrew police from the streets as extremists razed Sufi mosques and destroyed tombs. The anti-war movement and the anti-secrecy movement spearheaded by WikiLeaks were both damaged as result of the Libya intervention, as the clock was turned back. Moreover, the very meaning of "revolutionary" now came to include those who were the clients of imperial patrons. With the U.S. now speaking as if washed of all its sins in Iraq, recasting itself as an altruistic liberator of Arabs and protector of Muslims, the dynamics generated by the Libyan conflict were truly reactionary and retrograde.

The first steps in the Libyan civil war should have been to develop a peaceful transition, of the kind that the African Union advocated, for which it was never given a real chance. The friends of both sides of the

13. For a sample of the range of writings that dealt with the extended militarization of NATO states' foreign policies, the call for increased or maintained military spending, and the demand created for new generation fighters, see: Brewster, 2012/9/9; Bromund & Gardiner, 2011/4/19; BT, 2011/2/8; Emgler; 2011/3/28; Erlanger, 2011/10/5; FT, 2011/8/23; Gardner, 2011/3/25; Harding, 2011/3/28; Pincus, 2011/3/23; and, RGJ, 2011/3/13.

conflict should have exercised pressure on their respective sides to back away from escalating violence—that also did not happen, indeed, the opposite occurred on the insurgents' side. The result was a nation left in ruins, with continued bloodshed, and "healthy" prospects for much more violence in the future. However we may wish to salute all of this, "humanitarian" and "solidarity" do not recommend themselves as credible options, or ones that can sit well in the stomach.

As for those who hailed Libya's "reformist revolutionaries" (apparently without knowing who they were talking about, or worse yet, knowing full well), and who wrote to denounce anti-imperialist "polemics" (Shokr & Kamat, 2011) we would not hear from them again. Not a word was uttered when those they had supported lynched black Africans, or denounced gays as a threat to humanity at a meeting of the UN Human Rights Council to which Libya was reinstated after the ghastly murder of Gaddafi, nor when Law 37 and 38 respectively criminalized any speech supporting Gaddafi or criticizing the new Libyan government and banned anyone with any ties to the past government from political life.

CONCLUSION

The Aftermath: A New War on Africa

Sirte by all accounts continues to remain a city in ruins. Whatever will come of the African Union after Gaddafi is something that will largely come without Libya. While this has clearly blown wind into the sails of AFRICOM, NATO as an organization is faltering under the weight of military budget cuts as the European Union descends ever deeper into economic stagnation and financial crisis, and as streets protests greet NATO ministers and leaders whenever they meet. The U.S. finds itself increasingly under strain, unable to cope with a debt-fueled defence budget, but it continues with the hope that "humanitarianism" and "democracy promotion" will be the "soft power" tools that can ensnare enough international sympathy for coalitions to mobilize in defence of the U.S.' pursuit of ulterior aims. With its credibility shot, the U.S. hopes that it can recruit others to conduct indirect rule on its behalf, with these others presumably forgetting that they have their own interests to uphold. Even as AFRICOM finds itself invigorated, sustaining hopes for U.S. dominance for one day longer, it is not at all clear that the African Union will be content with merely being sidelined and diminished. In this respect Gaddafi's violent and brutal overthrow might have also blown some wind into the sails of a renewed anti-imperialism within the African Union, as it meets not in Sirte but in an even more astounding new assembly building in Addis Ababa.

African Reactions to Regime Change

"While the toothless bulldog of an African Union sat and watched so powerlessly

Libya was ransacked by mafias and ninjas so vehemently
What was his crime?
He wanted the African currency for his oil
He wanted to pay the price
He was slaughtered like a dog on his own soil
He rejected the Arab League and flocked with his African identity
He regretted his past and wanted to see Africa in total sanity
Muammar Al Gaddafi was a threat to western, hypocritical capitalists
Free food, shelter, healthcare and education, he gave to his people
As a champion of all African socialists. Huh!"—Blakk Rasta, "Gaddafi."

Gaddafi is Gone. Oh no!

"Gaddafi is gone, oh no! He was my brother, my father, my friend" These
and the words above came from a reggae band in Ghana and were presented in a professional music video made by Ghana Music as part of
Blakk Rasta's album, *Born Dread* (transcribed by Guanaguanare,
2012/4/21).[1] Blakk Rasta, born Abubakar Ahmed, novelist, playwright, and
a popular and sometimes "controversial" host of a radio show on Hitz
103.7 FM in Ghana, was responsible for greatly popularizing Barack
Obama in Ghana in 2008. He produced a hit song about Obama and then
met Obama in person in 2009 for a photo op in which they had their arms
around each other's shoulder (*The Buzz*, 2009/6/15).[2] Initially Blakk Rasta
even criticized Gaddafi in one of his songs, *The Libyan War*, saying that
Gaddafi had been "president for too long and would have to step down
but kicking him out should not be done through a coup d'état, murder,
assassination or killing." Then Blakk Rasta began to turn against his former idol, Obama (CitiFMonline, 2011/11/6).

Things changed radically once NATO began bombing Libya and trying to overthrow Gaddafi. From then on, and especially after the gruesome publicized murder of Gaddafi, Blakk Rasta went on "a war path with
the West for what he says is the deliberate assassination of an African
savior," Muammar Gaddafi. According to Blakk Rasta, "the West does
not want Africa's self-reliance and success thus killing the man who was

---

1. The music video can be seen at < http://www.youtube.com/watch?v=HXM
9JwSu2P4>.
2. See < http://www.ghanamusic.com/news/top-stories/blakk-rasta-meets-obama-
again-on-the-bbc/index.html>.

fighting for the continent's redemption." He explained that the West (the U.S. and NATO) killed Gaddafi because he "wanted Africa to have one currency known as the Gold Dinar which would have destabilised all the wicked who have been sponging on Africa's resources." Now Blakk Rasta spoke of Gaddafi as a martyr and devoted Pan-Africanist, who had rejected the Arab League. Further praising Gaddafi, he added:

> "He was giving his everything to see Africa strong remember he established three banks in Africa. He wanted to kick out the International Monetary Fund (IMF). The West was making a lot of money out of Africa and he didn't like that so he established these banks and was on the verge of introducing with the support of other countries the Gold Dinar which would have Africa freer. We [Africans] wouldn't have gone to the IMF to get any money, they [West] didn't want that." (Aglanu, 2012/1/14)

While it is difficult to know what depth of popular sentiment is represented by public figures prominent in African popular culture such as Blakk Rasta, there is no denying that there was an outpouring of grief in numerous cases recorded by African mass media and electronic media across the continent. At least that is one feature that distinguishes African reactions from those found on any other continent. There were actual expressions of pain and mourning for Gaddafi's death, with little of the Western moral dualism about Gaddafi not being a "good" guy, and none of the shocking bloodlust of some "Arab Spring revolutionaries" who were quick to dispatch Gaddafi even as their own "revolutions" became mired in plots and counter-plots by Western powers and their local political and military proxies. Africa was also the first continent where a concentration of voices were heard condemning the racist persecution of black people in Libya by rebels with a sharply racial agenda. In the meantime white Western liberals praised the rebels as democracy-loving reformists and "Arab Spring" activists, and simply avoided the issue of "racism," which is apparently not part of their vocabulary. In the Arab-African, North-South, white-black divides that became apparent as a result of AFRICOM's and NATO's war against Libya, it was Africa which stood out with the greatest mass of public expressions of dignity, grief over inhumane brutality, and demonstrations against imperialism. While they do not represent the full range of opinion, including very anti-Gaddafi perspectives, the following quotes are a sample of the public outcry in Africa.

In Nigeria the press reported the views of "eminent Nigerians" on the death of Gaddafi, and these reactions were recorded between one and two days after his murder. They typically described a good leader whose only flaw was to have overstayed in office. Balarabe Musa, a left-wing political leader and former Governor of Kaduna State, said:

> "The lesson we should draw from the death of Gaddafi is that the world is being recolonised by America and NATO under a new condition. In the case of Gaddafi, he ruled his country and ensured the security of his people. He also had influence on people's lives, particularly, Africa. He served his people all his life. Nigeria has a lot of lessons to learn from the way Gaddafi ended. Libya and Iraq were states of their own which western imperialism detest. They want to dominate the earth. The next target is Nigeria." (Adeseko, 2011/10/22)

Senator Suleiman Salawu, national chairman of the Action Alliance of Nigeria said that Gaddafi, "was engaged in a war against imperialists," adding that he was, "one of the finest African leaders we have. If we are to count three African leaders who can be said to be good, he was among them. He used the wealth of Libya for the welfare of the masses" (Adeseko, 2011/10/22). Tony Momoh, a Nigerian journalist and former Minister of Information and Culture, asserted that, "more than the average African leader," Gaddafi "took good care of the people of Libya," and he added: "that can never be erased from his record. Here is a man who said he would not have a personal house until all Libyans have houses. Here is a man who addressed a human condition in Libya and provided for average Libyans" (Adeseko, 2011/10/22). Ebenezer Babatope, Chair of the Peoples Democratic Party of Nigeria, saw Gaddafi as, "a very strong pan-Africanist....He should be given a state burial....I have always followed Gaddafi and I have always loved him" (Adeseko, 2011/10/22). Mujahid Dokubo-Asari, head of the Niger Delta Peoples Volunteer Force, said that, "Gaddafi spilled his blood as a martyr to rekindle the fire of revolution all over the world," and warned that, "those who murdered him will not go scot-free." Asari, who had studied in Libya under a scholarship and is alleged to have received military training there, remarked that under Gaddafi Libya had the "highest literacy rate and the best health care in the whole of Africa. As a foreigner, I saw with my eyes" (AFP, 2011/10/21).

In Ghana, on the same day that Gaddafi was killed, the press relayed the words of Dr. Nii Alabi, a consultant to the African Union, who expressed the view that Gaddafi was an "iconic figure" for Africa and one of the few who would stand up to the West:

"I think it is just unfortunate that one of the iconic figures, and I am using iconic advisedly because he has symbolised some of the proud moments of Africa by daring the West, telling them to the face that they have not treated us well even though his terrorist credentials cannot be something I would ever subscribe to. Having said that I think for Africa, we have lost somebody, who tried to say that *yes I love this continent.* Gaddafi symbolised a lot of things but his stand for the United States of Africa is something that Kwame Nkrumah stood for, is something that really endeared him to many other Pan-Africanists." (CitiFMonline, 2011/10/20)

While critical of Gaddafi's long hold on power and the way he seemed to institutionalize power with his family, Ghana's former president Jerry Rawlings still held that Gaddafi's belief in "the power of the masses was never in dispute" (Myjoyonline, 2011/10/22). Rawlings also condemned the brutal and inhumane manner that Gaddafi was killed (Gomda, 2011/10/24). Another former president of Ghana, John Agyekum Kufuor, said he felt that "Gaddafi's death is a historic sad day in Africa," but added that during his eight years in power he did not become close to Gaddafi (Awuah, 2011/10/24).

In Kampala, Uganda, a divided Muslim community came together with, "anger and tears" that "characterised the special prayers held at the Gaddafi Mosque in Old Kampala. Speaker after speaker praised the fallen Libyan leader who helped fund several projects in the country including the Gaddafi Mosque." Over 30,000 people packed the mosque. Sheikh Abdulkadir Mbogo, who led the Friday prayers, said, "Gaddafi has died a hero, because he has done a lot for the Muslim community and the country." Sheikh Amir Mutyaba, the former Ugandan ambassador to Libya, broke down when narrating his meeting with Gaddafi, and said that Gaddafi "had a dream to unite Africa," and that, "he has died as a hero and Allah will bless him for his kind heart and the oil diggers will be punished." Deputy Mufti Sheikh Abdul Hayyi Mukiibi praised Gaddafi for constructing the Gaddafi main Mosque, *Voice of Africa* Radio, Muslim schools and the Muslim Call Society, an organisation supporting Muslim programs in the country. At Kibuli Mosque, supreme Mufti Zubair Kayongo and Sheikh Obed Kamulegeya declared: "The Muslim community and the country at large have lost a brother and great leader" (Mugerwa & Ouma, 2011/10/22).

Blakk Rasta in his song about Gaddafi referred to "the toothless bulldog of an African Union [that] sat and watched so powerlessly." This too became an issue among members of the African Union, especially those from southern Africa who were upset with how the AU Chairperson, Jean Ping, handled issues arising from NATO's bombing of Libya and the killing of Gaddafi.

The war on Libya had considerable fallout for the AU. Jean Ping, as reported in classified U.S. Embassy cables, made his pro-U.S. stance painfully clear and was often amenable to American flattery. In one example, in a meeting between Ping and U.S. Assistant Secretary for African Affairs Johnnie Carson, Ping noted the close relationship between Gabon and the U.S. when speaking to Carson. Ping also expressed his strong support for Obama and added: "We count on you. We are ready to go with you." Then Carson attempted some not-too-subtle flattery and one can almost picture Ping blushing: "When asked about the possibility of his succeeding [Gabonese President] Bongo, Ping chuckled and said he was not unemployed" (USET, 2009/7/13).

In an interview with Agence France-Presse on his first visit to Libya after Gaddafi's overthrow, Jean Ping said "the African Union wants to turn the page in its ties with Libya's new rulers." Ping had nothing to say to AFP about the brutality of Gaddafi's murder in spite of the kind of evidence available and provided in this chapter and chapter 5. In fact, he

FIGURE 6.1 U.S. Secretary of State Hillary Rodham Clinton and African Union Commission Chairperson Jean Ping shake hands after their bilateral meeting, at the U.S. State Department on April 21, 2011. (Source: U.S. Department of State via Wikimedia Commons.)

devoted some time to challenging "notions" that Libya had ever been financially generous toward either the AU or African states. Regarding the NTC, "what I told the authorities firstly is that the past is the past," Ping said, "no matter what happened. We must turn the page and look to the future." Recounting how fast Gaddafi wanted to "push" the AU while others preferred more gradual development, Ping added that he expects "the debate will continue following the fall of Gaddafi" but that, "the difference is that the debate will not be influenced by someone like Gaddafi, who wanted to force through his vision" (Lamloum, 2012/1/16). Far from sympathy, or even shock, not just over the butchery of a key figure in the AU, and countless African citizens who were lynched, abducted, and tortured, even as Ping stood in Tripoli, the only sense one could get is of someone who privately must have been cheering for regime change all along. The West, it seems, had its man in the AU. But not for much longer.

In a speech condemning the AU's mishandling of the war against Libya under Ping's direction, Zimbabwean President Robert Mugabe warned that Africa might be recolonized if leaders failed to follow the example of leaders of Africa's independence movements. He said this during a session on Peace and Security at the AU summit in Ethiopia which saw Ping's reelection. Africans should have vehemently opposed the bombing of Libya by NATO, Mugabe said, and that due to Africa's silence, "Gaddafi was killed in broad daylight, his children hunted like animals and then we rush to recognize the NTC." He denounced the AU's Peace and Security Commission for recognizing the NTC, saying it was not its mandate to do so (News24, 2012/1/31).

Key members of the Southern African Development Community (SADC) sought to oust Ping later in 2012, after Ping failed to secure a two-thirds majority in the final round of voting in January. According to a senior diplomat in the South African Foreign Ministry's Department of International Relations, "most SADC member states, particularly South Africa, Zimbabwe, Angola, Tanzania, Namibia and Zambia which played a key role in the southern Africa liberation struggle, were not happy with the way Jean Ping handled the Libyan bombing by NATO jets." Their major criticism was that not enough was done to defend either Gaddafi or Libya. The South African diplomat told Lugenzi Kabale, the foreign editor of Tanzania's *The Citizen* that, "Gadaffi was a hero to South African liberation fighters. He offered unlimited military and financial support to them during the struggle. So when they saw their hero being hit, with the AU Commission deliberately holding back any diplomatic support to save him, they waited for the right time to come to punish Jean Ping." The South African diplomat further commented that, "Colonel Gaddafi and, by extension, Libya did everything to get the AU where it is today," and he asked: "How come such a dear son of Africa being left to fight alone a machination of foreign forces in the name of NATO?" Tanzania's Minister for Foreign Affairs and International Cooperation, Bernard Membe, also "reiterated Colonel Gaddafi's material, financial and diplomatic support to African freedom fighters." Membe also noted the unprecedented lack of respect shown by Ping in not allowing the AU assembly to observe a minute of silence for Muammar Gaddafi after he was killed: "It was out-rageous that he did not allow heads of states and governments to stand up in silence for a minute in honour of the late Colonel Gaddafi and Sanha. Yet he is the one who, during this session, has allowed the same to stand in honour of Malawi's Bakili Muluzi" (Kabale, 2012/7/25).

Punish Ping they did. He was pushed out in a complex series of nego-tiations and votes and replaced by Dr. Nkosazana Dlamini-Zuma, who had been "at the frontline in transforming the former Organisation of African Unity (OAU) to the current AU." She was also former South African President Thabo Mbeki's "right hand woman" as the country's Foreign Minister. On July 15, 2012, in the fourth round of voting, Dlamini-Zuma won the votes of 37 AU member states, while "Ping got nothing and two votes rejected him categorically with a big 'no' as 12 votes were spoilt" (Kabale, 2012/7/25).

In a banquet between Zimbabwe's President Robert Mugabe and Zambia's President Michael Sata, Mugabe saluted the victory of Dlamini-Zuma with words that revealed the kind of thrust that was behind the ousting of Ping, an indirect commentary on his failed leadership.

> "We want the new leadership to reassert that Africa is not only defined by geography, but also by a set of values and principles which we have freely adopted as independent states over the years. These values include freedom, respect for the sovereign will of the people, as well as sustainable development and the eradication of poverty, among others. We welcome the election of the new chairperson of the commission and look forward to the injection of new ideas and vigour into the affairs of our union." (News24, 2012/8/7)

The African Union: Denouncing an Unnecessary and Provocative War

Some African actors were determined to stand by the established prin-ciples of the African Union and find a peaceful solution and transition in

Libya. Their perspective on both NATO's military intervention and the role of the UN itself provided a sharp critique that is well worth considering in detail. It is especially important as it was either diminished or ignored outright in Western news media but also because such blatant disregard advanced the cause of war. The African Union's stand on NATO's invasion of Libya was presented at a meeting between the UN Security Council and the African Union Mediation Committee (High Level Ad hoc Committee on Libya) on June 15, 2011, led by Dr. Ruhakana Rugunda, Uganda's Permanent Representative to the UN. Dr. Rugunda began by noting that it was good that the UNSC was finally meeting with the AU for a candid exchange of views, and he criticized the UNSC for not doing so sooner and explained why:

> "This should have happened much earlier because Libya is a founding member of the AU. An attack on Libya or any other member of the African Union without express agreement by the AU is a dangerous provocation that should be avoided." (AU, 2011, p. 2)

Speaking for the AU, Rugunda pointedly added that, "the UN is on safer ground if it confines itself to maintaining international peace and deterring war among member states," and that foreign intervention in the "internal affairs of States should be avoided except where there is proof of genocide or imminent genocide as happened in Rwanda or against the Jews in Germany and the European countries that were occupied by the Third Reich" (AU, 2011, p. 2).

The AU representative then rightly questioned whether anything that had happened to the rebels and their supporters in Libya could be described as "genocide":

FIGURE 6.2 Dr. Ruhakana Rugunda, Uganda's Permanent Representative to the United Nations. Rugunda spoke on behalf of the African Union on the war in Libya. (Source: courtesy of the United Nations, photograph by Paulo Filgueiras.)

"Fighting between Government troops and armed insurrectionists is not genocide. It is civil war. It is the attack on unarmed civilians with the aim of exterminating a particular group that is genocide—to exterminate the genes of targeted groups such as the Jews, Tutsis, etc. It is wrong to characterise every violence as genocide or imminent genocide so as to use it as a pretext for the undermining of the sovereignty of States." (AU, 2011, p. 3)

The AU had to remind the UNSC about why sovereignty matters in Africa, and that the AU would not be prepared to simply let sovereignty be dismissed any time a Western power cried "genocide" from afar.

"Certainly, sovereignty has been a tool of emancipation of the peoples of Africa who are beginning to chart transformational paths for most of the African countries after centuries of predation by the slave trade, colonialism and neo-colonialism. Careless assaults on the sovereignty of African Countries are, therefore, tantamount to inflicting fresh wounds on the destiny of the African peoples. If foreign invasions, meddlings, interventions, etc, were a source of prosperity, then, Africa should be the richest continent in the world because we have had all versions of all that: slave trade, colonialism and neocolonialism. Yet, Africa has been the most wretched on account of that foreign meddling." (AU, 2011, p. 3)

Rugunda reminded the UNSC that the AU called for dialogue in Libya, both before and after the passage of UNSCR 1970, which imposed sanctions, and UNSCR 1973, which was used to authorize military intervention. The UN simply ignored the AU, however, as Rugunda noted. Thus, "going on with the bombings of the sacred land of Africa has been high-handed, arrogant and provocative" (AU, AU, 2011, p. 3). Directing his comments apparently at Western military powers grouped under NATO, Rugunda remarked: "It is unwise for certain players to be intoxicated with technological superiority and begin to think they alone can alter the course of human history towards freedom for the whole of mankind. Certainly, no constellation of states should think that they can recreate hegemony over Africa" (AU, 2011, p. 3).

Observing that the continuation of hostilities, caused by the intervention of the UN and NATO, was making the situation for civilians much worse, Rugunda prophetically stated, "what is happening in Libya will undermine future efforts of the UN in the protection of civilians" (AU, 2011, p. 5). In fact, with another foreign-backed insurrection brewing in Syria at the same time, which exploded into violence that dwarfed the early weeks of Libya's war, any notion of the UNSC backing intervention under the "responsibility to protect" doctrine was shattered and dashed repeatedly.

The AU stood against the continued war in Libya, calling it both unnecessary and provocative against the whole of Africa.

"There is, therefore, no need for any war-like activities in Libya because there is a peaceful way forward. There has been no need for these war activities, ever since Gadaffi accepted dialogue when the AU mediation Committee visited Tripoli on April 10, 2011. Any war activities after that have been provocation for Africa. It is an unnecessary war. It must stop." (AU, 2011, p. 5)

As for the rebels, "the story that the rebels cannot engage in dialogue unless Gadaffi goes away does not convince us." The AU representative then added:

"If they do not want dialogue, then, let them fight their war with Gadaffi without NATO bombing. Then, eventually, a modus vivendus will emerge between the two parties or one of them will be defeated. The attitude of the rebels shows us the danger of external involvement in internal affairs of African countries. The externally sponsored groups neglect dialogue and building internal consensus and, instead, concentrate on winning external patrons. This cannot be in the interest of that country. Mobutu's Congo as well as performance of all the other neo-colonies of Africa in the 1960s, 1970s, 1980s and their eventual collapse in the 1990s prove that foreign sponsored groups are of no value to Africa." (AU, 2011, pps. 5-6)

South Africa: The ANC against Regime Change, Recolonization

In South Africa, the reactions of both past and present ANC leaders were among the few sources of criticism of regime change to receive attention in the Western media, apart from occasional quotes of Russian officials. It was a series of criticisms in fact, in some cases rife with contradictory positions. Yet they collectively provided one of the few outlines of an early critique of the war that was heard in few other places. The exceptions were Venezuela, Cuba, Nicaragua and the other members of the Bolivarian Alliance of the Americas (ALBA), and a few anti-imperialist writings that were sidelined in North American public commentary, even as they tended to predict accurately the course and outcomes of the war in Libya.

At first, South Africa, to its regret and even when it had every reason not to, backed UNSCR 1973 authorizing military intervention in Libya. It was a non-permanent member of the UN Security Council in March 2011. In April 2011 the government of South Africa announced that Gaddafi had indeed accepted the AU's plan for peace, with President Jacob Zuma personally leading five members of the AU on a delegation to Libya to meet with all sides (see Figure 6.3). South Africa called on NATO to cease its bombings in order to give a negotiated ceasefire a chance of succeeding. NATO did not oblige, and its NTC collaborators almost instantly rejected the peace plan (Sherwood & McGreal, 2011/4/11). The public denunciations of NATO that followed stem perhaps from the evaporation of an inexplicable credulity on the part of the South African leadership or South Africa pulling back from a dangerous game of taking Libya down a peg, coupled with a late realization that NATO and the NTC had no interest in peace.

By June 2011, South African president Jacob Zuma went public with condemnations of NATO actions as exceeding the (very problematic) mandate of the UN: "We strongly believe that the resolution is being abused for regime change, political assassinations and foreign military occupation....These actions undermine the efforts of the African Union in finding solutions to the problems facing its member states" (CNN, 2011/6/14). Later in the same month Zuma also criticized the ICC for issuing indictments against Muammar and Saif Gaddafi, and chief of intelligence Abdullah al-Senussi. Zuma pointed out out how this move would short circuit the AU-negotiated peace plan by now offering Gaddafi no exit at all, and nothing to lose in staying and fighting (*Mail & Guardian*, 2011/6/27). Indeed, Zuma was entirely correct on this account.

As South Africa began to articulate more clearly an independent perspective on the actual course of events in Libya and the nature of foreign intervention, it was no surprise that right wing U.S. media, and particularly propagandists working for the U.S.-funded organ, "Radio Free Europe/Radio Liberty," started to lambast South Africa as a "rogue democracy" (Kirchik, 2011/9/6). They now had to confront something other than the choir of self-serving "humanitarian" shrieks about Libya (even as the U.S. continued to bomb and slaughter Afghans, Pakistanis, and

FIGURE 6.3 South African President Jacob Zuma meets with Muammar Gaddafi in Libya on May 30, 2011, as part of an African Union effort to find a peaceful resolution to the conflict. (Source: courtesy of the Government Communication and Information System, South Africa.)

Yemenis) or the self-assured band of imperial opportunists who evaded international accountability for their own war crimes while sounding off against Libya with pristine sanctimony. Quite expectedly, few in the U.S. mainstream reflected on their own "rogue democracy." Obama had violated the *War Powers Act* and dismissed Congressional votes opposing the war, thus taking the U.S. to war when not attacked by Libya and when there was no immediate threat to U.S. national security. He thereby completely broke his own 2008 campaign promises. Few paused to consider how their own democracy had been thwarted, their Constitution undermined, and their diplomacy militarized. Least of all did they concern themselves with the pain and suffering that they wrought on Libyans who dared not serve their ambitions, and how they fully colluded with the racist persecution of black Libyans and migrant black Africans in Libya. On the other hand, these are exactly the sorts of questions and problems that U.S.-funded propagandists are paid to avoid.

"The re-colonisation of Africa is becoming a real threat," said Dr. Chris Landsberg, head of the Department of Politics at the University of Johannesburg. With over two hundred prominent South Africans, Landsberg signed an open letter slamming NATO's violation of international law and its regime change agenda. Other signatories included: ANC national executive member Jesse Duarte, political analyst Willie Esterhuyse of the University of Stellenbosch, former intelligence minister Ronnie Kasrils, lawyer Christine Qunta, former deputy foreign affairs minister Aziz Pahad, former minister in the presidency Essop Pahad, Sam Moyo of the African Institute for Agrarian Studies, former President Thabo Mbeki's spokesman Mukoni Ratshitanga, and poet Wally Serote. Landsberg appropriately denounced the UK, France, and U.S. as "rogue states," noting that "a rogue is an errant state that does not live by rules… the tragedy is that they are not likely to be charged in the International Criminal Court" (SAPA, 2011/8/24; see also Concerned Africans, 2011/8/9).

Former South African President Thabo Mbeki, Mandela's successor, gave a lengthy lecture at Stellenbosch University that incisively outlined one of the most cogent critiques of NATO's war (followed perhaps by that of the politically compromised Yoweri Museveni of Uganda). As reported by the press, Mbeki observed that Western powers were, "bent on regime-change in Libya, regardless of the cost to this African country, intent to produce a political outcome which would serve their interests" (SAPA, 2011/8/26). Mbeki also faulted the ICC for ensuring that the fighting in Libya would be prolonged by indicting Gaddafi and seeking his capture at the same time as Western powers urged him to leave Libya. Those powers, Mbeki explained, "heard but did not want to listen to anything informed by the objective to address the real interests of the African people of Libya" (SAPA, 2011/8/26).

In February 2012, Mbeki made similar arguments at length, in his Dullah Omar Eighth Memorial Lecture at the University of the Western Cape (Mbeki, 2012/2/16). Although that speech contained statements about Libya's role in the fight against apartheid that contradicted his own earlier speeches (DFA, 2002/6/14) and those of Nelson Mandela, Mbeki nonetheless made many strong points about NATO's war.

Mbeki told his audience that on March 10, 2011 the AU had drafted a peace accord, to which Gaddafi agreed. It "provided for an end to the violent conflict in Libya and the institution of a process whereby the Libyan people would engage one another in inclusive negotiations freely to determine the future of their country, including its obligatory and genuine democratization." The agreement would have eliminated "further resort to force and therefore the needless killing of tens of thousands of Libyans and the destruction of valuable national infrastructure and other property." Yet, when the AU's Peace and Security Council forwarded its peace plan to the UN Security Council, it did not get a fair hearing. Instead the UNSC "wilfully elected to ignore the decisions of the African Union, treating these decisions relating to an African country, and therefore us, the peoples of Africa, with absolute contempt." Mbeki also condemned the UNSC for treating Libya as if it had ceased to be an African country, and referred to the Arab League instead as the source that supposedly (in its eyes) provided legitimacy for all of its decisions. The result was that, "NATO intervened not to impose a no-fly-zone to protect civilians, as prescribed by the UN Security Council, but to lead and empower the opposition National Transitional Council in a military campaign to overthrow the Gaddafi regime." In playing a part in this, the UN itself had violated its own charter and all of the prescriptions of international law against the use of force. Mbeki specifically cited the following violations by the UN:

"the UN Secretary General refused to accredit the representatives of the Libyan Government;

"the UN Secretary General failed to take action to insist that even his own peace Envoy, former Jordan Foreign Minister, Abdel-Elah al-Khatib, should have the space to facilitate a peaceful resolution of the Libyan conflict;

"the UN Security Council refused to ensure that NATO acted in a manner consistent with its own resolutions, thus declining to hold NATO to account;

"the UN Security Council surrendered its authority to oversee the future of Libya to a self-appointed 'Libya Contact Group', made up of countries and organisations committed to regime-change in Libya, in defiance of the Security Council decisions; and,

"as we have said, the UN ensured that in all respects Libya should be defined as other than an African country, insisting that the legitimacy of the regime-change agenda derived from its support by the League of Arab States, knowing very well that for many years Libya had become virtually only a nominal member of this regional organisation, thus earning the wrath of many of the Member States of the League."

Mbeki reminded his audience about how the U.S., the U.K., and France justified their "illegitimate military actions in Libya and…[their] regime-change agenda," on the basis of four propositions: 1) that they were acting to make peace in Libya; 2) that they supported the "legitimate representatives of the Libyan people," the NTC, which these powers opposed "to what they unilaterally decreed was an 'illegitimate' Government;" 3) that they sought to bring democracy to Libya by "liberating" Libyans from dictatorship; and, 4) that they were enacting the "responsibility to protect."

"In this context," Mbeki continued, "I would like to state that there is absolutely no evidence that the Gaddafi regime either committed or had any intention to commit any genocide or wage a war against civilians, justifying the evocation by the UN, the P3 [U.S., UK, France] and NATO of the so-called 'right [responsibility] to protect'." Citing Western analysts and the Pentagon itself, Mbeki tore to pieces allegations that Gaddafi was deliberately targeting civilians, that the opposition had been peaceful, and that NATO had intervened to prevent "genocide," since no such slaughter was in the offing or had occurred in any of the cities controlled by the Libyan government. Mbeki then, regrettably, proceeded to seemingly place blame on Libya for NATO's military intervention, making a critical analytical error common even to many who wrote against the war, namely that the nature of the regime can somehow ever justify foreign military intervention. The U.S. and its few allies did not bomb Libya because of its "human rights record" or because of the absence of "multi-party elections." Indeed, as Mbeki picks up the thread of the stronger part of his analysis, it was the so-called "welcome strategic outcomes" achieved by the West that instruct us on its objectives. Mbeki lists these as: 1) securing Libya as a "friendly state" in a globally strategic region that is extremely volatile; 2) placing Western powers, and especially the U.S., in "a strong position to intervene in the African Maghreb, including in Egypt;" 3) guaranteeing favourable access to Libyan oil; 4) shutting down Libya as a point of departure for African migration to Europe; and, 5) serving as a precedent that would enable them to intervene in all other African countries. Thus far, Mbeki's list of outcomes has indeed been validated.

Mbeki had clear warnings for the African continent as it was plunged into a new imperial scramble and subject to the Eurocentric secular religion of the new missionaries of the West centred on "good governance" and "human rights." First, Mbeki warned that in the post-Cold War setting, "the Western powers have enhanced their appetite to intervene on our Continent, including through armed force, to ensure the protection of their interests, regardless of our views as Africans." Second, these powers, "will use the argument that they are our unique friends as defenders of our democratic and human rights, obliged to act in this regard especially when our Continent, through the AU and our regional bodies, can be presented as having failed to act to defend these rights." Third, these powers "will act as they did in Libya especially if, in situations of internal conflict, which they would also foment, they can argue that they are implementing" the R2P doctrine. Fourth, "in all instances we must expect that such interventions will be supported by some native forces, our own kith and kin, which the world powers concerned will present as the genuine representatives of our peoples, without regard to the truth in this regard." Fifth, that Western powers will attempt to harness multilateral institutions to support their narrow interests, such as in applying sanctions against a given country, and they will especially "misuse" the UN Security Council. Sixth, Western powers "will also use the global media to demonise whomsoever they view as their enemy, and present in the best possible light whomsoever they determine is their friend." Seventh, disunity in Africa "opens the door to our 're-colonisation'," especially as Western powers seek to limit the possibility of Africans forming a strategic alliance with the People's Republic of China.

FIGURE 6.4 As the host of the 15th African Union Summit in 2010, held in Uganda, Uganda's President Yoweri Museveni welcomes Muammar Gaddafi at the Speke Resort, Munyonyo. (Source: courtesy of the Ministry of Foreign Affairs, Uganda.)

Uganda: The Rebels Condemn Themselves

Next to Mbeki (2012/2/16), one early critique from an African leader also had damning points to make about the Libyan rebellion itself, along with a comparatively balanced appraisal of Gaddafi's history in power. This came from Uganda's President, Yoweri Museveni. Given the extensive amount of Libyan investment in Uganda, plus aid, it would not be unexpected if some might be tempted to argue that this was Museveni paying back a patron. Quite the contrary is the case. According to the U.S. State Department's Assistant Secretary for African Affairs, Jendayi Frazer, in a cable which she wrote in 2008 and marked "secret," Museveni had strong criticisms of Gaddafi's role in the AU (Frazer, 2008/6/18). Relations between Museveni and Gaddafi were apparently so poor that the former feared Gaddafi might attack his plane:

"Museveni noted that tensions with Qadhafi are growing and as a result, and [sic] he worries that Qadhafi will attack his plane while flying over international airspace. Museveni requested that the USG and GOU coordinate to provide additional air radar information when he flies over international waters." (Frazer, 2008/6/18)

At the AU Summit in Uganda in 2010 (see Figure 6.4), according to journalists "a mass fistfight broke out between Gaddafi's and Museveni's presidential guards as leaders arrived for the opening of an AU summit in Kampala in July," and then, "the two heads of state later argued in full view of delegates and reporters" (Malone, 2010/12/8). It is with this in mind that we should better appreciate the import of Museveni's striking article in Foreign Policy (Museveni, 2011/3/24), from which the following references come. Indeed, in the same article, Museveni begins with several paragraphs devoted to criticizing Gaddafi's role in backing Idi Amin, what Museveni saw as his arrogance and haste in pushing for a United States of Africa, his historical ties to "terrorism," and so forth.

However, where Museveni offered a positive assessment of Gaddafi's time in power, this was strikingly rare in the Western media. First, Museveni wrote of Gaddafi's independent foreign policy, and independent internal policies, and then remarked: "I am not able to understand the position of Western countries, which appear to resent independent-minded leaders and seem to prefer puppets. Puppets are not good for any country." In the same vein, Musveni stated that Gaddafi, "whatever his faults, is a true nationalist," adding, "I prefer nationalists to puppets of foreign interests. Where have the puppets caused the [progressive] transformation of countries? I need some assistance with information on this from those who are familiar with puppetry." Museveni applauded Gaddafi for making "some positive contributions to Libya, I believe, as well as Africa and the Third World." Then Museveni credits Gaddafi with a monumental achievement that transformed the position of all oil-producing countries and empowered them:

"Before Qaddafi came to power in 1969, a barrel of oil was 40 American cents. He launched a campaign to withhold Arab oil unless the West paid more for it. I think the price went up to $20 per barrel. When the Arab-Israel war of 1973 broke out, the barrel of oil went up to $40. I am, therefore, surprised to hear that many oil producers in the world, including the Gulf countries, do not appreciate the historical role played by Qaddafi on this issue. The huge wealth many of these oil producers are enjoying was, at least in part, due to Qaddafi's efforts. The Western countries have continued to develop in spite of paying more for oil. It therefore means that the pre-Qaddafi oil situation was characterized by super exploitation of oil producing countries by the Western countries."

Gaddafi is also credited by Museveni for having "built Libya," and certainly transforming it from the ramshackle, deeply impoverished backwater that it was under the monarchy. Gaddafi also expelled the British and U.S. military bases from Libya. Moreover, Gaddafi was a *moderate* in Musveni's own words, and he elaborated: "Qaddafi is one of the few secular leaders in the Arab world. He does not believe in Islamic fundamentalism, which is why Libyan women have been able to go to school, to join the army, and so forth. This is a positive point on Qaddafi's side."

Speaking of the present crisis in 2011, Museveni does not have a very kind view of Gaddafi's opposition and their pleas for Western military intervention, or the role of foreign interests. Focusing on actual events in Libya Museveni pointed out that, "when rioters are attacking police stations and army barracks with the aim of taking power, then they are no longer demonstrators; they are insurrectionists. They will have to be treated as such. A responsible government would have to use reasonable force to neutralize them." Any change of government must come from internal forces, Museveni emphasizes, adding that, "it should not be for external forces to arrogate themselves that role; often, they do not have enough knowledge to decide rightly"—as, indeed, they did not. Why should external forces even be involved, Museveni asks, observing that any such foreign intervention is "a vote of no confidence in the people themselves." There is no "good" to foreign intervention in Africa, he wrote:

> "If foreign intervention is good, then, African countries should be the most prosperous countries in the world, because we have had the greatest dosages of that: the slave trade, colonialism, neo-colonialism, imperialism, etc. But all those foreign-imposed phenomena have been disastrous. It is only recently that Africa is beginning to come up, partly because we are rejecting external meddling. External meddling and the acquiescence by Africans into that meddling have been responsible for the stagnation on our continent."

Museveni expresses a justifiable disdain for the neocolonial character of the Libyan rebels and their dependency on foreign power. "Regarding the Libyan opposition," he commented, "I would feel embarrassed to be backed by Western war planes. Quislings of foreign interests have never helped Africa." Furthermore, "if the Libyan opposition groups are patriots, they should fight their war by themselves and conduct their affairs by themselves," after all, he continued, "they easily captured so much equipment from the Libyan Army, why do they need foreign military support? I only had 27 rifles. To be puppets is not good."

As for the African temporary members of the UN Security Council that voted for UNSCR 1973—Gabon, Nigeria, and South Africa—Museveni pointed out that, "this was contrary to what the Africa Peace and Security Council had decided in Addis Ababa recently. This is something that only the extraordinary AU summit can resolve." It's not just a betrayal of a fellow African state, but of the African Union itself. Indeed, even Germany—a NATO member—abstained on UNSCR 1973.

Zimbabwe: NATO Liars and Brutal Aggressors

Zimbabwe's President, Robert G. Mugabe, made a stinging condemnation of NATO, and the "responsibility to protect," in his address to the UN General Assembly on September 22, 2011, just under a month before the overthrow and murder of Gaddafi (see Mugabe, 2011). Some relevant parts of the speech are reproduced below, transcribed from his spoken presentation. Mugabe first insisted on the obligation of members to honour the principles of the Charter of the United Nations calling them "our set of Commandments." He then pointed out that in the case of Libya NATO was violating those principles and no efforts were made to mediate and negotiate peace in Libya.

"There was quick resort to invoking Chapter 7 of the Charter, with gross, deliberate misinterpretation of the scope of the mandate originally given NATO to oversee and protect civilians.

"Mr. President, bilateral hatreds and quarrels, or ulterior motives, must not be allowed to creep into considerations of matters pertaining to threats to international peace and security, or even to the principle of the 'responsibility to protect'. We are yet to be convinced that the involvement of the mighty powers in Libya's affairs has not hindered the advent of the process of peace, democracy, and prosperity in that sister African country.

"Our African Union would never have presumed to impose a leadership on the fraternal people of Libya, as NATO countries have illegally sought to do— and in fact have done. At the very least, the African Union would have wished to join those principled members of this august body who preferred an immediate ceasefire and peaceful dialogue in Libya....

"Mr. President, the newly-minted principle of the 'responsibility to protect,' should not be twisted to provide cover for its premeditated abuse in violating the sacred international principle of the Charter, which is the principle of

FIGURE 6.5 Robert Mugabe, President of the Republic of Zimbabwe, addresses the general debate of the 66th session of the General Assembly on September 22, 2011. (Source: courtesy of the United Nations, photograph by Lou Rouse.)

non-interference in the domestic affairs of states, because to do so amounts to an act of aggression and causes destabilization of sovereign states. Moreover, to selectively and arbitrarily apply that [R2P] principle, merely serves to undermine the general acceptability of it. Indeed, more than other states, all the five permanent members of the Security Council bear a huge responsibility in this regard for ensuring that their historical privilege is used more to protect the United Nations Charter than to breach it, as is happening currently in Libya through the blatant, illegal, brutal, callous, NATO's murderous bombings.

"There we see NATO bombing places, seeking, hunting, and hounding the children of Gaddafi. Have the alleged 'sins' of the father now visited the sons, the children? Have the children lost their right to life? They are no longer human beings? They are being hunted every day. Or is it because each of them is no longer worth the price of the barrel of oil?...

"Mr. President, we in Africa are also duly concerned about the activities of the International Criminal Court which seems to exist only for alleged offenders of the developing world—the majority of them, Africans. The leaders of the powerful Western states guilty of international crime, like Bush and Blair, are routinely given the blind eye. Such selective justice has eroded the credibility of the ICC on the African continent."

This was not the only condemnation, nor the only action, taken by Mugabe. In early August 2011 Mugabe publicly labelled NATO as a "terrorist organization," to cheers from a crowd of Zimbabwe's veteran fighters from the war against white minority rule. Mugabe added that NATO was defying international law, "it has no rules and goes out blatantly wanting to kill—that's brazen murder, assassination." He asked rhetorically: "who then can respect it as a law-abiding organisation?" (BBC, 2011/8/8). In the same month, Libya's ambassador to Zimbabwe, Teher Elmagrahi, defected to the opposition NTC. Mugabe immediately instructed the ambassador and his embassy staff to leave Zimbabwe after the Libyan ambassador and an assistant raised the flag of the NTC over the Libyan Embassy (Nyathi, 2011/8/28). For months after, most African states did not recognize the NTC regime. Mugabe also warned the AU not to rush to recognize the NTC as the government of Libya, "but look at exactly what happened in that country leading to the callous murder of Colonel Muammar Gaddafi" (News24, 2012/1/31).

Regional Destabilization in the Aftermath of NATO

Even if we restrict ourselves to current events alone, it would probably require more than one book solely focused on Mali to do justice to understanding what has recently unfolded. By necessity, the presentation here is brief.

Mali, viewed in the West as a stable democracy until March 2012, suffered a military coup against the democratically elected president, at least in part for his failing to suppress Tuareg rebels from seizing the northern half of the country. A U.S.-trained army officer seized power. In the chaos that ensued, the Tuareg fighters in the Movement for the National Liberation of Azawad (MNLA) cemented their control over "an area larger than France" (a comparison made by Western media), the north (Azawad), and then found themselves in a violent struggle for power against Ansar Dine, a fundamentalist group that writers and some Malians see as linked with Al Qaeda in the Maghreb (AQIM) which

immediately began a program of religious persecution, killing and beating protesters, and severe repression against women in the north. Some
locals have reported that Ansar Dine now looks like a "United Nations"
of Islamists, with a mix of Arab and African fighters. The Malian Army,
and its junta (now in disarray, even if still wielding indirect control over
a new civilian administration) has not fared any better than before in trying to defeat the rebellion. Over 300,000 refugees have fled from the north,
many to neighbouring countries (AP, 2012/7/14; Nossiter, 2012/7/17,
2012/7/18; Simons, 2012/7/18).

In the view of Robert Pringle, a retired Foreign Service officer who was
also the U.S. Ambassador to Mali during 1987-1990, the partition, government overthrow, violence, and chaos besieging Mali today is an immediate consequence of the war in Libya and the outflow of heavily-armed
Tuareg fighters: "because of our intervention, we and our NATO allies are
indirectly responsible for the overthrow of one of Africa's few genuine
democracies, with a record of three free and fair elections, and on the
verge of a fourth when the coup intervened" (Pringle, 2012/7/11). As if
entirely oblivious to irony, and innocent of culpability, and after so much
damage has already been inflicted on Mali, the European Union sought
to mobilize West African forces under ECOWAS—not the AU—to intervene in Mali as the EU is once more "concerned" by the presence of Al
Qaeda (AP, 2012/7/23), though that was not the case in Libya, where the
staunchest anti-Al Qaeda government was overthrown by the West. For
its part, ECOWAS announced that it planned to deploy troops to Mali,
thus expanding the regionalization of the war (ECOWAS, 2012/7/24). In
the process, the EU thus opportunistically capitalizes on the crisis to further two key aims: reinserting European interests further in Africa, having contributed to the crisis in the first place, and sidelining the AU even
more, while propping up ECOWAS as the EU's own economic and "security proxy" (see Nivet, 2006).

Though Mali is now regularly cited as the first "victim" of the war in
Libya, part of a growing chain of regional destabilization, this represents
both opportunities for further AFRICOM insertion, and further setbacks
as well. As West African heads of state cry out for "humanitarian intervention" to "protect civilians" in Mali's north, their cries have none of the
resounding volume that we heard for Libya in 2011, and that faded with
Syria in 2012.

Empire or Dignity

"May God bless them," U.S. Secretary of State Hillary Clinton spoke with affected piety the day after Christopher Stevens, the U.S. Ambassador to Libya, and three other Americans had been slaughtered in an armed assault on the U.S. consulate in Benghazi on September 11, 2012. Clinton sounded like a high priest of empire as she continued, "and may God bless the thousands of Americans working in every corner of the world who make this country the greatest force for peace, prosperity, and progress, and a force that has always stood for human dignity—the greatest force the world has ever known. And may God continue to bless the United States of America" (Clinton, 2012/9/12).

The greatest force for human dignity that the world has ever known: this surges far beyond hyperbole and into distant constellations of theological fantasy. Just the past decade witnessed the calamity that the U.S. wrought against Iraq, in another unprovoked and unjustified attack. That war brought the murder of hundreds of thousands of Iraqi civilians, accompanied by torture, mass displacement, impoverishment, and a vast spread of lethal sickness from both the destruction of civilian infrastructure and the dense amounts of depleted uranium dust unleashed by exploded U.S. ordnance. There too, the U.S. has created a vast training ground for Al Qaeda forces that are as active as ever, all in the name of denying Al Qaeda a safe haven and putatively avenging the attacks of September 11, 2001.

Even if we restrict ourselves to Iraq alone, it ought to be astounding that any U.S. official could feel that she had the legitimacy not just to claim the moral high ground, but the entire territory of morality and human dignity. But this is how imperial ideology produces its myths, exploiting moments when Americans are killed to invite domestic listeners into a state of collective amnesia, reassuring them of their greatness in the eyes of God, as they are the innocent people who can do no wrong. Every attack they suffer must therefore be explicable only in terms of the dysfunctionality and the congenital and innate perversity of others. In the words of Obama, the dead Americans in Benghazi, "exemplified America's commitment to freedom, justice, and partnership with nations and people around the globe, and stand in stark contrast to those who callously took their lives" (Obama, 2012/9/12a). Thus the empire of "dignity" comes full circle in denying dignity to all others, in the name of dignity.

Nobody ever said that myths had to be either rational or fair. The same is true of the myths of interventionist "humanitarian protection," with all of the mass mediated hypes of "genocide," the campaigns to "Save Darfur" as Americans committed massacres in Iraq and Afghanistan, and the absurd expeditions of Hollywood celebrities to bring warmth and comfort to those oppressed by others. With a heightened sense of their own entitlement as a people blessed by God and destined to rule the earth, their overweening estimation of their own dignity is accompanied by an equally lordly view of "justice." The basic structure of belief in providence in shaping empire has changed little since the U.S. wars against Indigenous resistance in the nineteenth century and its invasions and occupations of Central American and Caribbean nations.

In response to the killing of American diplomats and Marines in Benghazi, Hillary Clinton vowed, "nor will we rest until those responsible for these attacks are found and brought to justice" (2012/9/12). Obama added to that: "We will not waver in our commitment to see that justice is done for this terrible act. And make no mistake, justice will be done" (Obama, 2012/9/12b). By now, we should understand what the U.S. leadership can mean with such statements, which can include everything from secret detention, to torture, to extrajudicial executions via drone strikes. With a reelection to safeguard, Obama will want Libyan heads on platters. In the past decade, "bringing to justice" has rarely meant simply arresting persons and bringing them to face fair trials. When the U.S. kills its adversaries, it calls that "justice." Yet when Gaddafi acted against the same forces, often in response to attempted coups, armed revolts, and assassination attempts, his actions were instantly chalked up to the atrocious "human rights record" of a "brutal dictator." Likewise, the U.S. claims its counterinsurgency in Afghanistan is about nation-building and winning hearts and minds, but Gaddafi's counterinsurgency in 2011 was a "threat to civilians" that mandated international action to stop it. A hue and cry was raised when Gaddafi referred to his opponents as rats and cockroaches—returning the favour, I might add—but thus far none has protested the language of Hillary Clinton when referring to some of the very same people as "savage" (Clinton, 2012/9/12). Again, this contradictory dualism is the work of imperial mythology, where justice and dignity—like capital—accrue only to the dominant and are denied to the dominated.

If Clinton and Obama feel that they have the moral authority to publicly and internationally proclaim the dignity and justice of U.S. actions, it is not in small part due to how intervention in Libya was used to give the international image of the U.S. a cosmetic makeover. Apparently believing that its sins in Iraq, Afghanistan, Yemen, Somalia, Pakistan, and elsewhere would be forgiven and forgotten, U.S. soft power was painted over and redeployed, with the U.S. once again promoting itself as the liberator and protector of Arabs and Muslims. The majority of the North American and European left—reconditioned, accommodating, and fearful—played a supporting role by making substantial room for the dominant U.S. narrative and its military policies. Even here self-described anti-imperialists and Marxists conceded ground to the State Department which would then be used to amass support for intervention: Gaddafi, in their view, was a dictator, even a collaborator of the West, he should not be defended, and he had to go. They thus agreed to make an issue out of Gaddafi, not empire. The left joined the choir, and the State Department pointed to the choir in justifying the idea that "the international community" was speaking with one voice against Gaddafi. Other supposed anti-imperialists and "leftists" (including some Marxists, anarchists, and social democrats) even backed the military intervention to "save Benghazi." In both approaches, the U.S. and other NATO political and military leaderships would benefit from what was at the very least half-praise from supposed ideological opponents at home. These approaches were derided by Latin American socialists, Pan-Africanists and African nationalists alike, who were the only real bastions of anti-imperialism in this entire story. The "neither-nor" à la carte attitude—neither supporting Gaddafi nor supporting NATO (with some exceptions to the latter)—with prompt denunciations of "Stalinism," paid scarce attention to who stood up against U.S. and NATO intervention in Libya: it was not Benghazi, which played an active role in legitimating and boosting the makeover of the U.S. reputation among Arabs.

Turning a blind eye to Sirte, and a racist blind eye to the plight of black Libyans and other black Africans at the hands of the insurgents, the European and North American left did nothing to oppose imperialism. They have suffered an irreparable loss of international credibility while cementing a North-South dividing line among socialists. It seems that the left of the global North bought into the dominant U.S. self-image of being a "force for dignity," fearful that its status would be imperiled by seeming to support "dictators" and being aligned with "Stalinists." (They were quick to adopt the cherished epithets of the very same "neocons" that they claimed to loathe.) Instead, they effectively opted for imperialism and for the global dictatorship of the U.S., with far more blood on its hands than any number of such "dictators" combined. In denouncing

Gaddafi, just as the U.S. was gearing up to depose him, they legitimated the position that Gaddafi's leadership was somehow the root or the pivot of the intervention, thereby inevitably even if indirectly, supporting regime change. They spoke as if all political systems must be identical to ours to be deemed democratic. They treated us to jejune formulas, with fatuous warnings to "Gaddafi supporters": "the enemy of your enemy is not your friend." Somehow, they failed to heed their own warning as they embraced the "valiant revolutionaries" of Benghazi, paying heed to neither their racist outrages nor the presence of Islamic reactionaries. In this they shared the same exuberant naïveté of the rightwing militarist Senator John McCain who, after touring Benghazi himself, declared with total confidence: "I have met with these brave fighters, and they are not Al-Qaeda" (McCain, 2011/4/22). Yet, Al Qaeda's very own second-in-command was the Libyan Abu Yahya al-Libi, whose own brother is a senior commander in the Libyan Islamic Fifghting Group. In response to the killing of Ambassador Stevens, McCain could not avoid signalling a u-turn: "It [was] a planned enemy attack, and we all know who the enemy is" (Muñoz & Herb, 2012/9/12; EuroNews, 2012/9/14)—indeed, the enemy's enemy, who was your friend.

But then what enemy was Gaddafi? According to the historical revisionism of the left in the global North, who want to have their cake and eat it too, Gaddafi would now be promptly reinterpreted as a friend of the West, one who "collaborated" with the U.S. "war on terror." Yet, as we saw throughout this book, it was Gaddafi's war on Al Qaeda that not only long preceded that of the U.S., it was Gaddafi who was personally the target of assassination attempts by Islamic extremists. In the years Gaddafi's Libya fought such extremists, the U.S. and Britain actively collaborated with them, first in Afghanistan, then in Bosnia and Kosovo, and in their attempts to assassinate Gaddafi. It was not Gaddafi who collaborated with the West's "war on terror," it was Gaddafi who persistently, even obsessively sought to reorient the U.S. into supporting Libya's own war on terror. Numerous U.S. embassy cables show Gaddafi constantly lecturing against the U.S. and Saudi Arabia for their support of extremists and wanting to see a change in such policy. Also numerous were the times that U.S. embassy officials seemed entirely indifferent. It is true that the U.S. sent Libyan extremists back to Libya, on rare occasions. What especially irked those who funded and armed groups such as the Libyan Islamic Fighting Group was that, unlike the U.S. with its appeals to "democracy" and "human rights," Gaddafi could fight Islamic extremism on its own turf. Unlike the U.S., Gaddafi could deploy Muslim missionaries across the planet, developing networks through the World Islamic Call Society, and founding prominent mosques in numerous nations.

Given the attack on the U.S. consulate in Benghazi, it is worth recalling in more detail what U.S. diplomats recorded when Gaddafi was in power. In a 2005 meeting with Libyan diplomats and intelligence officials, U.S. diplomats were told "the Saudis were to blame for inciting trouble in Libya," that the Libyan opposition "derives from radical Islam," and the Libyans asked the U.S. to influence the Saudis and to "ask them to rein in the Islamists" (USET, 2005/8/15). In his meeting with Congressman Tom Lantos, the U.S. embassy recorded in a cable marked "secret" that Gaddafi went to great lengths to impress upon the visiting U.S. delegation the threats posed by Wahabi/Salafi extremism (see USET, 2006/8/31a). Gaddafi "dedicated the majority of time to an hour-long tête-à-tête with Representative Lantos focusing on Wahabism in Saudi Arabia, which has become one of his standard topics;" and, intelligence chief Abdullah Senussi "took credit for the GOL [Government of Libya] putting Osama bin Laden on an Interpol watch list in 1997, showing that they had an inkling of events to come far in advance of 9/11." We noted before how Gaddafi also accused the U.S., in a meeting with Senator Arlen Specter (USET, 2006/8/31b), of supporting Wahabi extremists.[3]

It is understandable that, in an uncritical reading of U.S. embassy cables, one could form the opinion that Gaddafi collaborated with the U.S., when it was more the other way around, and not always. It was the late Christopher Stevens himself who reported the following in a cable marked "secret":

"Libya has been a strong partner in the war against terrorism and cooperation in liaison channels is excellent. Muammar al-Qadhafi's criticism of Saudi Arabia for perceived support of Wahabi extremism, a source of continuing Libya-Saudi tension, reflects broader Libyan concern about the threat of extremism. Worried that fighters returning from Afghanistan and Iraq could destabilize the regime, the GOL has aggressively pursued operations to disrupt foreign fighter flows, including more stringent monitoring of air/land ports of entry, and blunt the ideological appeal of radical Islam. The Qadhafi Development Foundation brokered talks with imprisoned members of the

3. There is a naming controversy around how some attach the label "Wahabi" to the Salafis—the details go beyond the scope of this book, suffice it to say to the reader that "Wahabi" is another name for Salafi, but one that Salafis themselves normally reject.

THE AFTERMATH: A NEW WAR ON AFRICA

Libyan Islamic Fighting Group (LIFG) that led to the release earlier this year
of about 130 former LIFG members. The GOL considers the program an
important means to signal willingness to reconcile with former enemies, a
significant feature of Libya's tribal culture. Libya cooperates with neighboring states in the Sahara and Sahel region to stem foreign fighter flows and
travel of trans-national terrorists. Muammar al-Qadhafi recently brokered a
widely-publicized agreement with Tuareg tribal leaders from Libya, Chad,
Niger, Mali and Algeria in which they would abandon separatist aspirations
and smuggling (of weapons and trans-national extremists) in exchange for
development assistance and financial support. Libya also cooperates closely
with Syria, particularly on foreign fighter flows. Syria has transferred over
100 Libyan foreign fighters to the GOL's custody over the past two years,
including a tranche of 27 in late 2007. Our assessment is that the flow of foreign fighters from Libya to Iraq and the reverse flow of veterans to Libya has
diminished due to the GOL's cooperation with other states and new proced-
ures. Counter-terrorism cooperation is a key pillar of the U.S.-Libya bilateral
relationship and a shared strategic interest." (USET, 2008/8/29)

The Libya that the U.S. has now "created" after months of devastating
bombings is almost the exact opposite of what Stevens described above:
Libya now lacks the power that creates the agency necessary for "cooperation" and the Islamic extremists that Libya countered, through its own
network of African and Middle Eastern collaboration, have been
unleashed, killing the very author of the cable above. Michael S. Smith,
author of a report titled, "A View to Extremist Currents in Libya," argued
that, "the very extremist currents that shaped the philosophies of Libya
Salafists and jihadis like (Abd al-Hakim) Belhadj appear to be coalescing
to define the future of Libya" (Herridge, 2012/1/4). The significance of
Belhadj (Belhaj) is that he became the head of the Tripoli Military Council
following the overthrow of Gaddafi, his militia was backed by Qatar, and
he is a former head of the LIFG who fought in Afghanistan with Al Qaeda
and recently ran in Libya's elections (Smith. 2012/7/7). It's clear from the
U.S. embassy cables coming out of Tripoli that Christopher Stevens, author
of many of the cables on Islamic extremism, was keenly aware in considerable detail of the nature and degree of Islamic militancy in eastern Libya,
particularly in Derna (USET, 2008/2/15, 2008/4/8, 2008/4/10, 2008/6/2,
2009/2/2). When Gaddafi stated in an interview with the BBC, early in
the 2011 rebellion, that these "are not my people, they are al-Qaeda,"[4] he

---

4. One copy of the interview was found at: <http://www.youtube.com/watch?v=
tEq-n6ciuxc>.

was guilty of making a sweeping generalization at worst, but not of being completely wrong, and the U.S. would have known that at the time.

To cast the cooperation referred to in the cable quoted above in conspiratorial terms as a subordinate collaboration requires an even more fanciful position because why, after all, would the U.S. overthrow a valued partner? Why would Stevens himself actively work with rebels in Benghazi to overthrow Gaddafi? The question opens the door to the narrative that the U.S. was so shocked by Libyan human rights abuses, which it discovered in February of 2011, that it could do nothing but act against Gaddafi. In other words, here too the denunciation of Gaddafi as a "collaborator" can serve to legitimate Western intervention and regime change, and at the very least it seeks to silence opposition to regime change. When empire called, many were cowed.

After Hillary Clinton cast the U.S. as the greatest force for human dignity ever known, it was unsurprising to hear Obama dust off a statement from a former Secretary of State, Madeleine Albright, when he told Telemundo that the U.S. is an "indispensable" nation (Díaz-Balart, 2012/9/12). The U.S. plans to make itself "indispensable" to Libya's future, with a vengeance. After the killing of its embassy staff, State Department spokesmen announced that AFRICOM was rapidly deploying a Marine Corps "fleet antiterrorism security team" (FAST) and two warships ostensibly "to secure the diplomatic facility in Tripoli, our Embassy, and protect U.S. citizens as needed." But they also added, "the Department of Defense is ready to respond with additional military measures as directed by the President" (U.S. Department of State, 2012/9/12; AJE, 2012/9/13). The U.S. also dispatched CIA and FBI agents, as well as Predator and Reaper drones (Dozier, 2012/9/15). Obama notified Congress that forces "equipped for combat" were being sent to Libya, this time choosing to abide by the War Powers Resolution, which might also suggest a longer term commitment to have "boots on the ground" (Bruce, 2012/9/14).

From this point onwards, it should be obvious to all Libyans that with the destruction of the Jamahiriya, the U.S. will feel free to march in at will. Having begged for NATO intervention and emphasized the need for "protection," those Libyans who called for and relied upon foreign support cast themselves as helpless creatures, incapable of either self-defence, or other forms of resistance, or even flight. Extended to the present, the "helpless Libyan" has become the Libyan incapable of self-rule. This is a bleak vision of humanity that has been erected by the "humanitarians" and by some Libyans, one at odds with history, sociology, and anthropology, which are rich with countless cases of people who have been able to fight, resist, and practice multiple forms of self-protection; indeed, local actors struggling for change often prefer their own solutions over those imposed by outsiders. It's as if everything we had learned had been dismissed and erased by both NATO and the "responsibility to protect" crowd, forcing some to go back and relearn some very basic lessons, even if they do so with reluctance to sacrifice the agency of international interventionists (see for example IRIN, 2012/2/10 and South & Harragin, 2012). Whether it is the motive or outcome is an academic question, but this tenacious unlearning of resistance and self-protection is the basis for creating a neo-colonial relationship of dependency. Those who speak of the "responsibility to protect" of course never use terms such as "neo-colonialism," except maybe to mock it; no, instead their world is populated only by the victims of dictators, and themselves as the liberators.

The empire that speaks of "dignity" first invented the image of the helpless Libyan begging for us to "stop standing idly by"—because we, in the West, are tasked with authoring the history of Libyans, according to this logic—and after inventing the image the empire went about destroying Libya until the image could materialize. Now U.S. officials tell the media that, "the Libyans have barely re-established full control of their country," and that the post-Gaddafi government "has limited tools at its disposal," with Paul Pillar, a former senior CIA official adding that, "the Libyans in just about every endeavor are just learning to walk, let alone run" (Dozier, 2012/9/15). They are, in other words, infants. Hence Obama rushed in Marines, drones, and CIA agents to hunt down those that attacked the consulate in Benghazi. According to the U.S., the Libyans themselves do not know who the attackers are; this matter requires U.S. intelligence. Destruction is creation, and in the chaos ensuing from the U.S./NATO unravelling the country, interventionists feel free to inscribe their preferred myths of history—"where they make a desert, they call it peace" (Tacitus, 98, ch. 30).

It's also interesting to reflect on the contradictory and bifurcated image created of ourselves by the humanitarian imperialists. On the one hand, as civilized Westerners we are something akin to angels. Our actions and thoughts reign high above history, residing in an altostratus of unimpeachable rectitude. In our teleological view of our own progress, we are at the highest point of human cultural evolution, ours being the highest stage of human achievement. We are the standard by which others are measured. We are what the future of all humanity looks like. The absence of our

298

SLOUCHING TOWARDS SIRTE

institutions and values in other societies is a measure of their inferiority. We should help them. We should help them to become more like us. These various "savage" others can be raised to our level of dignity, if we help them to acquire "prosperity" through the advance of "opportunity." Fixated on providence and destiny, we of course resent history, because history carries the inevitability of change, and of the decline of empire. As much as we resent history, we find cultural particularity loathsome: some differences simply defy polite tolerance, and demand our corrective intervention. High up in the clouds, perched on the wings of our stealth bombers, we preach the ideology of universal, individual human rights.

On the White House blog, on "The Future of America's Partnership with Sub-Saharan Africa," the word "dignity" appears twice, in a short post (Harris, 2012/6/14). In Obama's speech in Ghana, he mentions "dignity" twice (Obama, 2009/7/11). In both cases, at least once the word "dignity" is paired with "opportunity." Dignity, paired with "lucky chances." In the May 2010 "National Security Strategy" published by the White House, the word "dignity" appears 14 times, and twice in relation to Africa or a part of Africa. (Of course some variation of "terror"—terrorism, terrorist, etc.—appears 57 times.) The document never spells out what the U.S. political leadership means by dignity. If there is any indication at all of a working assumption, it is that dignity is somehow the result of health programs, clean water and food security (pp. 5, 39)—as if it were a material condition of life. In other instances, dignity in U.S. national security strategy arises from "combating poverty" (p. 35), which produces the cringeworthy suggestion that somehow poor people lack dignity (and rich Americans, of course, must have an awful lot of dignity instead). The pattern is there, "the dignity that comes with development" (p. 36). Apparently underdevelopment is a threat to U.S. national security because it produces *The Peoples without Dignity* who get these crazy notions in their heads about attacking U.S. interests. So the bad news is that places like Africa currently suffer from a *dignity-deficit*, but the good news is that with enough investment Africans can bridge the *dignity gap* by achieving greater material prosperity, that is, becoming more like the preferred image we still hold of ourselves, in spite of unemployment, mortgage foreclosures, and child hunger.

On the other hand, both NATO propaganda and the public advocacy of humanitarian imperialists are based on certain assumptions of humanity thereby creating another image of ourselves that is not about dignity, but rather impulse—not even impulse, maybe more something like mere pulsation. This is an image of humanity that is fundamentally founded on consumerism and instant gratification. The vision of our humanity that liberal imperialists entertain is one which constructs us as shrieking sacks of emotion. This is the elites' anthropology, one that views us as bags of nerve and muscle: throbbing with outrage, contracting with every story of "incubator babies" (first in Iraq, now again in Syria [Abunimah, 2011//8/8]), bulging up with animus at the arrest of Gay Girl in Damascus, recoiling at the sound of Viagra-fueled mass rape (Murphy, 2011/6/13). From mass hysteria in Twitter to hundreds of thousands signing an online Avaaz petition calling for bombing Libya in the name of human rights (the same Avaaz that had a petition calling for the release of the non-existent "Gay Girl in Damascus"), we become nerves of mass reaction. We cannot "stand idly by" because that would be what thinking people would do. In our state of frenzy, we scream for action via "social media," thumbs furiously in action on our "smart" phones. What should we do? Whatever, "do something…stand up and be counted."

If we do not act, we should be held responsible for the actions of others. When we do act, we should never be held responsible for our own actions. Then again, our "action" merely consists of asking the supremely endowed military establishment to act in our name.

This is a vision of us as an audience, a body of public opinion harnessed to a feed bag. One image of us as such an audience was strikingly described in William Gibson's *Idoru* (1996):

> "Personally I like to imagine something the size of a baby hippo, the color of a week-old boiled potato, that lives by itself, in the dark, in a double-wide on the outskirts of Topeka. It's covered with eyes and it sweats constantly. The sweat runs into those eyes and makes them sting. It has no mouth…no genitals, and can only express its mute extremes of murderous rage and infantile desire by changing the channels on a universal remote. Or by voting in presidential elections."[5]

Lacking in any dignity in the political and media elites' constructions of us as reactive bags of emotion, their anthropology as I call it is also accompanied by NATO's implicit sociology: societies can be remade through a steady course of high-altitude bombings and drone strikes.

Remade into what? It was Obama's stated intention to "install democracy" in Libya through foreign military intervention, which is an amazing

---

5. My many thanks to Brendan Stone, host of CFMU 93.3 FM, "Unusual Sources," for bringing this quote to my attention.

indictment of what he means by democracy. Obama announced his "commitment to the goal of helping provide the Libyan people an opportunity to transform their country, by installing a democratic system that respects the people's will" (*Huffpost Hill*, 2011/3/22).

The question is though, do Libyans want democracy? What do Libyans understand by democracy? These questions persisted in spite of the July 2012 elections for a national congress. With a 62 percent turnout of registered voters—not a spectacular figure if we had believed that there was a massive and popular yearning for elections—and with 80 percent of eligible voters registered, this meant that the actual turnout of all those who were eligible to vote was little more than 48 percent. After supposedly being crushed by the tyranny of Gaddafi, less than half of Libyans bothered to vote. A British survey that preceded the elections, the "First National Survey of Libya" conducted by Oxford Research International in association with the Institute of Human Sciences, University of Oxford, and the University of Benghazi, presented some interesting results.[6] Only 13 percent of those surveyed said democracy (either "Libyan-style" or "Western-style") should be installed in a year's time, with the total number rising to only 25 percent when the time period was stretched to five years. The majority simply rejected democracy. The largest number, 26 percent, wanted to see a single, strong Libyan leader (with another 12 percent choosing a small group of strong leaders), for the next year; the numbers declined to only 22 percent plus nine percent respectively when choosing for the next five years. Also, 62 percent wanted to maintain a politically centralized nation, rejecting the demands for autonomy by eastern Libya. Just under 50 percent wanted to see any prosecution of former regime supporters, with 66 percent wanting this for former regime members. Also, 53 percent of respondents said that the Muslim Brotherhood should play no role in the political future of Libya—and indeed, religious parties fared poorly in the elections. A further 16 percent said they were prepared to use violence for political ends. It's also true that the survey reported that 80 percent of Libyans thought that regime change was "absolutely right;" the same number also reported being "very careful with people" out of a lack of trust, and with tens of thousands of armed men roaming the streets, one has to wonder if they would express outright disagreement with the revolution to British outsiders accompan-

---

6. I received data compiled by the survey, along with two written reports and two PowerPoint presentations, from the British authors of the report.

ied by academics from Benghazi. What is interesting is that roughly a third of those surveyed manifested an overall pattern of preference for the political system that they had lost, added to a predominant lack of trust overall, and a strong current that prefers violence.

For some, violence and elections worked well together. On the eve of the election, gunmen shot down a helicopter carrying polling materials near the eastern city of Benghazi, killing one election worker (BBC, 2012/7/6). Previously, an election candidate had also been murdered (Shuaib, 2012/5/14). Following the NTC's issuing of draft electoral laws, several tribal leaders and militia commanders in Libya's east declared self-rule, "set up their own council and formed their own army, while saying that they would boycott elections and even work to prevent Saturday's vote from taking place" (AP, 2012/7/6). Over 216,000 had registered to vote in Benghazi's own election in May 2012 for an autonomous Cyrenaica Congress (Reuters, 2012/5/19). Misrata, like Benghazi, also sacked its rebel city council, amidst plenty of complaints of corruption, and elected an autonomous one (AP, 2012/2/21). Days before the July national congressional election, militia members from eastern Libya took over oil refineries in the towns of Ras Lanouf, Brega and Sidr, shutting down the facilities to pressure the NTC to cancel the elections. As a result, protesters shut off half of all of Libya's oil exports (Gumuchian & Shuaib, 2012/7/6). Angry protesters and militia fighters attacked election offices, setting fire to ballot papers and other voting materials, in Benghazi and Ajdabiya (AP, 2012/7/6). In a sudden move to appease Islamists, the NTC even stripped the parliament waiting to be elected of its reposibility in drafting a constitutional panel, now saying this would be directly elected in a separate vote (BBC, 2012/7/6). On the day of the election itself, "acts of sabotage, mostly in the east of the country, prevented 101 polling stations from opening," according to the chairman of the electoral commission (AFP, 2012/7/7). With militias firmly in control of Libya's cities and towns, frequently engaged in deadly assaults on each other, British journalists could only conclude: "Gaddafi has been replaced by what is in effect a patchwork quilt of local dictatorships" (Oborne & Cookson, 2012/5/18).

After the NTC touted itself to foreign audiences as a force for democracy (AFP, 2011/3/23), it was interesting to see what it meant by democracy in the electoral and other laws that they decreed since January 2012. Workers could not run as candidates, given the requirement that candidates must have a professional qualification; anyone who ever worked at any level of the former government was barred, unless they could demonstrate "early and clear support for the February 17th revolution;" those with an academic degree that involved study of Gaddafi's Green Book, which was previously a prerequisite to professional advancement, were also barred; also, anyone who received any monetary benefit under Gaddafi could be prohibited from participation—as Massaoud El Kanuni, a Libyan constitutional lawyer, realized, these "criteria could be used against three-quarters of the country" (Morrow, 2012/1/13). The NTC would then continue its practice of holding meetings in secret, not even releasing the names of its ruling members. What was known was that Khalifa Hifter, a Libyan exile on the payroll of the CIA, was now Libya's most influential army officer, especially after Gaddafi defector, General Abdul Fatah Younes, was mysteriously assassinated by forces aligned with the NTC during the middle of NATO's war. NTC leaders who were officials in Gaddafi's government clearly exempted themselves from their own laws—they were above the law.

Meanwhile, the great mass of Libyans who benefited under Gaddafi or had any "connections" whatsoever, were to be forgiven nothing. Yet, insurgent militias guilty of widespread and ongoing atrocities, were to be forgiven everything: before the elections, the NTC passed a law granting immunity to all of the "revolutionaries." In addition, the NTC passed a series of laws that criminalized free speech and any ties to the former government in sweeping terms, as if to codify the reign of terror that had been unleashed since Gaddafi's overthrow. The authorities were to take action against individuals who participated in "official and unofficial bodies of the former regime," as they pose a "threat to the security or stability" of Libya, with punishments ranging from surveillance to travel bans to barring them from residence in certain parts of the country. "Glorification" of Gaddafi or the former regime was also criminalized and punishable by a prison sentence (that the anti-glorification law was later repealed meant little, it simply legalized the ongoing practice of de facto persecution, and its original passage would have been enough to scare some). Another law banned spreading "news reports, rumours or propaganda" that could "cause any damage to the state," with the penalty being "life in prison." There would also be a prison sentence for anyone spreading information of rumours that could "weaken the citizens' morale" during "conditions of war," and Libya was still defined as being at war. There would be prison sentences for anyone who "attacks the February 17 revolution, denigrates Islam, the authority of the state or its institutions." Another law confiscated all property and funds belonging to persons who served in the former regime, that is except for those passing this law (Soguel, 2012/5/3). NTC Chair, Mustafa Abdul Jalil, threatened: "we will be tough towards people who threaten our stability" (AFP, 2012/2/17). This language echoed that of interim Defence Minister, Osama al-Juwali, who threatened Bani Walid (a pro-Gaddafi bastion that liberated itself from NTC rule) that forces loyal to the NTC would strike it with an "iron fist" (BBC, 2012/1/25). Where's that anti-Stalinism now?

That this language, the repression and persecution, and the laws above, constitute a "democratic" transformation and "liberation from dictatorship" is something deserving of mockery and condemnation—especially as citizens of NATO states have literally paid to bring this about. But instead of either mockery or condemnation, Western leaders have offered celebratory congratulations. Obama called the elections "another milestone in the country's transition to democracy," a statement parroted by the media, while the European Union hailed Libya's "first free elections" as the "dawn of a new era," and UN Secretary General Ban Ki-moon declared that Libyans had "sacrificed their lives or suffered lasting injury in order to win the right of the Libyan people to build a new state founded on human dignity and the rule of law"—"as if this were now a reality" (Shaoul & Marsden, 2012/7/11).

What remains a reality is that Libya continues to be a society at war with itself, not just as a matter of interpretation, but as a matter of the new national security laws. Neither officially, nor in practice, has the war ended. Not only are there still militarily active resistance units that supported Gaddafi, and refuse to admit defeat, but the government and opposing militias themselves also live in fear of possible overthrow. With matters taken to an extreme, Gaddafi is blamed for virtually everything that has transpired since his death, including getting blame for the torture and mass detentions by those who overthrew him. When the U.S. diplomats were murdered in Benghazi, Libyan government officials immediately saw the hand of "Gaddafi sympathizers." If Gaddafi is to blame for everything, it would mean that he still has power over Libyans, and therefore there has been no real revolution. Worse yet, by consistently blaming Gaddafi, Libya's new rulers disclaim any responsibility for themselves, which once again is a defeat for dignity as a reiteration of the "helpless Libyan."

The "helpless Libyan" was of course very popular to those making careers of "helping" and "protecting" others. If Libyans were not helpless, then they would be made so. Once protected, they would be thankful:

"One, Two, Three, merci Sarkozy!" (AFP, 2011/3/23). Gratitude is good. Gratitude provides important symbolic capital, which can then be converted into actual capital: tales of success and victory in countering "genocide," when properly mass mediated and aided by viral Internet campaigns, can be used to appeal for donations from the public, offer paid memberships, and seek financial support from states, while retaining a dubious identity as a NGO. In the case of thanks offered to states, gratitude translates into something akin to subordinate acquiescence, offering legitimation and thus serving as a lubricant for power. Thus French President Nicolas Sarkozy could tell his warrior-philosopher, Bernard-Henri Lévy:

> "The role I am playing goes beyond my person, or my mandate. It is the position of France in the Arab world on which the dawn is rising. It is the world order, the style of international relations for the approaching decades that we are in the process of defining. It is an event of long-term import [de longue portée]. A slow earthquake. All this is worth a little patience. Let's keep in contact. Thank you for what you have done." (Walden, 2011/12/29)

Notions of protecting civilians, preventing genocide, ending human rights abuses, putting war criminals on trial, providing humanitarian relief, all of these are rarely even of secondary concern to the key Western actors in actual practice, except as weapons. Sarkozy is at least frank: this story is about empire. Lévy, anxious to show how much of an insider he was in the power group that crushed Libya, unfortunately makes the mistake of providing information that entirely nullifies all of his other claims, such as the grotesque ones that Gaddafi brought war on himself, or the need to prevent a massacre in Benghazi, and so on (Al Arabiya, 2012/1/6).

The worst thing one could do to the dogmatic upholders of the "responsibility of protect" doctrine, is to take them seriously and to judge the outcomes of the interventions they endorse, on the very same terms they have chosen. Rather than the protection of civilians that key R2P advocates applauded as the defining feature of the intervention in Libya, what we have seen is a wide range of systematic and recurring actions that demonstrate the exact opposite of civilians being protected. This book has demonstrated, though documented cases, a consistent pattern in NATO actions where the safety of civilians was either ignored, or civilians were themselves the chosen targets, or certain civilians were armed and supported in threatening the lives of other civilians. Apart from cases, and speaking in terms of a broader framework, war itself cannot but escalate the costs to human lives, and NATO's intervention not only prolonged the war, it escalated the war and destroyed countless civilian lives both directly and indirectly. If we really wanted to see "civilians" being "protected," then we needed a counter force to protect Libyans from NATO. Moreover, NATO's intervention did not stop armed conflict in Libya, as that continues to the present. Massacres were not prevented, they were enabled, and many occurred after NATO intervened and because NATO intervened. The only issue on which NATO spokespersons and R2P advocates can score a rhetorical "win" is on Benghazi having been "saved"—saved, that is, from a fictitious massacre that was not in the offing. Even then one must be possessed of a certain racist bend of mind to talk about lives "saved" in Benghazi when we know of the horrors committed there against countless black Africans and black Libyans. Only if the latter do not count, as if they were to be subtracted from the "humanity" that "human rights" advocates claim as their devout concern, can one possibly make a claim that lives were saved in Benghazi. In addition, it takes a determined partisan to simply dismiss the documented "revenge killings" that took place, and continue to take place in Benghazi against persons known or imagined to have been loyal to Gaddafi. The implicit agreement tacitly binding NATO and R2P advocates was simply that certain lives were worth saving, and many more were not. Their answer to the killing, real or imagined, that they claimed to find so abhorrent was to introduce more killing. If this intervention is what they imagine to be "humanitarian," does it mean that they are capable of even worse?

Dignity has now become a target of imperial appropriation, most likely because imperial ideologues recognize a concept and a bundle of moral and political values that they cannot control and that will undermine their preferred slant on "human rights." U.S. national security strategy documents seem to essentially equate dignity with having modern conveniences and cash—in other words, an instumentalist or transactionalist view of dignity that sits well with capitalist values, and makes for easy policy options. In addition to instrumentalizing dignity, U.S. policy documents Westernize it, by reducing dignity to the property of the individual, and writers in U.S. mainstream organs are very desperate to find individualism in Libya (eg. Marlowe, 2012/9/18). However, ideas such as national dignity, and black dignity, speak of dignity as the possession of large collectivities, nor are they reducible to pragmatic calculations and the quest for monetary gain. If U.S. policy documents speak of dignity, it is out of recognition that this concept matters to many, hence best for the U.S. to try to produce the representations that it hopes will stick and to define the field for everyone else.

One reason why dignity matters so much, as a concept, is that it goes beyond freedom and rights and thus there is a risk for the West that some of the cherished concepts in its intellectual armory, used to wage international propaganda, could evaporate back into the thin air from which they came. Rights, specifically human rights, tend to privilege the individual, which is one of the reasons for long-standing and widespread criticisms of the idea as a Eurocentric and capitalist one. Freedom, especially in the pronouncements of U.S. political leaders, clearly means free markets, free trade, free flows of capital, and it implies an equivalent system of government where influence, access, and votes are bought and sold, and marshalled by competing groups of entrepreneurs organized in self-serving entities we know as political parties.

Dignity, however, does not imply that any one system of political organization is better or more needed than another. Dignity can exist and thrive in a multi-party state, in a one-party state, in a no-party state, and in a non-state society. Moreover, the roots of dignity are fundamentally local, and given the very diverse ways in which it can be perceived and valued, it cannot easily be codified in legal instruments at the international level. In other words, we should not expect a United Nations Charter on the Dignity of Peoples anytime soon. Dignity has no universally agreed upon list of traits—so the concept defies measurement, and it escapes positivism, capitalism, and Western humanitarianism.

Imperialist logics are also defied by dignity, a term that often comes out in the open as a rallying cry in resistance and rebellion. Imperialist denials of self-determination are challenged by the idea and defence of dignity. Intervention, as the one that occurs in Libya, is fundamentally opposed to dignity: the very act of intervention implies that there is some deficit or deficiency that requires the curative power of foreign actors. The Libyans are somehow inadequate in this frame of mind, not even their numbers are sufficient; hence we "iPad imperialists" must join their struggle: "we are all Libyans now." Except we are not, and never can be, nor should we ever pretend to assume someone else's identity. Imperial hubris (wars seen as "cake walks") is well accompanied by imperial narcissism ("they will greet us as liberators") and imperial personality disorder ("I am them").

Once foreign military intervention occurs, it scorches the earth in a way that unleashes new forces, and creates new deadly consequences that can be exploited for the purposes of further intervention. As we see in the rapid, militarized response of the U.S. to the killing of its ambassador and staff in Benghazi, intervention begets intervention. More intervention is needed to solve the problems caused by intervention.

The next time that empire comes calling in the name of human rights, please be found standing idly by.

References

Abbas, Mohammed. (2011/3/14). "Libya Jets Bomb Rebels, French Press For No-Fly Zone." *Reuters*, March 14.

Ablordeppey, Samuel. (2012/4/10). "Armed Attack on Ghana Embassy in Libya." *Ghana-Web*, April 10.

Abrahams, Fred. (2011/8/24). "A New Libya Must Honor Human Rights." *CNN*, August 24.

Abu Henanah, Kamel Abdullah. (2009). "A Debate Over the Proposed Libyan Constitution." *Al-Ahram Center for Political and Strategic Studies*, (137), October 25

Abunimah, Ali. (2011/8/8). "How CNN Helped Spread a Hoax about Syrian Babies Dying in Incubators". *Electronic Intifada*, August 8.

Adeseko, Duro. (2011/10/22). "Eminent Nigerians Mourn Gadhafi." *NBF News/The Nigerian Voice*, October 22.

Adi, Hakim, & Sherwood, Marika. (2003). *Pan-African History: Political Figures from Africa and the Diaspora since 1787*. New York: Routledge.

AEDI. (2008). "Libya's Investments in North Africa." *Africa Economic Development Institute*, December.

Africa Bulletin. (2010/12/15). "Africa: The Creation of the African Monetary Fund." *Africa Bulletin*, December 15.

African Press Organization (APO). (2012/2/16). "Libya: Hardship and Danger Remain." *StarAfrica.com*, February 16.

African Union (AU). (1999). Fourth Extraordinary Session of the Assembly of Heads of State and Government. EAHG/Draft/Decl. (IV) Rev.1. September 8-9, Sirte, Libya.

—. (n.d.). "The Creation of the African Monetary Fund."

—. (2004a). Report of the Chairperson of the Commission on the Common African Defence and Security Policy. First Meeting of the African Ministers of Defence and Security on the Establishment of the African Standby Force and the Common African Defence and Security Policy, Addis Ababa, Ethiopia, January 20-21. Min/Def. & Sec. 5(I). Addis Ababa: African Union

—. (2004b). Draft Framework for a Common African Defence and Security Policy. First Meeting of the African Ministers of Defence and Security on the Establishment of the African Standby Force and the Common African Defence and Security Policy, Addis Ababa, January 20-21. Min/Def. & Sec. 3(I). Addis Ababa: African Union.

—. (2011). "African Union Calls for an End to Bombing and a Political, Not Military Solution in Libya." *African Union*, June 15. .

—(2012). "African Union: The Financial Institutions."

AFRICOM. (2011). "About United States Africa Command." *U.S. Africa Command*, August.

—(2011/3/5). "AFRICOM Supports U.S. and International Response to Libya Crisis." *U.S. Africa Command*, March 5.

—. (2012/5/24). "Fact Sheet: United States Africa Command." U.S. AFRICOM Public Affairs Office, May 24

Agence France Presse (AFP). (2011/2/16). "At Least 4 Dead in Libya Clashes: Opposition, NGOs". *Agence France Presse*, February

—. (2011/3/13). "Opposition Leader Calls for No-Fly Zone, Medicine." *Sydney Morning Herald*, March 13.

—. (2011/3/23). "Libyan Rebels Foresee Democratic Regime". *Herald Sun*, March 23.

—. (2011/6/8). "Kadhafi 'Ordered Mass Rapes' in Libya: ICC." *Agence France Presse*, June 8.

—. (2011/6/10). "Libya Rape Claims 'Hysteria' – Investigator." *Herald Sun*, June 10.

—. (2011/9/26). "Nato Blasts Gaddafi Hometown: NTC Holds Back After Making Advance." *The Daily Star*, September 26.

—. (2011/10/21). "Nigerian Militant Mourns 'Martyr' Gaddafi." *News 24*, October 21.

—. (2011/12/15). "Putin Accuses US in Murder of Gaddafi." *Information Clearing House*, December 15.

—. (2012/2/17). "Libya Marks Revolution Day amid New Warning". *ABC News (Australia)*, February 17.

—. (2012/4/21). "Libya Building up Case against Seif: ICC Envoy." *Agence France Presse*, April 21.

—. (2012/7/7). "Libya Unrest 'Prevents Voting in 101 Centres'". *Agence France Presse*, July 7.

Aglanu, Ernest Dela. (2012/1/14). "Blakk Rasta Hits Hard at West for Killing Africa's Redeemer, Gaddafi." *Ghana Music.com*, January 14.

AGOA. (2000). African Growth and Opportunity Act.

Air Afriqiyah. (2009). About the Airline. [Archive]

Ajami, Fouad. (2011/8/31). "From Baghdad to Tripoli." *The Wall Street Journal*, August 31.

Akuetteh, Nii. (2011/9/22). "Anti-Imperialist Rage Should Be Constructive." *Pambazuka News*, (548), September 22.

Al Akhbar. (2012). "3980511_MORE-Insight - Libya - Confirmation Gadhafi is dead - LY700." *Al Akhbar English*.

Al Arabiya. (2011/2/19). "Gaddafi Recruits 'African Mercenaries' to Quell Protests." *Al Arabiya*, February 19.

—. (2011/2/21). "'Massacre' in Tripoli As Jets Strike Civilians: Witnesses". *Al Arabiya*, February 21.

—. (2011/10/26). "Qatar Admits It Had Boots on the Ground in Libya; NTC Seeks Further NATO Help." *Al Arabiya*, October 26.

—. (2012/1/6). "Qaddafi Brought War upon Himself, Says Architect of Libyan Intervention". *Al Arabiya*, January 6.

—. (2012/10/1). "Qaddafi Was Killed by French Agent, Not Rebel: Report". *Al Arabiya*, October 1.

AlJazeeraEnglish. (2011/2/18). "Eyewitness Reports Protester Deaths in Benghazi" [Video]. *Al Jazeera English*, February 18.

—. (2011/3/1). "Black Africans in Libya Live in Fear" [Video]. *Al Jazeera English*, March 1.

—. (2011/4/9). "Rare Glimpse into Gaddafi Forces" [Video]. *Al Jazeera English*, April 9.

Al Jazeera English (AJE). (2011/2/17). "Libya Live Blog." *Al Jazeera English*, February 17.

—. (2011/2/21). "Libya Protests Spread and Intensify." *Al Jazeera English*, February 21.

—. (2011/3/12). "Libyan Rebels in Retreat." *Al Jazeera English*, March 12.

— . (2011/3/28). "Rape Used 'as a Weapon' in Libya." *Al Jazeera English*, March 28. ·

—. (2011/8/29). "Foreign Migrants at Risk Libya." *Al Jazeera English*, August 29.

—. (2011/10/20). "Muammar Gaddafi Killed as Sirte Falls." *Al Jazeera English*, October 20.

—. (2012/9/13). "US Warships Steam Towards Libya Coast". *Al Jazeera English*, September 13.

Al-Saadi, Yazan. (2012/3/19). "US Mercenary 'Took Part' in Gaddafi Killing; Sent to Assist Syrian Opposition." *Al Akhbar English*, March 19.

Al-Shalchi, Hadeel. (2011/8/25). "Intense Battles Erupt Near Gadhafi Seized Compound." *Associated Press*, August 25.

—. (2011/9/18). "Libya Ex-Rebels Advance on Bani Walid Again." *Associated Press*, September 18.

—. (2011/10/4). "Fleeing Gadhafi Bastion, Bitter at the New Libya." *Associated Press*, October 4.

—. (2011/10/5). "Libya Fighters Loot Gadhafi Tribe, Showing Divide." *Associated Press*, October 5.

Amnesty International (AI). (2011). *The Battle for Libya: Killings, Disappearances and Torture*. London, UK: Amnesty International. September.

—. (2011/2/23). "Libya: Organization Calls for Immediate Arms Embargo and Assets Freeze." *Amnesty International*, February 23.

—. (2011/6/23). "Document—African Union Must Prioritize the Protection of Civilians in Conflict Situations." *Amnesty International*, June 23

—. (2011/8/25). "Both Sides in Libya Conflict Must Protect Detainees from Torture." *Amnesty International*, August 25.

—. (2011/8/31). "Libya: Fears for Detainees Held by Anti-Gaddafi Forces." *Amnesty International*, August 31.

—. (2011/9/12). "Libya: NTC Must Take Control to Prevent Spiral of Abuses." *Amnesty International*, September 12.

—. (2011/10/3). "Warring Libyan Forces Must Allow Humanitarian Aid to Reach Sirte." *Amnesty International*, October 3.

—. (2011/11/17). "Amnesty International USA Announces Leadership Transition: Suzanne Nossel Selected as New Executive Director of Human Rights Organization." *Amnesty International-USA*, November 17.

—. (2012a). *Militias Threaten Hopes for New Libya*. London, UK: Amnesty International. February 16.

—. (2012b). *Libya: The Forgotten Victims of NATO Strikes*. London, UK: Amnesty International. March.

AMT/MF. (2012/1/28). "New Chinese-funded African Union HQ Inaugurated." *Addis Ababa Online*, January 28.

Anderson, Ewan W. (1987). "Water Resources and Boundaries in the Middle East. In Richard N. Schofield & Gerald Henry Blake (Eds.), *Boundaries and State Territory in the Middle East and North Africa* (pp. 85-97). Cambridgeshire: Middle East & North African Studies Press.

Anderson, Lisa. (1982). "Libya and American Foreign Policy." *Middle East Journal*, 36(4), Autumn, 516-534.

—. (1983). "Qaddafi's Islam." In John L. Esposito (Ed.), *Voices of Resurgent Islam* (pp. 134-149). New York: Oxford University Press.

Anuforo, Emeka. (2012/3/1). "AU Concludes Work on African Monetary Fund, Others." *The Guardian (Nigeria)*, March 1.

Asfaw, Tedla. (2011). "Ugly Racism in the Libya Uprising Live On TV." *ECADF: Ethiopian News & Opinions*.

Associated Press (AP). (1994/2/19). "ANC Draft Policy Paper Criticises 'New World Order'." *New Straits Times*, February 19.

—. (2011/2/26). "Libya Protests: Obama Says Muammar Gaddafi Must 'Leave Now'." *The Huffington Post*, February 26.

—. (2011/3/15). "Libyan Rebels Lose Last Stronghold West of Tripoli." *Ahram Online*, March 15.

—. (2011/4/27). "AP Interview: UN Diplomat Works against Gadhafi." *Fox News*, April 27.

—. (2011/8/5). "Media Group Urges UN Probe of Strike on Libya TV." *Associated Press*, August 5.

—. (2011/8/29). "AU: Libya Rebels Killing Black Workers." *CBS News*, August 29.

—. (2011/9/19). "Rebels Express Mix of Emotions in Siege of Qaddafi Bastion." *Fox News*, September 19.

—. (2011/10/25). "Qaddafi's Final Days: Rage and Despair." *CBS News*, October 25.

—. (2011/10/28). "Gadhafi Hometown Pays Heavy Price in Libyan Battle." *USA Today*, October 28.

—. (2012/2/21). "Elections in Libya's Misrata Show a Splintered Nation". *CTV News*, February 21.

—. (2012/7/6). "Fears of Violence, Calls for Boycott Threaten to Mar Vote in Libya". *CP24*, July 6.

—. (2012/7/14). "Islamists in Mali Detain Protesters." *The New York Times*, July 14.

—. (2012/7/23). "Mali: European Support for Intervention." *The New York Times*, July 23.

Awuah, I.F. Joe. (2011/10/24). "Kufuor in Tears. For Gaddafi." *Daily Guide Newspaper*, October 24.

—. (2011/12/13). "Otumfuo Succeeds Gaddafi." *Daily Guide Newspaper*, December 13.

Avni, Benny. (2011/3/30). "Astonishment Spreads at U.N. Over Chaos in Libyan Diplomatic Ranks." *New York Sun*, March 30.

Baker, David R. (2003/4/18). "Bechtel to Rebuild Iraq. Reconstruction: Politically Connected S.F. Firm Wins Bid." *San Francisco Chronicle*, April 18.

Bald, Margaret. (2000). "Libya/Nigeria: Xenophobia in Libya." *World Press Review*, 47(12), December.

Barigaba, Julius, & Khisa, Isaac. (2012/2/18). "Libya: Gaddafi Ghost Still Haunts Investments in East Africa." *AllAfrica/The East African*, February 18.

Bariyo, Nicholas. (2012/3/7). "Uganda to Return Libyan Assets." *The Wall Street Journal*, March 7.

Bastian, Marc. (2011/10/23). "Kadhafi's Last-Stand Hometown Littered with Bodies." *Agence France Presse*, October 23.

Basu, Moni. (2011/6/29). "Analysts Blame Faulty Assumptions for Prolonged Libya War". *Cable News Network*, June 29.

BBC. (1976). "Soldier for Islam" [Video]. *Adam Curtis_The Medium and the Message.*

—. (1979). "John Simpson Meets Gaddafi for First BBC Interview" [Video]. *BBC News-Africa.*

—. (1999/6/13). "World: Africa Mandela Welcomes 'Brother Leader' Gaddafi." *BBC News*, June 13.

—. (1999/6/14). "World: Africa Gaddafi Visits Robben Island." *BBC News*, June 14.

—. (2008/8/29). "Gaddafi: Africa's 'King of Kings'." *BBC News*, August 29.

—. (2010/6/8). "Libya 'Expels' UN Refugee Agency UNHCR." *BBC News*, June 8.

—. (2010/8/31). "Gaddafi Wants EU Cash to Stop African Migrants." *BBC News*, August 31.

—. (2011/2/16). "Libya Protests: Second City Benghazi Hit by Violence". *BBC News*, February 16.

—. (2011/2/21). "Libya Protests: Tripoli Hit by Renewed Clashes." *BBC News*, February 21.

—. (2011/3/29). "Libya: Pro-Gaddafi Forces Push Rebels Back From Sirte." *BBC News*, March 29.

—. (2011/4/29). "What Now for Colonel Gaddafi's Green Book?" *BBC News*, April 29.

—. (2011/6/8). "Libya: Gaddafi Investigated Over Use of Rape as Weapon." *BBC News*, June 8.

—. (2011/8/8). "Mugabe Labels NATO a 'Terrorist Group' over Libya." *BBC News*, August 8.

—. (2011/8/26). "Libya: Hundreds of Bodies Found at Tripoli Hospital." *BBC News*, August 26.

—. (2011/8/27). "Libyan Capital Tripoli Faces Water, Power Crisis." *BBC News*, August 27.

—. (2011/8/31). "Libya: 'Mass Killing' Sites in Tripoli." *BBC News*, August 31.

—. (2011/9/22). "Libya: NTC Says Key Oasis Towns Taken." *BBC News*, September 22.

—. (2011/9/27). "Libya Fighting: Fears Grow For Civilians in Sirte." *BBC News*, September 27.

—. (2011/10/7). "Libya NTC Forces Take Most of Gaddafi Stronghold Sirte." *BBC News*, October 7.

—. (2011/10/16). "Libya: Bulldozers Raze Gaddafi Bab Al-Aziziya Compound." *BBC News*, October 16.

—. (2011/10/20). "Libya's Col Muammar Gaddafi killed, says NTC." *BBC News*, October 20.

—. (2012/1/25). "Libyan Defence Minister in Restive Bani Walid for Talks". *BBC News*, January 25.

—. (2012/2/15). "Libyans Not Keen on Democracy, Suggests Survey." *BBC News*, February 15.

—. (2012/6/11). "Libya Unrest: UK Envoy's Convoy Attacked in Benghazi." *BBC News*, June 11.

—. (2012/7/6). "Libya Election Helicopter 'Shot Near Benghazi'". *BBC News*, July 6.

Beaumont, Peter; Blake, Gerald H.; & Wagstaff, J. Malcolm. (1988). *The Middle East: A Geographical Study.* London, UK: David Fulton.

Beeman, William. (2011/2/23). "Megalomaniac Gaddafi Out of Touch." *Press TV*, February 23.

Benesch, Susan. (2004). "Inciting Genocide, Pleading Free Speech (Media in Rwanda)." *World Policy Journal*, 21(2), Summer.

Biney, Ama. (2008). "The Legacy of Kwame Nkrumah in Retrospect." *Journal of Pan African Studies*, 2(3), 129-159.

Black, Ian. (2011/2/17). "Libya Cracks Down on Protesters after Violent Clashes in Benghazi". *The Guardian*, February 17.

—. (2011/10/26). "Qatar Admits Sending Hundreds of Troops to Support Libya Rebels." *The Guardian*, October 26.

Black, Ian, & Stephen, Chris (2011/9/18). "Libyan NTC Leaders Fail to Agree on Interim Cabinet as Fighting Continues." *The Guardian*, September 18.

Black, Ian, & Bowcott, Owen. (2011/2/18). "Libya Protests: Massacres Reported as Gaddafi Imposes News Blackout." *The Guardian*, February 18.

Black Star News (BSN). (2011/6/21). "Editorial: Ethnic Cleansing of Black Libyans." *Black Star News*, June 21.

Blomfield, Adrian; Squires, Nick; Samuel, Henry; and Sherlock, Ruth. (2012/9/30). "Bashar Al-Assad 'Betrayed Col Gaddafi to Save His Syrian Regime'". *The Telegraph*, September 30.

Borger, Julian, & Macalister, Terry. (2011/9/1). "The Race is on for Libya's Oil, with Britain and France Both Staking a Claim." *The Guardian*, September 1.

Bosco, David. (2011/10/24). "Foreign Policy: Was Killing Gadhafi A War Crime?" *NPR*, October 24.

Bowcott, Owen. (2011/6/9). "Libya Mass Rape Claims: Using Viagra Would Be a Horrific First." *The Guardian*, June 9.

Boyle, Francis A., & Bernstein, Dennis. (2002). "Interview with Francis Boyle: Amnesty on Jenin." *Covert Action Quarterly*, (73), 9-12, 27.

Boyle, Peter. (2011/3/13). "Gaddafi Tries to Crush Rising, West Threatens Attack." *Green Left*, March 13.

Branigin, William; Sheridan, Mary Beth; & Lynch Colum. (2011/2/23). "Obama Condemns Violence in Libya, Asks For 'Full Range of Options'." *The Washington Post*, February 23.

Brewster, Murray. (2012/9/9). "RCAF Fretted Over Libya Wear and Tear". *Metro*, September 9.

Bright, Martin. (2002/11/10). "MI6 'Halted Bid to Arrest Bin Laden': Startling Revelations by French Intelligence Experts Back David Shayler's Alleged 'Fantasy' about Gadaffi Plot." *The Observer*, November 10.

Bromund, Theodore, & Gardiner, Nile. (2011/4/19). "Libya Mission Demonstrates That British Defense Cuts Must Be Reversed". *The Heritage Foundation*, April 19.

Bruce, Mary. (2012/9/14). "Obama Notifies Congress of Troops Deployed to Libya and Yemen". *ABC News*, September 14.

Bruguière, Peggy. (2011/11/22). "'We Miss Gaddafi' Say Chadians." *France24*, November 22.

BT. (2012/2/8). "MPs Warn Over Libyan Operation". *Belfast Telegraph*, February 8.

Buchanan, Patrick J. (2011/3/8). "It's Their War, Not Ours." *Anti-War.com*, March 8.

Burchall, H. (1933). "Air Services in Africa." *Journal of the Royal African Society*, 32(126) January, 55-73.

Bureau of Investigative Journalism (BIJ). (2012/2/4). "Obama Terror Drones: CIA Tactics in Pakistan Include Targeting Rescuers and Funerals." *The Bureau of Investigative Journalism: Covert War on Terror*, February 4.

—. (2012/5/29). "Analysis: Obama Embraced Redefinition of 'Civilian' in Drone Wars." *The Bureau of Investigative Journalism: Covert War on Terror*, May 29.

—. (2012/6/4). "CIA 'Revives Attacks on Rescuers' in Pakistan." *The Bureau of Investigative Journalism: Covert War on Terror*, June 4.

Burns, Nicholas. (2008/10/24). "We Should Talk to Our Enemies." *The Daily Beast*, October 24.

Bush, George W. (2001). "U.S., Africa Strengthening Counter-Terrorism and Economic Ties: President Bush, Remarks to the African Growth and Opportunity Forum." Washington, DC: U.S. Department of State.

—. (2007). "President Bush Creates a Department of Defense Unified Combatant Command for Africa." Office of the Press Secretary, February 6.

The Buzz. (2009/6/15). "Blakk Rasta Gets His Obama Moment." *Ghana Music.com*, June 15.

Byers, Bruce K. (2011). "Diplomacy, Analysis, and Decision-Making—the Need for a New Paradigm." *American Diplomacy*, October.

Calgary Herald. (2012/3/9). "Grave Offence in Libya." Editorial, *Calgary Herald*, March 9.

Cameron, David. (2011/3/29). Prime Minister Opens London Conference on Libya. London UK: Foreign and Commonwealth Office, March 29.

Camilleri, Ivan. (2010/9/1). "EU Mum on Gaddafi's Request for €5 Billion." *Times of Malta*, September 1.

Campbell, Horace. (2011/3/24). "AFRICOM as Libya Bombing Motive." *Institute for Public Accuracy*, March 24.

—. (2011/3/31). "Libya: U.S. Military and Africom—Between the Rocks and the Crusaders." *AllAfrica.com*, March 31.

—. (2011/10/27). "The Execution of Gaddafi and the Attempted Humiliation of Africa." *Pambazuka News*, 554, October 27.

Campbell, Oliver. (2011). "Former Libyan PM Exposes US-NATO Machinations." *World Socialist Web Site*, November 24.

Canadian Press. (2011/2/25). "No Canadians at Airport: Military Evac Flight Leaves Tripoli Empty". *City News*, February 25.

Canestaro, Nathan. (2003). "American Law and Policy on Assassinations of Foreign Leaders: The Practicality of Maintaining the Status Quo." *Boston College International and Comparative Law Review*, 26(1), 1-34.

Carney, Jay. (2011/3/23). "Press Briefing by Press Secretary Jay Carney, Senior Director for Western Hemisphere Affairs Dan Restrepo and Deputy National Security Advisor for Strategic Communications Ben Rhodes." The White House, Office of the Press Secretary, March 23.

Carvin, Andy. (2011/2/21). "The Revolution Will Be Tweeted." *NPR*, February 21.

CBC. (2011/3/13). "Pro-Gadhafi Forces Gaining on Rebels." *Canadian Broadcasting Corporation*, March 13.

CEN-SAD. (n.d.). BSIC: Sahel-Saharan Investment and Trade Bank. Community of Sahel-Saharan States.

—. (2003a). Final Communiqué: 5th Ordinary Session of the Conference of Leaders and Heads of State, Niamey, March 14-15. Community of Sahel-Saharan States.

—. (2003b). Niamey Declaration on Conflict Prevention and the Peaceful Settlement of Disputes. Community of Sahel-Saharan States.

—. (2006a). Final Communiqué: 8th Ordinary Session of the Conference of Leaders and Heads of State, Tripoli, June 1-2. Community of Sahel-Saharan States.

—. (2006b). Report: 14th Ordinary Session of the Executive Council, Tripoli, May 30-31. Community of Sahel-Saharan States.

CERD. (1997/4/23). UN Committee on the Elimination of Racial Discrimination: State Party Report, Libyan Arab Jamahiriya, April 2, CERD/C/299/Add.13.

—. (1998/3/24). UN Committee on the Elimination of Racial Discrimination: Summary record of the 1272nd meeting: Armenia, Cameroon, Israel, Libyan Arab Jamahiriya, Netherlands, Rwanda, Yugoslavia, March 24, CERD/C/SR.1272.

—. (1998/3/30). UN Committee on the Elimination of Racial Discrimination: Concluding Observations, Libyan Arab Jamahiriya, March 30, CERD/C/304/Add.52.

—. (2003/6/18). UN Committee on the Elimination of Racial Discrimination: State Party Report, Libya, June 18, CERD/C/431/Add.5.

—. (2004/3/12). Concluding observations of the Committee on the Elimination of Racial Discrimination: Libyan Arab Jamahiriya, March 12, CERD/C/64/CO/4.

Channel 4. (2011/8/28). "Evidence of Libya Massacre as Remains of 50 People Found." *Channel 4 News*, August 28.

Charbonneau, Louis. (2011/3/16). "Libya Envoy: World Has 10 Hours to Act against Gaddafi." *Reuters*, March 16.

—. (2011/12/14). "U.N. Chief Defends NATO from Critics of Libya War." *Reuters*, December 14.

Chatterjee, Pratap. (2003/5/22). "Bechtel Drums Up War Business." *Asia Times*, May 22.

Chivers, C. J., & Schmitt, Eric. (2011/12/18). "In Strikes on Libya by NATO, an Unspoken Civilian Toll." *The New York Times*, December 18.

Chomsky, Noam. Chomsky, N. (2009). Statement by Professor Noam Chomsky to the United Nations General Assembly: Thematic Dialogue on the Responsibility to Protect. New York: United Nations.

—. (2012/1/7). "Recognizing the 'Unpeople'." *Truthout*, January 7.

Chowdhury, Jayanta Roy. (2011/2/23). "Text Message from a House in Libya: We Are Being Slaughtered Here". *The Telegraph (Calcutta)*, February 23.

Christensen, Thomas J., & Swan, James. (2008/6/4). "Policy Statement: China in Africa: Implications for U.S. Policy." *U.S. Africa Command*, June 4.

Christian Science Monitor. (2011). "Libya 101: A Primer on Key Battleground Cities—Sirte." *Christian Science Monitor*, nd.

—. (2011/10/20). "Editorial Board: How Qaddafi killing affirms Arab Spring principles." *Christian Science Monitor*, October 20.

CitiFMonline. (2011/10/20). "Gaddafi Was An African 'Icon'—Dr Alabi." *Daily Guide*, October 20.

—. (2011/11/6). "Blakk Rasta to Release Song for Gaddafi." *Ghana Music.com*, November 6.

Clinton, Hillary. (2009/3/28). "Secretary Clinton's March 24, 2009 Conversation with Australian Prime Minister Kevin Rudd." Cable from the Secretary of State, United States of America, March 28.

—. (2009/7/17). "Follow-up to African Union Summit (c-al9-01532)." Cable from the Secretary of State, United States of America, July 17.

—. (2012/9/12). "Remarks on the Deaths of American Personnel in Benghazi, Libya". *U.S. Department of State*, September 12.

CNN. (1997/10/21). "Mandela, Mubarak Exchange Awards: Libya's Standoff with West on Agenda at Meeting." *Cable News Network*, October 21.

—. (1997/10/22). "Nelson Mandela Visits Libya, Embraces Moammar Gadhafi." *Cable News Network*, October 22.

—. (2011/2/19). "Report: Helicopters Fire on Libya Protesters". *Cable News Network*, February 19.

—. (2011/2/25). Piers Morgan Tonight [Transcript]. *Cable News Network*, February 25.

—. (2011/5/17). "ICC to Investigate Reports of Viagra-Fueled Gang-Rapes in Libya." *Cable News Network*, May 17.

—. (2011/6/14). "South African President Blasts NATO Actions in Libya." *Cable News Network*, June 14.

—. (2011/8/19). "Brother of Libya's Information Minister Reported Killed in NATO Strike." *Cable News Network*, August 19.

Cockburn, Patrick. (2011/6/24). "Amnesty Questions Claim that Gaddafi Ordered Rape as Weapon of War." *The Independent*, June 24.

—. (2011/8/28). "Rebels Wreak Revenge on Dictator's Men." *The Independent*, August 28.

—. (2011/8/30). "The New Libya: Better Not Be Black." *CounterPunch*, August 30.

Coghlan, Tom. (2011/9/27). "Sirte Civilians Accuse NATO of Genocide." *The Australian*, September 27.

Collins, Michael. (2011). "Libya Is Not About Who Gaddafi Was. It's About What America Under Obama Has Become." *Stop War UK*, October 24.

Concerned Africans. (2011/8/9). "Libya, Africa and the New World Order: An Open Letter." *Pambazuka News*, (554), August 9.

CorpWatch. (2003). "Bechtel: Profiting from Destruction." *CorpWatch*, June 5.

Cowell, Alan. (2011/2/16). "Protests Take Aim at Leader of Libya". *The New York Times*, February 16.

Crawley, Mike. (2002/5/23). "With Mideast Uncertainty, US Turns to Africa for Oil." *Christian Science Monitor*, May 23.

Cremonesi, Lorenzo. (2012/9/29). "Un agente francese dietro la morte di Gheddafi". *Corriere della Sera*, September 29.

Crilly, Rob. (2011/3/19). "Libyan Refugees Flee Benghazi as Fighting Intensifies." *The Telegraph*, March 19.

—. (2011/3/21). "Libya: Rebels Push on to the Disputed Town of Ajdabiya." *The Telegraph*, March 21.

Crilly, Rob, & Evans, Martin. (2011/8/26). "Libya: RAF Jets Lead Strikes on Gaddafi's Home Town of Sirte." *The Telegraph*, August 26.

Crush, Jonathan, & Ramachandran, Sujata. (2009). "Xenophobia, International Migration and Human Development." United Nations Development Programme, Human Development Reports Research Paper 2009/47, September.

Dagher, Sam. (2011/6/21). "Libya City Torn by Tribal Feud." *The Wall Street Journal*, June 21.

Dallaire, Roméo, & Bernstein, Jeffrey. (2011/3/18). "Does the World Belong in Libya's War? Yes. Now Let's Hope It's Not Too Late." *Foreign Policy*, March 18.

Daly, Corbett B. (2011/10/20). "Clinton on Qaddafi: 'We came, we saw, he died'." *CBS News*, October 20.

Darwish, Adel. (1998). "Did Britain Plot to Kill This Man?" *The Middle East*, September, 4-6.

de Haas, Hein. (2011/2/21). "African Migrants Become Easy Target for Racist Violence in Libya." *Hein de Haas*, February 21.

Dembélé, Demba Moussa. (2011/10/27). "NATO Murdered Gaddafi." *Pambazuka News*, 554, October 27.

Democracy Now. (2011/4/19). "Phyllis Bennis: U.K. Sends Troops into Libya as International Coalition Expands Mission to Include Regime Change." *Democracy Now!* April 19.

Department of Foreign Affairs, South Africa (DFA). (1997). "Statement on the Visits to Libya, Egypt and Morocco by President Mandela, October 1997, 14 October 1997." South African Government Information.

—. (2002). "Statement on the State Visit to Libya, Tripoli, 12-14 June 2002." South African Government Information.

—. (2002/6/14). "Joint Communique between the Great Socialist People's Libyan Arab Jamahiriya and South Africa, 14 June 2002." South African Government Information.

Deutsche Presse-Agentur. (2011/3/31). "Rebels Blame Chad Troops for Loss of Key Libyan Cities." *Monsters & Critics*, March 31.

de Zayas, Alfred. (2012). "Foreign imposed 'Regime-Change' Violates the UN Charter in Letter and Spirit." *Current Concerns*, (11), March 12.

Díaz-Balart, José. (2012/9/12). "Exclusiva: Entrevista completa de Telemundo con presidente Obama". *Telemundo*, September 12.

DipNote. (2011/3/10). "U.S. Announces Additional Humanitarian Assistance in Response to Violence in Libya." *DipNote: U.S. Department of State Official Blog*, March 10.

Dozier, Kimberly. (2012/9/15). "US Scrambles to Rush Spies, Drones to Libya". *Associated Press*, September 15.

Dziadosz, Alexander. (2011/9/22). "Sirte Shows Rocky Path Ahead for Libya's New Rulers." *Reuters*, September 22.

—. (2011/9/30). "Ruined Libya Town Shows Danger of Postwar Vendetta." *Reuters*, September 30.

Duff, Gordon. (2011/3/21). "Libya a War of Lies: The 'Conspiratorial Veil' of Western Racism." *Veterans Today*, March 21.

Dziadosz, Alexander, & Golovnina, Maria. (2011/9/22). "Libya Rulers Says Gaddafi Running Out of Options." *Reuters*, September 22.

Economic and Political Weekly. (1986). "Pre-Emptive Strikes?" *Economic and Political Weekly*, 21(14) April 5, 553.

The Economist. (2000/10/12). "Libya and Africa: Pogrom." *The Economist*, October 12.

ECOWAS. (2012/7/24). "Emergency Meeting of Ecowas Committee of Defence Staff on Mali in Abidjan." *Economic Community of West African States*, Press Release No. 202.

El Gamal, Rania. (2011/10/2). "Libyans Run Gauntlet of Bullets To Escape Sirte." *Reuters*, October 2.

—. (2011/10/5). "Sirte Residents Turn Anger on Libya's New Rulers." *Reuters*, October 5.

—. (2011/11/4). "Gaddafi Kin Seethe, In Test for New Libya." *Reuters*, November 4.

El Gamal, Rania, & Gaynor, Tim. (2011/10/5). "Libyan Forces Plan 'Final' Attack On Gaddafi Hometown." *Reuters*, October 5.

—. (2011/10/6). "Sniper Fire Holds up Push into Gaddafi's Hometown." *Reuters*, October 6.

—. (2011/10/14). "Libyan Tanks Hope to Crush Sirte Resistance." *Reuters/The National Post*, October 14.

—. (2011/10/19). "Libya Forces Relaunch Sirte Assault after Setback." *Reuters*, October 19.

El Gamal, Rania, & Logan, Joseph. (2011/10/1). "Red Cross Gets Medicine into Libya's Besieged Sirte." *Reuters*, October 1.

El-Kikhia, Mansour O. (1997). *Libya's Qaddafi: The Politics of Contradiction*. Gainesville, FL: University Press of Florida.

El Madany, Sherine. (2011/9/20). "Ammunition Shortage Hampers Attack on Gaddafi Bastion." *Reuters*, September 20.

Engler, Yves. (2011/3/28). "Harper's 16 To 29 Billion Reasons for Sending Fighter Jets to Libya". *Rabble.ca*, March 28.

EO12333. (1981). Executive Order 12333—United States Intelligence Activities. *National Archives.*

Erlanger, Steven. (2011/10/5). "Panetta Urges Europe to Spend More on NATO or Risk a Hollowed-Out Alliance". *The New York Times*, October 5.

EuroNews. (2011/2/19). "Libyan City of Ajdabiya a 'Free City'." *EuroNews*, February 19.

—. (2011/3/20). "Libya Highway of Death 19 March 2011." [Video] March 20.

—. (2012/9/15). "Al-Qaeda: US Ambassador is Vengeance for Al-Libi". *EuroNews*, September 15.

Evans, Robert. (2011/9/26). "U.N. Says Cannot Get Supplies into Libya Stronghold." *Reuters*, September 26.

Fadel, Leila. (2011/8/22). "Libya Rebel Council Head Warns Battle Is Not Over, Urges Calm." *The Washington Post*, August 22.

Fahim, Kareem. (2011/5/10). "Killings and Rumors Unsettle a Libyan City." *The New York Times*, May 10.

Fahim, Kareem, & Kirkpatrick, David D. (2011/2/22). "Qaddafi's Grip on the Capital Tightens as Revolt Grows." *The New York Times*, February 22.

—. (2011/2/23). "Qaddafi Massing Forces in Tripoli as Rebellion Spreads." *The New York Times*, February 23.

Fahim, Kareem; Kirkpatrick. David D.; & Cowell. Alan. (2011/3/29). "As Diplomats Meet in London on Libya, Rebel Advance Stalls." *The New York Times*, March 29.

Fahim, Kareem; Shadid, Anthony; & Gladstone, Rick. (2011/10/20). "Qaddafi, Seized by Foes, Meets a Violent End." *The New York Times*, October 20, A1

FAIR. (2011/8/18). "Media Advisory: Libyan Deaths, Media Silence." *FAIR—Fairness and Accuracy in Reporting*, August 18.

Farmer, Ben. (2011/10/22). "Gaddafi's Final Hours: NATO and the SAS Helped Rebels Drive Hunted Leader into Endgame in a Desert Drain." *The Telegraph*, October 22.

Farmer, Ben, & Henderson, Barney. (2011/10/20). "Libya: 'Gaddafi Dies from Wounds' Suffered In Sirte Capture." *The Telegraph*, October 20.

Farmer, Ben, & Sherlock, Ruth. (2011/10/15). "Ruined Sirte Becomes a Killing Ground as Gaddafi Loyalists Face Destruction, But Mete out Death of Their Own." *The Sunday Telegraph*, October 15.

FFM. (2012). Report of the Independent Civil Society Fact-Finding Mission to Libya. Arab Organization for Human Rights, Palestinian Center for Human Rights, and the International Legal Assistance Consortium.

FIDH. (2011/2/21). "Massacres in Libya: The International Community Must Respond Urgently." *International Federation for Human Rights (FIDH)*, February 21.

Fitzgerald, Mary. (2011/8/31). "We Are Afraid . . . People Might Think We Are Mercenaries." *The Irish Times*, August 31.

Fletcher, Martin, & Haynes, Deborah. (2011/2/25). "Gaddafi Must Leave, West Tells Libya." *The Times*, February 25.

FORA.tv. (2011/10/3/). "Wesley Clark on America's Foreign Policy 'Coup'." San Francisco, CA: The Commonwealth Club.

Ford, Glen. (2011/8/17). "Black Libya City Said to Fall to Rebel Siege." *Black Agenda Report*, August 17.

Forte, Maximilian C. (2009/6/17). "America's Iranian Twitter Revolution." *Zero Anthropology*, June 17.

Fox. (2011/10/23). "Clinton Talks Iraq, Libya: Secretary of State on 'Fox News Sunday'." *Fox News Sunday*, October 23.

France24. (2011/2/21). "Witnesses Say African Mercenaries Have Been Captured in Libya." *France24*, February 21.

Frazer, Jendayi. (2008/6/18). "A/S Frazer's June 13 Meeting with Ugandan President Museveni." U.S. Department of State, Secretary of State, June 18.

Friedman, George. (2011/8/30). "Libya: A Premature Victory Celebration." *STRATFOR: Geopolitical Weekly*, August 30.

FT. (2011/8/23). Editorial: "Libyan Lessons". *Financial Times*, August 23.

Furuhashi, Yoshie. (2011/3/2). "Black Africans Live in Fear in 'Free Libya'." *MRzine*, March 2.

Gaddafi, Muammar. (1975). *The Green Book: Part Three, the Social Basis of the Third Universal Theory*. Tripoli, Libya: Public Establishment for Publishing, Advertising and Distribution.

—. (2005). "AlGathafi Tells African Leaders: 'If Only We Had Listened to Nkrumah'." *New African*, (443), August-September, 30-33.

Gamel, Kim, & Al-Shaheibi, Rami. (2011/10/15). "Libyan Capital Sees First Big Firefight in Months." *Associated Press*, October 15.

Gardner, Dan. (2011/3/25). "Libya Shows Why Canada Needs Jets". *The Vancouver Sun*, March 25.

Garlasco, Marc. (2012/6/11). "NATO's Lost Lessons from Libya." *The Washington Post*, June 11.

Garrett, William B.; Mariano, Stephen J.; & Sanderson, Adam. (2010). "Forward in Africa: USAFRICOM and the U.S. Army in Africa." *Military Review*, January-February, 16-25.

Gaynor, Tim, & El Gamal, Rania. (2011/10/2). "Shortages 'Killing Patients' on Libya Siege Hospital." *Reuters*, October 2.

Gearan, Anne. (2012). "In Africa, Clinton Takes Subtle Swipe at China." *The Washington Post*, August 1.

Gelb, Leslie H. (2011/3/8). "Don't Use U.S. Force in Libya!" *The Daily Beast*, March 8.

Ghanea, Nazila. (2011). "Prohibition of Incitement to National, Racial or Religious Hatred in Accordance with International Human Rights Law." *United Nations Office of the High Commissioner for Human Rights*.

Ghosh, Palash R. (2011/8/31). "Libyan Revolt Unmasks Lethal Racism against Black Africans." *International Business Times*, August 31.

Gibson, William. (1996). *Idoru*. New York: Berkley Books.

Gillette, Christopher. (2011/10/19). "Libyans Fight against Last Gadhafi Holdouts." *Associated Press*, October 19.

Gilligan, Andrew. (2011/9/11). "Gaddafi's Ghost Town after the Loyalists Retreat." *The Sunday Telegraph*, September 11.

Glazebrook, Dan. (2011/11/24). "Libya and the Manufacture of Consent." *Al-Ahram Weekly*, (1073), November 24-30.

—. (2012/5/25-27). "An Ongoing Disaster: Libya, Africa and Africom." *CounterPunch*, May 25-27.

—. (2012/6/14). "The Imperial Agenda of the US's 'Africa Command' Marches On." *The Guardian*, June 14.

GlobalResearchTV. (2012/1/12). "The Gaddafi Mercenaries and the Division of Africa." [Video] *Global Research TV*, January 12.

Gomda, A.R. (2011/10/24). "JJ Booms at Legon. We Flogged Women Naked." *Daily Guide*, October 24.

Gott, Richard. (2001/1/15). "The Reconquest of Africa." *New Statesman*, January 15.

Graff, Peter. (2011/8/25). "Thirty Gaddafi Fighters Found Dead at Tripoli Camp." *Reuters*, August 25.

Guanaguanare. (2012/4/21). "Gaddafi [Song]." *Guanaguanare: The Laughing Gull*, April 21.

Gumuchian, Marie-Louise. (2012/2/29). "Shattered Gaddafi Town Says Forgotten in New Libya." *Reuters*, February 29.

Gumuchian, Marie-Louise, & Shuaib, Ali. (2012/7/6). "Half of Libya's Oil Exports Hit by Protests". *Reuters*, July 6.

Hague, William. (2011/3/29). Statement from the Conference Chair Foreign Secretary William Hague Following the London Conference on Libya. London UK: Foreign and Commonwealth Office, March 29.

Ham, Carter. (2011). "Commander's Intent." Kelley Barracks, Stuttgart, Germany: Headquarters, United States Africa Command.

—. (2012). Statement of General Carter Ham, U.S. Army Commander, United States Africa Command, before the House Armed Services Committee. February 29.

—. (2012/3/9). "U.S. Command Fights Terrorists on African Soil." *NPR*, March 9.

—. (2012/6/26). "Transcript: Ham Discusses African Security Issues at ACSS Senior Leaders Seminar." *U.S. AFRICOM*, June 26.

Harding, Thomas. (2011/3/28). "Shortage of RAF Pilots for Libya as Defence Cuts Bite". *The Telegraph*, March 28.

—. (2011/10/20). "Col Gaddafi Killed: Convoy Bombed by Drone Flown by Pilot in Las Vegas." *The Telegraph*, October 20.

Harding, Thomas; Rayner, Gordon; & McElroy, Damien. (2011/8/24). "Libya: SAS Leads Hunt for Gaddafi." *The Telegraph*, August 24.

Harris, Grant T. (2012/6/14). "The Future of America's Partnership with Sub-Saharan Africa." *The White House Blog*, June 14.

Hart, Peter. (2011/8/24). "NYT Points Out 'Racist Overtones' in Libyan Disinformation It Helped Spread." *FAIR—Fairness and Accuracy in Reporting*, August 24.

Harter, Pascale. (2011/6/14). "Libya Rape Victims 'Face Honour Killings'." *BBC News*, June 14.

Harvey, David. (2003). *The New Imperialism*. New York: Oxford University Press.

Harvard Law Review. (2003). "International Law. Genocide. U.N. Tribunal Finds That Mass Media Hate Speech Constitutes Genocide, Incitement to Genocide, and Crimes against Humanity. Prosecutor v. Nahimana, Barayagwiza, and Ngeze (Media Case), Case no. ICTR-99-52-T (Int'l Crim. Trib. for Rwanda Trial Chamber I Dec. 3, 2003)." *Harvard Law Review*, 117(8), June, 2769-2776.

Hashem, Ali, & Jay, Paul. (2012/3/21). "Former Al Jazeera Reporter on Libyan Coverage". *The Real News*, March 21.

Head, Jonathan. (2012/2/9). "Should Libya Rebuild Gaddafi Hometown of Sirte?" *BBC News*, February 9.

Hedges, Chris. (2011/9/5). "Libya: Here We Go Again." *Truthdig*, September 5.

Hendawi, Hamza. (2011/3/28). "Gadhafi Hometown a Major Obstacle in Rebel Advance." *Associated Press*, March 28.

Herbert, Bob. (2003/4/14). "Ultimate Insiders." *The New York Times*, April 14.

Herridge, Catherine. (2012/1/4). "The Islamist Winter: New Report Suggests Extremist Views Winning in Libya". *Fox News*, January 4.

Hubbard, Ben. (2011/9/1). "Libyan Rebels Round up Black Africans." *Associated Press*, September 1.

Hubbard, Ben, & Al-Shalchi, Hadeel. (2011/9/24). "Libyan Forces Fight for Gadhafi's Hometown Sirte." *Associated Press*, September 24.

Huffpost Hill. (2011/3/22). "Obama: We're Promoting Democracy in Libya". *Huffpost Hill*, March 22.

Huffington Post. (2011/10/25). "Obama 'Tonight Show' Appearance: President Talks Gaddafi, GOP, Halloween (VIDEO)." *The Huffington Post*, October 25.

Human Rights Watch (HRW). (2006). "Stemming the Flow: Abuses against Migrants, Asylum Seekers and Refugees." *Human Rights Watch*, 18(5E), September.

—. (2011/7/13). "Libya: Opposition Forces Should Protect Civilians and Hospitals—Looting, Arson, and Some Beatings in Captured Western Towns." *Human Rights Watch*, July 13.

—. (2011/10/23). "Libya: Apparent Execution of 53 Gaddafi Supporters: Bodies Found at Sirte Hotel Used by Anti-Gaddafi Fighters." *Human Rights Watch*, October 23.

—. (2011/10/24). "Libya: Apparent Execution of 53 Gaddafi Supporters." *Human Rights Watch*, October 24.

—. (2011/10/30). "Libya: Militias Terrorizing Residents of Loyalist Town." *Human Rights Watch*, October 30.

—. (2012). *Unacknowledged Deaths: Civilian Casualties in NATO's Air Campaign in Libya*. New York: Human Rights Watch.

—. (2012/2/21). "Libya: Displaced People Barred from Homes." *Human Rights Watch*, February 21.

—. (2012/5/14). "NATO: Investigate Civilian Deaths in Libya—At Least 72 Dead in Air Attacks on Unclear Targets." *Human Rights Watch*, May 14.

Hussein, Mohamed. (2011/2/21). "Libya Crisis: What Role Do Tribal Loyalties Play?" *BBC News*, February 21.

ICFTU. (2000/10/12). "Racist Attacks on Migrant Workers in Libya." *International Confederation of Free Trade Unions*, October 12.

Immigration and Refugee Board of Canada (IRBC). (1998). "Libya: Information on an Attempted Attack on President Gaddafi by a Religious Group in 1996, Possibly Affiliated with A Group Called Al-Sahwa of Islam." *Refworld (UNHCR)*, July 1.

International Committee for the Red Cross (ICRC). (2011/10/27). "Libya: Detainees and the Dead Must be Respected." *International Committee for the Red Cross*, October 27.

International Organization for Migration (IOM). (2011). "Egyptian Migration to Libya." *International Organization for Migration (IOM) Cairo*.

IOL. (2011/3/19). "French Jets Destroy Tanks, Vehicles." *IOL News*, March 19.

Iqbal, Martin. (2011/6/8). "Viagra-Induced Rape: ICC Ups the Ante on Propaganda as Desperate NATO Struggles to Crush Libyan Resistance." *Empire Strikes Black*, June 8.

IRIN. (2012/2/10). "Security: New Report on R2P Challenges Humanitarians". *IRIN: Humanitarian News and Analysis* (UN Office for the Coordination of Humanitarian Affairs), February 10.

ITNews Africa. (2012/1/13). "Libyan Government to Review African Telecom Investments." *Balancing Act*, (587), January 13.

Jawad, Rana. (2010/6/17). "How Libya Became a Dead End for Migrants." *BBC News*, June 17.

Joffé, George. (2009). "Political Dynamics in North Africa." *International Affairs*, 85(5), 931–949.

Johnson, Trevor. (2000/10/28). "Ethnic Violence and Mass Deportations of Immigrants in Libya." *World Socialist Web Site*, October 28.

Juhasz, Antonia. (2006/8/4). "Bechtel Takes a Hit for War Profiteering." *AlterNet*, August 4.

Kabale, Lugenzi. (2012/7/25). "SADC Irked by Inaction on Libya." *The Citizen*, July 25.

Kaijun, Zheng, & Xiaolong, Zhu. (2011/10/26). "Gaddafi Spends Last Days in Fear, Humbleness." *Xinhua*, October 26.

Kamara, Ahmed M. (2011/8/26). "Black Africans Executed in Cold-Blood by Rebels in Libya." *The Zimbabwe Mail*, August 26.

Keaten, Jamey. (2011/3/24). "France: Libya Operation May Last Weeks, Not Months." *Associated Press*, March 24.

Kelley, Michael. (2012/3/20). "Leaked STRATFOR Emails: U.S. Government Sent Blackwater Veteran to Fight with Rebels in Libya and Syria." *Business Insider*, March 20.

Kerry, John. (2011/3/14). "We Must Not Wait For a Massacre." *Al Jazeera English*, March 14.

Khisa, Issac. (2012/6/4). "Libya Targets New Markets in Africa." *Africa Review*, June 4.

Kinsman, Jeremy. (2011). "Truth and Consequence: The Wikileaks Saga." *Policy Options*, February.

Kirchik, James. (2011/9/6). "South Africa Stands with Qaddafi." *The Atlantic*, September 6.

Kirkpatrick, David D. (2011/3/21). "Hopes for a Qaddafi Exit, and Worries of What Comes Next." *The New York Times*, March 21.

—. (2011/6/24). "Rebels Arm Tripoli Guerrillas and Cut Resources to Capital." *The New York Times*, June 24.

—. (2011/7/30). "NATO Strikes at Libyan State TV." *The New York Times*, July 30.

—. (2011/9/22). "U.S. Reopens Its Embassy in Libya." *The New York Times*, September 22.

Kirkpatrick, David D., & El-Naggar, Mona. (2011/2/21). "Qaddafi's Grip Falters as His Forces Take on Protesters." *The New York Times*, February 21.

Kirkpatrick, David D., & Nordland, Rod. (2011/8/23). "Waves of Disinformation and Confusion Swamp the Truth in Libya." *The New York Times*, August 23.

Koring, Paul. (2011/3/16). "No-Fly Zone over Libya Gets Scant Support at UN as Time Grows Short." *The Globe and Mail*, March 16.

Kramer, Reed. (2012/7/13). "Africa: U.S. Military Steps up 'Sustained Engagement' With Africa." *AllAfrica.com*, July 13.

Krause-Jackson, Flavia, & Alexander, Caroline. (2011/11/14). "Jibril Turns against Foreign Powers that Aided Qaddafi Overthrow." *Bloomberg*, November 14.

Kucinich, Dennis. (2011/8/21). "Time to End Nato's War in Libya." *The Guardian*, August 21.

Kuperman, Alan J. (2011/4/14). "False Pretense for War in Libya?" *Boston Globe*, April 14.

Labott, Elise, & Dougherty, Jill. (2011/8/2). "U.S. Warns Libyan Rebels to Get Their Act Together." *CNN*, August 2.

Lamloum, Imed. (2012/1/16). "AU Wants to Turn the Page with Libya Post-Kadhafi." *Agence France Presse*, January 16.

Landler, Mark. (2011/10/24). "Before Qaddafi's Death, U.S. Debated His Future." *The New York Times*, October 24.

Langford, Stephen. (1987). "Baselines and Historic Bays." In Richard N. Schofield & Gerald Henry Blake (Eds.), *Boundaries and State Territory in the Middle East and North Africa* (pp. 135-146). Cambridgeshire: Middle East & North African Studies Press.

LATimes . (1997/10/23). "Mandela Visit to Libya Gives Kadafi a Boost." *Los Angeles Times*, October 23.

Laub, Karin, & Al-Shalchi, Hadeel. (2011/2/7). "Egypt Protests Leave 297 Killed: Human Rights Watch." *The Huffington Post*, February 7.

Laub, Karin, & Schemm, Paul. (2011/8/30). "Libya Rebels Pledge Assault on Gadhafi Stronghold." *Associated Press*, August 30.

Laughland, John. (2008/3/12). "What Is Really Behind the Mediterranean Union?" *The Brussels Journal*, March 12.

Lauria, Joe. (2011/4/1). "Tripoli's Envoy at U.N. Hits Snag." *The Wall Street Journal*, April 1.

Lea, David. (2001). *A Political Chronology of Africa*. London, UK: Europa Publications.

Lederer, Edith M. (2012/3/12). "UN Extends Its Political Mission in Libya with a Mandate to Promote Democracy." *Associated Press/680 News*, March 12.

Lee, Jesse. (2011/3/3). "The President on Libya: 'The Violence Must Stop; Muammar Gaddafi Has Lost the Legitimacy to Lead and He Must Leave'." *The White House Blog*, March 3.

Lekic, Slobodan. (2011/10/6). "NATO: No Immediate End to Libya Bombing." *Associated Press*, October 6.

—. (2011/10/21). "NATO: It Didn't Know Gadhafi Was in Bombed Convoy." *Associated Press*, October 21.

Lobe, Jim. (2007/2/1). "Africa to Get Its Own US Military Command." *IPS News*, February 1.

Logan, Joseph, & El Gamal, Rania. (2011/9/30). "Civilians Surge Out of Sirte, Say Food Dwindling." *Reuters*, September 30.

Logan, Joseph, & Farge, Emma. (2011/9/16). "Erdogan to Visit Libya as Sirte Battle Rages." *Reuters*, September 16.

Lucas, Ryan. (2011/3/28). "Libyan Rebels Shelled Outside Gadhafi Hometown." *The Seattle Times*, March 28.

Lucas, Ryan, & Hadid, Diaa. (2011/3/15). "Gadhafi Forces Overwhelm Rebel City in March East." *Salon*, March 15.

Lynch, Colum. (2011/3/31). "Gaddafi Picks Nicaraguan for U.N. Post." *The Washington Post*, March 31.

MacAskill, Ewen. (2011/4/29). "Gaddafi 'Supplies Troops with Viagra to Encourage Mass Rape', Claims Diplomat." *The Guardian*, April 29.

MacDonald, Alistair. (2011/3/1). "Cameron Doesn't Rule Out Military Force for Libya." *The Wall Street Journal*, March 1.

MacDougall, Clair. (2011/3/6). "How Qaddafi Helped Fuel Fury Toward Africans in Libya." *Christian Science Monitor*, March 6.

MacLean, William. (2011/9/14). "RPT-Tripoli's New Normal - Bickering Politicians." *Reuters*, September 14.

—. (2011/9/29). "Civilians Flee Sirte Battle, Fighting Hampers Aid: U.N." *Reuters*, September 29.

MacSwan, Angus. (2011/3/19). "Refugees Flee Benghazi, Dreading Gaddafi's Revenge." *Reuters*, March 19.

Magdoff, Harry. (2003). *Imperialism without Colonies*. New York: Monthly Review Press.

Mail & Guardian. (2011/6/27). "Zuma Says Warrant against Gaddafi Undermines the AU." *Mail & Guardian*, June 27.

Malakata, Michael. (2012/3/20). "Libya's LAP Green Demands Restitution for Zambia Telco Stake." *Computerworld Zambia*, March 20.

Malone, Barry. (2011/11/11). "Insight: Africa to Miss Gaddafi's Money, Not His Meddling." *Reuters*, November 11.

—. (2010/12/8). "Ugandan Leader Feared Gaddafi Attack on Plane: Cable." *Reuters*, December 8.

Mandela, Nelson. (1999). "Speech by President Nelson Mandela at a Luncheon in Honour of Muamar Qaddafi, Leader of the Revolution of the Libyan Jamahiriya, Cape Town, 13 June 1999." South African Government Information.

Marghani, Amin B. (2012/4/6). "Libya: The Full Story behind Ban of Libyan Airlines from Operating in EU." *The Tripoli Post*, April 6.

Marlowe, Ann. (2012/9/18). "Hope Yet for Libya". *Wall Street Journal*, September 18.

Mathaba. (2012/3/31). "Nelson Mandela's Historic Visit to Great Jamahiriya." *Mathaba News*, March 31.

Mayer, Jane. (2003). "Dept. of Connections: The Contractors." *The New Yorker*, May 5.

Mazetti, Mark, & Schmitt, Eric. (2011/3/30). "C.I.A. Agents in Libya Aid Airstrikes and Meet Rebels." *The New York Times*, March 30.

Mbeki, Thabo. (2012/2/16). "Reflections on Peacemaking, State Sovereignty and Democratic Governance in Africa." Dullah Omar Eighth Memorial Lecture by Thabo Mbeki Foundation Patron, Thabo Mbeki, at the Community Law Centre of the University of the Western Cape, Belleville, February 16.

McCain, John. (2011/4/22). "Statement by Senator Mccain in Benghazi, Libya". U.S. Senator John McCain, Arizona: Press Releases.

McDermott, Anthony. (1973). "Qaddafi and Libya." *The World Today*, 29(9), September, 398-408.

McDonnell, Patrick J. (2011/9/16). "Libyan Rebels Launch 'All-Out' Attack On Sirte." *McClatchy Tribune-News*, September 16.

McGreal, Chris. (2011/3/14). "Libyan Rebels Urge West to Assassinate Gaddafi as His Forces Near Benghazi." *The Guardian*, March 14.

Médecins Sans Frontières (MSF). (2011/10/14). "Libya: Working With Shortages, Threats, and Shelling in Sirte." *Doctors Without Borders/ Médecins Sans Frontières*, October 14

—. (2011/10/19). "Sirte: The Integrity of Medical Facilities Must Be Respected." *Doctors Without Borders/ Médecins Sans Frontières*, October 19.

Melber, Henning. (2001). *The New African Initiative and the African Union: A Preliminary Assessment and Documentation*. Uppsala: Nordic Africa Institute.

Meo, Nick. (2011/2/20). "Libya Protests: 140 'Massacred' As Gaddafi Sends in Snipers to Crush Dissent". *The Telegraph*, February 20.

Micallef, Mark. (2010/11/30). "Gaddafi: Stop the Migration or Europe Turns Black." *Times of Malta*, November 30.

Michael, Maggie. (2011/3/16). "Moammar Gadhafi's Forces Close in on Libyan Rebels." *The Guardian*, March 16.

Michaels, Jim. (2011/12/7). "AFRICOM Chief: U.S. Wants to Help Libyan Forces." *Army Times*, December 7.

—. (2011/3/10). "Is U.S. Missing a 'Window Of Opportunity' In Libya?" *USA Today*, March 10.

Miles, Donna. (2011/11/4). "Obama: Libya Mission Underscores NATO's Effectiveness." *American Forces Press Service* (U.S. Department of Defense), November 4.

—. (2012/6/15). "Africom Forms Military Relationship with Libya." *American Forces Press Service* (U.S. Department of Defense), June 15.

Miles, Tom. (2011/2/20). "Libya's 'African Mercenary' Problem." *Tomathon*, February 20.

Milne, Seumas. (2011/10/26). "If the Libyan War Was About Saving Lives, It Was a Catastrophic Failure." *The Guardian (UK)*, October 26.

Mimboé, Prosper Rémy. (2010/12/16). "Cameroon: African Monetary Fund Operational in 2011." *Africa-info*, December 16.

Mirror. (2011/2/21). "Colonel Gaddafi Troops Gun Down 200 Protesters in Libya Bloodbath." *The Mirror*, February 21.

—. (2011/3/20). "Crack SAS Troops Hunt Gaddafi Weapons inside Libya." *The Sunday Mirror*, March 20.

Moeller, Robert. (2010/7/21). "The Truth About Africom." *Foreign Policy*, July 21.

Moonga, Choongo. (2001). "The Union Takes Shape." *New African*, April, 10.

Moraff, Christopher. (2007/9/19). "AFRICOM: Round One in a New Cold War?" *In These Times*, September 19.

Morrow, Will. (2012/1/13). "Libya: TNC Releases Anti-Democratic Draft Electoral Laws". *World Socialist Web Site*, January 13.

Mufson, Steven. (2011/6/10). "Conflict in Libya: U.S. Oil Companies Sit on Sidelines as Gaddafi Maintains Hold." *The Washington Post*, June 10.

Mugabe, Robert G. (2011). Statement by His Excellency the President of the Republic of Zimbabwe, Comrade Robert Gabriel Mugabe, on the Occasion of the General Debate of the 66th Session of the United Nations General Assembly, New York, September 22.

Mugerwa, Yasiin, & Ouma, Wandera. (2011/10/22). "Tears as Muslims Pay Respect to Col. Gaddafi." *Daily Monitor*, October 22.

Muhammad, Askia. (1997/11/4). "Mandela's Libya Visit Raises Questions about U.S. Policy." *Final Call News*, November 4.

Mulholland, Rory. (2011/10/4). "Civilians Flee Horror of the Battle for Sirte." *Agence France Presse*, October 4.

Mumisa, Michael. (2011/2/24). "Is Al-Jazeera TV Complicit in the Latest Vilification of Libya's Blacks?" *The Independent*, February 24.

Muñoz, Carlos, & Herb, Jeremy. (2012/9/12). "Al Qaeda's Hand Seen in Killings in Libya". *The Hill*, September 12.

Murphy, Dan. (2011/6/13). "The Gay Girl in Damascus Hoax, 'Mass Rape' in Libya, and Press Credulity." *Christian Science Monitor*, June 13.

Murray, Craig. (2011/8/26). "Sirte—the Apotheosis of 'Liberal Intervention'." *Craig Murray*, August 26.

Murray, Rebecca. (2012/3/31). "Libya: Rebels March Into New Libya With a Hangover." *AllAfrica.com*, March 31.

Museveni, Yoweri. (2011/3/24). "The Qaddafi I Know." *Foreign Policy*, March 24.

Myjoyonline. (2011/10/22). "Gadhafi Believed in the Power of Masses—Rawlings." *Daily Guide*, October 22.

National Democratic Institute (NDI). (2006). "The Libyan Political System and Prospects for Reform: A Report from NDI's 2006 Delegation." *National Democratic Institute*, April 25.

—. (2012). "Libya." *National Democratic Institute*.

NATO. (2011/2/21). "Statement by the NATO Secretary General on Events in Libya." *North Atlantic Treaty Organization*, February 21.

—. (2011/2/24). "NATO Secretary General's Statement on the Situation in Libya." *North Atlantic Treaty Organization*, February 24.

—. (2011/2/25). "Statement by the NATO Secretary General on the Situation in Libya." *North Atlantic Treaty Organization*, February 25.

—. (2011/4/14). Statement on Libya following the working lunch of NATO Ministers of Foreign Affairs with non-NATO contributors to Operation Unified Protector, April 14.

—. (2011/8/28). NATO and Libya: Operational Media Update for 28 August. Naples Media and Information Center.

—. (2011/8/30). NATO and Libya: Operational Media Update for 30 August. Naples Media and Information Center.

—. (2011/9/15). NATO and Libya: Operational Media Update for 15 September. Naples Media and Information Center.

—. (2011/9/16). NATO and Libya: Operational Media Update for 16 September. Naples Media and Information Center.

—. (2011/9/25). NATO and Libya: Operational Media Update for 25 September. Naples Media and Information Center.

—. (2011/9/27). NATO and Libya: Operational Media Update for 27 September. Naples Media and Information Center.

—. (2011/10/1). NATO and Libya: Operational Media Update for 1 October. Naples Media and Information Center.

—. (2011/10/2). NATO and Libya: Operational Media Update for 2 October. Naples Media and Information Center.

—. (2011/10/20). NATO and Libya: Operational Media Update for 20 October. Naples Media and Information Center.

—. (2011/10/23). NATO and Libya: Operational Media Update for 23 October. Naples Media and Information Center.

—. (2012/3/5). Monthly press briefing by NATO Secretary General Anders Fogh Rasmussen, March 5. *North Atlantic Treaty Organization*.

NBC. (2011/2/22). "Gadhafi: 'I'm in Tripoli, Not Venezuela'." *NBC News*, February 22.

—. (2011/3/27). "Gates: Libya Not a 'Vital' Interest for US." *Meet the Press*, March 27.

—. (2011/4/29). "US Intel: No Evidence of Viagra as Weapon in Libya." *MSNBC*, April 29.

Nebehay, Stephanie. (2011/6/10). "Rape Used as Weapon of War In Libya and Elsewhere - U.N.." *Reuters*, June 10.

—. (2012/2/16). "Assets of Subsidiaries of Libya's Investment Arm Freed: UN Panel." *Reuters*, February 16.

New York Times (NYT). (1997/10/23). "Despite U.N. Ban, Mandela Meets Qaddafi in Libya." *The New York Times*, October 23.

News24. (2012/1/31). "Don't Recognise Libya's NTC, Mugabe Tells AU." *News24*, January 31.

—. (2012/8/7). "We Want New Ideas, Mugabe Tells AU." *News24*, August 7.

Niblock, Tim. (2001). *Pariah States & Sanctions in the Middle East: Iraq, Libya, Sudan.* Boulder, CO: Lynne Rienner.

Nivet, Bastien. (2006). *Security by Proxy? The EU and (Sub-)Regional Organisations: The Case of ECOWAS.* Occasional Paper No. 63, March. Paris: European Union Institute for Security Studies.

Nolan, Robert. (2011/12/5). "The African Union After Gaddafi." *The Whitehead Journal of Diplomacy and International Relations*, December 5.

Nossel, Suzanne. (2012/2/10). "Why Pressuring Russia and China Is the Key to Ousting Assad." *The New Republic*, February 10.

Nossiter, Adam. (2012/7/17). "Jihadists' Fierce Justice Drives Thousands to Flee Mali." *The New York Times*, July 17.

—. (2012/7/18). "Fear Stalks Mali's Refugees Despite Escape to Safety." *The New York Times*, July 18.

Nowak, Manfred. (2003). Introduction to the International Human Rights Regime. Boston: Martinus Nijhoff.

Nyathi, Kitsepile. (2011/8/28). "Zimbabwe Throws Out Defected Libyan Envoy." *Pan-African News Wire*, August 28.

Obama, Barack. (2009/7/11). "Remarks by the President to the Ghanaian Parliament." The White House, Office of the Press Secretary, July 11.

—. (2011/3/18). "Remarks by the President on the Situation in Libya." The White House, Office of the Press Secretary, March 18.

—. (2011/3/28). "Remarks by the President in Address to the Nation on Libya." The White House, Office of the Press Secretary, March 28.

—. (2011/10/20). "Remarks by the President on the Death of Muammar Qaddafi." The White House, Office of the Press Secretary, October 20.

—. (2011/11/4). "Remarks by President Obama in Honoring the Alliance between the United States and France." The White House, Office of the Press Secretary, November 4.

—. (2012/9/12a). "Statement by the President on the Attack in Benghazi". The White House, Office of the Press Secretary, September 12.

—. (2012/9/12b). "Remarks by the President on the Deaths of U.S. Embassy Staff in Libya". The White House, Office of the Press Secretary, September 12.

Obama, Barack; Cameron, David; & Sarkozy, Nicolas. (2011/4/14). "Libya's Pathway to Peace." *The New York Times/International Herald Tribune*, April 14.

Oborne, Peter, & Cookson, Richard. (2012/5/18). "Libya Still Ruled by the Gun". *The Telegraph*, May 18.

O'Connor, Patrick. (2011/9/26). "US, European Corporations Rush To Secure Cut from Libyan War." *World Socialist Web Site*, September 26.

—. (2011/10/19). "The Destruction of Sirte." *World Socialist Web Site*, October 19.

OHCHR. (2011/4/8). "Committee on the Protection of the Rights of Migrant Workers Concludes Fourteenth Session." *United Nations Human Rights: Office of the High Commissioner for Human Rights*, April 8.

O'Neill, Brendan. (2011/2/25). "The Narcissism of the Ipad Imperialists Who Want to Invade Libya." *The Telegraph*, February 25.

OpenSecrets. (2012). Bechtel Group: Annual Lobbying, 2012. *OpenSecrets.org*.

Oppel, Richard A., & Henriques, Diana B. (2003/4/18). "A Nation at War: The Contractor; Company has Ties to Washington, and to Iraq." *The New York Times*, April 18.

Osborn, Andrew, & Spillius, Alex. (2011/12/15). "Vladimir Putin Blasts John McCain as a War Criminal." *The Telegraph*, December 15.

Owen, David. (1987). "State Terrorism, Internationalism and Collective Action." *Review of International Studies*, 13(2), April, 81-89.

Palmer, Alasdair. (2005/5/1). "Regime Change is Illegal: End of Debate." *The Telegraph*, May 1.

PANA. (2001/3/1). "OAU Opens Fifth Extraordinary OAU Summit in Sirte." *PanaPress*, March 1.

—. (2011/2/6). "Libya Cancels Guinea's US$24m Debt." *PanaPress*, February 6.

Paul, Ron. (2011/8/29). "'Mission Accomplished' in Libya?" *RonPaul.com*, August 29.

Pawlak, Justyna. (2011/9/30). "Analysis: Libya Endgame Carries New Risks for NATO." *Reuters*, September 30.

Payandeh, Mehrdad. (2012). "The United Nations, Military Intervention, and Regime Change in Libya." *Virginia Journal of International Law*, 52(2), 355-403.

PBS. (2000). "War in Europe Facts and Figures." *Frontline*, February 22.

Pelham, Nicolas. (2002). "Britain's New Friend Struts about in Fancy Dress and Throws Dollars to the Poor. But Will the Libyans Still Put Up with Him?" *New Statesman*, 131(4601), August 19, 18-19.

Perdue, William D. (1989). *Terrorism and the State: A Critique of Domination through Fear*. New York: Praeger.

Perrin, Jean-Pierre. (2011/6/22). "Il y a eu des dizaines de cas de soldats assassins." *Libération*, June 22.

Perry, Alex. (2011). "Libyan Leader's Delusions of African Grandeur." *TIME*.

Pincus, Walter. (2011/3/23). "U.S. Spending on Military Operations in Libya Drains Pentagon". *The Washington Post*, March 23.

Pizzey, Allen. (2011/10/23). "A Morbid Cleanup Left in Libya." *CBS News*, October 23.

—. (2011/10/25). "Signs of Ex-Rebel Atrocities in Libya Grow." *CBS News*, October 25.

Pollack, Kenneth M. (2002). *Arabs at War: Military Effectiveness, 1948-1991*. Lincoln, NE: University of Nebraska Press.

Pougala, Jean-Paul. (2011/4/20a). "Why the West Wants the Fall of Muammar Gaddafi, Part 1 of 5." [Trans. Sputnik Kilambi] *OleAfrica*, April 20.

—. (2011/4/20b). "Why the West Wants the Fall of Muammar Gaddafi, Part 2 of 5." [Trans. Sputnik Kilambi] *OleAfrica*, April 20.

—. (2011/4/20c). "Why the West Wants the Fall of Muammar Gaddafi, Part 3 of 5." [Trans. Sputnik Kilambi] *OleAfrica*, April 20.

—. (2011/4/20d). "Why the West Wants the Fall of Muammar Gaddafi, Part 5 of 5." [Trans. Sputnik Kilambi] *OleAfrica*, April 20.

Prensa Latina. (2011/3/31). "D'Escoto: The United Nations Is a Deadly U.S. Weapon." *MRzine*, March 31.

Pringle, Robert. (2012/7/11). "The Trouble in Mali." [Letter to the Editor] *The New York Times*, July 11.

Pugliese, David. (2012/2/17). "The Libya Mission One Year Later: Into the Unknown." *The Ottawa Citizen*, February 17.

Quinn, Andrew. (2011/2/28). "Clinton Says Gaddafi Must Go." *Reuters*, February 28.

Quist-Arcton, Ofeibea. (2011/2/25). "In Libya, African Migrants Say They Face Hostility." *NPR*, February 25.

Quoriana. (2011/7/18). "Gaddafi and Mandela: Brother Leaders." *Mathaba*, July 18.

Radio Free Europe. (2012/1/29). "African Union Opens New Headquarters Funded by China." *Radio Free Europe/Radio Liberty*, January 29.

Radio Netherlands Worldwide (RNW). (2011/3/2). "HRW: No Mercenaries in Eastern Libya." *Radio Netherlands Worldwide*, March 2.

Ramdani, Nabila. (2011/2/20). "Libya Protests: 'Foreign Mercenaries Using Heavy Weapons Against at Demonstrators'." *The Telegraph*, February 20.

Randall, David. (2011/10/23). "Gaddafi's Dream Capital for Africa Pulverised into a Ruin." *The Independent (UK)*, October 23.

Reuters. (1997/10/22-23). "Mandela's Visit to Libya to Discuss Lockerbie-affair." *Reuters*, October 22-23.

—. (2011/3/20). "Wreck of Gaddafi's Force Smoulders Near Benghazi." *Reuters*, March 20.

—. (2011/3/30). "Obama Signed Secret Libya Order Authorizing Support For Rebels." *The Huffington Post*, March 30.

—. (2011/4/3). "Chad Says Citizens Abused in Rebel-Held Libya." *Reuters Africa*, April 3.

—. (2011/10/1). "Libya's NTC Says Will Call Two-Day Truce at Sirte." *Reuters*, October 1.

—. (2011/10/5). "Civilian Safety Key to Ending Libya Mission: NATO." *Reuters*, October 5.

—. (2011/10/6). "NATO Campaign to Continue While Libya Resistance Lasts." *Reuters*, October 6.

—. (2011/10/16). "Sirte Residents Accuse Libya Fighters of Looting." *MSNBC*, October 16.

—. (2012/1/7a). "Libya NTC Says to Review Investments Worldwide." *Reuters*, January 7.

—. (2012/1/7b). "Zambia Refutes Reports It Will Reverse Zamtel Sale." *Reuters*, January 7.

—. (2012/1/31). "Libya Minister to Protect Investment in Zamtel." *Reuters Africa*, January 31.

—. (2012/5/12). "Libya Minister Warns Italy on Clandestine Immigration." *Reuters*, May 12.

—. (2012/5/19). "Vote in Libya's Benghazi Tests Support for Autonomy". *Reuters*, May 19.

—. (2012/6/16). "Second World War Graves in Libya Desecrated Again." *The Guardian*, June 16.

RGJ. (2011/3/13). "Editorial: The U.S. Can't Afford to Get Involved in Another Civil War". *The Reno Gazette-Journal*, March 13.

Rice, Condoleeza. (2006/7/21). "Secretary Rice Holds a News Conference." *The Washington Post*, July 21.

—. (2008/9/6). "Transcript: U.S. Secretary of State Condoleezza Rice, Libyan Leader Col Muammar Abu Minyar al-Qadhafi Discuss Africa Command." *U.S. Africa Command*, September 6.

Rice, Xan. (2011/2/6). "China's Economic Invasion of Africa." *The Guardian*, February 6.

Richter, Paul. (2011/3/18). "U.N. Security Council Authorizes Action against Moammar Kadafi." *Los Angeles Times*, March 18.

RightWeb. (2010). Henry Jackson Society. *RightWeb*, August 18.

Roberts, Andrew. (2011/3/2). "The Top 10 Quotes from Gaddafi's Green Book." *The Daily Beast*, March 2.

Ross, Sonya. (1998/3/27). "Mandela Has No Apologies: South African Leaders Defends Ties to Cuba, Libya." *Associated Press/The Free Lance-Star*, March 27.

Roth, Kenneth. (2011/3/19). "The Security Council Has at Last Lived Up To Its Duty." *Human Rights Watch*, March 19.

Rozenberg, Joshua. (2008/9/14). "Why the World's Most Powerful Prosecutor Should Resign: Part 2." *The Telegraph*, September 14.

RT. (2011/12/2). "Libyan In(Ter)Vention: False Facts Fatal For Gaddafi." *RT (Russia Today)*, December 2.

Russeau, Simba. (2011/3/21). "Libya: Uprising Revives Entrenched Racism Towards Black Africans." *AllAfrica.com/IPS*, March 21.

Samora, Mwaura. (2011/4/12). "Libya: What If Colonel Gaddafi Loses the Battle for Tripoli?" *AllAfrica*, April 12.

SAPA. (2011/8/24). "Concerned Africans Criticise NATO." *Daily News*, August 24.

—. (2011/8/26). "Mbeki Criticises West's Libyan intervention." *Times Live*, August 26.

Satter, Raphael G. (2011/10/21). "World Looks Warily to Libya's Future Post-Gadhafi." *Associated Press*, October 21.

Sawer, Patrick. (2011/7/2). "Gaddafi Threatens to Attack Europe over Airstrikes." *The Telegraph*, July 2.

Schell, Jonathan. (2011/6/21). "Say What You Will, It's a War in Libya." *Los Angeles Times*, June 21.

Schwarz, Peter. (2011/8/13). "NATO Allows Libyan Refugees to Drown in the Mediterranean." *World Socialist Web Site*, August 13.

Sengupta, Kim. (2011/8/27). "Rebels Settle Scores in Libyan Capital." *The Independent*, August 27.

Shabi, Rachel. (2011/8/25). "NATO Nations Set to Reap Spoils of Libya War." *Al Jazeera English*, August 25.

—. (2012/1/19). "NATO Accused of War Crimes in Libya: New Report Criticises Western Forces for Bombing Civilian Targets in Sirte During Conflict." *The Independent*, January 19.

Shane, Scott. (2011/10/28). "Western Companies See Prospects for Business in Libya." *The New York Times*, October 28.

Shaoul, Jean, & Marsden, Chris. (2012/7/11). "The Real Significance of Libya's Elections". *World Socialist Web Site*, July 11.

Shenker, Jack. (2011/5/8). "Aircraft Carrier Left Us to Die, Say Migrants." *The Guardian*, May 8.

Sheridan, Mary Beth. (2011/10/15). "Gaddafi Home Town Largely Destroyed." *The Washington Post*, October 15.

Sherlock, Ruth. (2011/9/28). "Libya: Exodus from Sirte as Thousands Flee Rebel Offensive." *The Telegraph*, September 28.

Sherwood, Harriet, & McGreal, Chris. (2011/4/11). "Libya: Gaddafi Has Accepted Roadmap to Peace, Says Zuma." *The Guardian*, April 11.

Shirien. (2011/8/23). "Gaddafi the Closet Imperialist." *Yansoon*, August 23.

Shokr, Ahmad; & Kamat, Anjali. (2011). "Libya's Reformist Revolutionaries". *Economic & Political Weekly*, 46(12), March 19, 13-14.

Shuaib, Ali. (2012/5/14). "Libya Election Candidate Killed in Remote South". *Reuters*, May 14.

Sidner, Sara. (2011/6/17). "Libyan Rebels Say Captured Cell Phone Videos Show Rape, Torture." *CNN*, June 17.

Simons, Geoff. (1996). *Libya: The Struggle for Survival.* 2nd ed. New York: St. Martin's Press.

Simons, Marlise. (2012/7/18). "Mali Asks International Court to Investigate Atrocities." *The New York Times*, July 18.

Simmons, Ann. (2000/12/16). "Migrant Workers from Ghana Who Fled Libya Cite Racism." *Los Angeles Times*, December 16.

Simpson, Victor L. (2011/8/5). "Italy Demands NATO Probe over Libya Boat Migrants." *Associated Press*, August 5.

Sinco, Luis. (2011/3/23). "Journalists Visit Prisoners Held by Rebels in Libya." *Los Angeles Times*, March 23.

Skinner, Danielle. (2011/3/30). "General Ham Discusses First Weeks as AFRICOM Commander at All-Hands Staff Meeting." *U.S. Africa Command*, March 30.

Sky News. (2011/10/2). "Libyan Children Killed Fleeing Sirte." *Sky News*, October 2.

Slackman, Michael. (2009/3/22). "New Status in Africa Empowers an Ever-Eccentric Qaddafi." *The New York Times*, March 22.

Smith, David. (2011/2/22). "Has Gaddafi Unleashed a Mercenary Force on Libya?" *The Guardian*, February 22.

—. (2012/8/1). "Hillary Clinton Launches African Tour With Veiled Attack on China." *The Guardian*, August 1.

Smith, Graeme. (2011/4/1). "A Rebellion Divided: Spectre of Revenge Killings Hangs Over Eastern Libya." *The Globe and Mail*, April 1.

Smith, Michael. (2012/7/7). "Outcome of Libyan Elections Could Spell Trouble for US". *Fox News*, July 7.

Soguel, Dominique. (2012/5/3). "Libya Grants Immunity to 'Revolutionaries'". *Agence France Presse*, May 3.

Solingen, Etel. (2007). *Nuclear Logics: Contrasting Paths in East Asia and the Middle East.* Princeton, NJ: Princeton University Press.

Solomon, Hussein, & Swart, Gerrie. (2005). "Libya's Foreign Policy in Flux." *African Affairs*, 104(416), 469-492.

Somaliland Press. (2011/2/23). "LIBYA: At Least Four Somali Refugees Are Killed and Many Forced Out To the Desert." *Somalilandpress*, February 23.

Sotloff, Steven. (2011/4/12). "Non-Starter: Why Libya's Rebels Don't Trust the African Union." *TIME magazine*, April 12.

SourceWatch. (2008). Jack Sheehan. *SourceWatch*.

—. (2011). Bechtel Group, Inc. *SourceWatch*.

South, Ashley, & Harragin, Simon. (2012). *Local to Global Protection in Myanmar (Burma), Sudan, South Sudan and Zimbabwe.* London, UK: Humanitarian Practice Network, Overseas Development Institute.

Squires, Nick. (2010/8/31). "Gaddafi: Europe Will 'Turn Black' Unless EU Pays Libya £4bn a Year." *The Telegraph*, August 31.

Stephen, Chris. (2011/6/18). "Muammar Gaddafi War Crimes Files Revealed." *The Observer*, June 18.

—. (2011/9/16). "Anti-Gadafy Forces Capture Sirte Stronghold." *The Irish Times*, September 16.

Stephen, Christopher, & Tiron, Roxana. (2011/8/28). "Libyan Rebels Say Qaddafi Using Human Shields to Defend Sirte Stronghold." *Bloomberg*, August 28.

Stevenson, Jonathan. (2011/5/9). "AFRICOM's Libyan Expedition." *Foreign Affairs*, May 9.

Stirewalt, Chris. (2011/10/21). "Obama Brandishes another Scalp." *Fox News*, October 21.

STRATFOR. (2011/3/14). "Special Report: Libyan Involvement in Africa." *STRATFOR Intelligence Report*, March 14.

Strausz-Hupé, Robert, & Possony, Stefan T. (1950). *International Relations in the Age of the Conflict between Democracy and Dictatorship*. New York: McGraw-Hill Book Company, Inc.

Sullivan, Kimberly L. (2009). *Muammar Al-Qaddafi's Libya*. Minneapolis, MN: Twenty-First Century Books.

Sunday Mail. (2012/3/5). "No Shame and No Gratitude in Lawless Libya: The Profoundly Disturbing Attacks on War Graves." Editorial, *Daily Mail*, March 5.

SWF. (2011). "Libyan Investment Authority." *SWF Institute*.

Tacitus, Publius Cornelius. (98). *De vita et moribus Iulii Agricolae*.

Taki, Jihad. (2011/2/21). "Libyan Ambassador to UN Urges International Community to Stop Genocide." *Global Arab Network*, February 21.

Tananbau, Duane. (1997). "Contempt for Congress: The Reagan Administration, Congress, and the War Powers Resolution." In Eric J. Schmertz, Natalie Datlof & Alexej Ugrinsky (Eds.), *Ronald Reagan's America, Vol. 2* (pp. 467-477). Westport, CT: Greenwood Press.

Tapper, Jake; Khan, Huma; & Raddatz, Martha. (2011/3/18). "Obama: U.S. Involvement in Libya Action Would Last 'Days, Not Weeks'." *ABC News*, March 18.

Tarimo, Judica. (2012/2/4). "Gaddafi Never Invested in Tanzania, Says Govt." *IPPMedia*, February 4.

Taylor, Jerome. (2011/8/24). "Dash for Profit in Post-war Libya Carve-Up." *The Independent*, August 24.

Teil, Julien. (2011). "Guerre Humanitaire en Libye : Il n'y a pas de preuve !" *La Guerre Humanitaire*, November.

Thomas, Gary. (2011/3/30). "US May Use Covert Action against Gadhafi." *Voice of America*, March 30.

Thomet, Laurent, & Lamloum, Imed. (2011/10/31). "Libya Elects New Govt Head, NATO Lifts Air Cover." *Associated Press*, October 31.

Times. (2011/2/16). "As it Happened: Libya Uprising February 25." *The Times*, February 26.

Times of Malta. (2010/12/9). "Editorial: Libyan Realities for Europe on Migration Flow." *Times of Malta*, December 9.

Timmerman, Kenneth R. (2004). "Breakthrough with Muammar Qaddafi; Libya's Leader Pledges to Give Up Weapons of Mass Destruction, Abandon Terror and Renew Ties with America. Can This Man Be Trusted?" *Insight on the News*, March 29, 18-21.

Timmermann, Wibke Kristin. (2006). "Incitement in International Criminal Law." *International Review of the Red Cross*, 88(864), December.

Tkachenko, Maxim. (2011/12/15). "Putin Points to U.S. Role in Gadhafi's Killing." *CNN*, December 15.

Tong, Sebastian. (2011/8/22). "Analysis: Investors Eye Promise, Pitfalls in Post-Gaddafi Libya." *Reuters*, August 22.

Touray, Omar A. (2005). "The Common African Defence and Security Policy." *African Affairs*, 104(417), 635-656.

Tripoli Post. (2012/1/2). "AU Summit to Decide Fate of Libyan Assets Held in Member States." *Tripoli Post*, January 2.

Turse, Nick. (2012/7/12). "Obama's Scramble for Africa: Secret Wars, Secret Bases, and the Pentagon's 'New Spice Route' in Africa." *TomDispatch*, July 12.

Tuttle, Robert, & Alexander, Caroline. (2011/9/27). "Libya Forces Halt Sirte Attack." *Bloomberg*, September 27.

UKSF News. (2011/10/25). "Did the SAS Help Catch Gaddafi?" *Elite UK Forces*, October 25.

United Nations (UN). (1948a). Charter of the United Nations.

—. (1949b). Convention on the Prevention and Punishment of the Crime of Genocide. New York: United Nations General Assembly.

—. (2003). Security Council Lifts Sanctions Imposed on Libya after Terrorist Bombings of Pan Am 103, UTA 772. UN Press Release SC/7868.

—. (2005). Resolution Adopted by the General Assembly: 60/1. 2005 World Summit Outcome. *United Nations General Assembly*, October 24.

—. (2006). Security Council Condemns Attacks against Journalists in Conflict Situations, Unanimously Adopting Resolution 1738. New York: United Nations Department of Public Information, News and Media Division.

—. (2009). Implementing the Responsibility to Protect: Report of the Secretary-General. *United Nations General Assembly*, January 12.

—. (2011). Security Council Approves "No-Fly Zone" Over Libya, Authorizing "All Necessary Measures" to Protect Civilians, by Vote of 10 in Favour with 5 Abstentions. New York: United Nations Department of Public Information, News and Media Division.

—. (2012/1/5). "Libya: UN Official Impressed by Pace of Returns to Cities Emerging from Conflict." *United Nations Organization*, January 5.

United Nations Development Programme (UNDP). (2009). *Human Development Report 2009*. New York: United Nations Development Programme.

United Nations Economic Commission for Africa (UNECA). (1983). "Establishment of an African Monetary Fund: Executive Summary." UNECA Meeting of the Conference of Ministers, Addis Ababa, Ethiopia, April 27-May 3.

United Nations Human Rights Council (UNHRC). (2012). *Report of the International Commission of Inquiry on Libya*.

United Nations Security Council (UNSC). (2011/3/17). Resolution 1973 (2011), Adopted by the Security Council at its 6498th meeting, on 17 March 2011. New York: United Nations Organization.

United Press International (UPI). (1990/5/19). "Mandela Visits Libya, Thanks Kadafi for Helping Train ANC." *Los Angeles Times*, May 19.

UN Watch. (2011/2/21a). "24 Rights Groups Urge US and EU to Confront Libyan Massacres in UN Security Council and Human Rights Council." *UN Watch*, February 21.

—. (2011/2/21b). "Urgent Appeal to Stop Atrocities in Libya." *UN Watch*, February 21.

Upstream. (2011/8/29). "ENI Chief Mends Libya Fences." *Upstream Online*, August 29.

U.S. Congress. (2000). An Act to authorize a new trade and investment policy for sub-Saharan Africa, expand trade benefits to the countries in the Caribbean Basin, renew the generalized system of preferences, and reauthorize the trade adjustment assistance programs. One Hundred Sixth Congress of the United States of America, Second Session, Washington, DC, January 24.

U.S. Department of Defense. (2011/3/1). "DOD News Briefing with Secretary Gates and Adm. Mullen from the Pentagon." Office of the Assistant Secretary of Defense (Public Affairs), News Transcript, March 1.

U.S. Department of State. (2011/3/24). "Implementing UN Security Council Resolutions on Libya". *DipNote: U.S. Department of State Official Blog*, March 24.

—. (2012/9/12). "Briefing by Senior Administration Officials to Update Recent Events in Libya". *U.S. Department of State*, September 12.

U.S. Embassy-Addis Ababa (USEAA). (2009/7/15). "African Union Summit Wrap-up: Qadhafi Pulls It Off, Barely." U.S. Embassy Cable, Addis Ababa, Ethiopia, July 15.

—. (2009/7/15). "African Union Summit Wrap-up: Qadhafi Pulls It Off, Barely." U.S. Embassy Cable, Addis Ababa, Ethiopia, July 15.

U.S. Embassy-Monrovia (USEM). (2009/12/22). "Libya Invests $30 Million in Liberian Rice Development." U.S. Embassy Cable, Monrovia, Liberia, December 22.

U.S. Embassy-Tripoli (USET). (2005/8/15). "Libyans Pleased with Saudi Decision". U.S. Embassy Cable, Tripoli, Libya, August 15.

—. (2005/8/31). "Senator Lugar's Meeting With Qadhafi August 20." U.S. Embassy Cable, Tripoli, Libya, August 31.

—. (2006/8/31a). "Congressman Lantos Stresses Bilateral Achievements and Regional Challenges with Libyan Officials." U.S. Embassy Cable, Tripoli, Libya, August 31.

—. (2006/8/31b). "Senator Specter Reviews Bilateral Relationship with Senior Libyan Officials." U.S. Embassy Cable, Tripoli, Libya, August 31.

—. (2006/9/24). "Libya Tells Exim –Trust Us, Our Credit's Good." U.S. Embassy Cable, Tripoli, Libya, September 24.

—. (2007/5/4). "Libya: Darfur Conference Atmospherics." U.S. Embassy Cable, Tripoli, Libya, May 4.

—. (2007/11/15). "Growth of Resource Nationalism in Libya." U.S. Embassy Cable, Tripoli, Libya, November 15.

—. (2007/11/27). "Libyan Organization Issues Statement Opposing Africom." U.S. Embassy Cable, Tripoli, Libya, November 27.

—. (2008/2/15). "Extremism in Eastern Libya". U.S. Embassy Cable, Tripoli, Libya, February 15.

—. (2008/3/3). "Libyan Parliament Convenes, Cabinet Changes Expected." U.S. Embassy Cable, Tripoli, Libya, March 3.

—. (2008/3/12). "GOL Still Bristling Over Victims of Terrorism Legislation, UTA Judgment." U.S. Embassy Cable, Tripoli, Libya, March 12.

—. (2008/3/17). "Back to the Future? Qadhafi Calls for Dramatic Socio-economic Change in GPC Speech." U.S. Embassy Cable, Tripoli, Libya, March 17.

—. (2008/4/8). "Assassination of Security Officer in Eastern Libya". U.S. Embassy Cable, Tripoli, Libya, April 8.

—. (2008/4/10). "MFA Discourages Idea of Soft Power Programming in Eastern Libya". U.S. Embassy Cable, Tripoli, Libya, April 10.

—. (2008/4/24). "Debt, Nuclear Energy, and Golf Carts: Putin Visits Libya." U.S. Embassy Cable, Tripoli, Libya, April 24.

—. (2008/5/8). "Libya's NSC Solicits U.S. Views on Civilian Nuclear Cooperation & Lethal Military Equipment Sales." U.S. Embassy Cable, Tripoli, Libya, May 8.

—. (2008/6/2). "Die Hard in Derna". U.S. Embassy Cable, Tripoli, Libya, June 2.

—. (2008/6/9). "Libya to Increase Peacekeeping Cohort in the Philippines." U.S. Embassy Cable, Tripoli, Libya, June 9.

—. (2008/7/22). "Thug Life: Hannibal Al-Qadhafi's Arrest Prompts Fissure in Swiss-Libyan Relations." U.S. Embassy Cable, Tripoli, Libya, July 22.

—. (2008/7/23). "A Commercial Cautionary Tale: Bechtel's Bid For Sirte Port Project Falls Flat." U.S. Embassy Cable, Tripoli, Libya, July 23.

—. (2008/8/25). "Libyan Reaction to Claims Settlement Agreement Positive, High Expectations for U.S. Influence on Al-Qadhafi." U.S. Embassy Cable, Tripoli, Libya, August 25.

—. (2008/8/28). "Saif Al-islam Al-Qadhafi Calls for Further Reform, Threatens to Withdraw from Politics." U.S. Embassy Cable, Tripoli, Libya, August 28.

—. (2008/8/29). "Scenesetter for Secretary Rice's Visit to Libya." U.S. Embassy Cable, Tripoli, Libya, August 29.

—. (2008/10/2). "Scenesetter for the Visit of SE Williamson to Libya." U.S. Embassy Cable, Tripoli, Libya, October 2

—. (2008/10/17). "Al-Qadhafi: To Russia, With Love?" U.S. Embassy Cable, Tripoli, Libya, October 17.

—. (2008/12/5). "Muammar Al-Qadhafi Quietly Involved in Process to Adopt a Libyan Constitution." U.S. Embassy Cable, Tripoli, Libya, December 5.

—. (2008/12/22). "Libya Commercial Round-up for November 2008." U.S. Embassy Cable, Tripoli, Libya, December 22.

—. (2008/12/31). "Libya Interested in U.S. Weapons, More Ambivalent on Other Military Cooperation." U.S. Embassy Cable, Tripoli, Libya, December 31.

—. (2009/1/15). "Senior Regime Figures Ambivalent about U.S.-Libya Relations". U.S. Embassy Cable, Tripoli, Libya, January 15.

—. (2009/1/21). "Uganda: Qadhafi's Crown Tarnished in Council of Kings Cancellation." U.S. Embassy Cable, Tripoli, Libya, January 21.

—. (2009/1/29). "Libya Expects to Win Chairmanship of AU Assembly." U.S. Embassy Cable, Tripoli, Libya, January 29.

—. (2009/2/2). "Libya: Meeting with Returned Gtmo Detainees Under USG-GOL Transfer Framework MOU". U.S. Embassy Cable, Tripoli, Libya, February 2.

—. (2009/2/11). "Al-Qadhafi's African Union: Obstacles to Success, Opportunities for Engagement." U.S. Embassy Cable, Tripoli, Libya, February 2.

—. (2009/2/18). "Libya's National Security Adviser: Looking for Signals of U.S. Intent." U.S. Embassy Cable, Tripoli, Libya, February 18.

—. (2009/2/27). "For Ordinary Libyans, It's the Economy, Stupid." U.S. Embassy Cable, Tripoli, Libya, February 27.

—. (2009/3/5). "Scenesetter for the Visit of General William Ward to Libya, March 10-11." U.S. Embassy Cable, Tripoli, Libya, March 5.

—. (2009/3/9). "Libya's Succession Muddled as the Al-Qadhafi Children Conduct Internecine Warfare." U.S. Embassy Cable, Tripoli, Libya, March 9.

—. (2009/3/11). "General People's Congress Shuffles Cabinet, Postpones Wealth Distribution Plan." U.S. Embassy Cable, Tripoli, Libya, March 11.

—. (2009/3/18). "U.S. Africa Command Head: Allaying Libyan Fears on the Mission." U.S. Embassy Cable, Tripoli, Libya, March 18.

—. (2009/3/23). "Libya Wants to Sign Aviation Agreement, Commence Flights to U.S." U.S. Embassy Cable, Tripoli, Libya, March 23.

—. (2009/4/9). "Libya Plans AU Ministerial April 15-16 to Discuss AU Integration, Possibly Darfur." U.S. Embassy Cable, Tripoli, Libya, April 9.

—. (2009/4/17). "Muatassim's Washington Debut: Burnishing His Image and Testing U.S. Waters." U.S. Embassy Cable, Tripoli, Libya, April 17.

—. (2009/5/3). "Musa Kusa Seeks Cooperation on Africa, Al-qaeda—and POTUS Meeting with Al-Qadhafi." U.S. Embassy Cable, Tripoli, Libya, May 3.

—. (2009/5/18). "Scenesetter for the Visit of General William Ward to Libya, May 21." U.S. Embassy Cable, Tripoli, Libya, May 18.

—. (2009/5/26). "Al-Qadhafi: No Longer Reluctant to Engage with Africom." U.S. Embassy Cable, Tripoli, Libya, May 26.

—. (2009/6/4). "Libya's Former Nuclear Center Director Resurfaces." U.S. Embassy Cable, Tripoli, Libya, June 4.

—. (2009/7/13). "AU Summit: A/S Carson's Meeting With AU Commission Leadership." U.S. Embassy Cable, Tripoli, Libya, July 13.

—. (2009/7/15). "Libya's AU Summit Scorecard: Victory (of Sorts) From Jaws of Defeat." U.S. Embassy Cable, Tripoli, Libya, July 15.

—. (2009/7/21). "The Cast of the Jamahiriya: Background Information for NEA AA/A Feltman's Visit to Tripoli." U.S. Embassy Cable, Tripoli, Libya, July 21.

Embassy Tripoli (Libya)

—. (2009/8/3a). "Caterpillar Negotiations Inching Along." U.S. Embassy Cable, Tripoli, Libya, August 3.

—. (2009/8/3b). "Two Steps Backward? GOL Enforces 2004 Law on Foreign Distributors." U.S. Embassy Cable, Tripoli, Libya, August 3.

—. (2009/8/5). "Prodding Libya to Action on Time Sensitive Issues—Corrected Copy." U.S. Embassy Cable, Tripoli, Libya, August 5.

—. (2009/8/19). "CODEL McCain Meets Muammar and Muatassim Al-Qadhafi." U.S. Embassy Cable, Tripoli, Libya, August 19.

—. (2009/9/8). "AU Summit Serves as Opening Act for Qadhafi's 40th Anniversary Celebration." U.S. Embassy Cable, Tripoli, Libya, September 8.

—. (2009/10/12). "Libyan MFA Seeks Progress on Political-military Issues." U.S. Embassy Cable, Tripoli, Libya, October 12.

—. (2009/10/26). "What Passes for Political Ferment in Libya." U.S. Embassy Cable, Tripoli, Libya, October 26.

—. (2009/11/2). "Muatassem Al-Qadhafi Asserts Anti-Libya Bias." U.S. Embassy Cable, Tripoli, Libya, November 2.

—. (2009/12/14). "Saif Al-Islam's Staff Reaches Out on Pol-Mil Issues." U.S. Embassy Cable, Tripoli, Libya, December 14.

—. (2010/1/27). "Senior Libyan Justice Official: Less Talk, More Action is Best". U.S. Embassy Cable, Tripoli, Libya, January 1.

Van Auken, Bill. (2011/10/24). "The US and Gaddafi: The Murderer Calls for an Investigation of the Crime." *World Socialist Web Site*, October 24.

Vandewalle, Dirk. (1998). *Libya since Independence: Oil and State-Building.* Ithaca, NY: Cornell University Press.

Van Langendonck, Gert. (2011/8/29). "In Tripoli, African 'Mercenaries' at Risk." *Christian Science Monitor*, August 29.

Varner, Bill. (2011/6/8). "Qaddafi May Be Charged With Systematic Rape, Prosecutor Says." *Bloomberg*, June 8.

Verkaik, Robert. (2011/5/1). "Bombs Hit Gaddafi Home." *Daily Mail*, May 1.

Viorst, Milton. (1999). "The Colonel in His Labyrinth." *Foreign Affairs*, 78(2), March-April, 60-75.

Walden, George. (2011/12/29). "How is Bernard-Henri Lévy Possible?" *The Times Literaruy Supplement*, December 29.

Wall Street Journal. (2011/4/4). "Review and Outlook: The Arab Revolt and U.S. Interests:

A U.S. Strategy Has to Begin by Distinguishing Between Friends and Enemies." *Wall Street Journal*, April 4.

Watson, Ivan, & Roth, Richard. (2011/3/31). "With Defections, Libya Has Tough Time Getting Envoy to U.N.." *CNN*, March 31.

White House. (2010). National Security Strategy. Washington, DC: The White House.

—. (2011). United States National Action Plan on Women, Peace, and Security. Washington, DC: The White House

—. (2012a). "Fact Sheet: Obama Administration Accomplishments in Sub-Saharan Africa." The White House, Office of the Press Secretary, June 14.

—. (2012b). "U.S. Strategy toward Sub-Saharan Africa." Washington, DC: The White House.

Williams, David, & Shipman, Tim. (2011/3/25). "Proof We Are Winning: MoD Release Footage of Airstrikes Wiping Out Gaddafi's Guns as Coalition Planes 'Fly Free Over Libya." *Daily Mail*, March 25.

Will, George F. (2011/3/8). "On Libya, Too Many Questions." *The Washington Post*, March 8.

Williams, Stephen. (2007). "Libya to Fund African Industry." *African Business*, October.

Winnett, Robert, & Watt, Holly. (2011/3/2). "Libya: SAS Ready to Seize Col Gaddafi's Stores of Mustard Gas." *The Telegraph*, March 2.

Witcher, Tim. (2011/12/19). "Russia Demands NATO Inquiry of Libya Civilian Deaths." *Agence France Presse*, December 19.

Woodward, Bob. (1987). *Veil: The Secret Wars of the CIA, 1981-1987*. New York: Simon & Schuster.

Worth, Robert F. (2011/3/30). "On Libya's Revolutionary Road." *The New York Times*, March 30.

Wright, Claudia. (1981-1982). "Libya and the West: Headlong into Confrontation?" *International Affairs*, 58(1), Winter, 13-41.

Wright, John. (1981). *Libya: A Modern History*. Beckenham, UK: Croom Helm Ltd.

Xinhua. (2010/1/31). "African Investment Bank to Be Launched Soon: AU Chief." *CRI English*, January 31.

York, Byron. (2011/3/23). "White House: Libya Fight is not War, it's 'Kinetic Military Action'." *Washington Examiner*, March 23.

Zirulnick, Ariel. (2011/6/9). "ICC: Evidence Shows that Qaddafi Ordered Rape of Hundreds." *Christian Science Monitor*, June 9.

Zucchino, David. (2011/3/24). "Libyan Rebels Appear to Take Leaf from Kadafi's Playbook." *Los Angeles Times*, March 24.

Index

MORE NONFICTION FROM BARAKA BOOKS

Trudeau's Darkest Hour
War Measures in Time of Peace, October 1970
Edited by Guy BOUTHILLIER & Édouard CLOUTIER

The Question of Separatism
Quebec and the Struggle over Sovereignty
Jane JACOBS

A People's History of Quebec
Jacques LACOURSIÈRE & Robin PHILPOT

Going Too Far
Essays About America's Nervous Breakdown
Ishmael REED

The First Jews in North America 1760-1860
The Extraordinary Story of the Hart Family
Denis VAUGEOIS (Translated by Käthe Roth)

America's Gift
What the World Owes to the Americas and Their First Inhabitants
Käthe ROTH & Denis VAUGEOIS

MIX
Paper
FSC® C100212

Printed by Imprimerie Gauvin
Gatineau, Québec